University of Washington
Publications on Asia
Sponsored by the Far Eastern
and Russian Institute

Power Relations within the Chinese Communist Movement, 1930-1934

A STUDY OF DOCUMENTS

by

Tso-liang Hsiao

UNIVERSITY OF WASHINGTON PRESS

Seattle · 1961

This book is sponsored by the Modern Chinese History Project of the Far Eastern and Russian Institute, whose members have taken an active interest in the work of the author.

Preface

The purpose of this study of documents is to prepare materials for a monograph on the Chinese Communist movement of 1930-34, viewed from the angle of intraparty conflicts with particular reference to their relations with Moscow.

As my annotations of documents grew to a considerable size, it was suggested to me that they be published for the benefit of those who might be interested. This seemed all the more necessary from the business point of view, since the financial support for my work was understandably not unlimited. Accordingly, I decided to have this study published first.

The search for documents for inclusion in this study was as thorough as possible within the limits of the two major collections of Chinese Communist sources now available in Taiwan, namely, Vice President Ch'en Ch'eng's personal files, called the Shih Sou collection (after his studio name), referred to hereinafter as SSC, and the Bureau of Investigation collection, referred to hereinafter as BIC. The former contains Communist sources from the Kiangsi Soviet, collected on the spot by Nationalist troops under the command of General Ch'en Ch'eng during the anti-Communist campaigns in Kiangsi in the early thirties. This collection was used to compile *A Collection of Red Bandit Reactionary Documents* for private circulation under his sponsorship in 1935. It had since remained in his personal files, unnoticed until I discovered it by chance on August 1, 1957, when I started the work of research which made this volume possible.

The latter collection contains materials issued by the Central

Headquarters of the Chinese Communist Party, which in the early thirties was first located in the Shanghai underground and later transferred to the Communist base in southern Kiangsi.

In addition, a small number of documents have been gathered from outside the two collections to fill important gaps.

Documents pertaining to intraparty power relations have been studied exhaustively and have all been listed in this work with the exception of a very small number of items which are obviously of little importance. Out of a great number of documents on military affairs which dominated the picture of the Kiangsi Soviet, only those relating to the intraparty debate over strategical and tactical problems have been selected.

All Comintern sources available in Taiwan covering the period under study are listed in this volume.

The full Chinese text of all documents listed in this work will be printed in a number of volumes for the benefit of those who may be interested. Where the originals of some documents cannot be found in Taiwan, but in the outside world, the originals will be gathered and included in the Chinese volumes as far as possible. For this purpose, the article numbers of the Li Lisan-sponsored land law of May, 1930, which are cited in this study, are based on the original text of the law available in the Hoover Library, but not on the reproduction of the text listed in this volume.

Some of the Chinese Communist organs in the period under study were first published in Shanghai and then in Kiangsi. If not otherwise indicated, the *Reconstruction of the Party* cited in this work refers to its Shanghai edition.

It is not easy to translate Chinese Communist expressions and terms into English. I suspect that some of the translations contained in this work are subject to debate, though not for lack of care in the effort to avoid it. Sometimes the Chinese Communists made a distinction between the Central Committee and the Central Politburo, but oftentimes they did not, simply employing the vague expression *Central* to denote either or both of the two different organs. Except in obvious cases, no particular effort was made to distinguish these terms from one another in translation.

Documents on the two land investigation drives in 1933 and 1934, which had a good deal to do with factional struggles, are reserved for another volume on the agrarian revolution in China in 1930-34.

Altogether 267 items containing a total of a little more than a

million Chinese characters are listed in this study. Items dealing with the same subject are grouped in one section and arranged in chronological order except where a change of the order seemed necessary.

This study is by no means final. Being a survey of documents,
it cannot be expected to do more than skim the surface of a vast
subject which is a challenge to modern scholarship. The annotations of the items listed were written at different times and not
necessarily in chronological order. Their differences in detail
and length do not necessarily imply any difference in importance.
Indeed, they are separate sketches joined together by a thin
thread. Many of the conclusions reached are wholly tentative.

References to imperfections of pioneer works as contained in
this volume were made for my own research purposes only.
When it was decided to have this preliminary study published
first, I found it very difficult to remove or change those references unless the whole manuscript was rewritten. Therefore, I
have had to leave them alone on the understanding that they will
not be printed in the text of the projected monograph. It need
hardly be pointed out that scholars, being human, are apt to
make mistakes and that it is often these mistakes which really
make academic progress possible.

I owe debts of gratitude to a number of friends and scholars
for aid and cooperation in the preparation of this work. Profes-
sors George E. Taylor, Earl Swisher, Franz Michael, and the
late Professor Shu-chin Ts'ui were the first to help me bring
about the research project which made the present volume possible. At various stages of my work, Vice President Ch'en
Ch'eng, Dr. Wang Shih-chieh, Messrs. Yü Ching-t'ang, Chi
Yuan-p'u, Wang Min, Ni Pao-kwen, and others gave invaluable
assistance in one form or another in response to my requirements. Both Dr. Hu Shih and Dr. Wang Shih-chieh read the manuscript and made helpful suggestions.

During the actual writing I was ably assisted by Professor
Chieng-ming Chu, Professor Tzu-ch'en Hsiao, and Mr. Abra-
ham E. Wu, who played a vital role in helping me select and
analyze documents. Professor Chu, who did the major part of the
research, contributed much toward making the book what it is.
He also prepared the glossary and bibliography, while Mr.
Liang-chang Hsiao assisted in clerical work.

Meanwhile, my wife and our beloved ones have sacrificed so
much to enable me to take a glimpse into an important part of
contemporary world history.

I am grateful to the Far Eastern and Russian Institute of the University of Washington for furthering the publication of this work.

This study is a part of the preliminary results of a research program made possible by funds granted by The Asia Foundation.

Needless to say, I am solely responsible for all statements, views, and possible errors in this volume.

Hsiao Tso-liang

Taipei, Taiwan
June 4, 1960

Contents

ix

Power Relations within
the Chinese Communist
Movement, 1930-1934

A Study of Documents

1

The Chu-Mao Type of Policies

A Single Spark Can Start a Prairie Fire (星星之火可以燎原. Hsing-hsing chih huo, k'o-i liao yüan), by Mao Tse-tung, January 5, 1930; printed in a pamphlet published by *The Mass Daily*, Sian, n. d., 008. 13/6063/C. 2, SSC; also printed in Mao Tse-tung, *Selected Works*, Chinese edition, Vol. 1, pp. 101-11, English edition, Vol. 1, pp. 116-28; approximately 6, 400 words including notes.

When 1930 opened, it saw a powerful Communist movement emerging from the rural districts in the hinterland of China. Mao Tse-tung, who withdrew to Chingkangshan, a mountain stronghold in western Kiangsi, in the fall of 1927 and who was joined by the soldier Chu Teh there in April or May, 1928, had become the political leader of this movement. These two men and their followers were generally called the Chu-Mao group, a term used not only in Chinese circles but in Comintern documentation as well. (See Comintern letter to the CCP dated October 26, 1929, fifth paragraph from the end.) This group was militarily the most powerful of all the factions in the Chinese Communist hierarchy since Chingkangshan.

Driven from Chingkangshan in January, 1929, the Chu-Mao group moved to southern Kiangsi and invaded western Fukien several times during the year. As a result, they managed to establish a territorial base in the Kiangsi-Fukien border area and scored substantial successes from January, 1930, on.

With January, 1930, as the starting point, the CCP Secretary-General, Hsiang Chung-fa, saw a riper growth of a new rising tide of the Chinese revolution which was believed to have

3

begun in June, 1929. During the ensuing eight months or so,
according to him, the CCP concerned itself with the transformation of the warlord strife into a revolutionary war and the
establishment of a Soviet regime. (See T'e Sheng's Report on
the Work of the Central Politburo, September, 1930.)

With this rapid progress of events in China, some of the
Comintern officials saw signs of a new revolutionary upsurge
in the Chinese Soviet movement and found the Moscow-made
CCP policy of 1929 no longer adequate to meet the new situa-
tion in 1930. (For the Comintern position, see remarks of Otto
Kuusinen during the "Discussion of the Li-san Line by the
Presidium of the ECCI, " printed in the CCP organ *Bolshevik*,
Shanghai, May 10, 1931, Vol. 4, No. 3, pp. 47-48.)

The present statement was a policy pronouncement of Mao
Tse-tung at the beginning of 1930. As indicated in an editorial
note attached to it, this statement was originally in letter
form, designed to counteract a pessimistic view then existing
in the CCP. In reality, however, the significance of this statement should be much greater than that. This was one of Mao's
key statements of the time, summing up his past experiences
and foreshadowing the subsequent development of the Chinese
Communist movement.

The central idea of this statement was in favor of the establishment of a Red regime, and, to that end, Kiangsi was considered in the circumstances the best possible choice for a
base. This was in contrast to another school of thought then
prevailing in the CCP that it was necessary only to carry on
mobile guerrilla activities in the borderlands of Fukien,
Kwangtung, and Kiangsi without taking the trouble to set up and
consolidate a political regime. In other words, according to
Mao, this school of thought considered it futile to make any serious attempt to form a Red regime when a revolutionary high
tide loomed still far off; rather, it favored extending political
influence by means of guerrilla tactics until the masses were
won over and were in a position to start a nationwide revolution with the support of the Red Army.

In analyzing the situation in China, Mao pointed out the seriousness of the peasant problem, the soundness of the slogan of
the democratic dictatorship of workers and peasants, the development of the Red Army and guerrilla forces, the existence
of Red areas, and what not. He took pride in what he called the
Chu Teh—Mao Tse-tung type of policies, saying that only that
type of policies was correct—policies which lay in the establish-

ment of revolutionary bases, build-up of political regimes, intensification of the agrarian revolution, expansion of the people's armed forces culminating in the Red Army, development of political power like the movement of a succession of waves, and so forth. (Mao also identified this type of policies with the policies advocated by Fang Chih-min, a Communist military leader, who was captured by KMT troops in January, 1935, and executed six months later. For an explanation of the Chu-Mao type of policies, see Ho Kan-chih, *History of the Contemporary Chinese Revolution,* Hongkong, 1958, pp. 129-30.)

One cannot fail to note how the Chu-Mao type of policies harmonized with the basic policies made by Moscow for the CCP since 1926, or rather since 1927. It will be recalled that since 1926 the Comintern prescribed the agrarian revolution as the main content of the Chinese revolution and that from 1927 on it urged the Chinese Communists to build up Soviets, Red Army forces, and territorial bases. These policies, as will be seen later in this study, found even fuller and more concrete expression in Comintern directives to the CCP dated July 23, 1930, November 16, 1930, and July, 1931, respectively, as well as in the Comintern Resolution on the Chinese Peasant Problem and the Comintern Eastern Department Draft Resolution on the Land and Peasant Problems in Soviet Areas, both of which were adopted in 1930. The basic nature of the Chu-Mao type of policies remained unaltered despite changes in party leadership during the Kiangsi period. (For the Moscow-made basic policies for the CCP before 1930, see Comintern Resolution on the Chinese Problem, November, 1926; Comintern Resolution on the Chinese Problem, May, 1927; Comintern Resolution on the Chinese Problem, February 25, 1928; Comintern Letter to the CCP on the Political Problem and Present-day Tasks, n.d., probably issued in early 1929; Comintern Letter to the CCP on the Peasant Problem, June 7, 1929; Comintern Letter to the CCP, October 26, 1929; also CCP Circular to All Party Members, August 7, 1927; Documents of the CCP Sixth National Congress, July 9, 1928.)

As to why the Communists should take Kiangsi and not other provinces, Mao gave a number of reasons in this statement. Kiangsi, unlike Kwangtung and Hunan, was the weakest link in the enemy chain of defense in South China, Mao declared. So, too, with western Fukien and western Chekiang, which belonged to the same Communist operational area with Kiangsi under Mao's plan. Mao claimed that the basis of Communist work in

Kiangsi and western Fukien was also strong correspondingly. The other reasons given for the seizure of Kiangsi were:

1. In Kiangsi the economy was predominantly feudalistic, and the armed units of the landlords were the weakest in South China.

2. Kiangsi had no troops of its own. Troops from other provinces were not familiar with local conditions and did not have as much interest in the anti-Communist fight as the native troops.

3. Kiangsi, unlike Kwangtung, was free from the influence of imperialism.

This statement should be read in conjunction with an earlier statement of Mao under the title of "Why Can China's Red Regimes Exist?" dated October 5, 1928. (See Mao Tse-tung, *Selected Works,* compiled by Mao Tse-tung Selected Works Publishing Committee, CCP Central Committee, published by the People's Publishing Company, distributed by Hsin Hwa Book Company. Chinese edition, first edition, Peking, 1953, Vol. 1, pp. 49-58; English edition, New York, International Publishers, 1954-56, Vol. 1, pp. 63-70.

According to Hu Chiao-mu, a Communist historian, these two statements provide a theoretical basis for two fundamental policies of the Chinese Communist movement, namely, the development of Red Army operations and the establishment of rural revolutionary bases. With a momentarily invincible, superior enemy in the city, Hu states, Mao developed the unique strategy of encircling the city with the armed countryside with a view to the ultimate capture of the city. The subsequent development of the Chinese revolution, Hu adds, has borne witness to Mao's farsightedness. (See Hu Chiao-mu, *Thirty Years of the Chinese Communist Party,* Peking, 1952, pp. 29-30.)

As is perhaps inevitable in any translation, the English version of the present statement has lost much of the clarity and vigor of the Chinese original, not to mention the errors of translation that occur. For instance, the sentence extending from page 122 to page 123 of the first volume of Mao Tse-tung, *Selected Works,* English edition, should be recast. This sentence, which is an often cited statement made by Mao in a letter addressed under the name of the Front Committee to the Central Committee on April 5, 1929, may be retranslated as follows:

The revolution in semicolonial China will fail only if the peasant struggle does not have the leadership of the workers, but in no case will it be disadvantageous to the revolution itself if the development of the peasant struggle goes beyond the influence of the workers.

Land Law (土 地 法 T'u-ti fa), promulgated by the Chinese Revolutionary Military Council, n. d. ; reprinted by the General Political Department, First Army Corps, Red Army, 1930; reproduced in *A Collection of Red Bandit Secret Documents,* Vol. 5, leaves 1-4, 008. 2129/4074, SSC, and in *A Collection of Red Bandit Reactionary Documents,* Vol. 3, pp. 912-18, 008. 2129/4077/V. 3, SSC; approximately 2, 200 words.

This land law was apparently the work of the Chu-Mao group, and some of its basic principles were introduced or reaffirmed in a conference held on February 7, 1930. Leaving a more detailed discussion of this law to another volume on the agrarian revolution in China in 1930-34, we would like to cite for our present purposes the Political Resolution of the (Central) Soviet Area First Party Congress, held in November, 1931, which reads on leaf 3, side 1:

Though the "February 7 Conference" objected to the undisguised rich peasant line and took a step forward in regard to the land problem, yet it obscured the class struggle in the agrarian revolution and also made the mistake of the rich peasant line by putting forward "draw-on-the-plentiful-to-make-up-for-the-scarce and draw-on-the-fat-to-make-up-for-the-lean, " and "distribute-land-to-all-the-people. "

Three points in this passage should be understood:
1. The "February 7 Conference, " as can be seen in the section on the Fut'ien incident in this volume, was a conference held on February 7, 1930, under the sponsorship of Mao. The land policies adopted by that conference were challenged by leading participants in the Second Plenum of the Southwest Kiangsi Special Committee held under the auspices of the Li Li-sanists in July, 1930.
2. The two principles of land redistribution "draw-on-the-plentiful-to-make-up-for-the-scarce and draw-on-the-fat-to-make-up-for-the-lean" can be found only in this land law. These

two principles, as can be seen later in this volume, became a subject of repeated debate and controversy among the Communists during the Kiangsi period. They represented Mao's ideas in the sphere of land redistribution and drew severe criticisms and attacks from other factions.

3. To distribute land to all the people was nothing new. It dated from Chingkangshan where Mao redistributed land equally among all villagers, irrespective of sex or age. (See "The Struggle in the Chingkangshan Mountains, " the section on the agrarian problem, contained in Mao Tse-tung, *Selected Works,* Chinese edition, Vol. 1, p. 73, p. 86, note 21; English edition, Vol. 1, p. 90, pp. 307-8, note 21.) It therefore seems clear that this criterion of land redistribution was only reaffirmed in the February 7 (1930) Conference.

It should be noted that the principle of equal land redistribution was laid down in section 3 of the Resolution on the Peasant Problem adopted by the CCP Sixth National Congress held under Comintern supervision in 1928 at Moscow. It was later reaffirmed in section 2 of the Comintern directive to the CCP dated July 23, 1930. The Comintern directive to the CCP dated July, 1931, declared in unmistakable terms, toward the end of section 27, that "in redistributing land, one should not only take into account whether the land is large or small but also whether it is fat or lean. " (See *Red Documents,* printed by Chiai-fang-she, February, 1938, p. 397.)

2

The Liquidationists

A Reply to the Communist International (答 國 際 的 信
Ta kuo-chi ti hsin), by Ch'en Tu-hsiu, February 17, 1930;
printed in *Le Proletaire* (Wu-ch'an-che), July 1, 1930, pp. 101-
8, on file in the Hoover Library, Stanford University; secured
in photograph through the courtesy of Professor David N. Rowe,
Yale University; approximately 2, 800 words.

On February 8, 1930, the CCP Central Politburo forwarded
a Comintern telegram to Ch'en Tu-hsiu, requesting him to go
to Moscow to participate in a Comintern discussion of the question of his expulsion from the CCP, which had occurred on November 15, 1929. In reply, Ch'en rejected the Comintern request on the ground that his views on some basic problems of
the Chinese revolution were irreconcilable with Moscow's and
that it would be useless for him to make the trip so long as it
was impossible to reconcile those irreconcilable views, not to
mention the risk of his personal safety that might be involved in
the trip.
Here is the text of Ch'en's reply to Moscow together with a
copy of the Comintern telegram and a brief message from the
CCP Central Politburo to Ch'en.
The crucial problem involved in this statement was one of
estimation of the Chinese revolution, the same problem that
had characterized the Trotsky-Stalin debate over China. Ch'en
spoke frankly in support of Trotsky and upbraided the Comintern for its opportunism. While Ch'en was generally depicted
as an opportunist in orthodox Communist literature, he employed the same abusive word "opportunism" to attack Moscow,

9

and each held the other responsible for the failure of the revolution in China.

Specifically, Ch'en brought forward two basic problems that separated him from Moscow:

1. Should the future form of government in China be a democratic dictatorship of the workers and peasants or a proletarian dictatorship?

2. Should the present task of the Chinese Communists be to prepare directly for armed uprisings or to raise interim political slogans (such as a national assembly) to carry on the democratic struggle?

As the policy-makers in the Kremlin had, according to Ch'en, not learned a good lesson from the failure of opportunism, they stood in favor of a democratic dictatorship of the workers and peasants. Likewise, they advocated preparations for armed uprisings and rural guerrilla activities, because they had not learned a good lesson from the failure of blind actionism (which characterized the Ch'ü Ch'iu-pai leadership of 1927-28). Ch'en admitted that he objected to all these basic Comintern policies in China.

Acting on Comintern instructions, the CCP branded Ch'en Tu-hsiu and his followers as Trotskyites, Liquidationists, and so on. Just as the Trotskyites were purged in Russia, Ch'en Tu-hsiu and his group were liquidated in China. Owing to Ch'en's prestige among the Communist ranks, the attack on him and his Liquidationists continued unabated during the period under study, though he was then already outside the party. It also often happened that people charged with liquidationism had nothing to do with him at all.

For a better understanding of this document some other relevant statements should be consulted. Examples:

1. CCP Central Politburo resolution concerning the expulsion of Ch'en Tu-hsiu and approving the expulsion by the Kiangsu Provincial Committee of P'eng Shu-chih, Wang Tse-chieh, Ma Yü-fu, and Ts'ai Chen-te, dated November 15, 1929.

2. Ch'en Tu-hsiu's letter to all comrades of the party, dated December 10, 1929.

Would the Liquidationists Liquidate the Chinese Revolution or the Chinese Revolution Liquidate the Liquidationists?—Comments on the "Political Program of the Chinese Left-Wing Communist Opposition" (是取消派取消中國革命，還是

中國革命取消取消派？ —— 評"中國左派共產主義反對派政綱" Shih ch'ü-hsiao-p'ai ch'ü-hsiao chung-kuo ko-ming, han-shih chung-kuo ko-ming ch'ü-hsiao ch'ü-hsiao-p'ai?—p'ing "chung-kuo tso-p'ai kung-ch'an chu-i fan-tui-p'ai cheng-kang"), by Szu Mei (Chang Wen-t'ien), April, 1931; printed in *Bolshevik*, Vol. 4, No. 3, May 10, 1931, pp. 76-96, 300. 805/804, BIC; reprinted in lithograph by the Minyüehkan (Fukien-Kwangtung-Kiangsi) Soviet Area Provincial Committee, July, 1931, 008. 252/6013, SSC; reproduced with some textual errors and with the name of the writer omitted in *A Collection of Red Bandit Reactionary Documents*, Vol. 2, pp. 399-418, 008. 2129/4077/V. 2, SSC; approximately 9, 000 words.

This is probably the most representative of all the available CCP anti-liquidationist statements issued during the period under study. Though written more than a year later, it fits as well here and contrasts sharply with Ch'en Tu-hsiu's reply to the Communist International described previously.

As its subtitle indicates, this article was intended to be a reply to the political program adopted and made known by the Liquidationists. The text of the political program is unfortunately not available. A Western source says that various opposition groups held a conference at Shanghai in January, 1931, upon the advice of Trotsky. A nine-man Central Executive Committee was set up with Ch'en Tu-hsiu serving as Secretary-General and concurrently Chairman of the Politburo, and P'eng Shu-chih as head of the Propaganda Bureau. (See Conrad Brandt, Benjamin Schwartz, and John K. Fairbank, *A Documentary History of Chinese Communism*, Cambridge, Harvard University Press, 1952, p. 36.) If what this source says is true, then the political program in question must have been a resolution adopted by that conference.

The present article cites some isolated and incomplete items of the political program of the Liquidationists, which, allowing for possible misrepresentations, may give some clues to what the Liquidationists had in mind. These items follow, to which the author of the present article takes exception:

1. Estimation of the revolutionary situation (section 1). To the mind of the Liquidationists, according to this article, the 1925-27 revolution had failed, while the prospects for a future proletarian revolution were dim. That would mean that the camp of the counterrevolutionary forces had become fairly

stable during the present transition period, i. e. , during the trough between two revolutionary waves.

2. The nature of the Chinese revolution (section 2). According to the Liquidationists, it was stated, China was no longer a feudal land. Consequently, the Chinese revolution was proletarian rather than bourgeois in character.

3. Tactics in the transition period (section 3). In the present transition period, according to this article, the Liquidationists advocated Communist participation in a KMT-sponsored national assembly through which to solve such problems as the eight-hour workday, land confiscation, national independence, and self-determination.

4. Opportunism in a united-front policy (section 4). While seeking collaboration with capitalists in a national assembly, the Liquidationists attacked the Comintern's opportunism in co-operation with capitalists in the 1925-27 revolution in China.

5. The Soviet problem (section 4). Although Trotsky had advocated the formation of Chinese Soviets in the mid-twenties, the Liquidationists now dismissed the idea of setting up Soviet regimes in China as premature.

It was charged that the Liquidationists were sowing seeds of dissension among the ranks of the Communist International. They called themselves the Left-Wing Communist Opposition as heir to Marxism-Leninism, and they branded the Stalinists as an intermediate group and the Social Democrats as rightists.

After criticizing the political program of the Liquidationists point for point, the writer of this article concluded that the Liquidationists could not liquidate the Chinese revolution but that the Chinese revolution would liquidate the Liquidationists.

The importance of this article in the eyes of the Communists can be seen from the fact that it represented not only the personal views of the author but the official position of the party leadership as well. The article was reprinted and circulated in Kiangsi with the name of the author omitted. This would give the impression that the article looked like an official statement of the party under the leadership of the so-called Russian Returned Student Faction.

It may be recalled that in the spring of 1930 Pavel Mif, president of the Sun Yat-sen University at Moscow, was appointed Comintern delegate to China. With him traveled a group of young Chinese Communists who had been studying in that institution since 1926. This group was imposed by Mif on the Chinese party leadership in January, 1931, and they were known

among party veterans as the Russian Returned Students, the
Chinese Stalinists, or the twenty-eight Bolsheviks. Centering
around Ch'en Shao-yü (Wang Ming), the group included Ch'in
Pang-hsien (Po Ku), Chang Wen-t'ien (Lo Fu, Szu Mei), Wang
Chia-ch'iang, Shen Tse-min, Ho Tzu-shu, and others. (See
Benjamin I. Schwartz, *Chinese Communism and the Rise of
Mao*, Cambridge, Harvard University Press, 1951, p. 148;
Robert C. North, *Moscow and Chinese Communists*, Stanford,
Stanford University Press, 1953, p. 140.)

According to Chang Kuo-t'ao during an interview in Hongkong
late in October, 1959, Pavel Mif and his group emerged victorious from a party purge which had taken place in the Soviet
Union from the fall of 1929 to February or March, 1930. This
event marked a turning point in his career and in his role in the
Chinese revolution. Since late 1927, Chang stated, Mif served
as chief of the Chinese Section of the Eastern Department of the
Communist International. In that capacity he played an important role in the shaping of Chinese affairs. As he later became
president of Sun Yat-sen University at Moscow, he had the
chance to contact Soviet government authorities, which enhanced
his prestige and power. Having achieved power in Moscow, he
came to China to direct the Chinese revolution personally. He
arrived in China as Comintern delegate probably in June, 1930,
and went back to Russia toward the end of 1930 or early in
1931. As it was the general trend at that time to see new faces
in the leadership of the Communist movements in the various
countries, Mif brought with him to China a group of young students centering around Ch'en Shao-yü. Backed and patronized
by Mif, this group of young students soon became an eyesore to
virtually all old cadres within the CCP. However divided they
might be on other questions, the old cadres were quite at one in
resisting these young protégés of Pavel Mif.

3

The Li-san Line

Letter from the Central to the Front Committee of the Fourth Army (中央致四軍前委信 Chung-yang chih szu-chün ch'ien-wei hsin), dated April 3, 1930; handwritten manuscript; 224. 2/804, BIC; approximately 1, 350 words.

In this letter Li Li-san and his associates in the Politburo endorsed the action of the Fourth Army as consistent with the party line when they learned from newspaper reports that the army had carried guerrilla warfare into Kiangsi with the apparent object of seizing the province in cooperation with local Communist units. However, they expressed concern over the latest report that the army was moving southward in the direction of Tayü and Hsinfeng bordering on Kwangtung province, for this move, if the report was true, ran counter to the over-all policy of the party at the time. The purpose of this letter was to tell the Fourth Army to march to the north instead of the south in anticipation of a great storm that was brewing.

It will be recalled that the Fourth Army was the basis of the rise of the Chu-Mao group to power within the Chinese Communist hierarchy. It was organized in the spring of 1928 with Chu Teh as commander and Mao Tse-tung as political leader. Present-day Communist leaders like Ch'en Yi and Lin Piao were among its founders. Pavel Mif, Comintern delegate to China in 1930, spoke highly of the role of the Fourth Army in the Chinese Communist movement. (For stories of the growth of the Fourth Army, as well as the Red Army, see *Red China*, organ of the Central Soviet Government, July 29, 1933, p. 6; *Revolution and War*, organ of the Central Revolutionary Military

14

Council, published by the General Political Department, Chinese Workers' and Peasants' Red Army, Juichin, No. 1, November, 1933, pp. 28 ff; Kung Ch'u, *The Red Army and I*, Hongkong, Southwind Publishing Co., 1954, pp. 103 ff.; *A Collection of Red Bandit Reactionary Documents*, compiled under the sponsorship of General Ch'en Ch'eng, June, 1935, reprinted May, 1960, Vol. 6, pp. 1698 ff.; for Mif's views, see his publication *Heroic China: Fifteen Years of the Communist Party of China*, Chinese version, 1936, sec. 1, chap. 6.)

The strategic thinking of the Li Li-san leadership as set forth in this paper consisted of the following points:

1. The entire nation was headed for a revolutionary upsurge, marked, among other things, by an even development of the struggle of workers, peasants, and soldiers.

2. It was time to win preliminary successes in one or more provinces, which were to be followed immediately by a direct revolutionary situation looking toward a nationwide victory.

3. The party must organize political strikes, stage local uprisings, incite mutinies among government troops, and build up the Red Army, so as to prepare and carry out a nationwide insurrection.

4. The principal task of the Red Army, for the moment, was to march on the key cities.

5. The target for immediate attack was the three provinces of Hunan, Hupeh, and Kiangsi, with Wuhan as the center.

Against this background, the Li Li-san leadership insisted that the Fourth Army in Kiangsi should proceed along the Kan River northward, in order to take Kiukiang in conformity with the over-all strategy of a nationwide sweep, with Wuhan as the initial destination. To that end, he rejected the following three schools of thought then existing among party ranks:

1. To create an independent local regime in the borderland of Kwangtung, Fukien, and Kiangsi. This idea was dismissed as erroneous, conservative, and defeatist. But the interesting thing is that while Li Li-san attributed this idea to the Chu-Mao group, Mao also attacked the idea in his statement "A Single Spark Can Start a Prairie Fire," described previously. Just who was really in favor of this idea is not clear.

2. To win political power in Kiangsi province. Li Li-san did not dismiss this idea as impracticable, but he emphasized that it must be realized within the framework of a general victory in the three provinces of Hunan, Hupeh, and Kiangsi as a prelude to a nationwide sweep.

3. To win initial successes in the three provinces of Kwangsi, Kwangtung, and Fukien, with Canton as the center. This
idea was suggested by a local party conference of Kwangtung
province and was considered sound in itself. But Li Li-san
took exception to the suggestion that the Fourth Army should be
used to accomplish this task, for this would do harm to a bigger
party mission lying ahead.

In addition, the Li Li-san leadership accused the Fourth
Army of its sluggishness in increasing Red Army strength.
This was said to be due to its conservatism and its mistaken
policy of arming the peasantry in a divided rather than concen-
trated manner.

Toward the end of this letter, the party leadership expressed
the hope that Mao would go to Shanghai without fail to attend a
Conference of Delegates from the Soviet Areas then in preparation.

Unfortunately, a number of characters and phrases in the
Chinese original of this paper are missing through wear and
tear.

*Letter from the Central to the Front Committee of the
Fourth Army and for Transmission to the General Front Committee of the Third, Fourth, and Fifth Armies* (中央給四軍
前委 —— 并轉三四五軍總前委 —— 的信
Chung-yang chi szu-chün ch'ien-wei—ping chuan san szu wu
chün tsung-ch'ien-wei—ti hsin), dated April 26, 1930; handwritten manuscript; 224.2/804, BIC; approximately 850 words.

The purpose of this letter was to urge Mao Tse-tung to attend the Conference of Delegates from the Soviet Areas to be
held in Shanghai. It was stated that events had moved so fast
that the party leadership had to consider a great change in the
responsibility of the Red Army, which had become a major
force in the shaping of the high tide of the revolution. It was
added that the significance of the change was too far-reaching
to be explained by correspondence.

Accordingly, Mao was urged to attend the conference as representative of the Fourth Army at all events. It would not matter, it was stated, even if he arrived after the close of the conference. It was pointed out that several invitations had been
sent to him without eliciting a reply.

The Li Li-san leadership suggested a number of interim ar-

rangements for the benefit of the Red Army during the absence
of Mao. Chu Teh was, for example, made commander of all
Communist forces in Kiangsi.

It is not clear whether Mao arrived in Shanghai after all.

In order to understand why Li Li-san was insistent on a conference with Mao, it may be helpful to know some of Li Li-
san's viewpoints as known to contemporary observers. In the
Red Flag of March 29, April 5, and May 24, 1930, Li Li-san
published three articles in which he refused to consider any assumption that the labor movement had lagged behind the peasant
movement and in which he said that all talk of "encircling the
city with the country" or of relying on the Red Army to take the
cities was sheer nonsense. (See Benjamin Schwartz, *Chinese
Communism and the Rise of Mao,* pp. 138-39; cf. Robert
North, *Moscow and Chinese Communists,* pp. 133-34.) In
commenting on the Conference of Delegates from the Soviet
Areas, the *Red Flag* of June 21, 1930, declared that the conference stressed the importance of proletarian leadership and
of preparing for armed uprisings in the cities and that it repudiated the incorrect line of neglecting the leadership of the
city and concentrating exclusively on the "encirclement of the
city by the country" through attacks on the cities by Red Army
forces. (See Schwartz, *op. cit.,* p. 141; cf. North, *op. cit.,*
p. 135.)

In 1936 Mao told Edgar Snow that the most important single
tactic of the Red Army was mobile rather than positional warfare and that the program of the Red Army favored a wavelike
or tidal development, rather than an uneven advance, gained by
"leaps," and without deep consolidation in the territories
gained. But these tactics, Mao stated, were opposed by Li Li-
san, who wanted attacks rather than concentration, advances
without securing the rear, sensational assaults on big cities,
accompanied by uprisings and extremism. (See Edgar Snow,
Red Star over China, New York, Modern Library edition, 1944,
p. 178.) Mao declared that Li Li-san overestimated the military strength of the Red Army and the revolutionary factors in
the national political scene, and expected an almost immediate
take-over of the entire country. But in the opinion of the Red
Army, according to Mao, it was no time for possibly disas-
trous putschism and adventures. *(Ibid.,* pp. 181-82.)

Now let us turn to the comments of Mao's own machine on Li
Li-san. In 1945 the Mao machine stated that Li Li-san dismissed Mao's policies of establishing rural bases, encircling

the city with the countryside, and expediting the revolutionary
upsurge with the bases as extremely wrong and typical of the
provincialism and conservatism of the peasant mentality. (See
"Resolution on Some Historical Problems," adopted by the CCP
Central Committee on April 20, 1945, as printed in Mao Tse-
tung, *Selected Works,* Chinese edition, Vol. 3, p. 962; English
edition, Vol. 4, p. 178; also reprint of the resolution, p. 10.)

Judging from the foregoing, one has reason to believe that Li
Li-san invited Mao to Shanghai to hammer out an agreement on
the strategy and tactics to be employed in the nationwide sweep
Li Li-san had in mind.

The Chinese Soviet Political Program (中國蘇維埃的政
綱) chung-kuo su-wei-ai ti cheng-kang) taken from the Political
Resolution of the Conference of Delegates from the Soviet Areas;
reproduced in *A Collection of Red Bandit Secret Documents,* Vol.
2, leaves 1-2, 008.2129/4074, SSC; also in *A Collection of Red
Bandit Reactionary Documents,* Vol. 3, pp. 655-56, 008.2129/
4077/V.3, SSC; approximately 420 words.

The National Conference of Delegates from the Soviet Areas
was jointly called by the CCP and the National Labor Federation. (See "Declaration Calling for the Convocation of the First
National Congress of the Chinese Workers', Peasants', and
Soldiers' Council [Soviet]," contained in *The Chinese Soviets,*
Vol. 1, compiled and printed by the Central Preparatory Commission for the National Soviet Congress, probably Shanghai,
November 7, 1930.) According to a Japanese source, the joint
call was issued on February 25, 1930. (See *History of the Chinese Communist Movement* [Shina Kyosanto Undoshi], compiled by the General Staff, Tokyo, 1931, p. 314, cited in Benjamin Schwartz, *Chinese Communism and the Rise of Mao,* p.
140.) Yakhontoff reports that the conference was held at Shanghai on May 31, 1930, and attended by delegates from the various Soviet areas and professional units. (See Victor Yakhontoff, *The Chinese Soviets,* New York, Coward-McCann, Inc.,
1934, pp. 130-31.)

A man by the name of Li published an article in the *Communist International* of April 9, 1930, setting forth a three-part
program for consideration by the conference: a general program for Soviet governments, labor laws, and land laws. (See
Li, "Der I Kongress der Vertreter der Sowjetgebiets Chinas,"

Die Kommunistische Internationale, April 9, 1930, pp. 712-20, cited by Robert North in his study, *Moscow and Chinese Communists,* p. 134.) When it finally took place, the conference adopted a political program, a land law, and a labor law. In addition, it called upon the masses of the nation to win preliminary successes in one or more provinces and establish a national Soviet regime as soon as possible. (See "Declaration of the Presidium of the Conference of Delegates from the Soviet Areas, July 7, 1930, " included in *The Chinese Soviets,* Vol. 1, compiled and printed by the Central Preparatory Commission for the National Soviet Congress on November 7, 1930; cf. Victor Yakhontoff, *The Chinese Soviets,* p. 131; Benjamin Schwartz, *Chinese Communism and the Rise of Mao,* p. 141; Robert North, *Moscow and Chinese Communists,* p. 135.)

As indicated in an editorial note, the present statement is taken from the Political Resolution of the conference. Unfortunately, the text of that resolution is not available. Some three years later, G. B. Ehrenburg declared that the political resolution in question contained a mistaken statement to the effect that there already existed a revolutionary situation in China. Therefore, he regretted the incorrect political slogan of the conference, namely, the call to an immediate armed uprising. (See G. B. Ehrenburg, *Sovetskii Kitai,* Moscow, 1933, pp. 25-26, cited by Robert North in his study, *Moscow and Chinese Communists,* p. 135.)

On the whole, the present statement is based on the Ten Great Demands of the Political Resolution of the CCP Sixth National Congress. (For an English version of the Ten Great Demands, see Conrad Brandt, Benjamin Schwartz, and John Fairbank, *A Documentary History of Chinese Communism,* p. 132.) It contains, however, significant additions which show the traits of Li Li-sanism. Like the Provisional Land Law adopted by the conference, for instance, this statement forbids the sale, lease, and mortgage of land and stands for the nationalization of land (clause 4).

However, there is an inexplicable difference between this statement and the Provisional Land Law, both of which were adopted by one and the same conference. While this statement, based on point 8 of the Ten Great Demands of the Political Resolution of the CCP Sixth National Congress, provides for allotment of land to soldiers in active service (clause 2), the Provisional Land Law prescribes that decisions on the redistribution of land to the Red Army men who have not been as-

signed land will not be made until the establishment of a national
Soviet government (article 5, note 14). As both texts are re-
productions, it is not clear whether misprints have crept in.

Labor Protection Law (勞 動 保 護 法 Lao-tung pao-hu
fa), adopted by the National Conference of Delegates from the
Soviet Areas, May, 1930; printed in *The Chinese Soviets*, Vol.
1, pp. 7-10; compiled and printed by the Central Preparatory
Commission for the National Soviet Congress, November 7,
1930, 052.2/804, BIC; approximately 1,300 words.

This labor law is divided into eight chapters and forty-two
articles, dealing with questions of working hours, wages, labor
unions, and so forth. As article 42 provides that the law comes
into force upon its approval by the First National Soviet Congress, it is doubtful whether it had formally been put into practice at all, because that congress was not held until November
7, 1931, about a year after the disgrace of Li Li-san. The
party leadership complained, on September 1, 1931, that the
system of eight hours of work in a day, as provided in this law,
had never been implemented in the Soviet areas. (See A Directive Letter of the Central to the Soviet Areas, September 1,
1931.)
Strangely enough, there are some textual discrepancies between this law and the Chinese Soviet Political Program, both of
which were adopted by the same conference. It is provided, in
clause 3 of the Chinese Soviet Political Program, for instance,
that the minimum wage of a worker in a month shall not be less
than forty Chinese dollars and that women workers shall be
granted an eight-week leave of absence with full pay during
childbirth. On the other hand, this law does not provide for a
minimum wage of forty dollars per month and it grants a total
of twelve weeks of rest to a woman worker before and after
childbirth (clause 22).

Provisional Land Law (土 地 暫 行 法 T'u-ti tsan-hsing
fa), adopted by the National Conference of Delegates from the
Soviet Areas; reproduced in *A Collection of Red Bandit Documents*, Vol. 1, pp. 11-17, 008.2129/4070/V.1, SSC; *A Collection of Red Bandit Reactionary Documents*, Vol. 3, pp. 918-21,
008.2129/4077/V.3, SSC; approximately 1,400 words.

This provisional land law was adopted by the National Conference of Delegates from the Soviet Areas held in May, 1930, under the sponsorship of the Li Li-san leadership. Leaving a fuller discussion of this law to another volume on the agrarian revolution in China in 1930-34, we wish to make clear the following points for our present purposes:

1. The striking features of this land law are, *inter alia:* (a) prohibition of the sale, lease, and mortgage of land, (b) collectivization, and (c) relative leniency to the rich peasantry. Whereas other laws decree confiscation of all land of the rich peasant, this one deprives him of only that portion of his land which he rents out on lease (article 1, note 2).

2. As described previously, this land law was supported by the Second Plenum of the Southwest Kiangsi Special Committee held in July, 1930, a plenum which set itself against the land policies of the February 7 (1930) Conference sponsored by the Chu-Mao group. The clash came into the open during the Fut'ien incident late in 1930.

3. This land law was denounced by a stream of subsequent Comintern statements: (a) Comintern letter to the CCP, dated July 23, 1930; (b) Comintern Eastern Department Draft Resolution on the Land and Peasant Problems in Soviet Areas, n. d., reprinted by the CCP Central Secretariat on November (?) 20, 1930; (c) Comintern letter to the CCP received November 16, 1930; (d) documents concerning the discussion of the Li-san line by the Presidium of the ECCI, published in the CCP organ *Bolshevik* on May 10, 1931; (e) Comintern letter to the CCP, July, 1931.

4. After the pattern of Comintern denunciations, Chinese Communist statements also attacked this land law following the receipt of the Comintern directive of July 23, 1930. Examples: (a) statements made in or by the Third Plenum of September, 1930; (b) proceedings of the CCP Politburo enlarged meeting, November 22, 1930; (c) resolution of the Fourth Plenum of the CCP Central Committee, January, 1931.

The New Revolutionary High Tide and Preliminary Successes in One or More Provinces—Resolution on the Present Political Tasks Adopted by the CCP Politburo on June 11, 1930 (新的革命高潮與一省或幾省首先勝利 —— 一九三○年六月十一日政治局會議通過目前政治任務的決議 Hsin ti ko-ming kao-ch'ao yü i-sheng huo chi-sheng

shou-hsien sheng-li-i-chiu-san-ling nien liu yüeh shih-i jih
cheng-chih-chü hui-i t'ung-kuo mu-ch'ien cheng-chih jen-wu ti
chüeh-i), reproduced by the Red Army Academy Party Committee, Kian, Kiangsi, October 10, 1930; mimeographed;
008. 235/5051, SSC; also in: *A Collection of Red Bandit Secret
Documents*, Vol. 3, leaves 12-24, 008. 2129/4074, SSC, and
A Collection of Red Bandit Documents, Vol. 7, pp. 4-37,
008. 2129/4070/V. 7, SSC; approximately 9,000 words.

This rather desperate document represented the ultimate
formation of the Li-san line which had been brewing since the
early months of 1930. It contains several basic ideas which
have distinguished the Li-san line from other schools of thought
within the Chinese Communist movement.

In the first place, Li Li-san assumed that in the global revolutionary wave of the time a revolution could first break out in
China and then engulf the whole world. Conditions were ripe for
a revolution in China, and the political and economic crisis
was growing equally acute in all parts of the country. It would
therefore be inevitable that once a gigantic struggle of workers
was started in key cities, it would immediately make for a
nationwide revolutionary upsurge—a direct revolutionary situation.

Second, preliminary successes in one or more provinces
could only be achieved within the framework of the general
revolutionary situation in the whole nation. The circumstances
of the time made it necessary to take Wuhan as a center for
winning such preliminary successes, since Wuhan occupied a
strategic position in Central China, holding the key to a success
of the revolution throughout the country.

Third, the struggle of workers in urban centers would be a
decisive factor in the nationwide revolutionary movement. To
be successful, it needed only to be aided by other forces such
as peasant uprisings, soldier insurrections, and Red Army assaults.

Fourth, the revolution at the present stage was essentially an
agrarian revolution led by workers, which was in the nature of
a democratic revolution. But where the present democratic
revolution succeeded, it should immediately pass to a socialist
revolution and there should not be any interval between them.
It would be a gross mistake to postpone the socialist revolution
until after the successful completion of the democratic revolution all over the country.

It has become apparent that the Li-san line was in conflict
with the basic policies of both Ch'en Tu-hsiu and Mao Tse-tung.
For example, Li Li-san rejected the idea of a national assembly as advocated by Ch'en Tu-hsiu. Again, Li disagreed with
Mao's policies of the rural base, guerrilla tactics, encircling
the city with the countryside, and the like.

As to the relation of the Li-san line to Moscow, the Chinese
Communist record contains diverse and contradictory interpre-
tations. As will be seen later, the Third Plenum of the CCP
Central Committee of September, 1930, decided that Li Li-san,
in relation to Moscow, had committed an error of tactics rather
than of line. In contrast, the Fourth Plenum of January, 1931,
reversed the position of the Third Plenum and proclaimed that
Li Li-san had committed an error of line rather than of tactics.
The party veteran Ho Meng-hsiung saw an error of line in Li
Li-san's policies even before the convocation of the Third
Plenum.

In March, 1932, Ch'en Shao-yü, leader of the Russian Returned Students, quoted the Trotsky-Ch'en Tu-hsiu group as
saying:

The Li-san line was exactly the Comintern line. The reason why the
Comintern objected to the Li-san line was because the Comintern
had wanted to remove the insubordinate Li Li-san and his associates
from the central leading organ to be replaced by members of the
Stalinist group under the pretext of the fight against the Li-san line.
Therefore, the struggle against the Li-san line within the CCP was
an unprincipled factional struggle; it was an underhand scheme of
the Stalinist group. . . .*

It may or may not be a mere coincidence, but a growing number of Western observers share the opinion of the Trotsky-
Ch'en Tu-hsiu group as cited above. The consensus is that the
Li-san line was essentially shaped in Moscow and that since it
ended in failure, Li Li-san was made a scapegoat. These
Western observers together with their studies may be arranged
in chronological order as follows:

1. Harold R. Isaacs, *The Tragedy of the Chinese Revolution*,
first edition, London, Sacker and Warburg, 1938; second edi-

---

*See Ch'en Shao-yü, *Struggle for the More Complete Bolshevi-
zation of the Chinese Communist Party*, postscript, I, C, 2, p.
135, first edition, Shanghai, February, 1931; second edition,
Moscow, March, 1932; third edition, Yenan, March, 1940.

tion, Stanford, Stanford University Press, 1951, p. 303. This book has often been identified in bibliographies as "Trotskyist. "

2. Benjamin I. Schwartz, *Chinese Communism and the Rise of Mao*, Cambridge, Harvard University Press, 1951, chaps. 9-10.

3. Conrad Brandt, Benjamin Schwartz, and John K. Fairbank, *A Documentary History of Chinese Communism*, Cambridge, Harvard University Press, 1952, pp. 179-84.

4. Robert C. North, *Moscow and Chinese Communists*, Stanford, Stanford University Press, 1953, chap. 9.

5. Karl Wittfogel, *A Short History of Chinese Communism*, an unpublished manuscript on file in the Far Eastern and Russian Institute, University of Washington, 1956, chap. 5.

However, a study of available Comintern directives to the CCP since 1928 has forced the impression upon us that the Li-san line can hardly be said to have been in agreement with the basic policies of the Comintern in China since 1928 in spite of the seemingly enigmatic and contradictory language of those directives. A particular document involved in the present case is the Comintern directive of July 23, 1930, which was issued between the formation of the Li-san line on June 11 and the Communist capture of Changsha on July 28. It has become apparent that this Comintern directive actually represented the Comintern reaction to the Li-san line before it was given full swing. Conrad Brandt, Benjamin Schwartz, and John Fairbank, who did not have a text of this Comintern directive but only learned of the document from a footnote in the Isaacs publication *The Tragedy of the Chinese Revolution*, found an identity of ideas between this Comintern directive and the CCP Politburo resolution of June 11 and held Moscow responsible for the Li-san line on the basis of that identity of ideas. (See Conrad Brandt, Benjamin Schwartz, and John Fairbank, *A Documentary History of Chinese Communism*, pp. 181, 182-83, and 488: Commentary I: 1. Isaacs, p. 403, and Document No. 16: 1 "This CI letter, the text of which is not available, is mentioned by Harold Isaacs. . . ."; cf. Benjamin Schwartz, *Chinese Communism and the Rise of Mao*, pp. 143, 145, 153, 160, 162, and p. 232, note 32.) Robert North, who apparently had a text of the Comintern directive, detected some differences between it and the CCP Politburo resolution of June 11 but decided that the differences concerned timing and not the fundamental strategy for which Li Li-san was later to be held responsible. (See Robert North, *Moscow and Chinese Communists*, p. 137.)

However, a close examination of the Comintern directive of July 23, 1930, and the CCP Politburo resolution of June 11, 1930, shows discrepancies which go beyond the scope of timing or tactics. This can be seen from the following comparison:

Politburo Resolution

1. The political and economic crisis in China is growing equally acute in all parts of the country and there is no basic difference whatever between one locality and another. Once a gigantic struggle of the workers breaks out in key cities, it will inevitably make for a revolutionary high tide all over the country (section 9).

2. People have only perceived the superficial unevenness of the revolutionary development in the cities and in the countryside but have overlooked the unusual acuteness of the struggle of the workers and what not (section 7). If a great struggle of the workers breaks out in an industrial or political center, it will immediately lead to a direct revolutionary situation (section 8).

3. Preparing armed uprisings and winning preliminary successes in one or more provinces centering around Wuhan constitute the general line of the Party strategy for the moment (section 22, cf. section 10).

Comintern Directive

The new rising tide of the Chinese revolutionary movement has become an indisputable fact (section 1). But it has a particular process all its own. It has emerged for the most part in the areas swept by the revolution of 1925-27. This would mean that the new revolutionary rising tide has a weakness in the initial stage: the struggling masses cannot occupy industrial centers at the outset (section 3).

In analyzing the present-day struggle we must note that we do not have for the moment an all-China objective revolutionary situation (section 4). The waves of the labor and peasant movements have not yet been combined and it is not certain that, even if combined, they are strong enough for an attack on the imperialist-KMT rule. The peasant revolutionary struggles which can hope to succeed are only those which are developing in a few provinces in South China (section 4).

According to the trend of recent events, the revolutionary situation can cover a few major provinces, if not the whole country. Much will depend on whether the Communist Party has a correct strategy and, above all, whether it is able to

Politburo Resolution

Comintern Directive

lead and develop the Soviet movement (section 4). All plans for uprisings without reckoning with the support of the broad masses are warned against (section 20).

4. The greatest obstacle to the accomplishment of the task of the Party is the "guerrilla" concept of the past, which favors attacking rather than occupying the cities and which lacks the determination to set up local Soviet regimes in the cities. This is a reflection of the peasant mentality and has nothing in common with the present Party line (section 27).

Guerrilla activities must be promoted as far as possible (section 20).

5. The Red Army, like the peasants and the rank and file of the KMT troops, is an ally of the workers and is required to act in collaboration with the workers who have been ordered to start a general rising (section 13).

The Red Army must be organized and strengthened in order that it may be able to take one or more key cities in the future according to political and military circumstances (section 5).

6. The beginning of a successful bourgeois-democratic revolution would pass immediately to a socialist revolution, and there should be no interval between them (section 18, 19).

It would be a long and tortuous way to transform a bourgeois-democratic revolution, and there would be numerous temporary expedients in between (section 27).

7. Only the Right deviation is attacked.

Both the Right and Left deviations are condemned, with the Right deviation as the main danger.

In addition, as has been noted, the Comintern directive of

July 23, 1930, lifts the ban on the sale and purchase of land
(section 8), as provided in the land law enacted under the sponsorship of Li Li-san in the National Conference of Delegates
from the Soviet Areas in May, 1930.

Interviewed in Hongkong in late October, 1959, Chang Kuo-
t'ao declared that the Comintern had been at variance with Li
Li-san since June, 1929, when Ts'ai Ho-shen published an article which Moscow endorsed and Li Li-san condemned. Because of that article, Ts'ai Ho-shen was banished by the Li Li-
san leadership to Moscow. Since then Li Li-san had not been on
good terms with the Kremlin. The important thing to remember
is that when Pavel Mif was appointed Comintern delegate to
China in 1930, his principal mission was to keep Li Li-san in
line. Charged with the responsibility of directing the work of the
CCP, Mif had the support of Stalin.

Complex as they were, Chang stated, the sources of the Li-
san line had primarily been home-grown rather than imported.
In making his putschist adventures, Li Li-san was prompted by
traditional Chinese heroism rather than by Marxism. Being personally ambitious, despotic, and vainglorious, he disbanded
party and mass organizations. Such behavior was typically Chinese and could find no precedent in Russian experience.

Of course, Chang added, Li Li-san was responsible for his
policy of taking big cities. But if one looked at the matter more
broadly, one would also find that Moscow could not shirk its responsibility for the Li-san line in two respects, namely, (1) the
policy of forming Soviets in China, and (2) the fight against the
Right deviation. These two things had a common feature of veer-
ing to the Left. The formation of Soviets was intended to intensify the revolution within the country rather than presenting a
united front against imperialist aggression. The general trend
of Moscow policy toward the Left had no doubt helped the growth
of Li Li-sanism.

There are slight verbal differences in the three available texts
of the present statement as listed above. The thirty-fifth and
last section of this statement as contained in the text reproduced
in *A Collection of Red Bandit Documents*, compiled by the
Fourth and later the Second Department, Nanchang Headquarters,
Chairman of the Military Council, July, 1933-October, 1934,
does not appear in the other two texts.

An English version of this statement, which contains the thirty-
fifth section, appears in the Harvard publication *A Documentary
History of Chinese Communism*, pp. 184-200. Unfortunately, the

translations of some of the key phrases have lost much of the
original meaning. For example, in the phrase "use village
(forces) to besiege the cities" (p. 191), the supplied word
"forces" must go. Again, the very first sentence of section 9 on
page 189, which reads, "The basic economic and political crisis in China is everywhere becoming more intense and there is
no fundamental difference in it (as regards locality), " has lost
much of the very essence of the Li-san line as embodied in the
original.

*Resolution on the Chinese Problem, Adopted by the ECCI
Political Secretariat on July 23, 1930* (中國問題決議案 —
— 共產國際執委政治秘書處 一九三○年七月二十
三日通過 Chung-kuo wen-t'i chüeh-i-an—kung-ch'an kuo-chi
chih-wei cheng-chih pi-shu-ch'u i-chiu-san-ling nien ch'i yüeh
erh-shih-san jih t'ung-kuo), Chinese version, printed in *Red
Documents,* published by Chiai-fang-she, February, 1938, n. p.,
pp. 346-61, 008. 2129/2703, SSC; reproduced in *A Collection of
Red Bandit Secret Documents,* Vol. 3, leaves 3-12, 008. 2129/
4070, SSC; mimeographed; approximately 7, 800 words.

This Comintern statement, issued between the CCP Politburo
resolution of June 11 and the Communist capture of Changsha on
July 28, 1930, represented the official reaction of the Comintern to the Li-san line. It was the most immediate Comintern
statement in connection with the Li-san line and must be studied before one attempts to form any judgment on the question of
Moscow's relation to the line. But, unfortunately, this document has generally been overlooked or misunderstood in the
West despite the fact that a text of the document, according to
a letter from Robert North under date of April 8, 1959, can be
found in the Chinese Communist organ *Shih-hua* (True Words),
No. 1, October 30, 1930, pp. 2-5, n. p., probably Shanghai, on
file in the Hoover Library, Stanford University.

The important thing to remember is that this document was
meant not only to keep the Li-san line in check but also to provide the CCP with a code of conduct. It has become apparent
that this Comintern statement has foreshadowed the whole subsequent development of the Chinese Communist movement.

Having compared this statement with the Li-san line point for
point in the previous entry, we think it useful to analyze this
piece at length and let it speak for itself as follows:

This Comintern directive is divided into three parts, namely, (1) the rising tide of the Chinese revolutionary movement, (2) major tasks of the party, and (3) the prospects and tasks of the Chinese revolution. The first part is a diagnosis of the Chinese situation, which has often been misquoted or misrepresented. It begins by reaffirming the inevitability of a new rising tide of the Chinese revolution as postulated by the Sixth National Congress of the CCP and the Sixth World Congress of the Comintern in 1928. As a rebuttal to rightists, it is stated categorically that the new rising tide of the Chinese revolutionary movement has become an indisputable fact.

It is, however, pointed out that the rising tide of the Chinese revolution would first come in the provinces swept by the revolution of 1925-27. It would be impossible to seize industrial centers in the first instance.

There is, it is added, no objective revolutionary situation on a national scale for the moment. The labor and peasant movements have not yet been combined; they are not strong enough for attacking the imperialist and KMT rule. The peasant revolution can hope to succeed only in a few provinces; the ruling classes have not reached a stage of total collapse. However, judging from the trend of recent events, the revolutionary situation would cover at least a few important provinces, if not the whole country. The furtherance of this process will depend largely upon whether the CCP has a sound program and whether it can first of all correctly perform its task of leading and developing the Soviet movement.

It can be seen from the foregoing that the Comintern, in its letter of July 23, wanted the Li Li-san leadership to make its main efforts on the Soviet movement in the rural districts first, but not on industrial cities with a view to a nationwide sweep. In this connection, it should be remembered that the term "Soviet Areas" as used in Communist literature of the period under study was generally employed to denote the Communist-controlled areas in the rural districts rather than those in the urban centers. This should have been due to the fact that the Soviet as a form of government existed only in the rural districts at that time. Hence, the second part of the present Comintern statement accords priority to CCP work in the Soviet areas.

As it is, the second part of this statement consists of a total of sixteen sections, among which seven sections deal with Communist work in Soviet areas, six sections with that in non-Soviet areas, and three sections with the ideological struggle.

The major tasks of the CCP in the Soviet areas are the following: (1) establishment of a central government, (2) formation and strengthening of a Red Army, (3) solution of the agrarian problem, (4) avoidance of premature economic policies
such as collectivization, (5) improvement of the livelihood of
labor. By far the most important is the agrarian problem
which is featured or touched upon in all sections except the one
on labor.

Almost equally stressed but less fully discussed is the question of the creation of a central government and the build-up of
a Red Army. A government, it is stated, cannot be strong
without the support of a Red Army. Attention must be focused
on the organization and strengthening of a Red Army so that one
or more industrial or administrative key cities can be occupied
according to political and military circumstances in the future.
Here the phrase "in the future" is the key idea. It means that
the Red Army cannot be used to attack urban centers just now,
though it may be used to do so in the future according to circumstances. But despite the Comintern injunction, Li Li-san
ordered the Red Army to attack Changsha as the first step of
his march on Wuhan. Strangely enough, some contemporary
Western observers, who did not seem to understand the meaning of this key phrase, cited the whole sentence as a proof of
Moscow's approval of the putschist strategy of Li Li-san. (See
Conrad Brandt, Benjamin Schwartz, and John Fairbank, *A
Documentary History of Chinese Communism*, p. 181.)

When the present Comintern directive went on to discuss CCP
work outside the Soviet areas, it emphasized the proletarian
leadership on a national scale. The specific tasks assigned to
the CCP in the KMT-controlled areas are as follows:

1. Labor movement: (a) political strike, (b) economic struggle, (c) strengthening work in yellow (i. e., neutral) labor unions, (d) consolidating Red labor unions.

2. Anti-imperialist movement.

3. Mass movement against (a) warlord strifes, (b) neutralist
groups like the Reorganizationists, the Third Party, and the Hu
Shih group, and (c) the Trotsky-Ch'en Tu-hsiu faction.

4. Peasant movement.

5. Minorities.

In addition, the Comintern imposed on the CCP an ideological
program of a two-front struggle against Right and Left deviations, placing emphasis on the Right deviation as the main dan-

ger. The Right deviation includes tailism, underestimation of guerrilla warfare, and pro-rich-peasant policy, while the Left deviation includes insurrections without support of the broad masses, mechanical nationwide strikes, leftist economic policies, and so forth.

The third part of this Comintern directive is a blueprint for the future development of the revolution in China. The Chinese revolution is defined as being a bourgeois-democratic revolution which has four major characteristics, namely, (1) removal of the imperialist rule, (2) abolition of landlords' private land-ownership, (3) destruction of the alliance between landlords and capitalists, and (4) establishment of a democratic dictatorship of the workers and peasants.

It is pointed out that the bourgeois-democratic revolution is socialist but not capitalist in nature. It will be transformed into a socialist revolution through a long transition period rather than overnight as suggested by Trotsky. Here, the question of the speed of the transformation of a successful bourgeois-democratic revolution into a socialist revolution has also been misunderstood by some contemporary observers in the West. (See Conrad Brandt, Benjamin Schwartz, and John Fairbank, *A Documentary History of Chinese Communism,* pp. 181-82.)

Questioned whether the present statement was issued as a direct Comintern reply to the CCP Politburo resolution of June 11, Chang Kuo-t'ao stated during an interview in Hongkong in late October, 1959, that he did not know, because he was absent on leave at that time. But he felt sure that the Comintern must have been kept informed of the Li-san line by telegraph even if Moscow had not received the text of the CCP Politburo resolution of June 11 by then.

4

Military Adventures

The Current Political Situation and the Tasks of the Party in the Preparation of Armed Uprisings (目 前 政 治 形 勢 與 黨 在 準 備 武 裝 暴 動 中 的 任 務 Mu-ch'ien cheng-chih hsing-shih yü tang tsai chun-pei wu-chuang pao-tung chung ti jen-wu), address delivered by Li Li-san before the Central Action Committee on August 6, 1930; printed in *Red Flag Daily,* Nos. 2-4, August 16-18, 1930, Shanghai, on file in BIC, bearing no call number; approximately 10,500 words.

The fall of Changsha, the capital of Hunan province, to the Red Army on July 28, 1930, marked the apogee of the Li-san line. Encouraged by this event, Li Li-san set up a Central Action Committee to bear the full responsibility of carrying out the nationwide insurrection with Wuhan as the immediate target of military attack. The present statement was the speech delivered by Li Li-san on the occasion of the inauguration of the Central Action Committee.

Li Li-san flattered himself that Changsha bore witness to the soundness of the party policy as set forth in the June 11 Politburo resolution. He was now more than ever convinced of the success of his military adventures.

Probably owing to their contribution to the capture of Changsha, Li Li-san attached greater importance to the peasants and the Red Army than before. The peasants in China, he said, played a greater role in the revolution than the peasants in Russia. The Red Army, he stated, was the product of the agrarian revolution. There were only guerrilla activities before the revolution in Russia, while there were not

32

only guerrilla activities but also the regular Red Army in China.

Li Li-san claimed that the CCP had won over the majority of the working class. He explained that this should not be taken to mean that the party must necessarily have control of 51 per cent of the members of the labor unions, because such control would be difficult to attain even in the industrial countries in western Europe. This should only be understood in the sense that the party had the subjective power of commanding the respect and support of the majority of the working class. In other words, this should be understood in a political rather than mechanical sense.

As the Red Army was generally regarded as representing the peasantry, the fear was expressed that the peasantry would possibly lead the working class if the Red Army were used to take Wuhan where the labor struggle had not yet reached the upsurge point. Li Li-san dismissed this notion as erroneous, saying that to rely on the Red Army for the seizure of Wuhan without the help of labor insurrections would be as vicious as to depend solely upon the political strikes and armed uprisings of the workers without making use of the Red Army.

Declaration of the CCP on the Current Situation (中國共產黨 對日前時局宣言 Chung-kuo kung-ch'an-tang tui mu-ch'ien shih-chü hsüan-yen), dated August 14, 1930; printed in *Red Flag Daily,* No. 1, August 15, 1930, Shanghai, on file in BIC, bearing no call number; approximately 7, 200 words.

Though issued after the Communist retreat from Changsha, this statement was still characterized by the burning ambitions of the Li Li-san leadership which showed no lessening of its exuberant assurance that the stage had been set for a nationwide, armed uprising. This statement differs in no way from the June 11 Politburo resolution in all basic assumptions.

What is new in this statement is a political program of twenty-nine items based professedly on the ten-point program enacted by the Sixth National Congress of 1928. As it is, this political program contains some traits of Li Li-sanism such as the prohibition of the sale of land. Compared with the 1928 enactment, this program contains a number of additional provisions which make it considerably more comprehensive and radical. For instance, while the 1928 statement confines its

xenophobia to the overthrow of the imperialist rule and the confiscation of the enterprises and banks of foreign capitalism,
this program adds these new items: repudiate all foreign land
and sea forces from China; get back all concessions and leased
or ceded territories.

The present statement ends with a call for direct action
couched in no less desperate terms than the June 11 Politburo
resolution.

*Organizing Political Demonstrations, Strikes, and Prepar-
ing Armed Uprisings* (組織 政治示威、罷工 與 準備
武裝暴動 Tsu-chih cheng-chih shih-wei, pa-kung yü chun-
pei wu-chuang pao-tung), a leading article by Li Li-san in *Red
Flag Daily*, No. 10, August 24, 1930, on file in BIC, bearing
no call number; approximately 950 words.

The purpose of this leading article is to give an explanation
of the relationships of political demonstrations, strikes, and
armed uprisings. Political demonstrations and strikes, it is
stated, are necessary steps to the preparation of armed uprisings. On the one hand, political demonstrations and strikes
must aim at the preparation of armed uprisings so that armed
uprisings will come about with accelerating force. On the other,
armed uprisings must presuppose political demonstrations and
strikes; otherwise armed uprisings would be mere lip service.

As is evident from this article, the failure at Changsha did
not discourage Li Li-san a bit from his ambition for a nationwide sweep. He had come to pin his hopes on the broad masses
rather than on a small number of workers. "An armed uprising, " said he, "is a most stupendous class struggle. It must depend upon the strength of the broad masses, not merely upon
the small number of advanced elements. "

*The Question of Organization before an Imminent Direct
Revolutionary Action* (迫近直接革命行動時之組織
問題 Pe-chin chih-chieh ko-ming hsing-tung shih chih tsu-
chih wen-t'i), by [Teng] Chung-hsia; printed in *Red Flag Daily*,
No. 12, August 26, 1930, Shanghai, on file in BIC, bearing no
call number; approximately 2, 200 words.

This article deals with the relation of a revolutionary upsurge

to the organization of the party and of the labor union. As in
other aspects of the Communist movement, the tenet of the two-
front struggle applies here.

The main target of attack is Right opportunism, according to
which the tide of the revolution rises in proportion as the organization of the party and of the masses grows in strength. It
follows that there was no revolutionary upsurge at that time
since the organization of that kind was weak. This is said to be
contrary to the teachings of Lenin, who was of the opinion that
revolution resulted from the impossibility of maintaining the
status quo between the oppressor and the oppressed rather than
from the organization of a political party.

On the other hand, Left opportunism belittles the role of organization in the furtherance of a revolutionary surge. Since the
high tide of the revolution comes anyway, it would be of little
use to make a point of strengthening organization.

As the principal purpose of this article was to attack Right
opportunism, it would appear that this article was inspired by
Li Li-san who was later to be condemned for having overlooked
organization.

Another Red Army Attack on Changsha and Our Task (紅軍
再攻長沙與我們的任務 Hung-chün tsai kung chang-
sha yü wo-men ti jen-wu), editorial of *Red Flag Daily,* No. 13,
August 27, 1930, on file in BIC, bearing no call number; approximately 800 words.

On learning that the Red Army was making another attack on
Changsha late in August, this editorial set forth what should be
done about it in the light of the lesson learned from the first
attack a month before.

The failure of the first attack on Changsha was believed to
have been due to the fact that the broad masses in the nation had
not come to the aid of the move by means of large-scale demonstrations and political strikes. For this reason, the masses
were cautioned that Changsha was only a part of the general
revolutionary effort in the entire country and that it must be
coordinated with a nationwide struggle to be successful. To
that end, it was considered essential to set in motion political
strikes in all cities and widespread insurrections among soldiers and in the countryside so that the Red Army might not be
in an isolated position in the revolution.

Western Fukien Looks Like Another World (另 一 個 世 界 的 閩 西 Ling-i-ko shih-chiai ti min-hsi), printed in *Red Flag Daily*, No. 14, August 28, 1930, on file in BIC, bearing no call number; approximately 1,700 words.

This newsletter spoke highly of the Communist work in western Fukien where the Chu-Mao group had gained a foothold during 1929. In the middle of 1930 this group again appeared in western Fukien, after several months of guerrilla activities in southern Kiangsi. The military strength of this group had now increased to more than 40,000 men as against three to four thousand men in early 1929.

Mao's machine claimed that Mao not only had never had a hand in the Li-san line but had tried to help correct it with the greatest possible patience. (See "Resolution on Some Historical Problems," adopted April 20, 1945, Mao Tse-tung, *Selected Works*, Chinese edition, Vol. 3, p. 963; English edition, Vol. 4, p. 179; reprint of the resolution, p. 11.) However, it was reported in this newsletter that Mao and Chu Teh played a major part in a mammoth, local mass meeting in western Fukien to bid farewell to Red Army men who were being sent north to march on Nanchang and Wuhan to help carry the Li-san line into execution. It was interestingly reported that more than twenty people addressed the meeting and that "they were all workers or peasants except Chu Teh, Mao Tse-tung, and a delegate from Taiwan."

"Left" Opportunism in the Preparation of Armed Uprisings (準備武裝暴動中之"左傾"機會主義 Chun-pei wu-chuang pao-tung chung chih "tso-ch'ing" chi-hui chu-i), editorial of *Red Flag Daily*, No. 17, August 31, 1930, on file in BIC, bearing no call number; approximately 850 words.

As an integral part of the Communist life, the principle of a two-front struggle against Right and Left deviations applies to any Communist move. Here the principle applies to the Li Li-san line, and it is noteworthy that it is directed against Left rather than Right opportunism.

This editorial proceeds from the assumption that the preparation for armed uprisings presupposes a political mobilization of the broad masses, accompanied by organizational and technical preparations. The precondition for armed uprisings is a political strike in key industrial centers; without a political strike an armed uprising would be a mere military conspiracy on the part of a small number of people. But opportunists, it is pointed out, have failed to adhere to this basic assumption under the cloak of a "Left" slogan. They have simply prepared for armed uprisings in the technical and organizational fields. Accordingly, it is the object of this editorial to call a halt to this Left trend while the fight against Right opportunism goes on.

Telegram of the Plenum of the Central Preparatory Committee for the National Soviet Congress Paying a Tribute to the Third, Fourth, Fifth, Eighth, and Twelfth Armies of the Red Army (全國蘇維埃大會中央準備會全體會議慰勞紅軍第三、四、五、八、十二軍電 Ch'üan-kuo su-wei-ai ta-hui chung-yang chun-pei-hui ch'üan-t'i hui-i wei-lao hung-chün ti-san, szu, wu, pa, shih-erh chün tien), dated September 12 (1930); printed in *The Chinese Soviets,* Vol. 1, 052.2/ 804, BIC; approximately 1,100 words.

This telegraphic message was sent to Red Army forces when their second attack on Changsha, it was stated, was in progress.

It was pointed out that, acting on the strategy decided by the National Conference of Delegates from Soviet Areas, the Fifth and Eighth armies captured and held Changsha for about a week over a month before and that a second attack on Changsha was being carried out on a more massive scale by the Third, Fourth, Fifth, Eighth, and Twelfth armies. It was made clear that the purpose of the military operations was to win preliminary successes in a few provinces around Wuhan and even in the whole country.

The Strategy of the Red Army in the Besieging of Changsha (紅軍團攻長沙的戰略 Hung-chün wei-kung chang-sha ti chan-lüeh), editorial of *Red Flag Daily,* No. 34, September 17, 1930, on file in BIC, bearing no call number; approximately 850 words.

By the time this editorial was published, all hope of a success of the Red Army's second attack on Changsha was gone.

Of necessity, gone also was the essence of the Li-san line—seizure of key cities and objection to encircling the city with the countryside.

As the Communists failed to take Changsha, it had become apparent that they were confronted with a possible long-drawn struggle. Under the circumstances, they had to reconsider their politico-military strategy designed to make the implementation of the Li-san line possible. As shown in this editorial, the Communists had now given up their idea of a direct attack on Changsha and decided to transfer their activities to the countryside in Hunan. They had come to realize that if they managed to establish themselves in the rural districts Changsha would inevitably become an isolated city. Says the editorial:

Accordingly, the present strategy of the Red Army in Hunan is not one of simple attack on Changsha; it must be a swift expansion of its own activities in all the counties in the province. The city of Changsha will automatically fall only if the Red Army can establish itself on a firmer basis in the various counties. In addition, the development of political influence along this line would be more significant than a simple military victory.

Thus, the Li-san line ended with a shift of the focus of Communist work from the cities to the countryside.

5

Plans for a Soviet Government

Declaration Calling for the Convocation of the First National Congress of the Chinese Workers', Peasants', and Soldiers' Council (Soviet) (號召中國農工兵會議（蘇維埃）第一次全國代表大會宣言 Hao-chao chung-kuo.kung-nung-ping hui-i (su-wei-ai) ti-i-tz'u ch'üan-kuo tai-piao ta-hui hsüan-yen), issued by the Presidium of the National Conference of Delegates from Soviet Areas, July 7, 1930; contained in *The Chinese Soviets,* Vol. 1, compiled and printed by the Central Preparatory Commission for the National Soviet Congress, July 7, 1930, 052.2/804, BIC; approximately 2,900 words.

This was the first official appeal of the Li Li-san leadership to the masses for their support for a national Soviet congress, looking toward the proclamation of a central Soviet government. This appeal was made in the name of the Presidium of the National Conference of Delegates from Soviet Areas about five weeks after the close of that conference.

It was recalled that the National Conference of Delegates from Soviet Areas adopted a land law, a labor law, and a polical program intended for a Soviet government to be formed in future. Acting on a resolution of that conference, the presidium of the conference in its last session decided to call the First Chinese National Soviet Congress on November 7, 1930, the thirteenth anniversary of the Russian revolution. To make necessary preparations for the establishment of a government, it was decided to set up a Central Preparatory Commission for the National Soviet Congress to be composed of representatives of the Chinese Communist Party, the Chinese National Labor

Federation, the various Soviet areas, the Red Army, and the various revolutionary (civic) organizations. Accordingly, the masses of the entire nation were called upon to give support to the proposed Soviet congress.

It may be recalled that in the last days of the first KMT-CCP collaboration in the twenties Trotsky pressed for the formation of Soviets in China while Stalin considered it to be premature. But Stalin had changed his mind and shifted to a policy of armed uprising and Soviet formation after the CCP's break with the KMT Left at Wuhan in the summer of 1927. From that time on the Stalin leadership had repeatedly urged the CCP to establish Soviet regimes in China. Under Comintern supervision the CCP Sixth National Congress of 1928 drew up elaborate preliminary plans for the formation of Chinese Soviets. (For a story of the Stalin-Trotsky debate over the creation of Chinese Soviets see Robert North, *Moscow and Chinese Communists*, pp. 98 ff.)

According to Chang Kuo-t'ao during an interview in Hongkong in late October, 1959, the slogan of the formation of Soviets was first raised by the CCP Politburo enlarged meeting of November, 1927. It remained to be investigated, he said, whether Moscow had exerted any influence on it. But if there was any Russian impact, he added, it must have come forth in September, 1927.

Struggle for the Establishment of an All-China Central Soviet Regime (為建立全中國) 中央蘇維埃政權而鬥爭 Wei chien-li ch'üan-chung-kuo chung-yang su-wei-ai cheng-ch'üan erh tou-cheng), a leading article by Hsiang Chung-fa in *Red Flag Daily*, No. 11, August 25, 1930, on file in BIC, bearing no call number; approximately 1,100 words.

The secretary-general of the CCP proceeded on the assumption that the Chinese party was not only possessed of several million armed peasants and more than 300,000 Red Army men but was also capable of combining the insurrections of workers and soldiers to seize economic and political centers in the country. The weakness, he said, lay in the fact that no central government had been set up, and therefore the CCP could not give a clear-cut impression of nationwide antagonism against the KMT government. The establishment of a central Soviet government, he reasoned, would greatly help the revolution on a national scale, though Communist authority had not extended to the whole country, not even the whole area of a key province.

Hsiang Chung-fa declared in unmistakable terms that the proposed government should have a central urban basis and that it should swiftly be established at Changsha, Nanchang, or Wuhan. Rapid preparations must be made before the capture of those cities, he said. The attention of the broad masses, especially the Soviet areas and the Red Army, was therefore invited to this important task.

As has been noted previously, Mao advocated the establishment of a power center in Kiangsi including the western part of Fukien while the Li Li-san leadership wanted to take Hunan, Hupeh, and Kiangsi with Wuhan as the urban center. It is obvious that the present article reflected the position of the Li Li-san leadership on this score.

According to Chou En-lai, the idea of establishing a central government at Wuhan or, at any rate, at Changsha or Nanchang originated with the National Conference of Delegates from Soviet Areas held in May, 1930. (See the Shao Shan Report made by Chou En-lai in the Third Plenum in September, 1930.)

This article of the secretary-general of the CCP was published more than a month after the Comintern directive of July 23, 1930, in which it was stated that the establishment of a central Soviet government in keeping with the Soviet movement in China was of the first importance. This Comintern directive must have given an added impetus to the rush of the Li Li-san leadership to the formation of a central government, though Moscow linked the proposed government closely to the Soviet movement in the rural districts and suggested that the Red Army, as a requisite to the proposed government, should be organized at the safest place.

Urgent Notice of the Central Preparatory Commission for the National Soviet Congress (全國蘇維埃代表大會中央準備委員會緊急通知 Ch'üan-kuo su-wei-ai tai-piao ta-hui chung-yang chun-pei wei-yüan-hui chin-chi t'ung-chih), dated September 10, 1930; printed in *Red Flag Daily,* No. 28, September 11, 1930, on file in BIC, bearing no call number; approximately 1, 100 words.

This communication contains two points:

1. To urge the representatives from all localities to reach the place of the meeting of the Central Preparatory Commission

quickly. The date as well as the place of the meeting was not
disclosed; it was only stated that the meeting was originally
scheduled to take place on August 20 but had been postponed
owing to obstructions from all sides.

2. To tell the party ranks to make necessary preparations in
the spheres of propaganda, organization, and so forth for the
First National Soviet Congress scheduled to convene on November 7.

*Support the Soviet Central Preparatory Commission and Es-
lublish an All-China Central Soviot Rogime* (擁護蘇維埃中
央準備委員會與建立全國中央蘇維埃政權Yung-hu
su-wei-ai chung-yang chun-pei wei-yüan-hui yü chien-li ch'üan-
kuo chung-yang su-wei-ai cheng-ch'üan), editorial of *Red Flag
Daily*, No. 30, September 13, 1930, on file in BIC, bearing no
call number; approximately 1,000 words.

This statement began by disclosing that the first meeting of
the Standing Committee of the Central Preparatory Commission
for the National Soviet Congress was held on September 12 at
Nanking, the seat of the National Government. This contradicts
a report in the *International Press Correspondence* of October
23, 1930, that the meeting took place that day in Shanghai. (See
Robert North, *Moscow and Chinese Communists,* p. 149.)

It was pointed out in the present statement that the primary
responsibility of the Central Preparatory Commission was to
draw up plans for the forthcoming National Soviet Congress, to
be held on November 7, with a view to the creation of a central
Soviet government. The importance of the proclamation of a
central Soviet government as a nationwide rival regime against
the KMT authority was stressed.

*Report on the Plenum of the Central Preparatory Commis-
sion for the National Soviet Congress* (全國蘇維埃大會中
央準備委員會全體會議經過Ch'üan-kuo su-wei-ai ta-
hui chung-yang chun-pei wei-yüan-hui ch'üan-t'i hui-i ching-
kuo), printed in *Red Flag Daily*, No. 36, September 19, 1930,
on file in BIC, bearing no call number; also in the appendixes to
The Chinese Soviets, Vol. 1, 052.2/804, BIC; approximately
1,500 words.

This is an official report on the meeting of the Central Preparatory Commission for the National Soviet Congress, held on September 12. The two texts, contained in the two different sources given above, are generally identical. A difference lies in the fact that one text gives the number of the members of the presidium of the Central Preparatory Commission as five, while the other gives it as seven.

As can be seen from this statement, a provisional standing committee of the Central Preparatory Commission started work in July. According to the *International Press Correspondence* of October 23, 1930, that provisional standing committee was organized on July 23. (See Robert North, *Moscow and Chinese Communists,* p. 149.) It would appear that much of the preparatory work was actually done by that provisional standing committee.

When the Central Preparatory Commission met, a total of thirty persons were present, which represented two-thirds of the forty-five persons originally included in the proposed list of delegates.

The meeting of the Central Preparatory Commission made the following decisions:

1. The Central Preparatory Commission was to move from the KMT-controlled areas to the Soviet areas to facilitate work.

2. The convocation of the National Soviet Congress was postponed from November 7 to December 11, the anniversary of the Canton Commune.

3. Regulations for the election of delegates to the proposed National Soviet Congress were enacted.

4. An agenda of the forthcoming National Soviet Congress was prepared.

5. Three draft laws introduced by the representatives of the CCP Central Committee were adopted, namely, (a) general principles of a constitution, (b) land law, and (c) labor law.

6. A blueprint of the organization of the Central Preparatory Commission was drawn up.

The Drive for Calling a National Soviet Congress (論召集全國蘇維埃大會的運動 Lun chao-chi ch'üan-kuo su-wei-ai ta-hui ti yün-tung), editorial of *Red Flag Daily,* No. 36, September 19, 1930, on file in BIC with no call number; approximately 1,200 words.

In publishing the previously described report on the meeting of the Central Preparatory Commission, the present issue of the *Red Flag Daily* hailed the meeting as an event of great significance and listed the major resolutions of the meeting as follows:

1. Regulations governing the elections of delegates to the Soviet Congress.
2. A suggested agenda of the Soviet Congress.
3. A draft constitution.
4. Postponement of the Soviet Congress until December 11.

Proclamation of the Plenum of the Central Preparatory Commission for the First National Congress of the Chinese Workers', Peasants', and Soldiers' Council (Soviet) (中國 工 農 兵 會 議（蘇維埃）第一次全國代表大會中央準備 委員會全體會議佈告 Chung-kuo kung-nung-ping hui-i (su-wei-ai) ti-i-tz'u ch'üan-kuo tai-piao ta-hui chung-yang chun-pei wei-yüan-hui ch'üan-t'i hui-i pu-kao), printed in *The Chinese Soviets*, Vol. 1, 052.2/804, BIC; approximately 3,100 words.

This proclamation urged the necessity of establishing a central Soviet government to unify command of more than three hundred scattered Soviet areas in the country, armed with an estimated 300,000 Red Army men. Preparations should be accelerated to make possible the convocation of the proposed National Soviet Congress, which had been postponed until December 11, the third anniversary of the Canton Commune. Preparatory commissions at all levels were ordered to be set up in the Soviet areas, while Communist work in the KMT-controlled areas should be strengthened and coordinated with that in the Soviet areas. Delegates to the forthcoming Soviet congress were to be elected both within and without the Soviet areas.

Regulations Governing the Elections of Delegates to the First National Congress of the Chinese Workers', Peasants', and Soldiers' Council (Soviet) (中國 工 農 兵 會 議（蘇維 埃）第一次全國代表大會選舉條例 Chung-kuo kung-nung-ping hui-i (su-wei-ai) ti-i-tz'u ch'üan-kuo tai-piao ta-hui hsüan-chü t'iao-li), adopted by the Central Preparatory

Commission; printed in *The Chinese Soviets*, Vol. 1, 052. 2/
804, BIC; approximately 1, 900 words.

It was made clear that these electoral regulations were
enacted on the assumption that the proposed Soviet congress
was not a constructive but a combative gathering. Among the
disenfranchised were all those who worked for religion, such
as Buddhist monks and nuns, Taoist priests, Christian mis-
sionaries, Catholic fathers. Elections were to be held within
and without the Soviet areas.

*Provisional Regulations Governing the Elections of Dele-
gates of the Soviet Areas to the First National Congress of the
Chinese Workers', Peasants', and Soldiers' Council (Soviet)*
(中華工農兵會議（蘇維埃）第一次全國代表大
會蘇維埃區域選舉暫行條例 Chung-hua kung-nung-
ping hui-i (su-wei-ai) ti-i tz'u ch'üan-kuo tai-piao ta-hui su-
wei-ai ch'ü-yü hsüan-chü tsan-hsing t'iao-li), adopted by the
Central Preparatory Commission, 1930; printed in *The Chinese
Soviets*, Vol. 1, 052. 2/804, BIC; approximately 3, 300 words.

A fairly detailed set of regulations for use in the Soviet areas
as distinguished from the non-Soviet areas.

*Letter to the Various Organizations in the Areas under Re-
actionary Rule concerning the Electoral Campaign* (致反動
統治區域各團體關於選舉運動公函 Chih fan-
tung t'ung-chih ch'ü-yü ko t'uan-t'i kuan-yü hsüan-chü yün-tung
kung-han) by the Central Preparatory Commission, September
21 (1930); printed in *The Chinese Soviets*, Vol. 1, 052. 2/804,
BIC; approximately 1, 200 words.

This communication contains the general principles of elections outside the Soviet areas.

Agenda of the National Congress (全國大會議事日程
Ch'üan-kuo ta-hui i-shih jih-ch'eng), adopted by the Central
Preparatory Commission, September 12, 1930; printed in *The
Chinese Soviets*, Vol. 1, pp. 1-2, 052. 2/804, BIC; approxi-
mately 700 words.

This is the text of the agenda prepared by the Central Preparatory Commission for the National Soviet Congress. It consists of the following five items together with explanatory notes:

1. Political report and a declaration of the congress.
2. Constitution.
3. Labor law.
4. Land law.
5. Election of members of the proposed government.

Draft General Principles of the State Fundamental Law (Constitution) of the Chinese Soviet Republic (中華蘇維埃共和國國家根本法（憲法）大綱草案 Chung-hua su-wei-ai kung-ho-kuo kuo-chia ken-pen fa (hsien-fa) ta-kang ts'ao-an), prepared by the Central Preparatory Commission for adoption by the National Soviet Congress; printed in *The Chinese Soviets*, Vol. 1, 052.2/804, BIC; approximately 2,500 words.

As has been noted previously, the National Conference of Delegates from Soviet Areas, held in May, 1930, adopted only a political program and not a constitution. The work of drafting a constitution was left to the Central Preparatory Commission for the National Soviet Congress. The present document is the text of the draft constitution written by the Central Preparatory Commission. It was to be formally adopted by the National Soviet Congress in contemplation. It was made clear that this draft constitution was introduced by the Central Committee of the Chinese Communist Party.

It was made clear that it was not possible to work out a body of detailed, specific articles of the constitution at a time of struggle. Therefore, only the basic principles of a constitution were worked out as follows:

1. To practice true democracy to be representative of the broad masses.

2. To establish a political regime of the laboring masses.

3. To bring about the emancipation of women and protect the political, cultural, and social position of women and the youth.

4. To recognize and carry out self-determination.

5. To fight for the complete political and economic liberation of China.

6. To practice the revolutionary democratic-dictatorship of the workers and peasants with a view to the ultimate realization of the proletarian dictatorship. All the exploiting classes are deprived of political rights.

7. To protect the interests of the workers, carry out the agrarian revolution, and suppress all feudal remnants.

Labor Protection Law (勞動保護法 Lao-tung pao-hu fa), adopted by the National Conference of Delegates from the Soviet Areas (in May, 1930) and reaffirmed by the Central Preparatory Commission; printed in *The Chinese Soviets,* Vol. 1, 052.2/804, BIC; approximately 1,300 words.

The Central Preparatory Commission accepted without any change the labor protection law adopted by the National Conference of Delegates from the Soviet Areas in May, 1930.

Provisional Land Law (土地暫行法 T'u-ti tsan-hsing fa), revised by the Central Preparatory Commission; printed in *The Chinese Soviets,* Vol. 1, 052.2/804, BIC; approximately 1,400 words.

As described previously, the provisional land law adopted by the National Conference of Delegates from the Soviet Areas has these characteristics, *inter alia:* (1) prohibition of the sale and purchase of land and (2) formation of collective farms.

When the Central Preparatory Commission convened on September 12, the CCP had already received the Comintern directive of July 23, 1930. The Comintern denounced Li Li-san's land policy as premature. It observed: "The party should avoid premature measures. . . . For the moment the purchase and sale of land must not be prohibited" (section 8). "The party should publicize the central slogan of land nationalization. To translate this slogan into practice must be linked with the rising tide of the revolution and the success of the revolutionary democratic dictatorship of the workers and peasants all over the country" (section 6).

In consequence, the above-mentioned characteristics of the land law of May, 1930, were removed from its revised text as adopted by the Central Preparatory Commission. It was

stated euphemistically that there were only "slight amend-
ments, but no changes in basic principles at all. " (See "Report on the Plenum of the Central Preparatory Commission
for the National Soviet Congress, " described in a previous
item.)

*Regulations Governing the Organization of the Preparatory
Commissions at All Levels for the First National Soviet Congress of the Workers', Peasants', and Soldiers' Council (Soviet)* (中國) 工農兵會議（蘇維埃） 第一次全國代
表大會各級準備委員會組織大綱 Chung-kuo
kung-nung-ping hui-i (su-wei-ai) ti-i-tz'u ch'üan-kuo tai-piao
ta-hui ko chi chun-pei wei-yüan-hui tsu-chih ta-kang), adopted
by the Central Preparatory Commission, printed in *Red Flag
Daily*, No. 37, September 20, 1930, on file in BIC, bearing no
call number, also in *The Chinese Soviets*, Vol. 1, 052. 2/804,
BIC; approximately 1, 600 words.

According to this document, the Central Preparatory Commission for the National Soviet Congress was to be situated in
a central place in the Soviet areas while its branch offices
might be set up in the KMT-controlled areas.

*A Circular Ordering the Organization of the Electoral
Campaign for the First National (Soviet) Congress* (為組織
全國蘇維埃第一次大會選舉運動通令 Wei tsu-
chih ch'üan-kuo su-wei-ai ti-i-tz'u ta-hui hsüan-chü yün-tung
t'ung-ling), issued by the Central Preparatory Commission,
September 17 (1930); printed in the appendixes to *The Chinese
Soviets*, Vol. 1, 052. 2/804, BIC; approximately 1, 700 words.

The Central Preparatory Commission called upon all the
Soviet areas, the Red Army, and the various mass organizations to do what they could to prepare for the proposed National Soviet Congress which was to be held on December 11.
They should elect their delegates and prepare their proposals
to the Congress before November 7.

A Letter to the CCP Central (致中共中央公函 Chih
chung-kung chung-yang kung-han), by the Central Preparatory

Commission, November 20 (1930); printed in the appendixes
to *The Chinese Soviets*, Vol. 1, 052.2/804, BIC; approximately 370 words.

By this letter the Central Preparatory Commission formally
invited the Chinese Communist Party to send its delegates to
the forthcoming National Soviet Congress on an equal footing
with other delegates. It was made clear that the CCP Central
should send two delegates, while the local party unit at the
seat of the congress should send one delegate.

*Step Up Work of Preparation for the National Soviet Con-
gress* (加緊準備全國蘇維埃代表大會的工作
Chia-chin chun-pei ch'üan-kuo su-wei-ai tai-piao ta-hui ti
kung-tso), a CCP Central circular printed in *Red Flag Daily*,
No. 40, September 23, 1930, on file in BIC, bearing no call
number; approximately 3,600 words.

In this circular the CCP leadership called upon the whole
party to step up preparations for the National Soviet Congress
scheduled to take place on December 11. Every rank-and-
file member should do what he could to help pave the way for
the congress through propaganda, organization, and other
conceivable means. He should leave no stone unturned to
arouse the masses to activity in the interests of the congress.
Though approaches to work inside and outside the Soviet areas
were different, the ultimate object was the same: to lay as
good a foundation for the proposed Soviet congress as possible.
   After this document nothing has been heard of the proposed
Soviet congress under the Li Li-san leadership.

6

The Ho Meng-hsiung Opposition

A Statement of the Views of Ho Meng-hsiung (何 孟 雄
意 見 書 Ho-meng-hsiung i-chien-shu), dated September 8,
1930; released by the Central Secretariat, January 6, 1931;
mimeographed; 262.9/159, BIC; approximately 6,700 words
plus an appendix of approximately 1,000 words.

Ho Meng-hsiung, of the Kiangsu Provincial Committee, set
himself in this statement openly against the Li-san line. When
he did this, he had heard of the arrival of some sort of Comintern instruction, but he definitely knew nothing about the
July 23 Comintern directive. It is interesting to note that his
basic ideas agreed with the Comintern directive.

Ho Meng-hsiung, a former follower of Li Ta-chao and
leader of the labor movement in North China, served on the
Kiangsu Provincial Committee at Shanghai from 1927 on. For
a time he was secretary to the peasant department of that
Committee. (See "Resolution on Some Historical Problems,"
April 20, 1945, note 10.) According to the present paper, he
served consecutively as secretary to the party units of the
Shanghai Eastern and Central Districts during the reign of
the Li-san line.

In a meeting of party secretaries of the Shanghai area on
September 1, 1930, Ho Meng-hsiung frankly expressed his
political views which incurred the displeasure of the delegates
from the Central present. A week later he addressed this
letter to the Central Politburo in order to make his position
clear.

Ho Meng-hsiung made it clear that he had held different

views from Li Li-san and company ever since the Kiangsu
Provincial Party Congress held early in 1930 and that he had
been at loggerheads with them in the National Conference of
Delegates from the Soviet Areas in May, 1930. In the present
statement, he made altogether twelve points, some concerning theory, others relating to strategy and tactics, and still
others with respect to procedure. The twelve points may be
summarized as follows:

1. The Chinese revolution and the world revolution. According to Ho Meng-hsiung, the Li Li-san leadership had
failed to appreciate not only the unevenness of the revolutionary movement in the world but also the relation between the
Chinese revolution and the world revolution. Ho thought that
Li Li-san had exaggerated the role of the Chinese revolution
on the world scene and at the same time frustrated the hope
of a successful revolution in China in the first instance.

2. Preparation of armed insurrections. It was charged that
Li Li-san had damaged the prospects of armed insurrections
by reason of his failure to appreciate the principles of armed
insurrections and the changes of class relationships. He had
actually isolated himself from the masses.

3. Uneven development of the Chinese revolution. During a
discussion of the June 11 Politburo resolution in the Kiangsu
Provincial Committee, Ho said, he had advocated (1) stepping
up work in provinces where the Communist revolution had not
yet been successful and (2) consolidating the Communist hold
of the provinces where preliminary successes had been
scored. He stated that Li Li-san had dismissed his ideas as
erroneous.

4. The labor movement. In view of the party's unsatisfactory relation to the working class, Ho Meng-hsiung was of the
opinion that the important thing to do for the moment was to
make use of the labor union to win over the workers. In contrast, Li Li-san approached the problem from the political
but not mechanical angle as described previously.

5. Political and economic strikes. Ho attached equal importance to political and economic strikes while Li stressed
political strikes alone.

6. The Red labor union. Ho maintained that a strike could
be successful only if it was led by the labor union, but Li
abolished the labor union when he organized the Action Committee.

7. The Yellow (i.e., neutral) labor union. While Li dis-

missed middle-of-the-road labor unions as useless, Ho insisted on exploitation of them by discrediting their leaders and
winning over their rank and file.

8. The Red Army. According to Ho, the Red Army was the
most important force in the agrarian revolution and one of the
main forces in the entire revolutionary movement in China.
In contrast, the Li Li-san leadership had talked merely about
the expansion of the Red Army, and this was considered inadequate.

9. The Communist Youth. Ho was against the policy of sacrificing the C.Y. in favor of the Action Committee. He favored the restoration of the youth organization.

10. The Communist Party. Ho was dissatisfied with the
status of party membership: 70 per cent peasantry and 5.5
per cent labor. He advocated absorption of workers in cities.
In the rural districts he favored expulsion of the rich peasants from the party, limitation of the middle peasants, absorption of the poor peasants, and admission of the hired
farm hands to party leadership.

11. Combating Liquidationists and Rightists. Although he
was branded a Liquidationist agent, Ho Meng-hsiung claimed
that he began fighting the Liquidationists long before they became a serious problem within the party. He viewed the
Right deviation as the main danger in the two-front struggle,
though he himself was stigmatized as a Right deviationist.

12. Complaint against maltreatment. Ho Meng-hsiung
strongly protested that he was stopped from talking and
scolded by Li Li-san in the September 1 meeting. He complained of his removal (on September 4) from the post as
secretary to the Shanghai Central District branch of the CCP.

To this document is appended a note of Ho Meng-hsiung on
a statement made by Chou En-lai in a meeting of activists. In
this appendix Ho repeated his opinion outlined above with particular reference to the question of uneven development of the
Chinese revolutionary movement. He admitted that he separated the CCP line from the Comintern line but stated that he
did not realize that this would undermine the faith of the rank
and file in the party leadership, as he was given to understand.

Benjamin Schwartz gives a brief account of Ho Meng-
hsiung's views in his book *Chinese Communism and the Rise
of Mao*, p. 164. It does not seem likely that the document at
his disposal, dated 1931, is another copy of the present

piece, though the few arguments ascribed to Ho in that book
can be found in points 4, 5, and 6 of the present document.

It should be noted that in commenting on Ho Meng-hsiung in
1945, the Mao machine showed a high opinion of him. (See
"Resolution on Some Historical Problems, " April 20, 1945,
reprint, p. 16.)

According to Chang Kuo-t'ao during an interview in Hongkong in late October, 1959, all opposition to Ho Meng-hsiung
was the work of Pavel Mif. Ho was a close friend of Chang
and spoke openly in favor of him. When Mif's protégés first
returned to China, they all worked under Ho, who was in
charge of the party in Shanghai and Kiangsu province. Though
they hated Li Li-san as much as Ho did, their position in the
party was too low for them to have their say at that time.

*Combat the Opportunistic Line Represented by Ho Meng-
hsiung and His Role As a Liquidationist Agent* (反對何孟雄
代表的機會主義路線與其取消派的暗探作用
Fan-tui ho-meng-hsiung tai-piao ti chi-hui chu-i lu-hsien yü
chi ch'ü-hsiao-p'ai ti an-t'an tso-yung), address by Lo Mai
(Li Wei-han) in a meeting of activists, September 10, 1930;
printed in *Red Flag Daily*, No. 41-42, September 24-25, 1930;
on file in BIC, bearing no call number; approximately 3, 500
words.

A rather informative and revealing document on the Ho
Meng-hsiung case from the point of view of the Central Politburo under the leadership of Li Li-san, throwing a good deal
of light on the crucial points at issue. It should be read in
conjunction with Ho's own statement of September 8, 1930,
noted previously.

To begin with, it was disclosed that Ho declared in a party
meeting at Shanghai on August 20 that the Central had vio-
lated the Comintern line and that therefore he wanted to object
to the Central under the pretext of the Comintern line. He was
reported to have made similar utterances on several occasions afterwards. For this reason, he was charged with following the compromising and opportunistic lines and identified
as a Liquidationist agent.

It was revealed that the party leadership had set itself
against Ho's ideas ever since the second party congress of
Kiangsu province held in January or February, 1930. At that

congress he was allegedly following a compromising line between the Central and the Liquidationists. Examples:

a. The party regarded the feudal forces as the dominant reactionary influence, while the Liquidationists pointed up the capitalists. Ho for his part saw a combination of feudalists and capitalists with the latter in a leading position.

b. The party saw a growing disintegration of the reactionary rule while the Liquidationists took pride in its stabilization. He took no sides, maintaining that the reactionary rule was shaky.

c. The party pointed out that the revolution was daily drawing near to a high tide, while the Liquidationists said the opposite. Ho doubted that the revolution had the prospect of a high tide.

d. The party was in favor of an offensive line while the Liquidationists went in for a defensive line. Ho for his part advocated an offensive for the sake of defense.

Furthermore, Ho Meng-hsiung was said to have degenerated into an opportunistic line in the eight months following the second party congress of Kiangsu province. Evidences:

a. In the estimation of the revolution, Ho openly denounced the position of Li Li-san as excessive.

b. As regards peasant warfare, Ho criticized the attacks on Changsha as a type of tribal insurrection.

c. With respect to the question of uneven development, he found it impossible for the Chinese revolution to grow into a world revolution.

d. Regarding armed insurrections, it was his belief that the superior armed force of the imperialists could suppress a revolution.

e. As concerns the mass movement, he regarded winning over the masses and preparing positively for armed insurrections as two different things.

f. In regard to the labor movement, he deemed it necessary to absorb the bulk of workers into labor unions before political strikes were organized.

g. Last but not least, he favored the preservation rather than increase of the revolutionary force.

Finally, Ho Meng-hsiung was branded a Liquidationist agent on the ground that he had allegedly tried what he could to undermine the party leadership by means of factional activity all the time. As discussion of tactical questions was going on between the Comintern and the CCP Central, it was charged, he lost no time in taking advantage of it to drive a wedge between them. Whatever his motives, he had actually performed the function of a Liquidationist agent. Worst of all, he had a following within the party.

The Offensive of Right Opportunism against the Correct Line (右傾機會主義對於正確路線的進攻 Yu-ch'ing chi-hui chu-i tui-yü cheng-ch'ueh lu-hsien ti chin-kung), editorial of *Red Flag Daily,* No. 39, September 22, 1930; on file in BIC, bearing no call number; approximately 900 words.

Judging from its tone, this editorial must have been directed against Ho Meng-hsiung and his group, though it does not mention them by name. The gist of the statement is as follows:

At a time when the party is reviewing its work and when it must needs practice self-criticism, Right opportunists avail themselves of this opportunity to sabotage the general party line by taking advantage of minor mistakes committed. But self-criticism must be carefully distinguished from attacks by the opportunists. The purpose of self-criticism is to eliminate imperfections or to correct errors within the framework of the general party line. On the contrary, rightist attacks aim to destroy the whole party line by exaggerating shortcomings and mistakes through opportunistic interpretation. One should, therefore, practice self-criticism and object to attacks by rightists against the party line.

Intraparty Struggle and Self-Criticism (黨內鬥爭與自我批評 Tang-nei tou-cheng yü tzu-wo p'i-p'ing), editorial of *Red Flag Daily,* No. 42, September 25, 1930; on file in BIC, bearing no call number; approximately 900 words.

This editorial laid down three guiding principles for self-criticism which was believed to be of paramount importance at a time when a two-front struggle was waged. The three guiding principles:

1. Self-criticism should be practiced within the framework of the general line of the Comintern and of the CCP alike. Any criticism outside the scope of this general line, such as the sort of criticism leveled by Ho Meng-hsiung, was not allowed.

2. Self-criticism should be confined to specific issues but not directed against persons.

3. Self-criticism should be made under the direction of superior authorities. It could not be made independently of the party.

A Statement of the Views of Ho Meng-hsiung, No. 2 (何孟雄注意見書 二 Ho-meng-hsiung i-chien-shu erh), dated October 2, 1930; released by the Central Secretariat, January 6, 1931; mimeographed; 262.9/159, BIC; approximately 500 words.

In reply to a letter of the General Action Committee, the text of which is unfortunately not available, Ho Meng-hsiung set forth three points in this statement as follows:

1. He refused to plead guilty as the General Action Committee demanded. He could not admit to what were not his mistakes.

2. He denied that he had tried to undermine the party and engage in personal attack. His open objection to the position of Li Li-san was, according to him, not a personal attack but a dispute over political policy.

3. He cautioned that it was time to forget about all old quarrels and set the party on the right path.

A Statement of the Views of Ho Meng-hsiung, No. 3 (何孟雄注意見書 三 Ho-meng-hsiung i-chien-shu san), dated October 9, 1930; released by the Central Secretariat, January 6, 1931; mimeographed; 262.9/159, BIC; approximately 1,900 words.

Under the pressure of the party leadership Ho Meng-hsiung pleaded guilty after all. But he did this with qualification—he admitted his error in separating the CCP line from the Moscow line but rejected the charge of opportunism which had been brought against him. Specifically, he brought forward the following two major points in reply to the Central:

1. He admitted that he made a great mistake when he said that the CCP line was different from the Moscow line. What he had in mind, he said, was actually the mistakes of estimation, standpoint, and tactics on the part of the CCP Central.

Moreover, he confessed to a number of mistakes in his way of struggle, namely, (1) making criticisms before the masses but not through the organization, (2) damaging the prestige of the party, (3) playing into the hands of Liquidationists, (4) being neither dispassionate nor objective.

2. He characterized his being branded an opportunist as sheer nonsense. To trump up charges against him, he said, was not the proper way of ideological struggle.

Finally, he complained that he had been removed from all party work. He was growing very impatient with his unemployment and asked for a new position, however low.

It should be noted that this letter was written after the Central Committee Third Plenum, which had apparently brought considerable pressure to bear upon Ho Meng-hsiung.

A Statement to Comrades (告 同 志 書 Kao t'ung-chih shu), issued by the CCP Central, October, 1930; reproduced by the Political Department, Fourth Army, Red Army; mimeographed; 008.222/4074, SSC; approximately 5,500 words.

This paper was primarily directed against Ho Meng-hsiung, whose challenge to the party leadership seemed to continue unabated after the Third Plenum.

It was stated that Ho Meng-hsiung had wilfully misrepresented the tactical error of the party leadership to be an error of line, had instigated personal attacks within the Politburo, and had contrasted the line of the CCP Central with that of the Comintern.

It was pointed out that the CCP Central had been in complete agreement with the Comintern line after the Third Plenum, which under Moscow's direction called for a shift in tactics and organization to carry on the ever-growing revolutionary movement in China. In order to carry out the new task of the party, it was said, there should be a determined effort to carry on the two-front fight against Right and Left deviations with the former as the main danger. This Right deviation was exemplified by Ho Meng-hsiung at the time. The whole party was therefore called upon to step up this ideological fight on the basis of the Comintern directive of July 23 and the resolution of the Third Plenum.

7

The Third Plenum

Preface to "The Third Enlarged Plenum of the CCP Central Committee" (中國) 共產黨 中央委員會 擴大的第 三次全體會議 —— 引 言 Chung-kuo kung-ch'an-tang chung-yang wei-yüan-hui k'uo-ta ti ti-san-tz'u ch'üan-t'i hui-i—yin-yen), printed by the Central Bureau of Soviet Areas (?) on October 6, 1930; reproduced in *A Collection of Red Bandit Secret Documents*, Vol. 3, leaves 1-3, 008. 2129/ 4074, SSC; mimeographed; approximately 1,100 words.

The Third Plenum of the CCP Central Committee was held during September 24-28, 1930.

This paper is a prologue to an official collection of documents of and concerning "The Third Enlarged Plenum of the Central Committee of the Chinese Communist Party," entitled "Reference Items of the Third Plenum." Three points in this paper are worthy of note.

First, it is pointed out that the Third Plenum was held in September, 1930, under the auspices of the ECCI. Among those present were fourteen members of the Central Committee and two members of the Supervisory Committee. The agenda included four items, namely: (1) political question—accepting the Comintern directive of July 23, 1930, and discussing Comintern Eastern Department resolutions on the Chinese peasant and Soviet problems; (2) organizational question—discussing the Comintern Eastern Department resolution on the organization of the CCP; (3) the labor movement; (4) election of new members of the Central Committee and the Politburo.

Second, as a number of members of the Central Committee
and of the Politburo had died since the Sixth National Congress of 1928, the Third Plenum not only brought about a reshuffle in the Politburo but also elected according to "Comintern custom" seven members of the Central Committee, eight
alternates, and two members of the Supervisory Committee.
As a result, there were altogether twenty-three members of
the Central Committee and seven alternates plus three members of the Supervisory Committee and two alternates.

Third, the following documents pertaining to the Third
Plenum were released:

(A) Comintern resolutions: (1) resolution on the Chinese
problem, dated July 23, issued by the Political Secretariat;
(2) resolution on the organizational question issued by the
Eastern Department; (3) draft program of the labor movement issued by the Eastern Department; (4) resolution on the
Soviet question issued by the Eastern Department; (5) resolution on the peasant movement issued by the Eastern Department.

(B) Papers on the political problem: (1) political resolution;
(2) resolution on the work of the Central Committee; (3) T'e
Sheng Report by Hsiang Chung-fa; (4) Shao Shan Report by
Chou En-lai; (5) remarks of Po Shan (Li Li-san); (6) remarks
of the Comintern delegate; (7) conclusion by Chih Fu (Ch'ü
Ch'iu-pai).

(C) Papers on the organizational problem: (1) resolution on
the question of organization; (2) report and conclusion; (3)
[not clear].

(D) Papers on the labor problem: (1) resolution on the labor
movement; (2) report and conclusion; (3) report of the Party
Corps of the National Labor Federation.

(E) Miscellaneous items: (1) statement to the people; (2)
statement to the Red Army; (3) telegram to Soviet Russia; (4)
telegram to Germany.

Unfortunately, a number of the documents listed above are
not available.

Questioned as to what the expression "Comintern custom"
referred to above meant, Chang Kuo-t'ao declared in an interview in Hongkong in late October, 1959, that he did not
know. On second thought, he stated that he thought it might
mean a temporary expedient in the sense that members of the
Central Committee should be elected by a national congress
according to the party constitution, but it was not the case in
the Third Plenum.

Report on the Work of the Central Politburo (中 央 政治局 工作報告 Chung-yang cheng-chih-chü kung-tso pao-kao), by T'e Sheng (Hsiang Chung-fa), September, 1930; mimeographed; 257/940, BIC; approximately 1,900 words.

This is the text of the report made by Hsiang Chung-fa, Secretary-General of the CCP, on behalf of the Central Politburo to the Third Plenum, generally known as the T'e Sheng Report. Judging by its tone, this piece does not seem to be an unabridged text.

The Secretary-General of the CCP began by pointing out that the Third Plenum was held at the summer resort Lushan in northern Kiangsi. However, another Communist source mentioned Nanking as the meeting place (see editorial of *The Red Flag Daily*, Shanghai, Organ of the Central Committee, CCP, No. 48, October 4, 1930, available in the Hoover Library), while a non-Communist source referred to Shanghai as the scene of the parley. (See *A Collection of Red Bandit Reactionary Documents*, Vol. 2, pp. 421-22.)

This statement is divided into two parts: (1) the bolshevization of the party and (2) from the Second Plenum to the Third Plenum.

T'e Sheng pointed out that there were two different phases of the revolutionary development from the Second Plenum of June, 1929, to the Third Plenum of September, 1930, with January, 1930, as the demarcation line. The first phase was marked by the beginning of a new rising tide of the revolution, during which the main work of the CCP was to deal with the crisis of the Chinese Eastern Railway and the civil strife of warlords. The second phase saw a riper growth of the new rising tide of the revolution, which could be seen from a number of factors: the worsening economic crisis, the expanding civil war, the growing plight of workers and peasants, the acute class struggle of urban workers, the developing peasant war, and the rapid progress of the Red Army. The task of the CCP during this second phase, it was said, was to turn the warlord strife into a revolutionary war and to work for the establishment of a Soviet regime.

The first half of 1930 was thought to be a crucial period. During this period, it was stated, the CCP line was in complete agreement with the Comintern line. Only there were an overestimation of the revolutionary situation and overlook of the uneven revolutionary development, with the result that tactical

errors had been made. However, it was pointed out, the Central
Committee had corrected its errors without hesitation after receiving the Comintern directive. Though not mentioned by name,
the Comintern directive referred to must be the one under date
of July 23, 1930.

It was revealed that the struggle against Ho Meng-hsiung began as early as the Conference of Delegates from Soviet Areas
held in May, 1930. This would suggest that Ho began to oppose
Li Li-san before the Politburo resolution of June 11, 1930.

Furthermore, the story of the struggle against Ch'en Tu-hsiu
constitutes an important part of this statement. The struggle
started, it was said, with the crisis of the Chinese Eastern
Railway, during which Ch'en favored turning the slogan of supporting Soviet Russia into one of opposition to the KMT betrayal
of the country.

Chang Kuo-t'ao told an interesting story of how Hsiang Chung-
fa became secretary-general of the CCP, a story which might
be helpful for an understanding of the line-up of the Third
Plenum as well as the relatively insignificant role of Hsiang
Chung-fa in it. Interviewed in Hongkong in late October, 1959,
Chang declared that Hsiang Chung-fa was picked by Mif during
the Sixth National Congress of 1928 to serve as secretary-general of the CCP. Chinese Communist leaders in the conference,
he said, fell into two groups. On the one side stood Chou En-lai,
Li Li-san, and Ch'ü Ch'iu-pai who formed the left wing. On the
other, Ts'ai Ho-shen, Hsiang Ying, and Chang Kuo-t'ao himself banded themselves together, and were popularly known as
the right wing. Inasmuch as the strength of both sides was practically equal and as one group could not get the upper hand of
the other, Mif picked Hsiang Chung-fa as the CCP secretary-
general, which fact did not satisfy all the leaders of the CCP.
With a worker background, Hsiang was simply not competent
for the job. It was rumored that he even betrayed Communist
comrades to the KMT while under arrest in 1931.

*The New High Tide of the Chinese Revolution and the Chinese
Communist Party* (中國) 革命新高潮與中國共產黨.
Chung-kuo ko-ming hsin kao-ch'ao yü chung-kuo kung-ch'an-
tang), address by Chou En-lai before the 16th Congress of the
CPSU, July 5, 1930; printed in *Red Flag Daily*, No. 24, September 7, 1930; on file in BIC, bearing no call number; approximately 3,800 words.

Chou En-lai made this statement in Moscow between the CCP Politburo resolution of June 11 and the Comintern resolution of July 23. While his basic ideas about the Chinese revolution harmonized with Moscow's as laid down in the Comintern directive of July 23, 1930, he agreed essentially with Li Li-san in one important respect, namely, the taking of urban centers.

Specifically, Chou's views as set forth in the present statement coincided with the July 23 Comintern directive in the following points:

1. The new revolutionary tide in China was growing ripe daily, but the development of the revolution was uneven. The peasant movement in North China was behind that in South China, and the labor movement had not been coordinated with the peasant movement. The revolution would break out in one or more provinces first.

2. Only through preparatory stages could the bourgeois-democratic revolution be transformed into a socialist revolution.

3. Both the Right and Left deviations were condemned, with the Right deviation as the main danger.

On the other hand, Chou En-lai was inclined toward the seizure of key cities, though he was not so outspoken as Li Li-san on this point. He wanted the Red Army to move in the direction of political or industrial centers. He regretted that no industrial and commercial centers had been occupied in the Soviet areas. He took the position that a central government would be set up only after the formation of a strong Red Army and the capture of a key industrial and commercial center.

Chou En-lai revealed that only eighty-one members of the Ch'en Tu-hsiu group and more than twenty members of the Trotskyite group were left at the time and that they had all been expelled from the party. In spite of that, he said, the Right deviation remained the principal danger within the party.

According to Chang Kuo-t'ao during an interview in Hongkong in late October, 1959, Chou En-lai was sent by the CCP to Moscow in the spring of 1930 at the behest of Pavel Mif, chief of the Chinese Section, Eastern Department, Communist International. After his arrival in Moscow, Chou En-lai took over practically all the business of the Chinese delegation in Moscow, conducting negotiations on behalf of the CCP at the bidding of Mif. Both Ch'ü Ch'iu-pai and Chang Kuo-t'ao were kept in the background by the Comintern on account of their hostility to Mif, which came to the fore in what was

known as the Sun Yat-sen University case, in which they attacked the educational policy of Mif as president of that university and thus were punished. Removed from the Chinese delegation, Ch'ü Ch'iu-pai returned to China soon afterwards. Chang
Kuo-t'ao himself retired from active political life on leave. In
fact, Chou En-lai had become the only responsible and influen-
tial man from China in Moscow at that time.

*The Shao Shan Report-Reference Item No. 9 of the Third
Plenum* (少山報告 —— 三中全會材料第九號
Shao-shan pao-kao—san-chung ch'üan-hui ts'ai-liao ti-chiu hao),
by Shao Shan (Chou En-lai), September, 1930; mimeographed;
255.21/934, BIC; approximately 11,000 words.

Having completed his mission in Moscow, according to Chang
Kuo-t'ao during an interview in Hongkong in late October, 1959,
Chou En-lai came back to China to deal with the situation created by the Li-san line. Backed by the Kremlin and being on
good terms with both the old cadres and the Russian Returned
Students within the CCP, he was actually the most important
man within the Chinese Communist hierarchy at that time. His
flexible and ever adaptable personality had a good deal to do
with his way of doing things. Though he had Comintern instructions to keep Li Li-san in line, he did not pour oil on the flames.
Though he should have sponsored the Third Plenum himself, he
preferred to give way to Ch'ü Ch'iu-pai who had been the party
boss in 1927-28.
      The present document is the text of the statement made by
Chou En-lai before the Third Plenum. Though he reiterated for
the most part the terms of the Comintern directive of July 23,
he had a slightly different emphasis in the interpretation of the
development of the revolutionary situation and a radically different conception of what was called a line.
      He admitted that there was some difference in the estimation
of the revolutionary development between Moscow and the Chinese Party. He said that the CCP did not attach importance to
the uneven development of the revolution though it had perceived
it. Accordingly, the CCP had made an incorrect overestimation
of the speed and degree of the revolutionary development, which
resulted in individual tactical errors.
      As a rebuttal to opportunists Chou En-lai cited the oft-quoted
phrase in the Comintern directive: "The new upsurge of the Chi-

nese revolution has become an indisputable fact. " Though he endorsed the Comintern position that there was not yet an objective revolutionary situation all over China, he declared that the
Comintern did not consider such a prospect to be far distant.
Here lay the different emphasis Chou put on the development of
the revolutionary situation.

Chou En-lai decided that there was no difference in line between the CCP and the Comintern. By line he meant the CCP
tasks of "winning over the broad masses, concentrating revolutionary forces, organizing revolutionary wars, and preparing
positively for uprisings, so as to overthrow the KMT rule and
establish a Soviet regime. " He stated that these CCP tasks were
in complete agreement with Comintern directives.

However, as defined in the Comintern directive received on
November 16, 1930, which was the official Comintern reaction
to the position of the Third Plenum, the term "line" had a much
wider meaning than what Chou En-lai had said.

As the Comintern understood, Li Li-san was unrealistic in
analyzing the political situation when he decided that there was
already a revolutionary situation in China and even throughout
the world and that a preliminary success in one or more provinces would be an all-China direct insurrectionary situation,
coupled with the Trotskyite theory of uninterrupted transformation from a bourgeois-democratic revolution to a proletarian
revolution. This erroneous line of Li Li-san, it was stated, resulted in a failure to understand these basic questions: (1) the
uneven development of the revolution in the nation, (2) the labor
movement lagging behind the peasant movement, (3) the strong
position of imperialists in cities, (4) inadequacies in the Soviet
movement, (5) deficiencies in the Red Army, and (6) dangers in
sacrificing political and economic struggles for outright insurrection and in disbanding party and mass organizations, and so
forth.

It should be remembered that Chou En-lai's position as out-
lined above actually reflected the official position of the Third
Plenum. As will be seen later, this official position of the Third
Plenum was denounced by the Comintern as compromise-ism.

It has become apparent that as a result of the Third Plenum
the Li-san line had practically come to an end. The Action
Committee which had been set up to implement the Li-san line
had ceased to work. Meanwhile, Li Li-san himself had been removed from his position of leadership. The Third Plenum and
the party leadership thereafter were actually under the charge

of Ch'ü Ch'iu-pai. Compromise-ism as it existed at the time existed in theory rather than in fact.

The Mao machine was right when it in 1945 commented on the Third Plenum along this line. The Third Plenum and the ensuing Central, it was stated, played an active role in calling the Li-san line to a halt. Though the records of that plenum showed signs of a compromising spirit, the plenum actually removed all the errors that had been characteristic of the Li-san line. In the plenary session Li Li-san admitted his errors and soon afterwards he left his position of leadership in the Central. (See "Resolution on Some Historical Problems," April 20, 1945, contained in Mao Tse-tung, *Selected Works*, Chinese edition, Vol. 3, p. 963; English edition, Vol. 4, pp. 179-80; reprint, pp. 11-12.)

It should be noted that the present paper suggests a practical reason behind the compromising attitude of the Third Plenum. That was the challenge from Ho Meng-hsiung who insisted that Li Li-san had deviated from the Moscow line. To guard the prestige of the party leadership against that challenge, the Third Plenum felt obliged to identify Li Li-san's policies with Moscow—in theory but not in practice.

As will be seen later, another reason behind the compromising attitude of the Third Plenum toward Li Li-sanism was affinity of putschist ideas between Li Li-san and Ch'ü Ch'iu-pai, as confessed by the former during his trial at Moscow in December, 1930.

It is interesting to note that Conrad Brandt, Benjamin Schwartz, and John Fairbank tell an almost entirely different story of the Third Plenum, which has little or no basis in documents under our study. (See Conrad Brandt, Benjamin Schwartz, and John Fairbank, *A Documentary History of Chinese Communism*, pp. 182-83; Benjamin Schwartz, *Chinese Communism and the Rise of Mao*, pp. 151-56.) They include an extract of the English version of the present statement in *A Documentary History of Chinese Communism*, pp. 200-8. Being an extract, this English text has too many omissions (see p. 499) for it not to lose much of its original meaning. For example, the challenge from Ho Meng-hsiung, as contained at the end of section 2 of the document, is omitted; therefore one misses the chance of finding an important reason why the Third Plenum chose to take a compromising attitude toward Li Li-sanism. In addition, there are a number of errors of translation, a few examples of which are given on p. 66.

Errors	*Corrections*
sporadic practical mistakes (p. 202, l. 5)	sporadic tactical mistakes
revolutionary objective situation (p. 202, l. 12)	objective revolutionary situation
centralize the scattered Soviet areas (p. 202, l. 8 from bottom)	combine the scattered Soviet areas
The Soviet Delegates' Conference (p. 203, l. 18)	Conference of Soviet Areas' Delegates
this was the only way . . . (p. 204, l. 5)	this was, according to Lenin, the only way . . .

Conclusion of Political Discussion in the Third Enlarged Plenum—Reference Item No. 12 of the Third Plenum (三中擴大全會政治討論的結論 —— 三中全會材料第十二號 San-chung k'uo-ta ch'üan-hui cheng-chih t'ao-lun ti chieh-lun—san-chung ch'üan-hui ts'ai-liao ti-shih-erh hao), by Chih Fu, September, 1930; mimeographed; 255.21/933, BIC; approximately 15,000 words.

This is the conclusion made by Ch'ü Ch'iu-pai after the discussion of the draft political resolution submitted to the Third Plenum. It consists of five major points which constituted the main subjects of discussion during the session, namely: (1) estimation of the rising tide of the Chinese revolution; (2) tactical questions during the rising tide; (3) main tasks during the rising tide; (4) organizational strength, mass organization, and the Red Army; (5) intraparty struggle, two-front struggle, and so forth.

The essentials of this paper are the same as those of Chou En-lai's report described previously. The authority on which this statement is based is the July 23 Comintern letter, and yet it is emphasized that Li Li-san was in agreement with the Kremlin in line. In other words, compromise-ism is the basic idea of this statement. What has been said of Chou En-lai's speech can also be said of this statement. On the whole, this statement is clearer and more comprehensive than Chou En-lai's report.

The most controversial question in the Third Plenum, as in previous CCP policy debates since 1927, was the question of the so-called estimation of the revolution, i.e., the assessment of the chances for the revolution. This question arose, according to Ch'ü, before the Sixth National Congress of 1928 and had since divided the party into two different schools of thought. On the one hand, some maintained that despite the 1927 defeat the revolutionary high tide would nevertheless come pretty soon. On the other, it was feared that the chances were that the advent of the rising tide would be indefinitely delayed.

This divergence of opinion, as Ch'ü put it, was the demarcation line between the party leadership and the rightists, and it was also the distinction between the Comintern and the Trotskyites.

Ch'ü took the position that the CCP's over-all estimation of the revolution was in complete agreement with the Comintern's and that it was the rightists like Ho Meng-hsiung and Chang Kuo-t'ao who distorted the Moscow line and branded the CCP leadership as its violator. The rightists did this, according to Ch'ü, because they wanted to take advantage of the matter to make havoc of the party.

Like Chou En-lai, Ch'ü Ch'iu-pai admitted that the Li Li-san leadership had made an incorrect estimation, but insisted that that had concerned the speed of the revolutionary development, being only a tactical error. He disclosed that Li Li-san admitted his miscalculation of the speed of the revolutionary development during the deliberations of the meeting.

In keeping with Moscow policy since early 1929, Ch'ü Ch'iu-pai reaffirmed the general idea of the two-front struggle with the Right deviation as the main danger. He singled out Ho Meng-hsiung and Chang Kuo-t'ao for attack. Ch'ü wanted a showdown with these two men, suggesting that their case be made known to the whole party with a view to a political settlement. It is noteworthy that Ch'ü did not threaten a showdown with Li Li-san despite the fact that the Third Plenum was called for the specific purpose of tackling the problem of Li Li-san.

According to Chang Kuo-t'ao during an interview in Hongkong in late October, 1959, Ch'ü Ch'iu-pai had no alternative but to return to China after his dismissal from the Chinese delegation in Moscow. Since he was a member of the CCP Politburo and since Hsiang Chung-fa was not a competent secretary-general of the party, Ch'ü Ch'iu-pai took charge of the Third Plenum. In doing this, Ch'ü Ch'iu-pai had also the support of Chou En-lai, who had made himself agreeable to everybody.

Chang Kuo-t'ao declared that whoever had the support of the majority of the Politburo controlled that organ and therefore the

whole party. Moscow's patronage was not a prerequisite, though
its support was an important factor for a party leader to maintain his position. Ch'en Tu-hsiu, for example, could manage to
get along for a while in spite of Moscow. Again, Li Li-san
achieved power in the party through his own effort independently
of Moscow. On the other hand, Ch'ü Ch'iu-pai was imposed by
the Kremlin upon the Chinese party in 1927; Wang Ming and his
group were outright protégés of Pavel Mif.

An old party leader like Ch'ü Ch'iu-pai, Chang added, would
certainly not give way to Mif and his protégés who had wanted
to get the upper hand of all old cadres. The tension between
Mif and Ch'ü Ch'iu-pai was the controlling factor in the power
relationships within the Chinese Communist movement during
the latter half of 1930, all other matters being side issues.

As to why Ch'ü Ch'iu-pai attacked Chang Kuo-t'ao, Chang explained that though they both were united against Mif, they were
divided on other questions. For example, Chang had the support
of Ho Meng-hsiung whom Ch'ü Ch'iu-pai did not like.

*Resolution on the Political Situation and the Party's General
Tasks—Resolution for Accepting the ECCI Political Secretariat
Resolution on the Chinese Question, July, 1930* (政治狀況和
黨的總任務議決案 —— 接受共產國際執行委
員會政治秘書處一九三〇年七月的中國問題議
決案的決議 Cheng-chih chuang-k'uang han tang ti tsung
jen-wu i-chüeh-an—chieh-shou kung-ch'an kuo-chi chih-hsing
wei-yüan-hui cheng-chih pi-shu-ch'u i-chiu-san-ling nien ch'i
yüeh ti chung-kuo wen-t'i i-chüeh-an ti chüeh-i), adopted by the
CCP Central Committee Third Plenum, September, 1930; mimeographed; 300.3/808, BIC; approximately 13,500 words.

This is the resolution adopted by the Third Plenum and is
thus the main document of that session. As its subtitle indicates, it solemnly accepts the Comintern directive of July 23
as a guide to CCP work. According to the Comintern Eastern
Department as well as Ch'en Shao-yü, this resolution was
drafted by Ch'ü Ch'iu-pai. (See "Report of the Comintern Eastern Department on the Mistakes Made by the CCP Third Plenum
and Comrade Li Li-san," reproduced in *Bolshevik*, Vol. 4, No.
3, May 10, 1931, p. 74; Ch'en Shao-yü, *Struggle for the More
Complete Bolshevization of the Chinese Communist Party*, part
2, par. 5, sec. 3a.)

It is understandable that the basic spirit of this resolution, like the statements of Chou En-lai and Ch'ü Ch'iu-pai, is compromise-ism. On the one hand, it accepts the Comintern directive of July 23; on the other, it finds the Li-san line to be in harmony with the Moscow line. Li Li-san was wrong, it is proclaimed, only in estimation of the revolution, which resulted in tactical errors. The definition of line, as understood in the Third Plenum, is different from what Moscow conceived.

It is important to note a textual distinction between the present resolution and the Comintern directive of July 23. It is made clear in the July 23 Comintern directive that the new rising tide of the Chinese revolutionary movement has become an indisputable fact, but that there is not yet an objective revolutionary situation on a national scale. Conversely, the present resolution asserts that there is not yet an objective revolutionary situation on a national scale, but that the new rising tide of the Chinese revolutionary movement has become an indisputable fact. This reversal of the order of the two clauses may well account for the point at issue between Moscow and the Third Plenum.

Of particular interest is perhaps an explanatory note on terminology placed at the end of this document. The term "high tide" *(kao ch'ao),* it is said, is different from the "rising tide" *(kao chang)* or, literally translated, "high flow." It is pointed out that since 1928 "high tide" has been interchangeably used with what Zinoviev called "direct revolutionary situation" or what Lenin called "objective revolutionary situation." But both the terms used by the Bolshevik leaders are said to be vastly different from what is known as "rising tide" which denotes the long process of growth rather than the breaking point of the revolution. For this reason, the Third Plenum abolished the term "high tide" and laid down the following two rules as a guide of nomenclature:

1. "Rising tide"—used in the general sense of the growth of the revolutionary movement.

2. "Objective revolutionary situation"—used to denote a situation in which an armed insurrection would occur as a direct attack against the ruling class. "Direct revolutionary situation" is declared an inappropriate term.

The above terminological distinction is significant in that it was utilized by Ch'en Shao-yü to attack Li Li-san on the ground that the latter did not understand the distinction and that that ignorance was responsible for the fatal error of the Li-san line. (See Ch'en Shao-yü, *Struggle for the More Complete Bolshevi-*

zation of the Chinese Communist Party, part 2, par. 3, sec. 2;
cf. Benjamin Schwartz, *Chinese Communism and the Rise of
Mao,* p. 160.)

In this connection, it must be remembered that it was often
the case during the period under study that the Chinese Communist leaders did not quite understand Comintern directives, not
even their own statements drafted on the basis of those directives. They acted on what they believed to be the intention of
Moscow, and it often happened that they understood and acted
differently from one another.

*The Recent Organizational Tasks of the CCP—Resolution of
the Comintern Eastern Department* (中國 共產黨 的 最近
組織任務 —— 共產國際東方部議決案. Chung-
kuo kung-ch'an-tang ti tsui-chin jen-wu—kung-ch'an
kuo-chi tung-fang-pu i-chüeh-an), dated August, 1930; a pamphlet 009.54/6032, SSC; also reproduced in *A Collection of Red
Bandit Secret Documents,* Vol. 3, leaves 24-33, 008.2129/4074,
SSC; mimeographed; approximately 8,000 words.

As its title indicates, this statement was the Comintern-made
program on the organization of the CCP as introduced to the
Third Plenum. Naturally, it concerned itself only with the question of improving the organization and work of the party. It
pointed out the many and varied weaknesses and shortcomings
of the party and suggested necessary corrections.

Many phrases and individual words in this piece are missing.
This detracts greatly from the value of the document.

*Draft of Comintern Eastern Department's Proposed Program
—the Tasks of the CCP in the Labor Movement* (共產國)際東
方部提綱草案. —— 中共在職工運動中的任
務 Kung-ch'an kuo-chi tung-fang-pu t'i-kang ts'ao-an—chung-
kung tsai chih-kung yün-tung chung ti jen-wu), reference item
No. 3 of the Third Plenum; reproduced in *A Collection of Red
Bandit Secret Documents,* Vol. 3, leaves 45-51, 008.2129/4074,
SSC; mimeographed; approximately 5,000 words.

As its title indicates, this statement was the Comintern-made
program on CCP work in the sphere of labor. Needless to say,
it has shaped the subsequent development of CCP labor policy.

But this is only a reproduction; the original text is not available.

Comintern Resolution on the Chinese Peasant Problem ([國] 際)
對 於 中 國 農 民 問 題 決 議 案. [Kuo-chi] tui-yü chung-kuo
nung-min wen-t'i chüeh-i-an), n. d. ; reprinted by the North
Route Sub-Committee, February 18, 1931; reproduced in *A Collection of Red Bandit Secret Documents,* Vol. 3, leaves 33-38,
008. 2129/4074, SSC; mimeographed; approximately 3, 400
words.

This Comintern resolution on the Chinese peasant problem
falls into two parts. The first part concerned itself with the organization of the peasantry in the Soviet areas. It comprised the
following items of work:
    1. To organize hired farm hand associations and to unite with
the poor and middle peasants.
    2. To organize industrial workers and handicraftsmen.
    3. To form poor peasant associations.
    4. To place guerrilla forces under the control of Communists.
    5. To lead the peasants to combat religions in a gradual and
sure way. The churches as tools of imperialism must be closed
and their properties confiscated.
    The second part of this document dealt with the peasant move-
ment in the KMT-controlled areas. It was stressed that both
peasant committees and peasant associations must be formed,
which were to serve as the bases of provisional Soviets during
the Communist take-over.
    Quite a few individual words and phrases in this paper are
missing.

*Draft Resolution on the Land and Peasant Problems in Soviet
Areas* (蘇 維 埃 區 域 土 地 農 民 問 題 決 議 案 草 案
Su-wei-ai ch'ü-yü t'u-ti nung-min wen-t'i i-chüeh-an ts'ao-an),
by the Comintern Eastern Department, n. d. ; reprinted by the
CCP Central Secretariat, November (?) 20, 1930; a pamphlet
008. 751/4424/C. 1, SSC; reprinted by the CCP Wan-t'ai Ho-tung
Committee, April 22, 1931, mimeographed, 008. 751/4424/C. 2,
SSC; reproduced in *A Collection of Red Bandit Secret Docu-
ments,* Vol. 3, pp. 38-45 and in *A Collection of Reactionary
Documents,* Vol. 4, leaves 1-8, mimeographed. 008. 2129/7120,
SSC; approximately 5, 200 words.

This document has a positive and a negative side. Negatively it attacks Li Li-san's land policy such as collectivization and the ban on the sale, lease, and mortgage of land. Positively it contains a number of specific measures which formed the basis of the land law of the Chinese Soviet government proclaimed in November, 1931. A very important document indeed.

This document bears no date. At its head is a note which reads: "Document no. 2 released after the Third Plenum—the Eastern Department of the Communist International." At the end of the document is printed a date of the printing of this document by the CCP Central Secretariat—November (?) 20, 1930. In addition, there is also a note toward the end of this document, which reads: "This document was received five days ago."

The Two-Front Struggle (兩 條 戰 線 的 鬥 爭 Liang-t'iao chan-hsien ti tou-cheng), editorial of *Red Flag Daily,* No. 41, September 24, 1930; on file in BIC, bearing no call number; approximately 1,000 words.

This editorial of the CCP organ was published on the day when the Third Plenum of the Central Committee opened. Based on sections 18-20 of the Comintern directive of July 23, it called for a two-front struggle against the Right and Left deviations, placing emphasis on the Right deviation as the main danger.

It may be recalled that since 1928 Moscow had issued a stream of directives to the CCP, calling for a two-front struggle with the Right deviation as the main danger. This move culminated in the Comintern directive of July 23, 1930. It paralleled the general trend toward the left in the Soviet Union since 1928, when a campaign against Bukharin as a rightist symbol was set on foot after Trotsky on the left had been purged the previous year.

The stereotype of arguments against the Right deviation includes: (1) incompatibility of the uneven development of the revolution with the general crisis, (2) overlook of the peasant war and the agrarian revolution, (3) fear of imperialism, (4) rich peasant mentality, (5) economic instead of political strikes, (6) tailism and narrow-mindedness.

On the other hand, the Left deviation was also attacked, which was believed to have manifested itself primarily in the overlook of the uneven development of the Chinese revolution, the misconception of a direct revolutionary situation throughout China, the overlook of the necessary transitional stages in advance of the armed insurrection, and the ruling out of the possibility of strike and demonstration short of an armed insurrection.

CCP Central Committee Circular No. 91—Result and Spirit of the Third Enlarged Plenum (〔共黨〕中央通告第九一號 —— 三全擴大會的總結與精神 [Kung-tang] chung-yang t'ung-kao ti-chiu-i hao—san-ch'üan k'uo-ta-hui ti tsung-chieh yü ching-shen), dated October 12, 1930; mimeographed; 294.2/804, BIC, approximately 2,400 words.

The purpose of this circular is to impart information concerning the Third Plenum to the party rank and file. Three points are worth noting:

1. It is disclosed that the meeting lasted five days, from September 24 to 28, that fourteen members of the Central Committee and twenty-two others were in attendance, and that seven new members of the Central Committee, eight alternates, and two members of the Supervisory Committee were elected.

2. There is no mention of the verdict of the Third Plenum that Li Li-san did not deviate from the Moscow line.

3. The Comintern letter of July 23 is brought home to the party rank and file at great length. Though a close scrutiny reveals a slight compromising spirit latent in the lines, it is not obvious to outsiders.

8

The Moscow Trial of Li Li-san

Letter from the ECCI to the CCP Central Committee, Re- ceived on November 16, 1930 (共產國際執行委員會給中國共產黨中央委員會的信　一九三〇年十一月十六日收到 Kung-ch'an kuo-chi chih-hsing wei-yüan-hui chi chung-kuo kung-ch'an-tang chung-yang wei-yüan-hui ti hsin, i- chiu-san-ling nien shih-i yüeh shih-liu jih shou-tao), Chinese version, printed in *Red Documents* published by Chiai-fang-she, February, 1938, n. p., pp. 362-75, 008. 2129/2703, SSC; re- produced in *A Collection of Red Bandit Reactionary Documents*, Vol. 2, pp. 434-47, 008. 2129/4077, V. 2, SSC; approximately 7, 000 words.

This is as important a Moscow-made code of conduct for the CCP as the Comintern directive of July 23 previously discussed. It is most unfortunate that this piece has also been misunder- stood or misrepresented despite the fact that its language is so clear and definite that there should be no room for misconcep- tion.

To begin with, we must realize two things about this docu- ment. First, this letter agrees with the Comintern directive of July 23, but does not conflict with it. The only difference is perhaps one of language. Drafted after Changsha and the Third Plenum, this letter was understandably couched in more un- mistakable terms than the July 23 statement.

Second, this Comintern statement is not so much a denuncia- tion of the Li-san line as it operated, because the implementa- tion of the line had already come to a stop by that time, as a rejection of the verdict of the Third Plenum that Li Li-san did not err in line but in tactics. That is to say, the point at issue was predominantly a question of theory. It must be remembered that to Communists theory is always a guide for action.

Replying to a CCP communication, this document begins by stating that the ECCI was gratified to note that the Chinese Politburo had rescinded its previous resolution (of June 11) following a report made by Wu Hao (alias of Chou En-lai). The Kremlin expressed the hope that the CCP would steadfastly and thoroughly carry out the political line embodied in Comintern resolutions.

However, it is stated, a most serious disagreement had occurred between the Comintern and Li Li-san at a critical moment in the Chinese revolution. The ECCI deemed it its duty to clarify once again the substance of this disagreement so as to make possible the development of the Comintern resolutions concerned. It is emphasized that the point at issue was not a minor disagreement on timing or tactics, but a contrast between two different political lines whose confusion would not only be harmful but would involve a great danger of repeating the mistakes committed.

Li Li-san was accused of having been unrealistic in analyzing the political situation. He was quoted as maintaining that a revolutionary situation had been ripe all over China—and even throughout the world as well. His idea was allegedly based on the formula: armed insurrections in Hongkong, Canton, Wuhan, Shanghai, Peiping, Dairen, and so forth; Red Army attacks on Changsha, Nanchang, and Wuhan; insurrections and revolutionary wars all over the world. It was thought to be his belief that a preliminary success in one or more provinces was an all-China direct insurrectionary situation, coupled with the Trotskyite theory of uninterrupted transformation from a bourgeois-democratic revolution to a proletarian revolution.

Then, this statement lists a total of six major mistakes inherent in the Li-san line. Explained fairly clearly and unmistakably, these six mistakes were supposed to be the lessons learned from the Li Li-san policy—lessons which have had far-reaching effect on the subsequent development of the Chinese Communist movement, but which have generally been overlooked in the non-Communist world. The six mistakes are as follows:

1. Uneven revolutionary development in the nation. As conditions vary in the different parts of China, the revolution can hope to succeed only in certain provinces of, say, southern

China first but not on a national scale all at once. But Li Li-san failed to understand this and made the mistake of thinking that a victory in one or more provinces would directly pass over into a nationwide sweep.

2. Labor movement lagging behind the peasant movement. The Kremlin notes that the speed and scale of the peasant movement in China have gone far beyond those of the labor movement and that the labor movement is weak even in the key cities like Wuhan and Shanghai. But Li Li-san held the opposite view.

3. Strong position of imperialists in cities. It is pointed out that the big cities are under the political and military control of the imperialists and that urban workers are weak. Under such circumstances, the Comintern reasons, urban insurrections without organizing and preparing the masses in advance would be nothing but blind actionism.

4. Strengths and weaknesses of the Soviet movement. Despite its strengths, the Soviet movement in the hinterland is fraught with weaknesses which remain to be overcome. Li Li-san, it is charged, did not even mention this question. To make matters worse, he even brought forward premature programs such as collectivization and national farms.

5. About the Red Army. Despite its many merits and accomplishments, the Red Army has not yet been well organized. It is still far from strong enough for an attack on big cities where modernized troops of the imperialists are in garrison.

6. Other errors. Li Li-san made the mistake of sacrificing political demonstration and economic struggle for outright insurrection. He abolished the C.Y. and the labor unions, and so forth.

After criticizing Li Li-san's errors point for point, the ECCI assigned the Chinese Communists the following tasks for their immediate action:

1. Immediate build-up of a genuine workers' and peasants' Red Army. Starting even with a humble 45,000 to 50,000 men, the Red Army should be composed of workers and peasants, commanded chiefly by workers, and led by Communists. It should be completely in the hands of the CCP and securely established in the Soviet areas which are the revolutionary bases. The party should try its best to accomplish this task without delay.

2. Immediate establishment of a strong and competent Soviet government. Manned mostly with Communists, joined by non-Communist workers, peasants, and soldiers, the Soviet gov-

ernment should be established in the revolutionary bases and
should be dependent on the Red Army. It should have a program
of its own—an anti-imperialist and agrarian revolution program.

3. Genuine revolutionary mass work. The masses should be
organized within and without the Soviet areas according to plan.
Certain policies of Li Li-san in this respect are rejected.

In addition, the CCP was told that it would be desirable to
deal with the imperialists, but was warned that it would be
harmful and dangerous to entertain any illusion of living together with them "peacefully."

Toward the end of this letter Moscow raised a question of
discipline. It was charged that Li Li-san had declared that the
Comintern did not understand the local conditions in China or
the theory of the development of the Chinese revolution. He
dared to contrast loyalty to the Comintern with that to the Chinese revolution. He was quoted as saying in a CCP Politburo
meeting on August 3 that it was one thing to be loyal to the Comintern and its discipline, but another thing to be loyal to the
Chinese revolution. He said it would be different to talk to the
Comintern after Wuhan had been occupied. The Kremlin declared that it was most dangerous for Comrade Li-san to talk
like that.

For a Western interpretation of the present Comintern letter,
see Benjamin Schwartz, *Chinese Communism and the Rise of
Mao,* pp. 156-63. (Cf. Robert North, *Moscow and Chinese
Communists,* pp. 142-43.)

*Report of the Comintern Eastern Department on the Errors
of the Chinese Party Third Plenum and of Comrade Li Li-san*
(國) 際 東 方 部 關) 於 中 國) 黨 三 中 全 會 與 李 立 三 同 志
的 錯 誤 的 報 告 Kuo-chi tung-fang-pu kuan-yü chung-kuo
tang san-chung ch'üan-hui yü li-li-san t'ung-chih ti ts'o-wu ti
pao-kao), dated December, 1930, Moscow; Chinese version as
appendix to "The Discussion of the Li-san Line by the Presidium of the ECCI," printed in the CCP organ *Bolshevik,* Vol. 4,
No. 3, May 10, 1931, pp. 66-75, 300.805/804, BIC; approximately 3,900 words.

Prior to the Comintern letter received on November 16, 1930,
Li Li-san was sent to Moscow to make a report at Comintern
request. While in Moscow, he was grilled first by the Eastern
Department of the Comintern and then by the Presidium of the

Executive Committee of the Comintern, both of which successfully extorted abject confessions from him. He was detained in
Russian exile until 1945, when he reappeared in Manchuria
with the Russian army of occupation.

According to Chang Kuo-t'ao during an interview in Hongkong
in late October, 1959, the Eastern Department of the Comintern
was headed by Otto Kuusinen.

The present statement is a written report made by the Eastern Department to the ECCI Presidium, condemning the mistakes of Li Li-san as well as those of the CCP Third Plenum
which took a compromising attitude toward him. On the whole,
this report is a repetition of the Comintern letter received on
November 16, and it does not seem necessary to restate the
same old arguments here. But despite the general analogy between the two statements, this piece contains some interesting
revelations and elaborations which are no doubt helpful for an
understanding of the Li Li-san case. The Eastern Department
pointed out, for instance, that in planning his adventures, Li
Li-san had reckoned with Russian and Mongolian intervention
which would, in turn, involve Japan and precipitate a world
war. (Cf. Benjamin Schwartz, *Chinese Communism and the
Rise of Mao,* pp. 143, 157; Conrad Brandt, Benjamin Schwartz,
and John Fairbank, *A Documentary History of Chinese Communism,* p. 181.)

Contrary to the consensus of opinion of contemporary observers, Li Li-san's labor orientation drew the most vehement attack from the Eastern Department. It was charged that he had
wanted to organize a government and a Red Army in the city as
distinct from the countryside and that consequently he had dismissed the Comintern's China policy based on uneven revolutionary development as "ascend mountainism, " a term used in
contempt for retreat into the mountainous countryside.

It was disclosed that Li Li-san refused to obey Comintern directives for quite a few weeks while he was pushing his policies
and that the Comintern delegate in China could talk to only a few
members of the Politburo but not to others.

Turning its fire on the Third Plenum, the Eastern Department
brought a series of charges against what was later labeled compromise-ism. Of course, the first attack was against the failure
of the Third Plenum to recognize a conflict of line between Li
Li-san and Moscow. It was charged that the Plenum did not
even attempt to set itself against Li Li-san but against Ho
Meng-hsiung, who was inappropriately identified with Right de-

viation, which was actually found in certain aspects of Li Li-sanism. Like Li Li-san, it was added, the Third Plenum did not understand the role of the Red Army, nor the land revolution, nor the strength of labor. It did not, as it should, bring home to the entire party the significance of Li Li-san's errors so as to prevent their recurrence in the future.

Finally, the Eastern Department branded Ch'ü Ch'iu-pai a double-faced man. It was pointed out that the fight against Li Li-sanism had already been under way before Ch'ü went back to China and that in Moscow he had indicated his complete agreement with the Comintern position against Li Li-san's policies. While back in China, however, he failed to live up to Comintern directives and assumed a compromising attitude instead. It was thought that Ch'ü was plagued by factionism and blind actionism which dated from 1927-28 under the influence of Besso Lominadze.

A few sentences of this document are cited by Robert North in his study *Moscow and Chinese Communists,* p. 141, under a faulty translation of the title of the document, "The Report of the Far Eastern Commission of the Comintern in Regard to the Third Plenum of the Chinese Party and the Errors of Comrade Li Li-san." Verbally, the translation error is slight, but it has grossly altered the meaning.

Li-san's Report (立 三 報 告 Li-san pao-kao), made before the ECCI Presidium, December, 1930; included in "The Discussion of the Li-san Line by the Presidium of the ECCI," printed in *Bolshevik,* Vol. 4, No. 3, May 10, 1931, pp. 2-13, 300.805/804, BIC; approximately 5,600 words.

After several days of trial in the Eastern Department, Li Li-san went to the Presidium of the ECCI for a final interrogation. The present statement is his public confession made before the examining board of that Presidium.

In this statement Li Li-san confessed to practically all the errors ascribed to him in both the Comintern letter received on November 16 and the report of the Eastern Department to the Presidium of the ECCI. He also testified against the Third Plenum as charged by the Eastern Department. As the contents of his confession have already been outlined under those two documents, it is not necessary to recapitulate them here. What sounds particularly interesting are perhaps the points not touched on or elaborated before.

Li Li-san admitted that his errors dated from some time before the June 11 Politburo resolution. He declared that Ho Meng-hsiung was the only one within the party who voiced public objection to his policy and that therefore Ho became the target of attack in the Third Plenum. Meanwhile, Li revealed that Ch'en Shao-yü, Ch'in P'ang-hsien, and other Russian Returned Students who had just come back from Moscow were punished by the party because they criticized the June 11 resolution.

A little more detailed but still rather incomplete is Li Li-san's account of the Ch'ü Ch'iu-pai clique mentioned toward the end of the Eastern Department report. Not until after his arrival in Moscow, said Li, did he know that Ch'ü Ch'iu-pai had a clique of his own. But Li declared that he had no connection with the Ch'ü Ch'iu-pai clique whatever, though he admitted that he had operated under the influence of Ch'üCh'iu-pai, who was, in turn, influenced by Lominadze. Li emphasized that intraparty factionism, which had been rampant within the CCP, should be eliminated by all means; otherwise the party would go to pieces. He said he would like to make a detailed report on intraparty factions to both the ECCI Presidium and Control Commission.

Finally, Li Li-san suggested the convocation of a fourth plenum of the CCP Central Committee to liquidate his errors and the Third Plenum's. He promised to lay down all arms against the Comintern and correct his errors under its direction.

Inadvertently Robert North mistook (Ts'ai) Ho-shen for Ho (Meng-)hsiung in Li Li-san's words on intraparty cliques. He also took Li Li-san's remarks on the distrust between the Chinese Communists in Moscow and those in China to mean the distrust between Russian and Chinese Communists. (See Robert North, *Moscow and Chinese Communists*, pp. 143-44.)

Remarks of Kuchumov (苦秋莫夫發言 Ku-chu-mov fa-yen), dated December, 1930, Moscow; Chinese version as a part of "The Discussion of the Li-san Line by the Presidium of the ECCI, " printed in the CCP organ *Bolshevik*, Vol. 4, No. 3, May 10, 1931, pp. 13-21, 300.805/804, BIC; approximately 3,200 words.

According to a sentence in this statement, the present member of the examining board of the ECCI Presidium seems to have drafted, or at any rate participated in the drafting of, the written report of the Eastern Department described previously. He said Li Li-san had now gone a step further than in the interrogation in the Eastern Department, where he confessed only to his political errors and refused to admit that a small group in the Chinese party had been waging a struggle against the Comintern. Now Li declared, as mentioned previously, that he would like to make a report to the Control Commission of the ECCI on the factional struggles which had been going on within the CCP in recent months.

However, this Russian examiner expressed doubt as to whether a mere confession on the part of Li Li-san would be sufficient or whether Li Li-san would not change his mind when he went back to China. He said there had been quite a few cases in which some comrades confessed to their errors under Comintern pressure in Moscow but changed their stand while back in China. Among the numerous cases in this respect he singled out Ch'ü Ch'iu-pai who, according to him, had agreed to all Comintern directives against Li Li-sanism while in Moscow but who sacrificed his principles to private personal relationships and wrongly led the Third Plenum after he returned to China. Accordingly, he wanted Li Li-san to give a full account of the intraparty conflicts for the good of the party so that they might not recur in the future. He said that Li Li-san had never made himself clear with respect to the anti-Comintern struggle within the Chinese leadership and that it was not sufficient for him to confess to errors in line alone. Judging from Li Li-san's remarks in the Politburo, he added, the anti-Comintern move was not only based on a set of fixed principles but also backed by organizational measures within the party.

Here the Russian interrogator reiterated the repeatedly cited charge that Li Li-san ventured the opinion that the Comintern did not understand the local situation in China and that talking to the Comintern would be different after the capture of Wuhan. He pointed out that this anti-Comintern move was still going on after the confession of Li Li-san. He complained that the Comintern delegate in China was unfavorably spoken of simply because he advised the CCP to refrain from risking an uprising at Wuhan, where the odds were as many as some twenty divisions of KMT and imperialist troops to barely two hundred Red labor unionists.

It was stated that a Chinese comrade who after a long stay in Moscow had been sent back to China to work was among those punished by the Li Li-san leadership for their upholding of the Comintern line. Li was therefore upbraided for wilfully destroying comrades. Though not mentioned by name, the man referred to was probably Ch'en Shao-yü, leader of the Russian Returned Student group.

Additional evidence of Li Li-san's calculated destruction of comrades was furnished by the report that a group of thirty Communist agents was once captured in Nanking and placed in the custody of a detachment of KMT troops which happened to be under Communist control. A dispute immediately developed between the CCP's Nanking Municipal Committee and Kiangsu Provincial Committee over the matter. The former wanted the whole detachment of troops to revolt so as to save the captives. In contrast, the latter favored connivance at their execution in order to facilitate the carrying out of the plan of a nationwide insurrection. As the latter's position prevailed, those Communist prisoners were soon executed by their own comrades. At last, that detachment of troops was also disarmed by Nationalists.

This Russian interrogator added that the tensions between the Comintern and the CCP had developed because the CCP had been handicapped by its failure to learn from past experiences. The errors of the Canton Commune of 1927, for instance, had been pointed out in the resolution of the ECCI Ninth Plenum on the Chinese question. But they had been forgotten when Changsha was attacked. Changsha did not have mass support any more than the Canton Commune did. It was deplorable that the Third Plenum also failed to learn a good lesson from these unhappy experiences.

The Li Li-san leadership had, it was stated, wrongly played at insurrection when the strength of labor was far from equal to that task.

In conclusion, the present interrogator declared that the Third Plenum not only did not come a step nearer to the Comintern line but drove the disease, as it were, of the Li-san line to the vital interior of the body of the CCP.

Remarks of Madyar (馬其亞爾發言 Ma-dy-ar fa-yen), dated December, 1930, Moscow; Chinese version included in "The Discussion of the Li-san Line by the Presidium of the ECCI," printed in the CCP organ *Bolshevik,* Vol. 4, No. 3,

May 10, 1931, pp. 21-27, 300.805/804, BIC; approximately 3,000 words.

This rather passionate statement contains two major ideas which are said to have had international significance. Actually they are mere repetitions of old Comintern arguments with slight difference in detail.

In the first place, the present interrogator was infuriated at Li Li-san's remarks that the Comintern did not understand the conditions in China. According to him, all Comintern rebels of different nationalities had made similar remarks in support of their actions. In defense of the Comintern he emphasized that Comintern officials knew the Chinese situation better than the Chinese Communists did and that if there was anything Moscow did not understand, it was the jugglings within the Politburo of the Chinese party. Li Li-san was urged to keep his promise to supply information on this score.

A second point, closely connected with the first, is that Li Li-san was charged with having ignored the Comintern's instructions against playing at insurrection as shown in the case of the Canton Commune. This was considered significant in that the CCP was the most important Communist party in the Orient. Operating under the influence of Lominadze, Li Li-san had allegedly also erred in his rich peasant and labor policies.

Accordingly, an adherence to Comintern directives—by all national Communist parties by implication—was urged.

Remarks of Chang Kuo-t'ao (張 國 燾. 發 言 Chang-kuo-t'ao fa-yen), dated December, 1930, Moscow; included in "The Discussion of the Li-san Line by the Presidium of the ECCI," printed in *Bolshevik*, Vol. 4, No. 3, May 10, 1931, pp. 27-29, 300.805/804, BIC; approximately 1,100 words.

Like other Comintern officials, Chang Kuo-t'ao brought out two major points in this statement concerning general policy and the power struggle.

In the sphere of general policy, Chang declared that Li-san had committed errors of both Right and Left deviations. In prosecuting his semi-Trotskyist, anti-Comintern line, it was stated, Li-san was under the influence not only of Lominadze but of Ch'en Tu-hsiu and Borodin as well. Li-san failed to carry out a thoroughgoing land revolution and combat rich peasant influence on it, just as Ch'en Tu-hsiu and Borodin objected to talking about a thoroughgoing land revolution before the capture of Peking. In the fight against the Li-san line, therefore, a two-front struggle should be waged with Right deviation as the main danger.

Along the foregoing line of thinking, the double-faced Ch'ü Ch'iu-pai and the compromising Third Plenum were also condemned.

As regards intraparty conflicts, Chang Kuo-t'ao regretted that the Third Plenum punished certain party members for their criticisms of Li-san's errors. He admitted to the tensions between the Comintern delegate and the CCP Central but did not enlarge on the subject on the ground that Kuchumov had already talked a good deal about it.

In Chang's opinion, the Comintern should aid the CCP the way Madyar suggested. The mistakes of the Chinese party leadership should be made a good lesson for the Communists of the world to learn, he concluded.

In an interview in Hongkong in late October, 1959, Chang Kuo-t'ao could no longer remember the names of the party members who had been punished by the Third Plenum for their criticisms of Li-san's errors.

Remarks of Safarov (薩 活 洛 夫 發 言 Sa-fa-rov fa-yen), dated December, 1930, Moscow; Chinese version as included in "The Discussion of the Li-san Line by the Presidium of the ECCI," printed in *Bolshevik,* Vol. 4, No. 3, May 10, 1931, pp. 29-35, 008.805/804, BIC; approximately 2,600 words.

A fairly clear and comprehensive explanation of the Comintern position vis-à-vis the Li-san line. Though on the whole a repetition of old arguments and containing practically nothing new, this statement can nevertheless help a good deal in clarifying the case.

This Comintern officer regarded the tensions between Moscow and the CCP with grave concern. The familiar Comintern viewpoints need hardly be recapitulated here. Two points seem to be of particular interest.

First, Li Li-san was lashed for having belittled the gigantic, spontaneous peasant movement in China. It was pointed out that even imperialists considered the peasant movement to be of greater dimensions than the Taiping Rebellion and that capitalist newspapers were astonishedly looking for parallels in history. Instead of strengthening the Red Army, Li-san had actually pulled the rug from under it by denying Red Army men as well as hired farm hands land allotments in his land policy.

Second, it was revealed that Ch'ü Ch'iu-pai did participate in the Comintern discussion of the Chinese Politburo resolution of June 11 and that he did say himself that Li-san had gone mad. But he took a turn of 180 degrees after he had returned to China.

Remarks of Ts'ai Ho-shen (蔡 和 森 發 言 Ts'ai-ho-shen fa-yen), dated December, 1930, Moscow; included in "The Discussion of the Li-san Line by the Presidium of the ECCI," printed in *Bolshevik,* Vol. 4, No. 3, May 10, 1931, pp. 35-37, 008.805/804, BIC; approximately 620 words.

Ts'ai Ho-shen made two points in this brief statement:
First, the CCP was said to be facing a crisis. After the arrival of Li-san in Moscow, he stated, the anti-Comintern move was still going on within the Chinese party leadership. Since rank-and-file comrades rose against the party leadership, they were repressed on charges of factionism and Right deviation.

Second, Ch'ü Ch'iu-pai was identified as a real factionist. Eliminating dissidents, favoring intimates, he was looked upon as a double-faced enemy. Ts'ai confessed to his own double-faced, unprincipled struggle against the party in the past. Since he promised to correct his own mistakes, he expressed the hope that Li-san on his part would confide to the Comintern all he knew about the cliques within the CCP.

Remarks of Manuilsky (馬 努 伊 斯 基 發 言 Ma-nu-il-sky fa-yen), dated December, 1930, Moscow; Chinese version as included in "The Discussion of the Li-san Line by the Presidium of the ECCI," printed in the CCP organ *Bolshevik,* Vol. 4, No. 3, May 10, 1931, pp. 37-43, 008.805/804, BIC; approximately 2,750 words.

Dimitri Manuilsky, chairman of the examining board, made three points in this statement, namely, (1) estimation of the world situation, (2) the CCP as a model of all Communist parties in colonies, and (3) detention of Li Li-san in Russian exile.

The first point was an unproportionately long theoretical formulation of the world revolution, in which it was stressed that the world in the third period of postwar capitalism was not yet ripe for a successful revolution on account of the inadequate strength of the labor movement. Without an over-all view of the world situation, Li Li-san had run the risk of a nationwide sweep. His lack of a global perspective lay at the basis of all his errors. Without uprooting this basic ignorance, there would be no hope for really correcting his errors and preventing their recurrence. This seemed all the more necessary since Li Li-san had confessed to his errors so easily.

Blind to the world situation, Li Li-san had displayed a strong regionalism, which, to the chagrin of Manuilsky, had been responsible for the tension between Moscow and the CCP. Li Li-san was quoted as complaining that the Soviet Union had a "narrow national prejudice" and that the Russians did not understand Chinese affairs. He was once again upbraided for his oft-cited allegation that talking to the Comintern would be different after the seizure of Changsha and other big cities. He was told that this was not like the language of Communists but the language of the League of Nations in which people respected power. Like other Comintern officials, Manuilsky also attacked the double-faced cliques within the CCP and wanted Li Li-san to make a report on this score.

Second, Manuilsky advocated the convocation of a plenary session of the CCP Central Committee to practice self-criticism, for the CCP was an example for all Communist parties in the colonies to follow. According to him, the position of the CCP in relation to the Communist parties in colonies was like that of the Communist party of the Soviet Union in relation to all members of the Communist International.

Third, Li Li-san was not allowed to return to China despite the fact that he had been sent to Moscow only to make a report. He was told to attend a Bolshevik school in Moscow for a few months to learn the substance of his errors through daily work under the supervision of the Comintern rather than in a quick, half-hearted way.

With the exception of the second point, the present statement is quoted fairly extensively by Robert North in his study *Moscow and Chinese Communists*, pp. 144-45. The second point, which is omitted, throws considerable light on the position of the the CCP in the Communist movement in Asia in recent years.

Remarks of Bela Kun (白 臘 昆 發 言 Be-la-kun fa-yen),
dated December, 1930, Moscow; Chinese version as contained
in "The Discussion of the Li-san Line by the Presidium of the
ECCI, " printed in the CCP organ *Bolshevik,* Vol. 4, No. 3,
May 10, 1931, pp. 43-47, 008.805/804, BIC; approximately
1,900 words.

According to this Hungarian Communist leader, it was a section of the CCP leaders, not the Comintern, that did not understand the conditions in China. The question involved was not
only one of Comintern discipline but one of basic revolutionary
policy.

Bela Kun stated that both Li Li-san and Ch'ü Ch'iu-pai did not
understand the agrarian revolution in China any more than Ch'en
Tu-hsiu and Tan Ping-shan did. It was pointed out that the errors of Li Li-san's land policy, as shown in his land law of May,
1930, were actually a repetition of the mistakes made by Bela
Kun himself during the abortive Hungarian revolution—and also
of those made in Latvia, Lithuania, and the Ukraine. While the
Comintern had gained valuable experience from these mistakes,
Li Li-san simply ignored them and ventured the opinion that
Moscow did not understand Chinese affairs. This Hungarian then
enumerated the specific errors made by Li Li-san, which need
not be recapitulated here since they have repeatedly been discussed before.

In addition, Bela Kun attacked Li Li-san for his failure to
win the support of the broad masses. Without adequate preparation in mass work, it was charged, Li Li-san decided to stage
seven strikes within a month. This was as good as a scheme to
destroy the revolutionary vanguard, a euphemism for the Communist cadres.

Naturally, Ch'ü Ch'iu-pai was accused of double-facedness,
which, in the opinion of this Hungarian interrogator, should be
removed from the Chinese party once for all.

Remarks of Kuusinen (苦 烏 西 寧 發 言 Ku-u-si-nen fa-
yen), dated December, 1930, Moscow; Chinese version as contained in "The Discussion of the Li-san Line by the Presidium
of the ECCI, " printed in the CCP organ *Bolshevik,* Vol. 4, No.
3, May 10, 1931, pp. 47-51, 008.805/804, BIC; approximately
1,700 words.

This Finn focused his attack on the Right deviation of Li Li-
san for fear that concentrating charges on his Left deviation
alone might leave the impression of conniving at the Right deviation of which he had also been guilty.

Otto Kuusinen declared that the CCP, acting on Comintern instructions, had adopted a relatively unambitious and cautious
policy in 1929 but that it had required a reorientation in 1930,
which was marked by a rapid progress of the Soviet movement.
No doubt the important thing for the CCP to do under the circumstances was to prepare the masses for insurrection. In
fact, however, Li Li-san made little or no effort to prepare the
masses except on the technical side. He abolished the party, the
labor union, the C.Y., and even the strike. All these bore witness to his Right deviation, and the rightists in China should not
be allowed to repeat it.

Moreover, Ch'ü Ch'iu-pai was criticized for what was called
his oriental type of diplomacy. It was confirmed that he was
dismissed from the Chinese delegation to the Comintern in the
summer of 1930, owing to his implication in a factional struggle
in the Sun Yat-sen University in Moscow. He was not even
thought to be as frank as Li Li-san in making public confessions.

Remarks of Huang P'ing (黄 平 發 言 Huang-p'ing fa-yen),
dated December, 1930, Moscow; included in "The Discussion of
the Li-san Line by the Presidium of the ECCI," printed in *Bolshevik,* Vol. 4, No. 3, May 10, 1931, pp. 51-54, 008.805/804,
BIC; approximately 1,650 words.

This Chinese member of the Comintern examining board repeated almost entirely the arguments advanced by other inter-
rogators before him. Three minor points sound interesting:

First, it was discovered that in the factional struggle in the
Sun Yat-sen University the Chinese delegation under Ch'ü Ch'iu-
pai defied the leadership of the Eastern Department of the Comintern. That is to say, he defied the leadership of the Russian
Communist Party as well as the Comintern within the bounds of
the university.

Second, it was pointed out that the Comintern delegate in
China could not talk about political questions, because the CCP
leadership did not permit him to do so.

Third, the residue of the Ch'en Tu-hsiu leadership still remained in the party organs, it was claimed.

Remarks of Comrade P'i (皮 同 志 發 言 P'i t'ung-chih fayen), dated December, 1930, Moscow; Chinese version as contained in "The Discussion of the Li-san Line by the Presidium of the ECCI, " printed in the CCP organ *Bolshevik*, Vol. 4, No. 3, May 10, 1931, pp. 54-61, 008.805/804, BIC; approximately 4, 000 words.

Though for the most part repeating old Comintern arguments, this interrogator brought out some new ideas or elaborations that are at once revealing and illuminating. In quite a few cases, he cited Russian experience to discredit Li Li-san's policies and the compromising attitude of the Third Plenum.

Perhaps the most important charge against Li Li-san's policies was his neglect of the agrarian problem. According to this interrogator, the Comintern wanted the Chinese Communists to place the land and peasant problems at the forefront of their program, for the future of the revolution would, as he put it, depend on whether the land problem could be correctly solved and whether the support of the peasantry could be assured. The October Revolution of Russia was successful because it had the support of the peasants who were assigned land. On the other hand, the 1927 revolution of China failed because it did not have the support of the peasants who were denied land allotments. Li Li-san had isolated himself from the peasants by championing land redistribution according to tools of production and by refusing to give land to hired farm hands and coolies. Since the peasants constituted by far the greatest part of the population of China as well as Russia, their support was indispensable to a successful revolution.

In addition, this Comintern official made interesting disclosures concerning the tensions between Moscow and the CCP as follows:

1. Having learned that the CCP had adopted a "resolution, " the Comintern immediately tried to correct it and objected to its release. But Li Li-san refused to yield, saying that the Comintern did not understand the Chinese situation.

2. Shortly after Li-san's arrival in Moscow, the Chinese Politburo wrote to urge that he return to China after winding up

his mission on some organizational questions in Russia. But this interrogator rejected this demand on the ground that Li Li-san was sent to Moscow at the request of the Comintern with a view to an investigation of his line.

3. When the Comintern sent representatives back to China, the first thing for them to do was to eliminate Li Li-san and probably also his important supporters. Like the British party leadership following the ninth enlarged session of the Comintern, these representatives failed to do their duty and chose to cover up Li-san's errors instead, as was shown in the Third Plenum.

Comrade P'i felt concern at the failure of some well-trained Russian returned students to obtain leading positions in the Chinese Communist hierarchy because of intraparty conflicts. He was unhappy that some members of the CCP Politburo had not even visited the Soviet areas. He said they should go to the Soviet areas instead of Changsha and Wuhan.

Judging by the content and tone of this statement, Comrade P'i was probably not a Chinese despite the name. But Robert North took him for a Chinese. (See Robert North, *Moscow and Chinese Communists*, p. 145.) In an interview in Hongkong in late October, 1959, Chang Kuo-t'ao could not remember a Chinese member of the examining board by the name of P'i.

It should be noted that when Comrade P'i referred to representatives sent back by the Comintern to China, he used the plural of the personal pronoun in the third person "they." Does that mean that Ch'ü Ch'iu-pai was also sent back to China by the Comintern as contemporary Western observers have reported, or that the word "representatives" was employed in a very general sense? As has been noted previously, Chang Kuo-t'ao declared in unmistakable terms that when Ch'ü Ch'iu-pai returned to China in 1930, he was not on a Comintern mission.

The truth seems to lie in between. It was probable that Ch'ü Ch'iu-pai had to return to China after his removal from the Chinese delegation at Moscow. It was also probable that he was told by Comintern officials to work for the party along the Moscow line while back in China, though he was not an official agent of the Comintern. That he participated in discussions of the Li-san line and of the July 23 directive in Moscow does not necessarily mean that he was sent back to China by the Comintern on an official mission.

Li-san's Conclusions (立三的結論 Li-san ti chieh-lun),

dated December, 1930, Moscow; included in "The Discussion of the Li-san Line by the Presidium of the ECCI," printed in *Bolshevik,* Vol. 4, No. 3, May 10, 1931, pp. 61-66, 008.805/804, BIC; approximately 2,200 words.

This statement represented the conclusions reached by Li Li-san after he had heard the charges brought against him by members of the examining board of the ECCI Presidium. For convenience in discussion, the statement may be paraphrased into the following five points:

First, Li Li-san admitted that his errors were not accidental. According to him the CCP had paid no respect to the Comintern for a number of years—notably under the leadership of Ch'en Tu-hsiu, who claimed that the Comintern did not understand the practical conditions in China. Li-san conceded that he had shared this mistake with Ch'en Tu-hsiu. But after his interrogation in Moscow, Li-san stated, he had come to realize that he had been wrong in the past. He had now become aware that the Comintern was really the leader of the world revolution and that it had crystallized all the experiences of the world revolution.

Second, Li Li-san confessed that he knew from the very beginning that his line was totally different from that of the Comintern. But he thought that his line was more correct than the Comintern's. He considered his own line to be a special line.

Third, after their return to China, according to Li Li-san, Chou En-lai and Ch'ü Ch'iu-pai told him that it was incorrect for him to contrast his line with the Comintern's and that he had no grasp of the Comintern line if he really meant to have a special line of his own. Considering that both men, having just returned from Moscow, must know more about the Comintern position, Li Li-san had agreed with them. Meanwhile, according to Li Li-san, Chou En-lai and Ch'ü Ch'iu-pai advised him not to state his own mistakes and weaken the prestige of the party leadership. Accordingly, he refused to admit his mistakes in order to maintain the prestige of the Central. Li Li-san pointed out that not only he himself thought that way but that many other Politburo members also considered it advisable not to speak in terms of two different lines. This, he explained, was his attitude during the Third Plenum. It was not until after he had read the Comintern letter to the CCP (received November 16) after his arrival in Moscow that he recognized that the Comintern was perfectly right. But still he refrained from criticizing the

Third Plenum in his testimony in the Eastern Department for fear of injuring the prestige of the Chinese party leadership. This, he admitted, was a mistake. He had come to realize that only the Comintern line could lead the Chinese party and bring the Chinese revolution to a successful conclusion.

Fourth, Li Li-san recognized the seriousness of the intra-party conflicts, which had gone from bad to worse. If left alone, he said, they would lead to the destruction of the whole party. According to him, Ch'ü Ch'iu-pai had been primarily responsible for these factional struggles ever since the CCP Sixth National Congress of 1928.

Fifth, Li Li san reaffirmed his devotion to the Comintern line by promising to correct his mistakes in action. He declared that he would fight for the Comintern line and that he would go back to China to put this line into practice.

Li Li-san had hardly thought that he would have to spend fifteen years in Russian exile before he was sent back to China at the close of World War II.

Some passages of this statement are quoted in English translation by Robert North in his book *Moscow and Chinese Communists*, pp. 144-45. Apparently owing in part to the ambiguity of the Chinese version of the document, some errors of translation have crept in. The quoted passages concern the second and third points outlined above.

9

Re-emergence of Ho Meng-hsiung

and Mif's Protégés

Minutes of the Politburo Enlarged Meeting (政治局擴大會紀 錄 Cheng-chih-chü k'uo-ta-hui chi-lu), dated November 22, 1930; mimeographed; 255.21/809, BIC; approximately 16,900 words.

After receiving the Comintern letter on November 16, the CCP Politburo met for a preliminary discussion, as a result of which Ch'ü Ch'iu-pai was charged with the responsibility of preparing necessary data for another meeting. On November 22 an enlarged meeting of the Politburo took place with a total of ten persons from both the CP and CY leadership in attendance and with Ch'ü Ch'iu-pai, Chou En-lai, and Hsiang Chung-fa as the dominant figures. This document is the minutes of that meeting.

The consensus during the meeting was that the Third Plenum had operated within the scope of the Moscow line but that it had not sufficiently exposed Li Li-san's errors of Left deviation. It was conceded that the Third Plenum had adopted a compromising attitude.

Understandably, the errors of the Li-san line were portrayed as monstrous. But as a program for action, it was stated, they had already been brought to an end at the Third Plenum. Only as an issue of theory, it was conceded, they remained to be identified and divulged. According to Chou En-lai, five major theoretical questions were involved relating to (1) unevenness, (2) high tide, (3) relative class strengths, (4) organization, and (5) transformation of the revolution. Chou En-lai, like other conferees, based his explanations of these five questions on the Comintern letter under discussion.

It was disclosed that Ch'en Shao-yü and Shen Tse-min, two

leading members of the Russian Returned Student group, made a bid for power after the arrival of the Comintern letter on November 16, just as Ho Meng-hsiung did after the receipt of the Comintern directive of July 23. These two Russian Returned Students were quoted as perceiving a difference of line between Moscow and the CCP. Their demand for an open discussion of the Li-san line outside the party leadership was turned down.

Over and above, this document contains some scattered points which are at once revealing and illuminating. Examples:

1. Ch'ü Ch'iu-pai pointed out that in the Third Plenum even the Comintern delegate did not have a full grasp of the kernel of the question of line.

2. According to Ch'ü Ch'iu-pai, the General Action Committee was set up on August 1. Two days later, it was charged with the responsibility of directing a nationwide sweep. On August 3 the hope was expressed that Mongolia and Russia would come to the aid of China. In this atmosphere Li Li-san said defiantly that the Comintern did not understand the Chinese situation when he received telegrams from Moscow trying to keep him in check.

3. Hsiang Chung-fa held himself responsible for the establishment of the General Action Committee because Li Li-san made that decision with his blessing. Hsiang attached the greatest significance to the Comintern letter received on November 16, which, he said, provided the CCP with a new life. Ch'ü Ch'iu-pai agreed.

4. Quoted as stating that the question involved was one of line, Chang Kuo-t'ao at Moscow was said to have pressed for the adoption of a resolution under the cover of the Comintern line.

5. According to Ch'ü Ch'iu-pai, Li Li-san branded Chou En-lai a Right deviationist. Ch'ü Ch'iu-pai stated that he committed errors of a compromising nature under the influence of others including Chou En-lai.

Central [Politburo] Resolution Rescinding the Punishment of the Four Comrades Ch'en Shao-yü, Ch'in Pang-hsien, Wang Chia-ch'iang, and Ho Tzu-shu. (中央關於取消陳韶玉、秦邦憲、王稼薔、何子述四同志的處分問題的決議 Chung-yang kuan-yü ch'ü-hsiao ch'en-shao-yü ch'in-pang-hsien wang-chia-ch'iang ho-tzu-shu szu t'ung-chih ti ch'u-fen wen-t'i ti chüeh-i), adopted December 16, 1930; printed in *Reconstruction of the Party,* No. 1, January 25, 1931, pp. 29-30, 052.1/804, BIC; approximately 600 words.

This Politburo resolution rescinded a former party decision by which Ch'en Shao-yü and three other Russian Returned Students were punished for their attack on the June 11 Politburo resolution popularly known as the Li-san line.

In a meeting of staff members of the Central Committee held in late June or early July, 1930, Ch'en Shao-yü and others, who had just returned from Moscow, objected to the June 11 Politburo resolution. As a result, Ch'en Shao-yü was placed on probation as a party member for six months and Ch'in Pang-hsien, Wang Chia-ch'iang, and Ho Tzu-shu were reprimanded most severely.

By the present Politburo resolution all the four convicts were rehabilitated. Naturally, Li Li-san was blamed for his misjudgment which had flowed from his ideological errors as pointed out in the Comintern letter received on November 16.

Central [Politburo] Resolution concerning the Question of Comrade Ho Meng-hsiung (中央關) 於 (何孟雄同志 問題 的決議 Chung-yang kuan-yü ho-meng-hsiung t'ung-chih went'i ti chüeh-i), December 16, 1930; printed in *Reconstruction of the Party,* No. 1, January 25, 1931, pp. 30-31, 052.1/804, BIC; approximately 400 words.

In the December 16 Politburo meeting, in which the four leading Russian Returned Students were rehabilitated, earlier party decisions inflicting penalties on Ho Meng-hsiung were also reversed. His statement of September 8 was re-examined and given a new explanation in the light of the Comintern line.

It was found that the views of Ho Meng-hsiung were correct and that his objection to the Li-san line was in agreement with Moscow's policy. It was therefore resolved that the decisions of the Kiangsu Provincial Action Committee to remove Ho from party work and dismiss him as an alternate committeeman were rescinded. It was further decided that this Politburo resolution and Ho's statement alike were to be released. But actually these were not released until the Fourth Plenum of January, 1931.

Letter from Ho Meng-hsiung to the Dalburo (何孟雄致

遠東局 函 Ho-meng-hsiung chih yüan-tung-chü han), dated December 24, 1930; handwritten manuscript, 262/159, BIC; approximately 700 words.

In this letter to the Far Eastern Office of the Comintern, otherwise known as the Dalburo, Ho Meng-hsiung made two points:

1. He demanded the release of all his statements as well as the whole record of his dispute with the Li Li-san leadership so that he might not be misunderstood through smears by a section of Politburo members.

2. Removed from all jobs on September 4, he became impatient with his continued unemployment. He was anxious to get a new position.

According to Chang Kuo-t'ao during an interview in Hongkong in late October, 1959, the Dalburo was not a constituent part of the Comintern. It was an *ad hoc* organ established by the Comintern at one place or another in the Far East to deal with matters of a temporary nature in that region. Its jurisdiction and terms of reference varied. It had a wider authority while headquartered in Irkutsk than in Shanghai. Actually it consisted only of the Comintern delegate and a few assistants. (Cf. David J. Dallin, *Soviet Russia and the Far East,* New Haven, Yale University Press, third printing, 1953, p. 106.)

Program for Action of the Ho Meng-hsiung Faction (何 孟 雄派別行動綱領 Ho-meng-hsiung p'ai-pieh hsing-tung kang-ling), n. d. , handwritten manuscript, 262/159, BIC; approximately 200 words.

A transcript of an eight-point program of Ho Meng-hsiung, drafted probably in late December, 1930. The outstanding feature of this professedly Comintern-oriented program is the call for an emergency meeting to reorganize the party leadership. The eight points may be summarized as follows:

1. Support the Comintern line.

2. Eliminate the Li-san line and oppose the compromising line.

3. Reverse all resolutions of the Third Plenum.

4. Call an emergency meeting to be attended by practical work cadres under the auspices of the Comintern delegate to accept Comintern resolutions and reorganize the party at all levels.

5. Remove all those responsible for the organization of uprisings in Wuhan and Nanking.

6. Establish a central Soviet government immediately.

7. Organize a strong Red Army.

8. Lead and organize the everyday economic and political struggles of the masses.

Letter from Ho Meng-hsiung to the Central Politburo. (何 孟 雄 給 中 央 政 治 局 的 信 Ho-meng-hsiung chi chung-yang cheng-chih-chü ti hsin), n. d. ; handwritten manuscript; 262/159, BIC; approximately 700 words.

In this letter Ho Meng-hsiung suggested the convening by the Dalburo of an emergency party meeting like the August 7 (1927) Conference to accept Comintern resolutions and reorganize the CCP Politburo. If it took place after all, the meeting should, in his opinion, be attended by: (1) members of the Central Committee elected by the Sixth National Congress, (2) resolute opponents of the Li-san line in the various provinces, and (3) practical work cadres and activists.

Ho brought a variety of charges against the Politburo: lacking faith in Comintern resolutions, shaping and developing the Li-san line, and punishing comrades recklessly. He made an open bid for power by calling for a complete reorganization of the Politburo.

This letter was probably written about the same time as Ho's letter to the Dalburo dated December 24, described previously, since both contain the same statement: Ho's statements had not been released.

10

The Fut'ien Incident

Statement by Chu Teh, P'eng Teh-huai, and Huang Kung-lüeh on the Fut'ien Incident (朱德 彭德懷 黄公略為富田事變宣言 Chu-te p'eng-te-huai huang-kung-lüeh wei fu-t'ien shih-pien hsüan-yen), December 17, 1930, at Huangp'i, Kiangsi; reproduced by the Hsinkuo County Soviet Government, January 23, 1931; mimeographed; 008.222/3065, SSC; approximately 1,500 words.

The disgrace of Li Li-san had immediate repercussions in the Soviet areas. This found expression in the Fut'ien incident.

The Fut'ien incident occurred probably on December 8, 1930, when Liu Ti, a battalion political commissar of the Twentieth Army, rose in revolt at Tungku, a town about sixty miles to the southeast of Kian, Kiangsi, and led his unit of a few hundred men in an attack on Fut'ien, a neighboring town and a Communist stronghold. The rebels set free a group of Communist leaders of southwest Kiangsi, such as Tuan Liang-pi, Li Po-fang, and Chin Wan-pang, who had been arrested by the Mao machine on charges of being agents of the A-B League and Liquidationists. They overthrew the Kiangsi Provincial Soviet Government, forced its chairman to flee, and arrested Liu T'ieh-ch'ao, commander of the Twentieth Army, and others.

The three military leaders Chu Teh, P'eng Teh-huai, and Huang Kung-lüeh were involved in this case because the rebels declared their continued support for these military leaders while opposing Mao. In order to remove all possible misunderstandings, the military trio issued the present statement to make clear their attitude toward this matter.

The three military leaders in this statement declared their unequivocal support for Mao and denounced the rebels as members of the A-B League. They censured the rebels for seeking to drive a wedge between Mao and themselves and stated that they found no fault on the part of Mao, whose work notably on the General Front Committee was in agreement with the party line laid down by the CCP Third Plenum. They pledged their continued collaboration with Mao to the last.

It is significant to note that this statement contains points involving crucial issues of land policy and military strategy over and above personal attacks. It is pointed out that the rebel leaders had objected to land redistribution for the past two or three years and that they had decided against equal land redistribution during the Second Plenum of the Southwest Kiangsi Special Committee in July, 1930, a decision which ran counter to the land policy of the February 7 (1930) Conference held under the sponsorship of Mao. It should be noted that the land program of the Second Plenum in question was tailored along the broad lines of the land law enacted under the Li Li-san leadership in May, 1930.

With regard to military strategy, according to the present statement, the rebels advocated swift action and decisive war on enemy territory, while Mao reputedly stood for maneuvering the enemy deep into Communist areas so as to beat him by means of guerrilla tactics. When the Red Army returned to Kiangsi in October, 1930, from an abortive second attack on Changsha under the Li-san line and contemplated an assault on Kian in the guerrilla areas of southwest Kiangsi, it met with a considerable amount of resistance from the rebel leaders who favored a direct attack on Nanchang and Kiukiang in the north of the province. In this respect the rebel leaders obviously reflected Li Li-san's strategic thinking.

Accordingly, we have reason to believe that Mao was right when he told Edgar Snow in 1936 that Fut'ien was essentially a conflict with Li Li-sanism in the Soviet areas. But Mao's account as related to Edgar Snow contains a few obvious mistakes. For example, Liu Ti, a battalion political commissar of the Twentieth Army, who started the armed revolt, was confounded with Liu T'ieh-ch'ao, commander of the Twentieth Army, who was arrested by the former. Again, the chairman of the Kiangsi Soviet government named Tseng Shan was dislodged from Fut'ien, but not arrested by the rebels, as Edgar Snow was given to understand. Of course, it was possible that the mistakes were caused by a misunderstanding on the part of Edgar Snow during the interview. (See Edgar Snow, *Red Star over China*, p. 182.)

In addition, the present document reveals that the rebels had collected private arms of the people to build up a military force of their own and that they had contrived to penetrate into the Red Army. If true, this must have also incurred the enmity of the Mao group.

A brief story of the Fut'ien incident is told by Benjamin Schwartz in his book *Chinese Communism and the Rise of Mao*, pp. 175-78, but with numerous mistakes, including the basic one that he wants to absolve Li Li-san from implication in the incident in spite of the Edgar Snow account.

An ex-Communist by the name of Lu Ch'iang, who claims to have been on the spot during the Fut'ien incident, gives a brief account of the event in his book *The "Hero" on the Chingkang-shan*, Hongkong, the Liberty Press, 1951, pp. 33-38. This account is also not free from mistakes, including the basic one made by Benjamin Schwartz.

Incidentally, it should be noted that the A-B League was the abbreviation of the Anti-Bolshevik League which was an anti-Communist group in the Kuomintang in Kiangsi, formed and led by Tuan Hsi-p'eng shortly before the KMT-CCP split in 1927. This group played a considerable role in the fight against the Communists in Kiangsi.

An Open Letter from Chu Teh, P'eng Teh-huai, and Huang Kung-lüeh to Tseng Ping-ch'un and Others (朱德、彭德懷、黃公略給曾炳春等一封公開的信 Chu-te p'eng-te-huai huang-kung-lüeh chi tseng-ping-ch'un teng i-feng kung-k'ai ti hsin), December 18, 1930, at Ningtu, Kiangsi; reprinted by the Hsinkuo County Soviet Government at P'ingchuan, Kiangsi; mimeographed; 008.222/3065, SSC; approximately 2,100 words.

Close upon their statement on the Fut'ien incident described previously, the three military leaders addressed this open letter the next day to some of the rebel leaders and through them to the officers and soldiers of the Twentieth Army with a view to pacifying them. The main arguments in this letter are essentially the same as in their previous statement but are brought out more clearly.

Since the main charge against Mao was his Right deviation,

the military trio began by making a comparison between Mao and the rebels and decided that the truth was the other way around. The trio based their argument on the fact that Mao advocated equal land redistribution, objected to the political leadership and economic exploitation of the rich peasantry, and sought to strengthen the Soviet regime by arming the masses properly, whereas the rebel leaders adhered to the rich peasant line by favoring land redistribution according to labor power and refusing to expropriate the rich peasantry.

As regards military strategy, the trio pointed out that it was always a good idea to get the enemy to fight in Communist areas. If the fighting had been carried as far north as Kiukiang in non-Communist areas, as the rebel leaders demanded, it would have been doomed to failure, for the overwhelming power of the enemy in non-Communist areas and the counterrevolutionary activities of the A-B League in Communist areas would have combined to make this inevitable. Above all, this strategy was decided upon by the General Front Committee, not by Mao alone.

In this connection, the three military leaders gave an interesting account of the mysterious combination of the A-B Leaguers and Liquidationists who were considered to have pulled the wires behind the scenes in the Fut'ien incident. They said that the party leadership of southwest Kiangsi had made the mistake of following the liquidationist line in the past and that consequently the rich peasantry had exploited the land revolution. This played into the hands of the A-B League which had sought to undermine the revolution. In other words, the Liquidationists had been exploited by the A-B League in the sphere of policy, and one could not be distinguished from the other in the sphere of organization. For this reason, the fight against the A-B League had turned out to be a fight against the Liquidationists at one and the same time.

The trio claimed that a batch of leading members of the A-B League had been discovered in the Red Army, such as Liu T'ien-yo and others, who testified that Tuan Liang-pi, Li Po-fang, and Hsieh Han-ch'ang were leading members of the A-B League also. The latter group was quoted as confessing that their A-B League was "a new faction not so feudalistic as the A-B League led by Tuan Hsi-p'eng."

Meanwhile, the rebel leaders complained that Mao was given to playing political tricks and that he had built up a personal machine for himself. Dismissing this as backbiting, the trio retorted to the rebels, saying that since differences of political opinion could be composed by conference, it was entirely unthinkable for them to resort to rebellion. Therefore, all people connected with the Twentieth Army, including the rebels, were called upon to rally to the banner of the General Front Committee to carry on the revolution.

A Confidential Letter of the Rebels (叛逆的秘密信 P'an-ni ti pi-mi hsin), by the Kiangsi Provincial Action Committee, Yungyang, December 20, 1930; reproduced in A Collection of Reactionary Documents, Vol. 3, leaves 16-18, 008. - 2129/7120, V. 1, nos. 3-4, SSC; mimeographed; approximately 1, 200 words.

Released from Fut'ien prison, Tuan Liang-pi and others escaped to Yungyang, a town about sixteen miles to the southwest of Kian on the west side of the Kan River, beyond easy reach of Mao's machine. They had failed in their first attempt to contact the leaders of the Red Army owing to interception of their correspondence on the way. They were now trying another time, dispatching several messengers on different routes, in the hope that they might be heard from eventually. This letter, written under the name of the Kiangsi Provincial Action Committee, was delivered by one of these messengers in disguise to the addressees in Huangp'i north of the district seat of Ningtu. Upon receiving it, Chu Teh made it known to all concerned. With it was enclosed a copy of a mysterious note purporting to have been written by Mao to his henchman named Ku Po. Tuan Liang-pi and others wrote to request that Mao and his henchman be detained.

This letter was filled with grievances against Mao. Charging that Mao was bent on eliminating all party cadres of southwest Kiangsi under the plea of the A-B League, the rebel leaders grew impatient at the apathy of the military leaders in regard to the matter. They said they had tried their utmost to restrain their feelings of revenge, but they wondered if there would never be justice in the party.

Except for two henchmen of Mao, according to this letter, practically all the members of the Kiangsi Provincial Action Committee were arbitrarily identified as members of the A-B League and dealt with accordingly. Charges were simply trumped up. Confessions were exacted by torture. Nevertheless the victims did not know what it was all about.

It may be recalled that during the period of the Li-san line all agencies of the party, the CY, and the labor unions were merged into what was known as the action committees charged with the responsibility of bringing the line into practice. It was likely that the Kiangsi Provincial Action Committee was appointed by the Li Li-san leadership for the express purpose of carrying out the line in Kiangsi. The leading spirits of the Fut'ien rebellion, such as Tuan Liang-pi, Li Po-fang, and Ts'ung Yün-chung were all members of the Kiangsi Provincial Action Committee, with Tuan Liang-pi as secretary-general and Ts'ung Yün-chung as head of the department of organization. It was understandable that with the fall of the Li Li-san leadership these men were left in a totally exposed position.

However, the interesting thing is that these poor creatures did not seem to understand the implications of the change in the party leadership. They did not seem to realize that their connection with the Central Committee and its land and strategic policies since the days of the Li-san line was the very thing which was a thorn in Mao's side and a principal factor of their own destruction. Naïvely, they complained:

The Kiangsi Provincial Action Committee has operated in accordance with the correct directions of the Central Committee. Above all, the two comrades Li Wen-lin and Tuan Liang-pi have been to the Central Committee, and this time they have been strongly for a swift action against the enemy. For this reason they have been the first persons branded as members of the A-B League.

Furthermore, it should be remembered that the Southwest Kiangsi Special Committee was a regional party branch of the Central Committee as distinguished from the party branch in the Red Army known as the General Front Committee. The former was dominated by men probably connected with the Li Li-san leadership while the latter was controlled throughout by Mao and his group. It was therefore by no means accidental that Mao was quoted in this letter as saying "the Second Plenum of the Southwest Kiangsi Special Committee was dominated by the A-B League," while the rebels charged that, "in short, all cadres in southwest Kiangsi who had expressed some (different) views were branded as members of the A-B League."

As to their alleged connection with the A-B League, Tuan Liang-pi and others had the following to say:

We do not deny that the A-B League has a widespread organization in Kiangsi and that it has penetrated into the Soviet areas—for we have been active fighters against the A-B League in the past ourselves. But the inside story of the fight against the A-B League this time is a very painful one, indeed. . . . Comrade Tuan Liang-pi was the first to combat the A-B League in the Southwest Kiangsi Special Committee. . . . (As late as) two weeks ago, Comrade Tuan attacked Lo Shou-nan of the twenty-second (?) army for his compromising with the A-B League. . . . (Now) two weeks later, he is branded a member of the A-B League himself.

According to this letter, a low-ranking political officer like Liu Ti would not have been so audacious as to stage a revolt but for the fact that he had learned from Mao's agent Li Shao-chiu that "this is not a question about the A-B League, but a political question." Whatever its historical significance, Liu Ti performed a bold act without which the mass purge of that time would probably have never become known to the outside world.

Copy of a Letter from Mao Tse-tung to Ku Po (毛澤東給 古柏的信 Mao-tse-tung chi ku-po ti hsin), December 10, 1930; reproduced in *A Collection of Reactionary Documents,* Vol. 3, leaf 18, 008.2129/7120, V.1, nos. 3-4, SSC; mimeographed; approximately 300 words.

This is a copy of a mysterious letter purporting to have been written by Mao to his henchman Ku Po and enclosed in the afore-cited confidential letter of the rebels to the military leaders under date of December 20, 1930, as evidence of an alleged plot of Mao to eliminate fellow Communist leaders. While the rebels claimed that it was a genuine copy and not a forgery, the Mao group challenged its authenticity. The fact is that it was only a transcript and that the original letter was never produced.

In this communication Mao divulged three principal ideas. In the first place, he had decided to arrest and execute the so-called "C" cadres in the army and in the local regional party headquarters simultaneously. Just what sort of people were the "C" cadres was not made clear. Second, Ku Po was ordered to accomplish his mission with respect to West Kiangsi and the Kiangsi Provincial Action Committee within three days. Third, Tuan Liang-pi and others must be forced to confess that Chu Teh, P'eng Teh-huai, Huang Kung-lüeh, and T'eng Tai-yüan were leading members of the A-B League in the army so that they might be arrested and executed at an early date.

Judging from all documentary evidences available, one has the impression that this letter was in all probability forged.

A Reply of the General Front Committee (總前委答辯 的一封信 Tsung-ch'ien-wei ta-pien ti i-feng hsin), n. d., n. p. ; reproduced in *A Collection of Reactionary Documents,* Vol. 3, leaves 10-16, 008. 2129/7120, V. 1, nos. 3-4, SSC; mimeographed; approximately 4, 800 words.

In response to the confidential letter of the rebels dated December 20, 1930, the General Front Committee issued the present statement in defense of Mao. As Mao was in charge of the General Front Committee, this statement was tantamount to his own.

This statement is divided into five parts grouped under five headings, namely: (1) Who have really betrayed comrades? (2) Who are really the underhand plotters? (3) Did the action of Liu Ti not represent the intrigue of the A-B League? (4) Was the Second Plenum not controlled by the members of the A-B League and the Liquidationists? and (5) Who have trespassed against the middle peasantry?

The present statement repeats, for the most part, the arguments of the three military leaders with regard to the Fut'ien incident as described previously. The difference lies in detail rather than in nature.

Proceeding on the assumption that the Fut'ien incident was a creation of the A-B League and the Liquidationists, this document reveals that more than 4, 400 members of the A-B League were first discovered and arrested in the Red Army, with all their own organization and chain of command. It was learned from some of these people that Tuan Liang-pi, Li Po-fang, and Hsieh Han-ch'ang were leading members of the A-B League. These persons in turn implicated others, such as Chin Wan-p'ang and Ts'ung Yün-chung, in the charge. It is stressed that when it was decided to arrest these ringleaders, the decision was made by the General Front Committee, not by Mao alone. In contrast, this statement adds, the rival leaders went so far as to forge a letter from Mao to Ku Po, using it as evidence in order to drive a wedge between Mao and the military men. Such being the case, who were then really betraying comrades?

It is interesting to note that the General Front Committee did
not see any intrinsic demerit in the political trick of "playing
off one against another," of which Mao had been accused. All
depended, it was said, on the purpose to be served. If it was
used, as in the case of Mao, for the cause of the revolution, it
would be all to the good. If it was used, as in the case of the
rebels, it should be condemned.

The General Front Committee denied that the object of Liu
Ti's revolt at Fut'ien was to come to the rescue of comrades,
as he and his group claimed. If such had been the case, the
Committee contended, he would have behaved differently. He
would have, for instance, sought a solution by conference or
stopped with the release of the captives. As a matter of fact, he
had gone beyond all this. Over and above all atrocities committed, he had brought forward issues of policy and strategy.

It will be recalled that two major party conferences were
held in Kiangsi in 1930. One was the February 7 Conference
sponsored by Mao and attended by delegates from the Southwest
Kiangsi Special Committee and from the Fourth, Fifth, and
Sixth armies under Chu Teh, P'eng Teh-huai, and Huang Kung-
lüeh respectively. The other was the Second Plenum of the
Southwest Kiangsi Special Committee held in July and sponsored
exclusively by the group led by Tuan Liang-pi, Li Po-fang, and
Hsieh Han-ch'ang. These two conferences were widely divided
on land policy. While the former advocated the redistribution of
land, the latter denounced it as a concept of private landowner-
ship. Consequently, the former discharged a delegate by the
name of Chiang Han-po who had objected to land redistribution,
while the latter removed a delegate named Liu Shih-chi who had
steadfastly followed the line of the February 7 Conference. For
this reason, the General Front Committee decided that the Second Plenum was controlled by members of the A-B League and
Liquidationists.

The General Front Committee claimed to have worked toward
strengthening the alliance with the middle peasantry all the
time. On the contrary, it was charged, the rebel leaders had
originally objected to equal land redistribution in favor of land
redistribution according to labor power. This, the General
Front Committee reasoned, represented the interests of the
rich peasantry who, thanks to their superior labor power made
possible by their richer capital and better farming implements,
could obtain more land than the lower strata of the peasantry.
Seeing the danger involved in such a policy, it was stated, the

rival leaders later turned around and brought forward an "ultra-leftist" program of giving good land to poor peasants and hired farm hands and poor land to middle peasants. In so doing, it was pointed out, they had actually cut the throat of the middle peasantry and driven them to the side of the rich peasantry.

In conclusion, the General Front Committee emphasized that the question at issue was not one concerning Mao alone. The entire cause of the revolution was at stake. Since Mao was representing the correct line and actually leading the revolution of the nation, he had become the target of attack.

A study of this document brings out two major points which are particularly worthy of note:

1. It was Mao who had actually struck the first blow under the name of the General Front Committee. He first eliminated more than 4,400 men in the Red Army and then arrested the leaders of the Kiangsi Provincial Action Committee. Not until after the happening of all these did Liu Ti rise in revolt and attack Fut'ien prison. Moreover, Mao did not produce any evidence in support of these mass arrests. Had there been any such evidence at all, it would have been cited or mentioned in the present document. The charge that the rebel leaders were all members of the A-B League and Liquidationists had no basis in this document as elsewhere.

2. The story of the two conferences of 1930 suggests that the clash between the Mao machine and the rebel leaders was one of long standing. Mao controlled the Red Army and thereby dominated the February 7 Conference. The rebel leaders controlled the Kiangsi Provincial Action Committee as well as the Southwest Kiangsi Special Committee; they sponsored the Second Plenum in the heyday of the Li-san line and repudiated the land policy adopted by the February 7 Conference. In addition, they had made some headway to penetrate into the Red Army (for example, the Twentieth Army) which was the basis of power for Mao and his group in the Chinese Soviet movement.

It is interesting to note that nine months later, on September 1, 1931, the party Central under the leadership of the Russian Returned Students, who held no love for Mao Tse-tung or Li Li-san, pointed out that not only was the Second Plenum glaringly guilty of Li Li-sanism but also that the February 7 Conference made mistakes of Right and Left opportunism. (See A Directive Letter of the Central Committee to the Soviet Areas, September 1, 1931, p. 8.)

Circular Note No. 2 of the Central Bureau—Resolution on the Fut'ien Incident (中央局通告第二號 —— 對富田事變的決議 Chung-yang-chü t'ung-kao ti-erh hao—tui fu-t'ien shih-pien ti chüeh-i), January 16, 1931; reprinted by the CCP Branch of the Fourth Army, January 23, 1931; mimeographed; 008. 2107/5044, SSC; approximately 6,500 words.

Immediately after its coming into being on January 15, 1931, the Central Bureau adopted this resolution the following day approving a report submitted by the General Front Committee in regard to the Fut'ien incident. By this resolution the five rebel leaders Tuan Liang-pi, Li Po-fang, Hsieh Han-ch'ang, Chin Wan-pang, and Liu Ti were expelled from the party.

This resolution was issued as a circular to all party members in the Soviet areas. It consists of six parts, to wit, (1) the development of the Fut'ien incident, (2) objective causes, (3) subjective causes, (4) a counterrevolutionary move, (5) proper ways of fighting the A-B League and the Liquidationists, and (6) correcting past errors in the fight against the A-B League and the Liquidationists.

The story about the development of the incident is a concise one. When a large group of members of the A-B League, it was stated, was unearthed in the army, it was found that Tuan Liang-pi and Li Po-fang, both members of the Kiangsi Provincial Action Committee, and Hsieh Han-ch'ang, political commissar of the Twentieth Army, were leading members of the League. The General Front Committee in association with the Kiangsi Provincial Soviet Government had them arrested. Thereupon, Liu Ti of the Twentieth Army led his battalion in open revolt at Tungku, arresting the commander of the Twentieth Army and others. He then took Fut'ien, releasing Tuan Liang-pi and company, bringing forward anti-Mao slogans, and what not. At last he led his group to the west of the Kan River, attacking the Red Army Academy.

According to a Communist axiom, the more the revolution grew in intensity, the more active the reactionary forces became. With the KMT First Campaign against the Communists in full swing at that time, the A-B League and the Liquidationists were allegedly given a great impetus. This was looked upon as basic among the objective causes of the revolt.

It was conceded that the Fut'ien incident was not an accidental happening but an outcome of errors in the party line in southwest Kiangsi. It was charged that the composition of the party structure in southwest Kiangsi was based on petty bourgeois intellectuals who had managed to gain control of party and political leadership. In consequence, the rich peasant line was the order of the day, as could be seen from the fact that the anti-rich peasant policy of the February 7 Conference was simply repudiated by the Second Plenum sponsored by the rebel leaders. These petty bourgeois and rich peasant elements were given to factionism; they engaged themselves in unprincipled intraparty struggle. This eventually led to the Fut'ien incident.

As to the role of the mysterious A-B League in the incident, this document has the following to say:

No doubt the Fut'ien incident was in fact an act directed against the party and the revolution. Though it has not yet been proved that they (rebel leaders) organizationally are all members of the A-B League and the Liquidationists, their action against the party and against the revolution has objectively been in agreement with the reactionary behavior of the A-B League and the Liquidationists.

Toward the end of the present document, the mass line and the ideological struggle were stressed as the two principal ways to correct past errors in fighting the A-B League and the Liquidationists. There were indications that wanton beatings and killings led to a reign of Red Terror during the course of the incident. In a very real sense, this document was meant to call a halt to such excesses.

According to ex-Communist sources, the Central Bureau was set up as a device of the Central Committee to keep Mao in check. But Mao managed to wield power owing to the incompetence of the secretary of the new setup, Hsiang Ying. (See Lu Ch'iang, *The "Hero" on the Chingkangshan,* p. 43; Kung Ch'u, *The Red Army and I,* Hongkong, South Wind Publishing Co., 1954, p. 256.)

A Letter from the Central Bureau to Comrades of the West Route (中央局給西路同志的信 Chung-yang-chü chi hsi-lu t'ung-chih ti hsin), February 4, 1931; reproduced in *A Collection of Reactionary Documents,* Vol. 3, leaves 19-30, 008. 2129/7120, V. 3, nos. 3-4, SSC; mimeographed; approximately 8, 600 words.

Following their expulsion from the party, the five rebel leaders became more than ever recalcitrant and continued their resistance against Mao at their base of operations west of the Kan River. Apparently a large number of individual Communists were still under their direction, and it was for the purpose of winning these Communists over that the present letter was addressed to them.

The body of this letter is divided into four parts, namely, (1) a reappraisal of the Fut'ien incident, (2) main causes of the incident, (3) labor mentality versus peasant mentality, and (4) the counterrevolutionary character of the incident and errors in handling it. Needless to say, most of the points in this letter are repetitions of old arguments, and it is unnecessary to reproduce them all here except those that seem to throw some fresh or additional light on the subject.

According to this letter, the Communist ranks west of the Kan River had agreed to rally to the party leadership, but they persisted in their political stand against Mao. This was dismissed by the Central Bureau as being not objective in terms of Leninism because it was simply impossible to distinguish between party and political life. The Central Bureau said of the rebels:

> Though there are no members of the A-B League and the Liquidationists in their midst, their action has practically brought about what the A-B League and the Liquidationists want to perform. In other words, though they are not members of the A-B League and the Liquidationists themselves, their practical action has at least been exploited by the A-B League and the Liquidationists.

It was disclosed in this letter that after the occurrence of the Fut'ien incident the Kiangsi Provincial Action Committee held two enlarged sessions to discuss it. The first session attributed the incident to the intrigue of Mao, while the second pointed up the conflict between the labor and peasant mentality. Understandably, the Central Bureau decided that the intrigue came from the rebels rather than from Mao. As evidence in support of this, the forged letter from Mao to Ku Po was again singled out for discussion and explained at greater length than before. Mao, of course, was acquitted.

As to the question of labor mentality versus peasant mentality, it involved a subtle dispute over the ideological line, which, according to the Central Bureau, the rebels had utilized to build a theoretical basis for their counterrevolutionary activities. The point was that the rebels claimed to represent the laborers in contradistinction to the peasants, for whom Mao was looked upon as the spokesman. On this score, Mao was branded a Right opportunist. The Central Bureau took the position that to speak of a dispute over leadership between the labor and peasant mentality was in itself a theoretical error, for it denied the proletarian or party leadership in the agrarian revolution which had been going on in the country for a number of years. The main content of the Chinese revolution was a land revolution, which had to be led by the proletariat or rather the party. The fact was that Mao had throughout led the agrarian revolution on behalf of the party and that the rebels, for their part, stood for collectivization and objected to land redistribution.

The Central Bureau conceded that there had been many errors in the ways of handling the Fut'ien incident, but stressed that they were not errors of the party line. Seven months later, on September 1, 1931, the Central Committee under the leadership of the Russian Returned Student Faction commented that the Fut'ien incident was doubtless an uprising of the counterrevolutionaries but that in the course of handling it there was little ideological struggle or educational work among the masses. (See A Directive Letter of the Central Committee to the Soviet Areas, September 1, 1931, p. 6.)

Although the rebel leaders were still fighting on more than two months after the occurrence of the Fut'ien incident, their days were numbered. From the very beginning they had fought against heavy odds. With a handful of troops at their command they had no hope at all for a military victory. This was all the more true in view of the fall of Li Li-san. However, people have tended to exaggerate the significance of the incident as if the fate of Mao had been at stake. For example, Mao was quoted by Edgar Snow to the effect that "to many it must have seemed that the fate of the revolution depended on the outcome of this struggle. " (See Edgar Snow, *Red Star over China*, p. 182; also quoted in Benjamin Schwartz, *Chinese Communism and the Rise of Mao,* p. 175.) Again, some contemporary Western observers have ventured the opinion that "with this victory (in Fut'ien) Mao emerged as the main leader of this rural Communist base. " (See Franz H. Michael and George E. Taylor, *The Far East in the Modern World*, New York, Henry Holt and Company, 1956, p. 416.) As a matter of fact, Mao emerged as the main leader of the Communist movement in Kiangsi ever since his days on Chingkangshan in 1927-28, and the Fut'ien incident did not basically affect his position. On the contrary, it was after Fut'ien that his leadership in Kiangsi was seriously challenged by the Russian Returned Students throughout the period of 1931-34.

Circular Note No. 11, Central Bureau, Soviet Areas, CCP—
Correcting the Errors of Party Headquarters at All Levels in
Implementing Decisions of the Central Bureau (中共蘇區中
央局通告第十一號 —— 糾正各級黨部執行
中央局決議的錯誤 Chung-kung su-ch'ü chung-yang-
chü t'ung-kao ti-shih-i hao—chiu-cheng ko chi tang-pu chih-hsing
chung-yang-chü chüeh-i ti ts'o-wu), issued February 19, 1931;
mimeographed; 008.2107/5044, SSC; approximately 2,000
words.

While the Fut'ien incident was drawing to an end, there was
still political unrest in the Communist areas in Kiangsi. On the
one hand, the wave of rebellion among the Communist ranks
did not disappear altogether after the adoption by the Central
Bureau of the January 16 resolution aimed to stop it. On the
other, there were numerous speeches and actions directed
against the rebels, which had gone beyond the control of the
party. These extraparty activities continued unabated and even
spread to areas close to the seat of the Central Bureau. It was
for the purpose of putting a stop to these extraparty activities
that the present circular was issued.

Drafted against such a background, this circular begins by
citing democratic centralism as a guiding principle for enforc-
ing the party discipline. Democratic centralism, it is stated,
demands absolute obedience to decisions made by superior authority. But it happened, it is added, that this was not the case
in the handling of the Fut'ien incident.

The Central Bureau recalled that the January 16 resolution
decided that "No doubt the Fut'ien incident was in fact an act
directed against the party and the revolution," and that ". . .
their (rebels') action against the party and against the revolution
has objectively been in agreement with the reactionary behavior
of the A-B League and the Liquidationists." But the Central
Bureau was quick to stress that it had not jumped to the conclusion that "the Fut'ien incident was literally an insurrection of
the A-B League and the Liquidationists." Nor had it claimed to
have any substantial evidence to prove that "the leading spirits
of the Fut'ien incident are all members of the A-B League and
the Liquidationists" or that "they have consciously and openly
allied themselves with the A-B League and the Liquidationists
in a united front against both the party and the revolution."

This circular points out that the position of the Central Bureau, as outlined above, was clear and definite and that it was

made explicit to all party members in a couple of official statements. But what happened subsequently, it is stated, turned out to be different. For example, many party documents still contained the words "The Fut'ien insurrection of the A-B League and the Liquidationists. " Frequently there were trumped-up charges: "So and so is a member of the A-B League or a Liquidationist. " In addition, numerous party headquarters and party members had issued independent statements setting forth their own standpoints relative to Fut'ien. All these, it is pointed out, were contrary to the party line as decided by the Central Bureau. If unchecked, they would intensify intraparty conflicts and make for party dissensions; they would undermine party discipline and organization.

Accordingly, all subordinate party units were ordered by this circular to obey decisions made by the Central Bureau. Disobedience might lead, it was warned, to the disbandment of the party headquarters concerned.

About a month later, Hsiang Ying, secretary of the Central Bureau, testified that in investigating the Fut'ien incident the Central Bureau had made the mistake of pointing out merely the plot of the A-B League, the Liquidationists, and so forth, forgetful of the Li-san line as the principal factor. (See "Resolution and Report, First Enlarged Session of the Central Bureau, Soviet Areas, " reproduced by Wan-t'ai-tung Committee, CCP, May 8, 1931, leaf 9.) Interestingly, a document in the Russian official publication *Soviety v Kitae* ascribed the Fut'ien incident to the A-B League but not to the Li Li-sanists. (See Benjamin Schwartz, *Chinese Communism and the Rise of Mao,* p. 177.)

11

The Fourth Plenum

Resolution of the Enlarged Fourth Plenum of the CCP Central Committee (中國) 共產黨 中央委員會擴大會第四次 全體會議議決案 Chung-kuo kung-ch'an-tang chung-yang wei-yüan-hui k'uo-ta-hui ti-szu-tz'u ch'üan-t'i hui-i i-chüeh-an), January, 1931; 008.235/5948/C.1, SSC; reproduced by Wan-t'ai Ho-tung Committee, CCP, April 21, 1931, 008.235/5948/C.2, SSC; *Red Documents*, pp. 235-44, 008.2129/2703, SSC; *A Collection of Red Bandit Reactionary Documents*, Vol. 2, pp. 424-34, 008.2129/4072/V.2, SSC; approximately 5,300 words.

By this resolution the Li-san line, which had ceased to be a party policy since the Third Plenum of September, 1930, was formally liquidated by the Fourth Plenum as a revolutionary theory. The importance of this resolution in the ideological sphere is more apparent than real since this paper is no more than a rubber stamp affixed by the CCP to the Comintern directive received on November 16, 1930. The important thing is the program of action contained in the resolution, which consisted in both the fight against the Right deviation and the reorganization of the leading organs of the party at all levels. (See "Resolution on Some Historical Problems," April 20, 1945, contained in Mao Tse-tung, *Selected Works*, Chinese edition, Vol. 3, pp. 865 ff.; English edition, Vol. 4, pp. 182 ff.; reprint of the resolution, pp. 14 ff.) This program of action actually foreshadowed the whole subsequent development of the intraparty power struggle unleashed by the new party leadership throughout the 1931-34 period.

Like the Comintern directive received on November 16, this

resolution is a catalogue of monstrous blunders committed by Li Li-san: ignoring the uneven development of the revolution, attacking Changsha prematurely, pressing for collectivization, failing to establish a Soviet regime, and what not. Meanwhile, the compromising line of the Third Plenum is also denounced.

The Fourth Plenum was held at Shanghai early in January, 1931. It was sponsored by the Comintern delegate Pavel Mif with the support of Moscow. A total of thirty-nine representatives were present. As a result, a Politburo of sixteen members and alternates was elected. Li Li-san and Ch'ü Ch'iu-pai were eliminated, while Hsiang Chung-fa was re-elected after making a public confession. (See Ch'en Shao-yü, *Struggle for the More Complete Bolshevization of the CCP*, part 4, sec. 2, chap. 2, "The Counter-revolutionary Activities of Lo Chang-lung after the Fourth Plenum.") Those who had played a major role in shaping or following the Li-san line received a crushing blow. Thus, Li Wei-han, Ho Ch'ang, Kuan Hsiang-ying, and others were removed. (See editor's note, dated January 13, on Wei Jen's article entitled "The Fight Against Li-sanism should be Linked with the Reform of the Party Leadership," printed in *Reconstruction of the Party*, No. 1, January 25, 1931, pp. 17-21.) On the other hand, the Russian Returned Students were set up in leadership. These included Ch'en Shao-yü, Chang Went'ien, and Shen Tse-min. The ever adaptable Chou En-lai was also re-elected. (See Conrad Brandt, Benjamin Schwartz, and John Fairbank, *A Documentary History of Chinese Communism*, p. 36; cf. Robert North, *Moscow and Chinese Communists*, p. 146.)

As will be seen elsewhere in this study, Ho Meng-hsiung and Lo Chang-lung led a stubborn opposition against the Fourth Plenum called under the auspices of Pavel Mif. From the very beginning they questioned the desirability of such a plenary session. They reasoned that the party leadership, which as a whole shared the errors of Li-sanism, was not fit for the responsibility of bringing about a party reform. A new leadership should be created by an emergency party conference along the line of the August 7 Conference of 1927. When it was found that Pavel Mif brought forward a plan to reorganize the party leadership with strong prejudices in favor of his protégés, the Ho Meng-hsiung-Lo Chang-lung group withdrew from the meeting. These people in the opposition, branded as rightists, presented on their part a list of candidates for the Politburo, but to no avail. Thereupon they broke with the party leadership.

To judge from the views expressed by some of the Comintern officials during the Li Li-san trial at Moscow, the rise of the Russian Returned Student group to power in China seemed to be a foregone conclusion. It must be remembered that Moscow's purge of Li Li-san was not only a question of policy and theory but also a question of discipline and loyalty. From the latter point of view, the Russian Returned Students were uniquely suited to the tastes of Moscow. This seems all the more true in view of the fact that 1930 was marked by a tendency of the accession to power of 100 per cent Stalinist supporters everywhere in the Communist world. (See Leon Trotsky, *The Third International after Lenin,* translated by John G. Wright, New York, Pioneer Publishers, second edition, 1957, p. 329.)

Echoing the anti-rightist trend in the Soviet Union since 1928, the present document provides that the Right deviation remained the principal danger within the party at the moment. This provision had a very great practical value for the new upstart leadership which used it as a bludgeon to beat all their opponents, lumped under one appellation "rightists, " apart from the Li Li-sanists.

It transpired that the Russian Returned Students, once imposed on the party leadership, launched a party-wide reshuffle on all levels. Under the patronage of Pavel Mif, they built up a powerful machine of their own and dealt serious and in many cases fatal blows to their opponents. They eliminated practically all the rightists in the broad area of Shanghai. They challenged the leadership of Mao in Kiangsi to the extent that it looked as if he had lost all power on the eve of the Long March.

In 1945, the Mao leadership declared that the struggle against the Russian Returned Student line was the longest and most desperate of all the three intraparty anti-leftist struggles during the period of 1927-34, the other two being against Ch'ü Ch'iu-pai in 1927-28 and Li Li-san in 1930. With regard to the Fourth Plenum in particular, it was stated that the plenary session had no positive, constructive accomplishments at all and that it merely put into effect two faulty political programs, namely, (1) combat the Right deviation as the principal danger, and (2) reorganize and replenish party units at all levels. (See "Resolution on Some Historical Problems, " April 20, 1945, contained in Mao Tse-tung, *Selected Works,* Chinese edition, Vol. 3, p. 965; English edition, Vol. 4, p. 182; reprint of the resolution, p. 15.) It was pointed out that Mao and his group were throughout against this third Left line and that consequently their lead-

ership in various places was removed by the Russian Returned
Student group or its agencies or individual representatives.
(See Mao Tse-tung, *Selected Works*, Chinese edition, Vol. 3,
p. 970; English edition, Vol. 4, pp. 187-88; reprint of the resolution, p. 21.)

In its letter to the CCP Central Committee in July, 1931, the
Comintern was gratified to note the accomplishments of the CCP
Fourth Plenum. Meanwhile, it stressed the importance of taking
immediate steps to strengthen the leadership of the party in the
Soviet areas. There could be little doubt that this Comintern attitude had encouraged the Russian Returned Students to extend
their influence to the Soviet areas in the subsequent years. But
this should not necessarily be taken to mean that Moscow meant
to pull the rug from under Mao. In fact, the Comintern had a
high opinion of Mao as well as of the Soviet movement led by
him. It was declared in section 22 of this Comintern letter that
"the Communist Party should propagate the positive experience
of Comrade Mao Tse-tung in organizing short-term training
classes to train the White troops held captive."

According to Charles B. McLane, the Comintern retreated
from China after the Fourth Plenum, which was the last identi-
fiable instance of outright Soviet intervention in the internal affairs of the Chinese Communist Party. (See Charles B. McLane,
Soviet Policy and the Chinese Communists, 1931-1946, New
York, Columbia University Press, 1958, pp. 6 ff.) However,
the fact was that the Russian Returned Students, set up in CCP
leadership by Pavel Mif in the Fourth Plenum, remained in
power right up to the end of the Kiangsi regime in 1934 and that
Pavel Mif himself returned to Moscow to continue to head the
Chinese Section of the Eastern Department of the Comintern,
which was directing Chinese affairs. Meanwhile, Wang Ming,
leader of the Russian Returned Students, remained in Moscow
during the early thirties. In addition, the Comintern sent a directive to the CCP in July, 1931, which governed CCP policies
and intraparty struggles for a number of years. Also, the resolutions of the ECCI Eleventh, Twelfth, and Thirteenth Plenums
assigned concrete tasks or guiding principles of work to the
CCP, which solemnly accepted them. The resolution of the
ECCI Twelfth Plenum, for instance, represented the Comintern
impact on the fight against the Lo Ming line of 1933-34 and on
the CCP Fifth Plenum of January, 1934.

The present document begins with the statement that Li Li-
san made his adventures without regard to the Comintern direc-

tive of July 23, 1930, in addition to previous directives. It is interesting to note that despite this statement, as described previously, some contemporary observers still take the position that Li Li-san was made a scapegoat for the mistakes made by Moscow.

An English version of the text of this document appears in the Harvard publication by Conrad Brandt, Benjamin Schwartz, and John Fairbank, *A Documentary History of Chinese Communism*, pp. 209-16. There are numerous textual discrepancies between the English version and the Chinese original, some of which are basic in nature. Examples:

Errors	*Corrections*
1. cell (p. 215, l. 22)	all
2. who have fomented various anti-party, detrimental tendencies (p. 215, l. 25 f.)	who have laid the foundation of various anti-party tendencies and deviations
3. supplement (p. 216, l. 3)	replace
4. (6) (7) (8) (9) (p. 216)	(f) (g) (h) (i) (But the meaning of the context is ambiguous.)
5. that it be ready to make a careful summation of the experiences of Party work in industrial centres (p. 216, l. 11 f.)	(This clause does not appear in the original.)
6. The political resolutions of the Third Plenum amply prove this point (p. 212, l. 17 f.)	The political resolution of the Third Plenum and a number of documents relating to the Third Plenum all prove this point.
7. provincial committee members of the Kiangsu [original characters Chiang-nan, i.e., Kiang-nan, are presumably a misprint] . . . (p. 213, l. 19 f.)	Kiangnan Provincial Committee

A List of Candidates for Membership of the Central Committee Recommended by Ho Meng-hsiung (何孟雄提議之中委名單 Ho-meng-hsiung t'i-i chih chung-wei ming-tan), n. d. ; handwritten manuscript, 262/159, BIC; approximately 150 words.

An incomplete list of names in an incomplete transcript of an

undated document attributed to Ho Meng-hsiung. The content of
this piece seems to be authentic. Judging from its title, this
list of candidates must have been submitted about the time of
the Fourth Plenum held in January, 1931; but judging from its
content, it was not submitted directly to the Central Committee,
though it was not clear to whom it was addressed.

Apart from the missing part of this list, the twenty-one
names mentioned in it were for the most part little known at the
time. Of particular interest is a statement placed in parentheses
to the effect that Ch'en Shao-yü, leader of the Russian Returned
Students, was not included in the list on the ground that it was
reported that during a meeting he leaked the secret about the
seat of the Central Propaganda Department. An investigation of
this matter was requested, and it was suggested that if the report regarding the leakage was found untrue, the name of Shen
Tse-min, another Russian Returned Student, be removed from
the list in favor of Ch'en Shao-yü.

*Resolution of the CY Central Bureau regarding the CP
Fourth Plenum* (團) 中 央 對 黨 四 中 全 會 的 決 議
T'uan chung-yang tui tang szu-chung ch'üan-hui ti chüeh-i),
dated January 12, 1931; reproduced by the CY Wan-t'ai Ho-tung
Committee, April 21, 1931; mimeographed; 008.235/6055, SSC;
approximately 1,700 words.

The Central Bureau of the CY adopted this resolution after
hearing the report of its delegation to the CP Fourth Plenum. It
is understandable that the CY expressed itself satisfied with the
resolution of the CP Fourth Plenum, since by that time the CY
Central Bureau seemed to have already been reorganized by the
Russian Returned Students and brought under their complete
control. (See Resolution of the Fourth Plenum of the CCP Central
Committee, January, 1931, sec. 5, par. 8.)

This statement reveals two major points:

1. Lo Chang-lung and Ho Meng-hsiung led a move against the
Fourth Plenum both during and after it. They advocated an
emergency party conference to repudiate the plenum and the new
Politburo elected by it.

2. The rightists, who were identified with the Lo Chang-lung-
Ho Meng-hsiung group, included Wang K'e-ch'üan, Yü Fei,
Hsü Hsi-ken, Wang Feng-fei, Kuo Miao-ken, Ts'ai Po-chen,
and Ch'en Yu. These men voiced their opposition in the Fourth

Plenum, the All-China Federation of Labor, the Federation of Maritime Workers, and so forth.

It may be recalled that Lo Chang-lung, like Ho Meng-hsiung, was a member of the CCP from the very beginning, associated with the scholar and co-founder of the CCP Li Ta-chao. He was a leader of the labor movement. In opposition to the party leadership created by Pavel Mif, he played a leading role in setting up independent party leadership on various levels known as the Central Emergency Committee, the Second Provincial Committee, the Second District Committee, the Second Party Corps of the Labor Union, and so forth. He was described in 1945 by the Mao machine as having discredited the Red Army and the Red bases and having disclosed the names of party cadres to the KMT by distributing leaflets. He was dismissed from the party in January, 1931. (See "Resolution on Some Historical Problems," April 20, 1945, note 2, contained in Mao Tse-tung, *Selected Works*, Chinese edition, Vol. 3, p. 999, reprint of the resolution, p. 59.)

Statement of the Enlarged Fourth Plenum of the CCP Central Committee to All Party Members (中國共產黨中央委員會第四次擴大的全體會議告全體同志書 Chung-kuo kung-ch'an-tang chung-yang wei-yüan-hui ti-szu-tz'u k'uo-ta ti ch'üan-t'i hui-i kao ch'üan-t'i t'ung-chih shu), dated January 15, 1931; printed in *Reconstruction of the Party*, No. 1, January 25, 1931, pp. 5-8, 052.1/804, BIC; approximately 1,400 words.

The purpose of this statement was to inform the party members of the accomplishments of the Fourth Plenum, which not only abandoned the Li-san line but also routed the rightists such as Kuo Miao-ken, Ho Meng-hsiung, and P'eng Tse-hsiang. All these things were done in the name of the Comintern line, and, to ensure the execution of that line, the party leadership was reorganized. The Right deviation was emphasized as the main danger to guard against.

Resolution of the Central Inspectors' Conference in Support of the Fourth Plenum (中央巡視員會議擁護四中全會的決議 Chung-yang hsün-shih-yüan hui-i yung-hu szu-chung ch'üan-hui ti chüeh-i), n.d., printed in *Reconstruction of the Party,* No. 1, January 25, 1931, pp. 33-35, 052.1/804, BIC; approximately 1,050 words.

In keeping with the general line of the party leadership at the time, this statement lent support to the program of the Fourth Plenum with particular reference to the Right deviation as the main danger. Hsü Hsi-ken, Wang K'e-ch'üan, and Ho Meng-hsiung were mentioned by name as targets of attack.

In the course of the struggle against the Li-san line, it was said, there had developed two basically opposing lines in the party, to wit, the line of the Central Committee under the leadership of the Comintern and the opposition line of Right opportunism.

Moreover, this statement made these specific charges: The rightists declared against the Comintern delegate. They refused to believe that the Comintern had sent telegraphic instructions to the Fourth Plenum. They complained that the Comintern delegate had monopolized the Fourth Plenum. They claimed that the central party leadership had informed against certain party members.

The Fight against Li-sanism Should Be Linked with the Reform of the Party Leadership (反 立 三 主 義 要 與 改 造 黨 的 領 導 機 關 聯 系 起 來 Fan li-san chu-i yao yü kai-tsao tang ti ling-tao chi-kuan lien-hsi ch'i-lai), by Wei Jen, December 23, 1930; printed in *Reconstruction of the Party,* No. 1, January 25, 1931, pp. 17-21, 052.1/804, BIC; approximately 1,000 words, with editor's note of approximately 1,100 words.

Written late in December, 1930, this article was in favor of the convocation of an emergency party conference and the complete reorganization of the party leadership following the disgrace of Li Li-san. This seems to have reflected the views of Ho Meng-hsiung, and there is nothing new about it. What is new is that the article was released after the Fourth Plenum and printed in the party's official organ with an editor's note under date of January 14 designed to refute the points of view of the article. According to the editor, the issues raised by this article continued to be the subjects of debate within the party after the Fourth Plenum. Evidently, what is important is not the article itself but the editor's note which no doubt reflected the official views of the new upstart party leadership.

The editor's note brings out three major points as follows:

1. Enlarged plenum vs. emergency conference. According to the editor, the Fourth Plenum was held under the sponsorship of the Comintern delegate with the blessing of the ECCI. Moscow did not dismiss the idea of an emergency conference as false, but considered that such a conference would require some time for preparation, which would necessarily relax the party's efforts at its urgent tasks for the moment. The editor therefore suggested that the question at issue should not be one of contrast between the Fourth Plenum and an emergency conference, but one of whether the Fourth Plenum had solved the problem of the party line correctly. If the plenum was found in agreement with the Comintern line, it must certainly be supported in the continued struggle of the party.

2. Reform of the party leadership. In the editor's opinion, this question had been as good as settled. The leading spirits of both the Li-san and the compromising lines, such as Li Li-san, Ch'ü Ch'iu-pai, Hsiao Kuan (Kuan Hsiang-ying), Lo Mai (Li Wei-han), Ho Ch'ang, had been removed from the Politburo or the Central Committee. Their fellow travelers in the Central, who had confessed to their errors in the Fourth Plenum, should not be treated in the same manner. The question about the fellow travelers was to see whether they could really amend themselves in practice.

3. Reform of the party. As the editor pointed out, there was a great gap in the present article in that it did not go in for a reform of the entire party though it favored a reorganization of the party leadership. The errors of Li-sanism, it was stated, were so deeply rooted in the party that they could not be removed without a complete reform of the party as a whole. The Fourth Plenum, dedicated as it was to the reshuffle of the top leadership, was merely the first step in this direction. A long-range struggle was called for, it was stated, to carry the task of party reform to completion.

The Current Political Situation and the Central Tasks of the CCP (目前政治形勢與中國共產黨的中心任務 Mu-ch'ien cheng-chih hsing-shih yü chung-kuo kung-ch'an-tang ti chung-hsin jen-wu), originally printed in *Shih-hua*, No. 8, February 2, 1931; reproduced by the Wan-t'ai Ho-tung Committee of the CY, April 19, 1931; mimeographed; 008.222/6081-2, SSC; approximately 7,000 words.

Though not stated, this document must have been the new program adopted by the new Central Politburo, with a listing of specific major tasks to be done both inside and outside the Soviet areas.

This new program was described to be a forward line which, unlike the Li-san line, was based on the strength of the masses as prescribed by Moscow. The Nationalist campaign against the Communists which was started late in 1930 provided the setting of the drafting of this document. There can be little doubt that in the drawing up of the program three important documents had been consulted, namely, the resolution of the Fourth Plenum, the Comintern letter to the CCP received on November 16, 1930, and the Comintern letter of July 23, 1930.

As it is, the present document contains items concerning both Soviet and non-Soviet areas. Items on the Soviet areas may be summarized as follows:

1. To bring about close relationships between the party and the masses.

2. To build up a real Red Army of workers and peasants, establish its political commissar system, tighten its discipline, and so forth.

3. To coordinate the various Soviet areas so as to set the stage for a strong Soviet government.

4. To invalidate the land policies of Li Li-san and introduce an equal land redistribution program.

5. To organize labor and the poor peasantry.

6. To substitute proper economic policies for the premature measures of Li Li-san.

7. To step up the anti-imperialist movement.

8. To advance with the support of the masses rather than to retreat or stick to one place in the face of an enemy attack.

As for the program of the new leadership with respect to non-Soviet areas, it contains briefly the following items:

1. To lead the struggle of workers in issues of daily life such as wages, working hours, and so forth.

2. To foment peasant sabotage according to the uneven development of the peasant movement.

3. To instigate desertions in enemy troops.

4. To rouse the masses to the fight against imperialism, and

to bring home to them that the KMT anti-Communist campaign
was inspired by the imperialists.

5. To promote class struggle in minorities and work for their
emancipation.

6. To restore the original structure of the party, the CY, and
the trade unions, all of which were amalgamated into action
committees under the Li Li-san regime.

*Statement of Comrade Li-san to the Politburo and the Fourth
Plenum* (立 三 同 志 給 政 治 局 與 四 中 全 會 的 聲 明
書 Li san t'ung-chih chi cheng-chih-chü yü szu-chung ch'üan-
hui ti sheng-ming-shu), printed in *Reconstruction of the Party,*
No. 3, February 15, 1931, pp. 44-45, 052.1/804, BIC; approximately 450 words.

Judging by its tone, this statement must have been sent by Li
Li-san to China from Moscow before the convening of the Fourth
Plenum. In it Li Li-san repeated all his confessions made in
Moscow in December, 1930, but in a much simpler way. Specifically, he confessed to these errors: incorrect estimation of
the situation; misconception of the Comintern viewpoints of establishing bases, Red regimes, and the Red Army; nationwide
uprisings; uniting with the rich peasantry; nationalization and
collectivization of land; rejection of a united front from below;
distrust of the strength of workers and peasants. In a word, he
admitted, he had adopted a semi-Trotskyite, putschist line as
opposed to the Comintern line. He therefore requested the
Fourth Plenum to denounce his erroneous ideas, the compromising position of the Third Plenum, and the sham criticism of
Ch'ü Ch'iu-pai.

In publishing this statement in the official organ of the new
party leadership, *Reconstruction of the Party,* a party organ
formed after the Fourth Plenum, the editors regarded this
confession as "far from adequate" on the ground that Li Li-san
had not confessed to errors systematically.

12

The Mif-created Leadership

Defeats Li Li-sanists and Rightists

Resolution of the Kiangsu Provincial Committee with Regard to the Move of Comrade Wang K'e-ch'üan to Split the Party (江蘇省委關於王克全同志分裂黨的行動的決議 Chiang-su sheng-wei kuan-yü wang-k'e-ch'üan t'ung-chih fen-lieh tang ti hsing-tung ti chüeh-i), adopted January 17, 1931; printed in *Reconstruction of the Party*, No. 2, February 5, 1931, pp. 34-36, 052.1/804, BIC; approximately 1,400 words.

Pavel Mif had no sooner imposed his protégés on the Chinese party than a whole host of old cadres in the area of Kiangsu and Shanghai rose against the new leadership.

On January 17, 1931, Wang K'e-ch'üan withdrew from the Kiangsu Provincial Committee and threatened to form an independent provincial setup of his own. Immediately the Standing Committee of the Kiangsu Provincial Committee adopted this resolution, asking him to stop his separatist move, or else he would be held responsible for serious consequences.

Meanwhile, Wang was told to supply more information about the so-called CSS clique which, he said, had been found both in China and abroad. As will be seen later, CSS was the abbreviation of what was known as China Stalin's Section *(sic)*—a group of Chinese Communists who were believed to have won the special favor of Stalin.

Open Fire on the Rightist Faction (向右派開火 Hsiang yu-p'ai k'ai-huo), by Hsiang Ying, January 19, 1931;

printed in *Reconstruction of the Party,* No. 1, January 25, 1931, pp. 23-24, 052.1/804, BIC; approximately 800 words.

This article disclosed that the Party Corps of the National Labor Federation declared against the Fourth Plenum on January 17, 1931. Hsü Hsi-ken, Yü Fei, and Wang K'e-ch'üan were mentioned by name as the leading spirits of the move. As its title indicates, this article was aimed at denouncing this move.

Resolution concerning the Reports of the Meeting of the Party Corps of the National Labor Federation and the Kiangsu Provincial Committee Both Taking Place on January 17 (關) 於 一月十七日全總黨團會議與江蘇省委報告的決議 Kuan-yü i yüeh shih-ch'i jih ch'üan-tsung tang-t'uan hui-i yü chiang-su sheng-wei pao-kao ti chüeh-i), adopted by the Central Politburo, January 20, 1931; printed in *Reconstruction of the Party,* No. 2, February 5, 1931, pp. 29-31, 052.1/804, BIC; approximately 2,000 words.

This document represented the official reaction of the Politburo to the separatist movement on the part of the Kiangsu Provincial Committee and the Party Corps of the National Labor Federation, both of which broke with the new party leadership on on January 17.

This statement begins with a brief account of the actions of the so-called rightist rebels. Under the leadership of Lo Chang-lung, Hsü Hsi-ken, and Yü Fei, it was said, the Party Corps of the National Labor Federation openly objected to the Fourth Plenum and the leadership of the Comintern delegate, so much so that the recall of Pavel Mif was requested. Wang K'e-ch'üan, it was stated, set up another Kiangsu Provincial Committee in opposition to the one created by the Russian Returned Student leadership. Acting under the new independent chain of command, Wang Feng-fei formed a Second Chapei District Committee of Shanghai. In addition, other party units, such as that in the Federation of Maritime Workers, declared against the resolution of the Fourth Plenum.

It was pointed out that the anti-Comintern tendencies of the rightists were not accidental, dating from the Sixth National Congress of 1928. During the Fourth Plenum, it was stated, Lo Chang-lung and Ho Meng-hsiung obstructed the progress of the meeting and, in cooperation with Yü Fei, objected to the new party leadership. On the Committee for the Amendment of the Resolution of the Fourth Plenum, it was said, Hsü Hsi-ken supported Lo Chang-lung in sabotaging the resolution.

Accordingly, the Politburo in the present resolution took the following specific steps to deal with the rightists:

1. Approving the decisions of the Kiangsu Provincial Committee with respect to Wang K'e-ch'üan and Wang Feng-fei and calling upon them to stop their separatist movement forthwith.

2. Denouncing resolutions of the various party units which supported a separatist movement.

3. Removing Wang K'e-ch'üan, Lo Chang-lung, Hsü Hsi-ken, and Yü Fei from the party units in Kiangsu, Shanghai, and labor organizations.

4. Calling for a cessation of all separatist activities forthwith and an obedience to the decisions of the new Politburo pending a decision of Moscow.

My Political Attitude (我 的 政 治 態 度 Wo-ti cheng-chih t'ai-tu), by Ho Ch'ang, January 20, 1931; printed in *Reconstruction of the Party*, No. 3, February 15, 1931, pp. 51-52, 052. 1/804, BIC; approximately 1, 000 words.

Ho Ch'ang was a leading member of both the CCP North Bureau and the Shunchih (now Hopei) Provincial Committee during the reign of Li Li-san. Though he had confessed in the Fourth Plenum to his errors in aiding and abetting the Li-san line, he was found to compromise openly with the rightists when the anti-rightist campaign was in full swing. Accordingly, he was forced to make this public confession.

This confession covered three points: (1) admitting errors in helping develop Li-sanism, (2) supporting the Fourth Plenum, and (3) denouncing the separatist move of the rightists. He expressed his satisfaction with the new party leadership which he believed would be able to consolidate the party. He also recognized the Right deviation as the main danger and singled out Lo Chang-lung, Hsü Hsi-ken, Yü Fei, Wang K'e-ch'üan, and others for attack.

However, the editors of the party organ in which this statement was published found Ho Ch'ang's confession far from adequate. It was charged that he had not pointed out his errors systematically and that he did not know precisely where his errors lay. He was therefore requested to make a fuller and more systematic confession of his errors to be published in the party organ.

Combat the Rightist Faction Who Are Bent on the Split of the Party under the Plea of the Fight against the Li-san Line (反 對 藉 口 反 立 三 路 線 專 門 分 裂 黨 的 右 派 Fan-tui chieh-k'ou fan li-san lu-hsien chuan-men fen-lieh tang ti yup'ai), by P'u Ch'ing; printed in *Reconstruction of the Party*, No. 1, January 25, 1931, pp. 25-27, 052.1/804, BIC; approximately 1,000 words.

On the basis of two events which, as described previously, occurred on January 17, 1931, this article suggested that intraparty conflicts had reached a critical stage. The two events:

1. Wang K'e-ch'üan, a leading member of the Standing Committee of the Kiangsu party branch, withdrew from the Kiangsu Provincial Committee on the ground that he had found the party split. He argued among other things that a clique called CSS had been found in Shanghai with a three-point program: combating the Li-san line, supporting the Comintern line, and calling a Seventh National Congress. He said that the counterparts of this clique had been discovered in Germany, Poland, Annam, Korea, and so forth.

According to another source, immediately after the close of the Fourth Plenum, Lo Chang-lung brought forward a slogan of "combating the CSS clique." It was quickly made known that CSS was the abbreviation of "China Stalin's Section" *(sic)*, a group of people whom Stalin had specially designated to monopolize the Chinese party and the Chinese revolution. They were called the Stalinist clique in China. It was also said that the counterparts of this clique had been discovered in Germany, France, Poland, Japan, and elsewhere. (See Ch'en Shao-yü, *Struggle for the More Complete Bolshevization of the Chinese Communist Party*, postscript, sec. 2, par. 2.) This report seems significant in view of the fact that 1930, as has been noted previously, was marked by a tendency toward the rise to power of 100 per cent Stalinist supporters everywhere in the Communist world. (See Leon Trotsky, *The Third International after Lenin*, p. 329.)

2. It happened that a group of leading Communists who had fought against the Fourth Plenum was arrested by the British police at Shanghai. Wang K'e-ch'üan was quoted as stating that

this group had been informed against by those who supported the Fourth Plenum.

In view of the two incidents mentioned above the present article called for the unity of the party by combating the separatist movement of the rightists.

A Statement of the CCP Central Committee to All CP and CY Members (中國) 共產黨 中央委員會告全體黨員 和青年團) 員 書 Chung-kuo kung-ch'an-tang chung-yang wei-yüan-hui kao ch'üan-t'i tang-yüan han ch'ing-nien t'uan-yüan shu), dated January 25, 1931; printed in *Reconstruction of the Party*, No. 3, February 15, 1931, pp. 1-7, 052.1/ 804, BIC; reproduced by the Wan-t'ai Ho-tung Committee of the CY, April 12, 1931, and the Southwest Kiangsi Special Regional Committee of the CY, April 29, 1931; mimeographed; 008.222/ 8079, SSC; approximately 3,300 words.

This statement of the CCP Central Committee was directed against the rightist rebels and designed to urge them to rally around the banner of the party leadership.

It begins by stating that the Fourth Plenum removed associates of Li Li-san from the party leadership and dealt a serious blow to Lo Chang-lung and Ho Meng-hsiung.

It was revealed that Lo Chang-lung issued a pamphlet entitled "A Program for Pressing an Emergency Conference in Opposition to the Fourth Plenum," which was directed against the new party leadership. This pamphlet is unfortunately unavailable.

In addition to Lo Chang-lung, the rightist rebels mentioned in this statement included Kuo Miao-ken, Liao Mu-ch'ün (alias of Ho Meng-hsiung), P'eng Tse-hsiang, Wang Chung-i, and Wang K'e-ch'üan. Among the charges against these rightist rebels were:

1. Forming independent party leadership such as the Second Kiangsu Provincial Committee and the Second District Committee.

2. Holding party meetings and distributing pamphlets without the permission of the Central.

3. Speaking against the Fourth Plenum and the Comintern delegate during a party meeting in the National Labor Federation.

4. Discrediting the Red Army, the Soviet movement as well as the Comintern directive of July 23, 1930.

5. Pressing for an emergency party conference in substitution for the Fourth Plenum.

It was disclosed that the Central Committee passed a resolution on the action of the rebels on January 20, as a result of which some of them, such as Yü Fei, repented their mistakes.

Accordingly, the Central Committee made an urgent appeal to the rebels for obedience. Specifically, Wang K'e-ch'üan and Wang Fan-i (alias of Wang Feng-fei) were called upon to stop forming independent party organizations such as the Second Provincial Committee and the Second District Committee. Lo Chang-lung was told to discontinue his separatist activities in the National Labor Federation. The rank and file, for their part, were warned against participation in secret meetings and discussions sponsored by rebel leaders.

It was pointed out that some of the rebels held meetings at places unknown to the party leadership with the result that they were discovered and arrested by the enemy. Presumably, this must have referred to the discovery and arrest by the British police of Ho Meng-hsiung and others in a secret meeting at Shanghai on January 17. After their delivery to the Nationalists, they were all executed on February 7. After this event, the rebel group centering around the Central Emergency Committee disintegrated. It was rumored that Ch'en Shao-yü, chief of the Russian Returned Student leadership, was implicated in this incident. (See Benjamin Schwartz, *Chinese Communism and the Rise of Mao*, p. 166.)

Chang Kuo-t'ao declared during an interview in Hongkong in late October, 1959, that the chief purpose of his return to China from Russia was to seek an understanding with Ho Meng-hsiung, with whom Chang had developed a good friendship. Chang left Moscow early in January, 1931, and arrived in Shanghai in April. But before his arrival in China, Ho Meng-hsiung had already been executed.

Statement of Comrade Lo Mai (羅邁 同志 聲明書 Lo-mai t'ung-chih sheng-ming-shu), dated January 26, 1931; printed in *Reconstruction of the Party*, No. 3, February 15, 1931, p. 50, 052.1/804, BIC; approximately 300 words.

In this public confession Lo Mai (Li Wei-han), who had just been removed from the Central Politburo and the Kiangsu Provincial Committee, condemned Wang K'e-ch'üan and company for their forming an independent party apparatus in Kiangsu. He was made to support the Kiangsu Provincial Committee set up by the Russian Returned Student group, though that committee had toppled him. Understandably, he declared for the Politburo resolution of January 20 and a Kiangsu Provincial Committee resolution directed against himself.

The editors of the CCP organ in which this statement was published found it unsatisfactory and wanted Lo Mai to make another public confession. (See *Reconstruction of the Party*, No. 3, February 15, 1931, p. 53).

Resolution and Statement in Support of the Fourth Plenum against the Rightist Faction (擁護四中全會反對右派的決議案和聲明書 Yung-hu szu-chung ch'üan-hui fan-tui yu-p'ai ti chüeh-i-an han sheng-ming-shu), adopted by the Standing Committee of the Party Corps in the National Labor Federation on January 26, 1931; printed in *Reconstruction of the Party*, No. 3, February 15, 1931, pp. 42-44, 052.1/804, BIC; approximately 900 words.

The party unit which adopted this resolution was the unit set up by the Russian Returned Student leadership to take the place of the Lo Chang-lung group in the National Labor Federation. It was understandable that, as its title indicates, this statement was in favor of the Fourth Plenum against Lo Chang-lung, Hsü Hsi-ken, and others.

The arguments advanced in this statement against Lo Chang-lung and his group were the same old arguments described before. Above all, Lo and his associates were declared guilty of contravention of the Comintern line.

Resolution on the Question of Comrade Ho Ch'ang and Others (關於賀昌等同志問題的決議案 Kuan-yü ho-ch'ang teng t'ung-chih wen-t'i ti chüeh-i-an), adopted by the Central Politburo on January 27, 1931; printed in *Reconstruction of the Party*, No. 3, February 15, 1931, pp. 39-40, 052.1/804, BIC; approximately 450 words.

The Politburo claimed to have discovered that the Li-sanists had joined forces with the rightists in an effort to oppose the Comintern and split the CCP. It was said that many evidences

of the attack from both the Right and the Left had been found and
that Ho Ch'ang was just one of the cases in question.

Ho Ch'ang, who after his work in the party in North China was
in charge of the Kiangsu Provincial Committee before the Fourth
Plenum and who was considered to have never made any satisfactory confessions since the Fourth Plenum, was now found to
associate with the rightists. Accordingly, the Politburo decided
to give him this warning with the request that he make his attitude clear and correct his errors in practice.

In addition, Ch'ü Ch'iu-pai and Lo Mai were also called upon
to submit statements on their attitude toward the fight against
both the rightists and the Li-san line.

*Resolution concerning the Removal of Wang K'e-ch'üan from
the Central Politburo and the Central Committee and of Wang
Feng-fei from the Central Committee and Other Questions*
(關 於 開 除 王 克 全 中 央 政 治 局 委 員 與 中 央 委
員 王 鳳 飛 中 央 委 員 等 問 題 決 議 案 Kuan-yü
k'ai-ch'u wang-k'e-ch'üan chung-yang cheng-chih-chü wei-yüan
yü chung-yang wei-yüan wang-feng-fei chung-yang wei-yüan
teng wen-t'i chüeh-i-an), adopted by the Central Politburo,
January 27, 1931; printed in *Reconstruction of the Party,* No.
3, February 15, 1931, pp. 35-38, 052.1/804, BIC; approximately 1,400 words.

By this Politburo resolution Wang K'e-ch'üan was removed
from both the Central Politburo and the Central Committee and
Wang Feng-fei from the Central Committee. This decision was
to be sent to the Comintern for approval.

Paradoxically, the Central Politburo, which according to the
constitution of the CCP was elected by the Central Committee,
could dismiss a member of the Central Committee and even a
member of the Politburo itself.

Wang K'e-ch'üan was said to have led a movement against the
central leadership since the spring of 1929 when the so-called
Kiangsu problem arose, while Wang Feng-fei was denounced as
a persistent Li-sanist. The principal charges against them
both were the same: opposition to the Comintern, the Fourth
Plenum, the new central leadership, and the existing Kiangsu
Provincial Committee.

Specifically, Wang K'e-ch'üan was responsible for the Second
Kiangsu Provincial Committee and Wang Feng-fei for the Sec-

ond Chapei District Committee, Shanghai. They did not discontinue their separatist activities after the Politburo resolution of January 20 which, as described previously, was designed to keep them in line. Wang K'e-ch'üan, for instance, had set himself to organize a variety of independent local party units and yet he presumed to disobey an order of the central leadership summoning him for a trial.

In addition, several others were punished in one way or another by this resolution.

The Story of the Struggle against the Li-san Line (反對立三路線鬥爭的經過 Fan-tui li-san lu-hsien tou-cheng ti ching-kuo), by (Wang) T'ieh-chang, January 27, 1931; printed in *Reconstruction of the Party*, No. 3, February 15, 1931, pp. 16-30, 052.1/804, BIC; approximately 7,500 words.

This is a general story of the struggle against the Li-san line on the part of the Russian Returned Student group, told by a member of the group. The last part of the story is directed against the so-called rightists who made an open bid for power after the disgrace of Li Li-san. Though a one-sided story, this article sheds considerable light on the anti-Li-san campaign from beginning to end.

The whole story is divided into three phases centering respectively around the Politburo resolution of June 11, the compromising line of the Third Plenum, and the Comintern line of the Fourth Plenum.

1. First phase. The drive against the Li-san line, it was stated, did not begin with the June 11 resolution. Before the adoption of that resolution, Li Li-san published several articles which sounded like a political program. Thereupon, Ch'en Shao-yü, Wang Chia-ch'iang, Ch'in Pang-hsien, and Ho Tzu-shu approached the Politburo with the request that the ideas contained in those articles not be written into a formal party resolution. But their efforts were in vain.

After the resolution of June 11 had been passed, it was stated, the four men again expressed their dissenting views in a top party meeting in late June or early July. For that they were all punished. Ch'en Shao-yü was placed on probation as a party member for a period of six months and removed from the central party headquarters to take up a propaganda job in Kiangsu. The other three each got a reprimand. In addition, Wang Chia-

ch'iang was virtually exiled to Hongkong, Ho Tzu-shu banished
to North China, and Ch'in Pang-hsien sent to the bottom echelon
of the party to "study."

That these Russian Returned Students expressed themselves
against the Li-san line around the time of the adoption of the
Politburo resolution of June 11 was confirmed by Chang Kuo-t'ao
in an interview in Hongkong in late October, 1959. But their position in the party, according to Chang, was then too low to
carry any weight.

2. Second phase. Prior to the Comintern letter received on
November 16, Shen Tse-min raised the question of the wisdom
of the Third Plenum line in a top party meeting on November 1.
But he was branded a counterrevolutionary. There was no sign
of policy switch even in the Politburo resolution of November
25 which, while accepting the Comintern directive in question,
considered the position of the Third Plenum to be generally
right. It was not until the party circular number 96, issued on
December 23, that the party line began to change. But this
change did not take place overnight; a series of pioneering efforts had prepared the way beforehand. The most important
single event which had a direct bearing on circular number 96
was a top party meeting held on December 14, in which it was
decided among other things: (1) to call a Fourth Plenum to give
effect to the Comintern line, (2) to remove all those who had
helped to create or underwrite the Li-san line, (3) to denounce
the compromising line of the Third Plenum.

Unfortunately, a text of circular number 96 is not available.

3. Third phase. Circular number 96 which marked the turning point in the switch of the party line was stigmatized by
rightists as vicious. Lo Chang-lung and Ho Meng-hsiung insisted on the calling of an emergency parley patterned after the
August 7 (1927) conference. Despite their obstruction, the
Fourth Plenum convened under Comintern auspices after all and
was crowned with success. In the wake of the Fourth Plenum,
the rightists continued to sabotage. Lo Chang-lung and his group
opposed the Comintern delegate and the resolution of the Fourth
Plenum. Wang K'e-ch'üan set up an independent party structure
known as the Second Kiangsu Provincial Committee. The intran-
sigence of these rightists continued to be a thorn in the side of
the Russian Returned Student leadership after the liquidation of
the Li-san line.

Resolution concerning the Removal of Lo Chang-lung as a Member of the Central Committee and of the Party (關 於 開 除 羅 章 龍 中 央 委 員 及 黨 籍 的 決 議 案. **Kuan-yü** k'ai-ch'u lo-chang-lung chung-yang wei-yüan chi tang-chi ti chüeh-i-an), adopted by the Central Politburo on January 27, 1931; printed in *Reconstruction of the Party*, No. 3, February 15, 1931, pp. 31-35, 052.1/804, BIC; approximately 2,500 words.

As its title indicates, this Politburo resolution removed Lo Chang-lung as a member of the Central Committee and of the party. This decision was to be reported to the Comintern for approval. The charges:

1. On January 1 Lo was responsible for a resolution of the Party Corps of the National Labor Federation in opposition to the convocation of a Fourth Plenum.

2. On January 17 he led the said Party Corps to oppose the Fourth Plenum as well as the Comintern delegate and sent agents to the various provinces to carry on factional activities.

3. He refused to abide by the Politburo resolution of January 20 by which he should surrender his office in the National Labor Federation. In addition he circulated a vicious pamphlet entitled "A Program for Pressing an Emergency Conference in Opposition to the Fourth Plenum."

4. He had persistently objected to the Sixth National Congress. The January 1 resolution of the Party Corps mentioned above was viewed as the embodiment of Lo's basic ideas on the revolution. In it he stood for an emergency party conference proceeding "from down upward" as distinguished from up downward. Lo's ideas were held to be identical with those of the Liquidationists.

But most objectionable to the Russian Returned Student leadership was Lo's pamphlet in question, in which the Fourth Plenum was described as dictatorial and undemocratic and even more compromising in spirit than the Third Plenum, and in which the recall of the Comintern delegate, who was held primarily responsible for the errors of the Fourth Plenum, was requested. The Politburo charged that Lo's open attack on the Comintern delegate was tantamount to confiding to the enemy police just who was leading the party's plenary session.

Six months later the Presidium of the ECCI expressed itself satisfied with the expulsion of Lo Chang-lung from the CCP. (See Letter from the Presidium of the ECCI to the CCP, July,

1931, section 9.) In 1945 the Mao leadership also spoke ill of Lo
Chang-lung. (See "Resolution on Some Historical Problems,"
note 2.)

Judging from this document, Pavel Mif did not return to Russia until after the Fourth Plenum. According to Chang Kuo-t'ao
during an interview in Hongkong in late October, 1959, Mif did
not come back to China after his return to Russia. Some articles
from his pen were still seen appearing in periodicals in 1934 or
shortly thereafter. It was rumored that he was executed by order of Stalin during the purge of 1936. Whenever asked about
this rumor, Ch'en Shao-yü, his protégé, simply evaded the
question.

Statement of Comrade Ch'iu-pai (秋白 同 志 聲 明 書
Ch'iu-pai t'ung-chih sheng-ming-shu), printed in *Reconstruction
of the Party*, No. 3, February 15, 1931, pp. 45-48, 052.1/804,
BIC; approximately 1,700 words.

In this statement Ch'ü Ch'iu-pai confessed to all the errors
ascribed to him by the Comintern during the discussion of the
Li-san line at Moscow late in 1930. It was but natural that he
told his story in greater detail than did the Comintern. Specifically, he made the following four major points:

1. He fully accepted the verdict of the Fourth Plenum that he
should be primarily responsible for the compromising attitude
of the Third Plenum and for its disrespect for the Comintern
delegate. It was revealed that both before and after the Third
Plenum the Comintern delegate repeatedly pointed out the danger
that by following his putschist policies Li Li-san might one day
go the way of militating against the Comintern. Ch'ü admitted
that he and the Politburo did not agree with the Comintern delegate on this score, with the result that the Comintern delegate
did not have a chance to correct the error of the compromising
position of the Third Plenum in time.

In this connection, it is interesting to note a different attitude
assumed by Ch'ü Ch'iu-pai toward Pavel Mif on a former occasion. As has been pointed out previously, Ch'ü declared in a
Politburo meeting on November 22, 1930, that in the Third
Plenum even the Comintern delegate did not have a full grasp of
the kernel of the question of line.

2. The new party leadership emerged from the Fourth Plenum
with a program to continue to fight the Li-san line, the com-

promising attitude, and all types of Right or Left opportunism with particular reference to Right deviation as the main danger. Ch'ü Ch'iu-pai pledged to do what he could to support this program and correct his own mistakes under the direction of both the ECCI and the Chinese leadership.

3. Ch'ü Ch'iu-pai admitted that his compromising position was not accidental but that it dated back before the Sixth National Congress of 1928. From his adventures in 1927 through the Third Plenum in 1930, he stated, he had shared many basic ideas about the Chinese revolution with Li Li-san, ideas which centered around the question of the "Third Period," the relations between the Chinese revolution and the world revolution, the contradictions within the Chinese ruling class, the uneven development of the revolution, the question of the rich peasantry, the role of reformism, the united front from below, the question of armed insurrections, and so forth. In consequence, he admitted that he made the mistake of confusing Li Li-san's policies with the Moscow line despite the fact that he took part in the discussion of the Comintern directive of July 23, 1930, before it was adopted.

Ch'ü confessed that his conception of intraparty factional conflicts was also absolutely wrong. During his stay in Moscow as representative of the CCP, he admitted, he not only failed to help the Communist Party of the Soviet Union to eliminate the quarrels among the Chinese Communists in Moscow, but became involved in the quarrels himself. After his return to China, he witnessed all sorts of intraparty strife: workers versus intellectuals, pragmatists versus theorists, old cadres versus new cadres, home-grown party workers versus returned students. But instead of opposing such strife from the political angle, he made the mistake of offering his good offices in an attempt to bring the conflicting cliques together.

This statement was addressed to both the ECCI and the Chinese party leadership. To them Ch'ü Ch'iu-pai admitted his errors which he summed up in a single phrase—coward, corrupt opportunism.

This statement was issued some time between the Fourth Plenum and the last days of January, 1931. A Western source gives its date as January 17, 1931, which is probably true. (See Harold Isaacs, *The Tragedy of the Chinese Revolution,* revised edition, 1951, p. 363, 1. 5.) Ch'ü Ch'iu-pai had already been removed from the Chinese leadership when he made this public confession.

Statement of Comrade Ch'iu-pai (秋 火 白 同 志 聲 明 書
Ch'iu-pai t'ung-chih sheng-ming-shu), dated January 28, 1931;
printed in *Reconstruction of the Party*, No. 3, February 15,
1931, pp. 48-50, 052.1/804, BIC; approximately 600 words.

This brief statement was written in accordance with a Politburo resolution adopted on January 27, in which Ho Ch'ang,
Ch'ü Ch'iu-pai, Lo Mai, and others were called upon to make
known their attitude toward the fight against the rightists. (See
"Resolution on the Question of Comrade Ho Ch'ang and others,"
printed in *Reconstruction of the Party*, Shanghai, No. 3, February 15, 1931, pp. 39-40.) Therefore, the emphasis of this
statement was on the decision of the party leadership against the
rightists, though Ch'ü Ch'iu-pai's errors in his compromising
position and in his approach to intraparty conflicts were briefly
reiterated.

Specifically, Ch'ü Ch'iu-pai in this statement gave his unre-
served support to these party decisions: dismissal of Lo Chang-
lung and Wang K'e-ch'üan from the Politburo and the Central
Committee, dismissal of Wang Feng-fei from the Central Committee, reprimand for Ho Ch'ang, and what not.

After his removal from the party leadership in January, 1931,
Ch'ü Ch'iu-pai was engaged in the left-wing cultural movement
at Shanghai in cooperation with the noted novelist Lu Hsün until
1933, when he went to Kiangsi to serve as education commissar
of the Soviet Government at Juichin. He was left behind when
the Long March began late in 1934. Captured by Nationalist
troops in western Fukien in March, 1935, he was executed at
Ch'angting, Fukien, on June 18, 1935. (See "Resolution on
Some Historical Problems," April 20, 1945, note 5, contained
in Mao Tse-tung, *Selected Works*, Chinese edition, Vol. 3, pp.
999-1000, reprint, note 7; for a different story of Ch'ü's movements immediately after his disgrace and for a different date of
his execution, see Robert North, *Moscow and Chinese Communists*, pp. 146, 165.)

*Resolution Settling the Controversy over the Honan Problem
and Removing the Punishment Inflicted on Comrade Ch'en Yüan-
tao, and Others* (解 決 河 南 爭 論 問 題 及 取 消 陳
原 道 等 同 志 處 罰 決 議 案. Chiai-chüeh ho-nan cheng-
lun wen-t'i chi ch'ü-hsiao ch'en-yüan-tao teng t'ung-chih ch'u-
fa chüeh-i-an), adopted by the Central Politburo, January 29,

1931; printed in *Reconstruction of the Party,* No. 3, February 15, 1931, pp. 40-41, 052.1/804, BIC; approximately 550 words.

At the zenith of the Li-san line a section of the Communist leaders in Honan province went in for adventures regardless of the practical difficulties facing them. Another group led by Ch'en Yüan-tao objected to such putschist adventures. Under instructions of the North Bureau of the CCP, Ch'en and company were removed from office on charges of Right opportunism and factionism. After the Third Plenum, Ch'en was even placed on probation as a party member. With the installation of the new leadership after the Fourth Plenum, things took an abrupt turn. By this resolution Ch'en was rehabilitated and all former measures taken by the party leadership in connection with the Honan problem were abolished.

Resolution concerning the Dismissal of Wang K'e-ch'üan from the Party (關) 於 開) 除 王 克 全 黨 籍 決 議 案 Kuan-yü k'ai-ch'u wang-k'e-ch'üan tang-chi chüeh-i-an), adopted by the Central Politburo on January 30; printed in *Reconstruction of the Party,* No. 3, February 15, 1931, pp. 38-39, 052.1/804, BIC; approximately 500 words.

By this resolution Wang K'e-ch'üan was dismissed as a member of the Chinese Communist Party. This was done, it was charged, because he had increased his insurgent activities after his removal from the central party leadership by distributing Lo Chang-lung's pamphlet and sabotaging lower party units and party-sponsored labor conferences and because he had rejected another party summons for trial.

The Fourth Plenum and the Two-Front Struggle (四 中 全 會 與 兩 條 戰 線 的 鬥 爭 Szu-chung ch'üan-hui yü liang-t'iao chan-hsien ti tou-cheng), by (Shen) Tse-min; printed in *Reconstruction of the Party,* No. 2, February 5, 1931, pp. 1-13, 052.1/804, BIC; approximately 6,500 words.

This article throws a good deal of light on the intraparty conflicts during and after the Fourth Plenum. Being an active member of the Russian Returned Student group, the writer naturally pleaded for the new upstart leadership.

Understandably this article was directed against the rightists as well as the remnants of Li-sanists as they stood at the time. The writer maintained that the anti-Li-san struggle as a constructive party reform program should be continued after the Fourth Plenum. He explained how the two opposing factions—rightists led by Lo Chang-lung and Ho Meng-hsiung and the Li-sanists represented by Lo Mai (Li Wei-han), Ho Ch'ang, Li Ch'iu-shih, and Wang K'e-ch'üan—had buried the hatchet to present a united front against the new party leadership.

The writer proceeded on the assumption that the Fourth Plenum had successfully solved two basic problems, namely, the party line and party organization. This could be seen from the fact that the Comintern line had been accepted and the party leadership reorganized, and that there had also been an extensive move to reorganize the party units at lower levels.

However, it was stated, there were party members who held that the Fourth Plenum had not satisfactorily solved the two problems mentioned above, and therefore they had come to object to the plenum.

It was pointed out that there were three different schools of thought within the party in regard to the Fourth Plenum. One school bluntly opposed it, maintaining that it had not reached any settlement of the questions confronting the party and that it actually represented no less a compromising line than the Third Plenum. Lo Chang-lung and Ho Meng-hsiung were identified as spokesmen of this group.

Another school claimed to support the Fourth Plenum, but in a wrong way. They had made the mistake of thinking that the plenum was held merely to bring the struggle against the Li-san line to an end—no more, no less. Lo Mai (Li Wei-han) and Ho Ch'ang belonged to this group.

Still another school was given as true supporters of the Fourth Plenum who believed that the plenum had not only solved the party's problems of the past but paved the way for continued struggle against the enemies in the future. Though not mentioned by name, the Russian Returned Students were regarded as belonging to this group.

The present writer called the first group rightists and the second group Li-sanists. He summed up the viewpoints of the rightists as follows:

1. Since the old party leadership as a whole had been guilty of errors, its members certainly should all leave the position of leadership. But the fact was, it was charged, that some of its

members still retained their posts in the party leadership.

2. A party meeting like the Fourth Plenum should not be called by a party leadership which had been found faulty itself. The faulty party leadership should have been dissolved beforehand. That done, an emergency conference like the August 7 (1927) Conference should be convened to solve the party's problems.

It was disclosed that the Lo Chang-lung-Ho Meng-hsiung group questioned the very desirability of the Fourth Plenum before it opened, and that they withdrew from the meeting, attacking the party leadership reorganization plan introduced by Pavel Mif. They for their part suggested a list of candidates for the Central Committee who were adherents to the political ideas of Lo Chang-lung.

As to the group called the Li-sanists, their views were given as follows:

1. The Fourth Plenum was looked upon as an end of the Li-san line rather than a starting-point for future plans.

2. Since they had already confessed to their errors, they felt they should not be criticized again.

3. The struggle against the Li-san line should be stopped after the Fourth Plenum.

Needless to say, the present writer disagreed with both the rightists and Li-sanists and took pains to refute their points of view one by one. Before he concluded, he gave a brief account of how these two groups had combined to challenge the new leadership.

Combat Organizational Opportunism, Struggle for Party Reform (反對組織上的機會主義為黨的改造而鬥爭 Fan-tui tsu-chih-shang ti chi-hui chu-i wei tang ti kai-tsao erh tou-cheng), by (Wang) Chia-ch'iang; printed in *Reconstruction of the Party,* No. 2, February 5, 1931, pp. 14-19, 052.1/804, BIC; approximately 2,800 words.

This article was directed against the opportunism of party organization on the part of Li Li-san and the rightists, both of whom, it was said, held opposing views in this sphere.

According to the writer, Li Li-san contravened Marxism-Leninism in the field of party organization as follows:

In the first place, Li Li-san did not realize that the revolution called for organization and that the party was essential to the

organization of the masses. To him, the party was there to
"monopolize" the revolution out of all relations with the masses.

Second, Li Li-san did not understand the role of other organizations of the working class, such as the labor unions and the
CY, and their relations with the party. Therefore, he merged
the party and the CY into the Action Committees and substituted
the "Industrial Committees" for the labor unions.

Third, he failed to comprehend the real meaning of democratic
centralism and adhered to the patriarchal rule instead. This
gave rise to a whole host of malpractices within the party, such
as commandism, routinism, exclusively appointive system,
blind obedience, and lack of incentives.

Fourth, Li Li-san had no grasp of the significance of the fight
against incorrect tendencies within the party. He took advantage
of the ideological struggle to play havoc among comrades and
simply suppressed self-criticism.

On the other hand, this writer also attacked the conception of
party organization of the rightists and made an interesting comparison between it and the theory of Li Li-san, both of which
were regarded as two extremes. Specifically, the rightists
stood for these things: extreme democracy, factionism, slack
discipline, pure election, disobedience to superior authority,
laissez-faire, objection to the appropriate form of struggle,
and so forth.

Determined Objection to the Rightist Faction (堅 決 的 反
對 右 派 Chien-chüeh ti fan-tui yu-p'ai), by (Cheng) Hung
Yi; printed in *Reconstruction of the Party*, No. 2, February 5,
1931, pp. 20-23, 052. 1/804, BIC; approximately 1, 300 words.

Apart from a brief prologue and epilogue in condemnation of
the rightist insurgency, the body of this signed article is a concise account of the political program and practical action of the
rightists. It seems clear that the most important point at issue
was the controversy over the Fourth Plenum and an emergency
conference.

The political program of the rightists, according to the article, consisted of the following four points:

1. The party as well as the revolution was thought to have
been destroyed. It followed that the situation facing the party
now resembled the situation at the time of the August 7 (1927)
conference.

2. The Soviet movement was not yet a real mass movement; therefore the struggle for a Soviet regime should not be a task of first importance to the party. Economic struggle should take the place of political struggle.

3. The party line since the Sixth National Congress of 1928 had been a wrong one.

4. There was no danger of Right deviation within the party.

As to the practical action of the rightists, the following five points were listed:

1. The Party Corps of the National Labor Federation openly objected to the Fourth Plenum and the Comintern delegate.

2. Wang K'e-ch'üan formed the Second Provincial Committee and Wang Feng-fei the Second Chapei District Committee, Shanghai.

3. Lo Chang-lung appealed for an emergency conference in opposition to the Fourth Plenum, and distributed a pamphlet.

4. Open collusion with the Liquidationists, seeking the participation of the expelled rightist Wang Chung-i in the proposed emergency conference.

5. Making open defamatory statements against the party.

In addition, the rightists had displayed the following tendencies:

1. Extreme democratization and disobedience to superior authorities.

2. Trumping up a story of an intraparty faction at the expense of the pro-Comintern cadres and engaging in unprincipled personal struggles.

3. Arbitrary and indiscriminate application of the terms of "patriarchy" and "commandism" to those whom the rightists disliked.

Resolution on the Question of the Action of the Delegation of the CCP Central Committee to the Communist International in 1929-1930 (關 於 一 九 二 九 至 一 九 三 ○ 年 中 共 中 央 駐 國 際 代 表 團 行 動 問 題 的 決 議 案 Kuan-yü i-chiu-erh-chiu chih i-chiu-san-ling nien chung-kung chung-yang chu kuo-chi tai-piao-t'uan hsing-tung wen-t'i ti chüeh-i-an), adopted by the CCP Politburo on February 20, 1931, printed in *Reconstruction of the Party*, No. 4, March 8, 1931, pp. 20-22, 052.1/804, BIC; approximately 1,400 words.

This is an extremely important document on CCP intraparty

conflicts, but it simply cannot be understood by itself or even when read in conjunction with other available documents. It would be impossible to annotate this document at all but for the fact that Chang Kuo-t'ao threw a good deal of light on it during an interview in Hongkong in late October, 1959.

This document reveals a number of isolated and unintelligible points: The Comintern adopted a resolution on the action of the Chinese delegation in 1930; Wu Hao (alias of Chou En-lai), as CCP representative to Moscow, had accepted this Comintern resolution; in consequence, the Chinese delegation was reorganized with the result that Ch'ü Ch'iu-pai, Teng Chung-hsia, and Yü Fei were recalled to China. Against this background, the CCP Central Politburo adopted the present resolution in which it made the following observations:

1. The factional struggle waged by the Li Chien-ju-Yü Tu-san group against the party unit in the Sun Yat-sen University at Moscow had had its repercussions in China. Within the framework of this factional struggle Ch'ü Ch'iu-pai had exerted influence on the CCP Politburo, which had in turn operated at the expense of Ch'en Shao-yü and company. Likewise, Teng Chung-hsia and Yü Fei had been given to factional struggle after their return to China.

2. Since the majority of the Chinese delegation at Moscow supported the Li Chien-ju-Yü Tu-san group, it was natural that the head of the Chinese delegation Ch'ü Ch'iu-pai had adopted a compromising attitude in the CCP Third Plenum and disrespected the Comintern delegate. Meanwhile, Teng Chung-hsia and Yü Fei had acted against the party leadership. For all these Chou En-lai was also held responsible.

3. In this context Lo Chang-lung, Wang K'e-ch'üan, and so forth had come to stigmatize Pavel Mif and Ch'en Shao-yü as belonging to one faction which sought control of the Chinese party. This was described in the present document as groundless.

Interviewed in Hongkong in late October, 1959, Chang Kuo-t'ao disclosed the background of this factional struggle like this: Ch'ü Ch'iu-pai and Chang Kuo-t'ao, as noted previously, objected to the educational policy of Pavel Mif as president of the Sun Yat-sen University in Moscow. Consequently, there was no love lost between them and the Russian. The party unit in the university was then under Pavel Mif's control. Li Chien-ju and Yü Tu-san were both workers from Shanghai and were mere tools in the power struggle. It had turned out that Mif was vic-

torious in the tussle. Accordingly, the Comintern passed a
resolution in condemnation of the Chinese delegation. Chou En-
lai was called to Moscow to take over all the duties of a liaison
officer between the Kremlin and the Chinese party. Both Ch'ü
Ch'iu-pai and Chang Kuo-t'ao fell into disgrace. Chang immediately went away on leave, while Ch'ü Ch'iu-pai returned to
China.

Statement of Wang K'e-ch'üan (王 克 全 的 聲 明 書
Wang-k'e-ch'üan ti sheng-ming-shu), dated May 3, 1931;
printed in *Red Flag Weekly,* No. 12, July 1, 1931, pp. 20-27,
052. 1/809, BIC; approximately 3,000 words.

Since he could not stand the sort of solitary life he was leading after his expulsion from the party, Wang K'e-ch'üan wrote
this letter to the Politburo requesting a restoration of party
membership after abjectly confessing to past errors.

To begin with, he acknowledged his factional prejudices in the
reign of the Li-san line. He claimed that he raised objections
to that line when it was in its best time. But he was irresolute
and succumbed to the patriarchal repression of Li Li-san after
all. He said he was dissatisfied with the disciplinary punishment inflicted by Li Li-san on the Russian Returned Students.
But he cowardly refrained from touching upon the question of
line at all before and during the Third Plenum.

Wang K'e-ch'üan admitted that he had made the mistake of
insisting on the convocation of an emergency conference and
that he did not change his mind even after the Fourth Plenum.
He confessed that he had complained of the ignorance of the
Comintern delegate of the practical conditions in China and that
such a disrespectful attitude toward the Comintern delegate was
even "more dangerous than the Li-san line."

According to the present confesser, he was one of those who
had been primarily responsible for the Emergency Committee
and the Second Kiangsu Provincial Committee. But he said he
did all this under the influence of others. He said he was in his
heart against such a step and so, too, with Ho Meng-hsiung;
but he gave in when others, like Lo Chang-lung (alias Wen Hu)
and Hsü Hsi-ken, insisted. He disclosed that he served as secretary of the Emergency Committee in succession to Hsü Hsi-
ken for three days.

After everything had been said and done, Wang K'e-ch'üan

now became aware that he had been wrong in the past. He had come to realize that the Fourth Plenum was perfectly right. Accordingly, he requested that the Politburo rescind his expulsion as a party member and come to his rescue through education.

Central [Politburo] Resolution regarding the Statement of Wang K'e-ch'üan (中央關於王克全聲明書的決議案. Chung-yang kuan-yü wang-k'e-ch'üan sheng-ming-shu ti chüeh-i-an), adopted by the Standing Committee of the Central Committee on June 1, 1931; printed in *Red Flag Weekly*, No. 12, July 1, 1931, pp. 27-29, 052.1/809, BIC; approximately 700 words.

By this resolution the Politburo rejected the request of Wang K'e-ch'üan for readmission to the party. It was argued that he in his appeal had ascribed his past errors solely to factionism and patriarchal repression rather than exposing his opportunist viewpoints politically and that he had not laid bare all that he knew about the counterrevolutionary activities of the rightists.

Order of the Council of People's Commissars of the Soviet Provisional Central Government to Arrest the Deserter of the Revolution Ku Shun-chang (蘇維埃臨時中央政府人民委員會通令——為通緝革命叛徒顧順章事 Su-wei-ai lin-shih chung-yang cheng-fu jen-min wei-yüan-hui t'ung-ling—wei t'ung-ch'i ko-ming p'an-t'u ku-shun-chang shih), dated December 10, 1931; printed in *Red Flag Weekly*, No. 27, December 17, 1931, 052.1/809, BIC; approximately 1,600 words.

This was perhaps the most sensational of all stories of Communist desertion during the period under study. The hero in the play was a young Communist by the name of Ku Shun-chang who was captured by KMT detectives at Hankow on April 25, 1931. According to the information provided by him, Communist cells at Hankow were wholesale discovered and raided, and a number of Communist agents were executed.

Taken to Nanking, the story went, Ku Shun-chang informed KMT authorities of all that he knew about Communist personnel and their activities. He proved the identity of the well-known

Communist writer Yün Tai-ying, who had been imprisoned
under an assumed name, and immediately this man was shot.
He leaked out the underground addresses of Chou En-lai, Ch'ü
Ch'iu-pai, Li Wei-han, and others in Shanghai, and by good
luck these people had just left Shanghai when the KMT-imperialist police arrived. It was through the help of Ku's relatives
that Hsiang Chung-fa, secretary-general of the CCP, was arrested and executed. Interestingly, Ku even put up an adver-
tisement in the newspapers asking the general public to help
arrest Chou En-lai.

In view of the foregoing, the Soviet Government at Juichin,
Kiangsi, ordered the capture or murder of the renegade Ku
Shun-chang wherever he turned up in the country.

According to a Chinese Communist source, Hsiang Chung-fa
was executed on June 24, 1931, a date about which foreign observers are generally misinformed. (See the Weekly Service
Program in Memory of Comrade Hsiang Chung-fa, issued by
the Yung-chi-tai Special Committee, August 23, 1931; see Benjamin Schwartz, *Chinese Communism and the Rise of Mao*, p.
185; Conrad Brandt, Benjamin Schwartz, and John Fairbank, *A
Documentary History of Chinese Communism*, p. 36; Shigezo
Yoshikawa, *Handbook on Current China* (Chukyo Soran), Tokyo,
1950, p. 329.)

Letter from Comrade Li Li-san (李 立 三 同 志 來 信
Li-li-san t'ung-chih lai-hsin), dated March 1, 1932; printed in
Struggle (Shanghai), No. 14, May 28, 1932, leaves 12-13;
mimeographed; 052.1/809, BIC; approximately 2,500 words.

In this letter Li Li-san confessed to three major errors he
had committed during the Li-san line and the fight against it.
He made the present confession at a time when he was supposed
to understand his errors much better after more than a year of
study at Moscow. The three errors related to the crisis of the
party, the struggle against the Li-san line, and the question of
the rightists.

Li Li-san recognized that he used to think that the party
leadership and, indeed, the whole party structure would have
been shaken if he had admitted his error to be an error of line.
But now he found this thought to be entirely wrong. He now realized that any departure from the Comintern line would be
bound to fail and that a new leadership born out of party strug-

gle could only lead to the strengthening rather than the weakening of the party.

As to the question of the anti-Li-san struggle, Li Li-san himself was strongly prejudiced in favor of the Russian Returned Students against the rightists Lo Chang-lung and Ho Meng-hsiung. He characterized the former as the earliest genuine fighters against the Li-san line and the latter as mere rightist crooks.

He regretted that he had failed to place emphasis on the fight against the rightists in the past, with the consequence that they had managed to grow in strength in the party under the cloak of anti-Li-sanism.

It is interesting to note that Li Li-san in this letter betrayed two things which seemed to be sheer machinations of the Russian Returned Students in pursuit of their own object but which, contrary to their expectations, have served to cut their own throats.

In the first place, it was revealed that in an earlier letter to the Politburo after his interrogation by the Eastern Department at Moscow, Li Li-san criticized the leader of the Russian Returned Student group, Ch'en Shao-yü, for his "engagement in unprincipled intraparty factional struggles, " and what not. So far as is known, prior to the present letter Li Li-san had sent back from Moscow no other letter than the one described in a previous item entitled "Statement of Comrade Li-san to the Politburo and the Fourth Plenum, " which was printed in the CCP organ *Reconstruction of the Party,* Shanghai, No. 3, February 15, 1931, pp. 44-45. That statement, it will be recalled, contains no specific criticisms against Ch'en Shao-yü; it contains only brief repetitions of the familiar confessions made by Li Li-san in Moscow. In publishing that statement, however, the official Communist organ added an editor's note which found the statement to be "far from adequate. " This editor's note seems to be significant. It seems to suggest a number of possibilities. It was possible that the statement in question would have originally contained criticisms against Ch'en Shao-yü, which would have been deleted when the statement was published. It was also possible that Li Li-san had been asked to prepare another public confession couched in terms suited to the taste of the Russian Returned Student leadership and that the present letter was the one prepared under these circumstances and also adulterated when published.

Second, the present letter claims that Ho Meng-hsiung, like

Lo Chang-lung, did not begin to attack the Li-san line until after the Third Plenum. This is certainly not true. As has already been noted, Ho Meng-hsiung was the most vociferous opponent to the Li-san line before and during the Third Plenum; he issued his famous statement on this score as early as September 8, 1930, that is, more than half a month before the opening of the Third Plenum.

The two points mentioned above raise an important question as to how far statements by individuals as published in Communist organs can be relied upon as criteria for judgment of their real intentions. This is all the more true of the statements of those who are tortured by the party.

This letter claims that Ch'en Shao-yü began his attack against the Li-san line before the adoption of the Politburo resolution of June 11. That happened when Li Li-san published an article entitled "The Various Questions Prior to the Rising Tide of the Chinese Revolution." It was not stated precisely when and where that article was published. Unfortunately, the article in question is not available.

13

The Russian Returned Students

Seek to Control Soviet Areas

Circular No. 1 of the CCP Central Bureau of the Soviet Areas—Establishment of the Central Bureau of the Soviet Areas and Its Tasks (中共蘇區中央局通告第一號 —— 蘇維埃區中央局的成立及其任務 Chung-kung su-ch'ü chung-yang-chü t'ung-kao ti-i hao—su-wei-ai ch'ü-yü chung-yang-chü ti ch'eng-li chi ch'i jen-wu), January 15, 1931; mimeographed; 008.2107/5044, SSC; approximately 2,200 words.

Though set up about a week after the Fourth Plenum of the Central Committee held early in January, 1931, the Central Bureau of the Soviet Areas of the CCP apparently owed its birth to the Third Plenum, which took place in September, 1930. Much of the language of the present circular was drawn from the political resolution of the Third Plenum.

At the head of a list of a nine-man membership stood Chou En-lai, who was followed by Hsiang Ying, Mao Tse-tung, Chu Teh, Jen Pi-shih, Yü Fei, Tseng Shan, and two others.

According to ex-Communist sources, Hsiang Ying, who had a worker background, served as the secretary. They say the Bureau was created with a view to holding Mao in check, who had become increasingly insubordinate in the rural Soviet districts. But because of the low ability of the secretary Hsiang Ying, Mao wielded real power. (See Kung Ch'u, *The Red Army and I,* p. 256; Lu Ch'iang, *The "Hero" on the Chingkangshan,* p. 43.)

The purpose of the present circular was to announce publicly the inauguration of the Central Bureau, which took place on January 15, 1931. According to this circular, the Soviet dis-

tricts throughout the country were divided into six areas, namely: (1) the Central Area, comprising the southwestern Kiangsi
Special Area and the Hunan-Hupeh-Kiangsi (called Hsiangokan
for short) Border Special Area, designated as the seat of the
central government when established; (2) the Hunan-Hupeh
(called Hsiango for short) Border Special Area; (3) the Hupeh-
Honan-Anhwei (generally known as Oyuwan for short) Border
Special Area; (4) the Kiangsi-Fukien-Anhwei (called Kanmin-
wan for short) Border Special Area; (5) the Fukien-Kwangtung-
Kiangsi (called Minyüehkan for short) Border Special Area;
and (6) the Kwangsi Area, which consisted of the Right and Left
River Soviets.

These six areas were to be party, administrative, and military areas alike.

As its title indicates, the Central Area was made the center
of all rural Soviet districts in the country. Three major factors
in the Central Area had contributed to this decision, to wit, (1)
a broad mass base resulting from the agrarian revolution, (2) a
strong military establishment, and (3) a convenient base from
which to take one or more urban centers.

In the meantime, the Red Army was reorganized into seven
armies. Political commissars of the army were created. In addition, the Action Committee and the General Front Committee
were formally abolished.

According to this circular, the Central Bureau had charge of
all party units in the various Soviet areas in the nation, including the party branches in the army. Like the South Bureau and
the Yangtse Bureau, it was made responsible to the Central
Politburo of the CCP.

It was made clear that the Soviet areas that had not yet been
brought into geographical contact with the Central Area were
not placed under the control of the Central Bureau for the moment. It would appear that the Oyuwan Soviet was not subject to
the jurisdiction of the Central Bureau.

According to Chang Kuo-t'ao during an interview in Hongkong
in late October, 1959, the creation of the Central Bureau was
intended to prepare the way for the transfer of the Central Committee from Shanghai to Kiangsi. After the formation of the
Central Bureau, Mao's power in Kiangsi gradually decreased.

Interviewed in Hongkong toward the end of October, 1959,
Kung Ch'u, formerly chief-of-staff of the Chinese Central Red
Army and author of *The Red Army and I,* published in Hongkong
in 1954, declared that Mao wielded all power in Kiangsi before

the establishment of the Central Bureau, that Hsiang Ying in the
capacity of its secretary had a say in party affairs after the
creation of that setup, and that Mao lost practically all power
after the removal of the headquarters of the Central Committee
from Shanghai to Kiangsi.

*Stepping Up the Reorganization of Our Party in the Soviet
Areas* (加 緊 改 造 蘇 維 埃 區 域 內 我 們 黨 的 組
織 Chia-chin kai-tsao su-wei-ai ch'ü-yü nei wo-men tang ti
tsu-chih), by Hung Yi; printed in *Reconstruction of the Party*,
No. 4, March 8, 1931, pp. 1-6, 052.1/804, BIC; approximately 2,700 words.

This article cites a fairly long report on the extremely unsatisfactory work of the party in the western Hupeh Soviet area
as a warning to all party members, and states that it was also
true of southwestern Kiangsi. This was an obstacle, it is said,
standing in the way of a successful revolution and must be removed in order to consolidate the Chinese Communist Party. It
would therefore be a matter of the first importance to step up
the work of party reform in the Soviet areas and all party members there should do what they could to accomplish this task.
    This article seems to suggest that the Russian Returned Stu-
dent leadership was extending its tentacles into the Soviet areas
after the defeat of the rightists.
    The significance of this article can be seen from the fact that
Mao's machine declared in 1945 that the reorganization of party
leadership ranging from the central to local units inside and
outside the Soviet areas was one of the two erroneous programs
of the Russian Returned Student leadership, the other being the
fight against the Right deviation. (See "Resolution on Some Historical Problems," contained in Mao Tse-tung, *Selected Works*,
Chinese edition, Vol. 3, pp. 965-67; English edition, Vol. 4,
pp. 182-83; reprint of the resolution, pp. 14-16.)

*Resolution and Statements Adopted by the First Enlarged
Meeting of the CCP Central Bureau of the Soviet Areas* (中 共
蘇 區 中 央 局 第 一 次 擴 大 會 議 決 案 與 報 告
Chung-kung su-ch'ü chung-yang-chü ti-i-tz'u k'uo-ta-hui i-
chüeh-an yü pao-kao), adopted probably in late March, 1931;
reproduced by the CCP Wan-t'ai-tung Committee, May 8, 1931;

mimeographed; 008.235/5048-2, SSC; approximately 11,000 words.

By virtue of the present documentation the Central Bureau of the Soviet Areas formally liquidated the Li-san line. It did this in the wake of the Central Committee, which eliminated the Li-san line more than two months earlier by resolution of the Fourth Plenum.

Like the resolution of the Fourth Plenum, the present documentation was based on the Comintern directive received on November 16, 1930. Understandably, it was for the most part a repetition of the same old arguments.

The present documentation records that the Li-san line did not emerge overnight—it dated from the elimination of the Liquidationists in 1929 and culminated in the Politburo resolution of June 11, 1930.

In fact, the present item contains two different statements by Hsiang Ying, secretary of the Central Bureau. One was his opening speech before the Central Bureau's first enlarged meeting then in session. The other was his main statement, based on a draft resolution of the Central Bureau, to accept the Comintern directive received November 16, 1930. Missing is a third piece which might well be the resolution mentioned in the title of this pamphlet.

The two statements in the present item were most probably issued in late March, 1931, as can be seen from section 4 of the main statement, which begins by saying that "The Central Bureau of the Soviet Areas has been established for more than two months,"—it being recalled that the Central Bureau was established on January 15, 1931.

It is interesting to note that less than half a year later, on September 1, 1931, the Russian Returned Student leadership charged that the enlarged meeting of the Central Bureau, before which the present two statements were made, had committed errors of both Right and Left opportunism. (See a Directive Letter of the Central Committee to the Soviet Areas, September 1, 1931, p. 8.) In November, 1931, it was further charged that the enlarged meeting was guilty of the most serious error committed by the Central Soviet area, namely, the absence of a clear and definite class line as well as adequate mass work. (See Political Resolution Adopted by the First Party Congress of the [Central] Soviet Area, November, 1931, leaf 5.)

Resolution of the Eleventh Plenum of the ECCI (共產國) 際執委第十一次全會決議案. Kung-ch'an kuo-chi chih-wei ti-shih-i-tz'u ch'üan-hui chüeh-i-an), adopted in April, 1931; Chinese version appearing in *The International Line,* printed by the Central Bureau, Soviet Areas, December, 1932, pp. 1-26, 009.54/0676, SSC; approximately 13,000 words.

This ECCI resolution proceeded on the assumption that the time was fast approaching when the stability of capitalism would come to an end. On the basis of this assumption, the present statement shaped the course of a number of major Communist policies in China which, thanks to the presence of the Soviets and the Red Army, was standing "in the forefront of the national revolutionary movements of the colonial world." Examples of Communist policies of this kind may be given below:

1. Intensification of the contradictions of the two systems of capitalism and socialism.

This premise prepared the way for the CCP's uncompromising position in Kiangsi that the future of China would be either a colony or a Soviet land and that there would be no third road lying ahead.

2. Preparations of imperialists for an armed attack against the Soviet Union.

The Comintern warning of an armed attack against the Soviet Union was nothing new. It dated from the days before the period under study. But this statement was the most immediate source of the CCP's policy of protecting Russia after the Japanese attack on Manchuria on September 18, 1931.

3. The united front from below.

The Comintern strategy of a united front from below was first mentioned, during the period under study, by Li Li-san and Ch'ü Ch'iu-pai in their confessions printed in the CCP organ *Reconstruction of the Party* of February 15, 1931, Shanghai, described previously. The present statement made mention of this Comintern strategy several times, defining it as a policy of enlisting the broad masses of workers, employees, and other semiproletarians in the cause of the struggle. This determined the pattern of the CCP's united front policy during the Kiangsi period to be a united front from below, thus ruling out the possibility of interparty collaboration between the KMT and the CCP.

It is interesting to note that in accepting this Comintern resolution in August, 1931 (see *The International Line,* probably
Juichin, printed by the Central Bureau, Soviet Areas, CCP,
December, 1932, pp. 27-42), the CCP brought about a slight
but significant change in the wording of this statement by quoting it to the effect that "the stability of capitalism has already
reached the end of its journey" *(ibid.,* p. 27). As will be seen
later, the Comintern reappraisal of capitalism did not reach
such a radical stage as the CCP described until the Twelfth
Plenum of the ECCI, held in September, 1932.

Letter of the ECCI Presidium to the CCP (共 產 國) 際
執 委 主 席 (團) 給 中 國 共 產 黨 的 信 Kung-ch'an kuo-
chi chih-wei chu-hsi-t'uan chi chung-kuo kung-ch'an-tang ti
hsin), dated July, 1931; Chinese version printed in *Bolshevik*
(Kiangsi), No. 1, July, 1934, pp. 1-41, 008.105/4013, SSC;
also printed in *Red Documents,* pp. 376-404, 008.2129/2703,
SSC; approximately 15,000 words.

This document represented Moscow's program for China
after the ECCI Eleventh Plenum of April, 1931, which found
the Chinese revolution ranking first among all revolutionary
movements in the colonial world because of the presence of the
Chinese Soviets and the Red Army. Though ideologically this
statement was in agreement with the two previous Comintern
directives dated July 23 and November 16, 1930, it had a radically different application to the new situation in China following the CCP Fourth Plenum.

In this document as in its predecessors, the Kremlin assigned the CCP three main tasks: (1) forming a secure base and
a Red Army, (2) establishing a central Soviet government, and
(3) promoting the mass movement in non-Communist areas.
These tasks, it was stated, would have been accomplished in
the summer of 1930 but for the misdeeds of Li Li-san. This deposed Communist leader was said to have objected to these
tasks under cover of the leftist language.

It is vital to note that this Comintern directive governed the
power relationships within the Chinese Communist hierarchy
throughout the period 1931-34. On the one hand, it endorsed the
decisions of the Fourth Plenum and their subsequent execution.
On the other, it was the most immediate Comintern authorization for the convocation of the First National Soviet Congress on

November 7, 1931, which proclaimed the Central Soviet Government at Juichin, Kiangsi.

Specifically, Moscow appreciated the CCP Fourth Plenum in these respects: (1) beating the rightists; (2) liquidating Li Lisanism and the compromising attitude toward it; (3) rectifying the party line, reorganizing the party leadership, and reorienting party work; (4) electing the new Politburo and removing Lo Chang-lung and his followers. Meanwhile, this directive stressed the fight against Right opportunism as the main danger at the time.

As to the Soviet areas in particular, this Comintern letter called for the taking of immediate steps to strengthen the party leadership and lower echelons there, including the party in the Red Army.

It must be remembered that Mao and his group were diametrically opposite to Moscow in their evaluation of the Fourth Plenum. In 1945 the Mao machine declared that the Fourth Plenum accomplished nothing positive or constructive and that it merely marked the beginning of the third Left line putting forward two interrelated erroneous programs: (1) fight against the Right deviation as the main danger and (2) reorganization of the party leadership at all levels. Though opposed to the Li-san line and the compromising attitude in form, it was stated, the plenum actually had for its principal object the fight against the "Right deviation." In consequence, the plenum had dealt the Lisanists and compromisers too heavy a blow. The party leadership created by the plenum had improperly hit most of the so-called "rightists." (See "Resolution on Some Historical Problems," April 20, 1945, contained in Mao Tse-tung, *Selected Works*, Chinese edition, Vol. 3, pp. 965-67; English edition, Vol. 4, pp. 182-83; reprint of the resolution, pp. 14-16.)

Moreover, the Mao leadership pointed out that Mao and his associates were throughout opposed to the third Left line led by the Russian Returned Students. Because of this, the leadership of the Mao group in various places was removed by the Central Committee and its agencies or representatives after the Fourth Plenum. *(Ibid.*, Chinese edition, Vol. 3, p. 970; English edition, Vol. 4, pp. 187-88; reprint, p. 21.)

In view of these divergences between Moscow and the Mao group there seems to be little doubt that the challenge of the Russian Returned Students to the leadership of Mao in the Soviet areas from 1931 on was wittingly or unwittingly supported by the Kremlin. However, there is no evidence to suggest that

Moscow wanted to remove Mao from all his political power. In fact, as described previously, the Comintern in section 22 of the present directive spoke highly of Mao's positive experiences in, say, training KMT captives. Rarely in Comintern documents were Chinese Communist leaders mentioned by name as heroes.

This Comintern directive urged the CCP to set up a central Soviet government in the safest area with dispatch. There can be little doubt that this must have given a great impetus to the proclamation of the central government at Juichin five months later. That this document was a direct Comintern authorization for the creation of the Juichin government is even more firmly substantiated by the fact that the present document contains detailed instructions for the solution of the Chinese land problem, instructions which were copied almost wholesale and verbatim by the land law enacted by the First National Soviet Congress in November, 1931.

There is every reason to believe that Pavel Mif, who had returned to Russia by this time, must have played a very great role in the drafting of the present document. That is why Chang Kuo-t'ao, during an interview in Hongkong in late October, 1959, called the whole Kiangsi period beginning from the summer of 1930 a period of the reign of Pavel Mif. As far as is known, Mao's machine has scrupulously avoided mentioning Pavel Mif and the Comintern in discussions of the power struggle of the Kiangsi period, merely calling it the third Left line or, more recently, the Wang Ming line.

Questioned whether or not Moscow supported Mao during the Kiangsi period, Chang Kuo-t'ao declared during the Hongkong interview that there was no evidence to indicate Moscow's support or nonsupport of Mao. Comintern directives were customarily addressed to the central leadership of the CCP, not to individuals. The general feeling was that Mao was capable of doing something.

[CCP] Resolution on the Resolution of the Eleventh Plenum of the ECCI (關於國際執委第十一次全會總結的決議 Kuan-yü kuo-chi chih-wei ti shih-i-tz'u ch'üan-hui tsung-chieh ti chüeh-i), adopted in August 1931; printed in *The International Line*, pp. 27-42, 009.54/7076, SSC; approximately 7,300 words.

Hereby the CCP Central Committee accepted the resolution

of the Eleventh Plenum of the ECCI and pledged to carry it out
in practical work.

Central (Politburo) Resolution on the Question of Cadres
(中央關) 於幹部問題的決議   Chung-yang kuan-yü
kan-pu wen-t'i ti chüeh-i), dated August 27, 1931; printed in
Red Flag Weekly, No. 18, October 13, 1931, pp. 35-44, 052.1/
804, BIC; approximately 4, 700 words.

The question of cadres had a good deal to do with the intraparty struggle after the Fourth Plenum. After the fall of Li Li-
sanists and rightists, the struggle was primarily between the
Russian Returned Students and the Mao group.

The significance of this question can be seen by comparing
the present statement issued by the Russian Returned Student
group with the "Resolution on Some Historical Problems"
adopted in 1945 by the Mao machine.

This statement contains a whole list of charges against the
traditional misconceptions of the question of cadres, one of
which is, for instance, that the party in the past was wont to
favor old cadres and fear new ones.

By contrast, the 1945 statement lists the reorganization and
replenishment of the party leadership at all levels as one of the
two major faulty policies of the Russian Returned Students.
Through this policy, it is stated, the party leadership eliminated its opponents within the party. Says the 1945 statement:

> Instead of regarding the veteran cadres as valuable assets of the
> party, the sectarians [i. e. , the Russian Returned Students] perse-
> cuted, punished, and deposed large numbers of these veterans in the
> central and local organizations, comrades experienced in work and
> closely connected with the masses but who proved uncongenial to
> them and were unwilling to follow them blindly or chime in with
> them. They did not give proper education to new cadres, nor did
> they handle the promotion of such cadres seriously (especially ca-
> dres of working-class origin), but carelessly replaced veterans in
> the central and local organizations with new cadres or cadres com-
> ing from other places who either lacked experience in work or had
> no close contact with the masses, but who proved congenial to them
> and did nothing but follow them blindly and chime in with them. In
> this manner, they not only disheartened the old cadres but also
> spoiled the new ones.

(See Mao Tse-tung, *Selected Works,* Chinese edition, Vol. 3,

p. 987; English edition, Vol. 4, pp. 206-7; reprint, p. 43.)

A Directive Letter of the Central to the Soviet Areas (中 央 對 蘇 區 指 示 信 Chung-yang tui su-ch'ü chih-shih-hsin), September 1, 1931; 008.222/5053, SSC; approximately 11,500 words.

In September, 1931, the mantle of the Russian Returned Student leadership was cast over the shoulders of Ch'in Pang-hsien, who formed and headed the so-called Provisional Central Politburo. He, like his fellow Russian Returned Students since January, 1931, was engaged in a desperate struggle for power with the Mao group in the Soviet areas. It was not until after the Communist evacuation of Kiangsi, in a conference at Tsunyi, Kweichow, in January, 1935, that Mao got the upper hand of Ch'in and achieved control of the party. Mao's machine described this power struggle as the longest and bitterest one he had ever had within the party during the 1927-34 period. (See full text of the "Resolution on Some Historical Problems, " April 20, 1945, contained in Mao Tse-tung, *Selected Works,* Chinese edition, Vol. 3, pp. 955-1002; English edition, Vol. 4, pp. 171-218; also reprint of the resolution published in March, 1953; Hu Chiao-mu, *Thirty Years of the Chinese Communist Party,* p. 35. Relevant sections of Hu Chiao-mu's account were included by Robert North in his book, *Moscow and Chinese Communists,* pp. 166-67, but unfortunately the most important passage, which appears in literal translation on page 167, is an almost impossible version with much of the real meaning of the original lost.) It seems clear that the present document marked the beginning of the power struggle between Ch'in and Mao during this period. Though nominally addressed to all Soviet areas, this document was actually directed against the Central Soviet Area over which Mao had direct control.

As is routine in a Communist paper of the kind, the present letter begins with a perfunctory recognition of the achievements made in the Central Soviet Area: (1) resisting the Nationalist campaigns, (2) expropriating landlords and implementing equal land redistribution, (3) establishing Soviet regimes in conquered areas, (4) building up a disciplined Red Army, (5) combating counterrevolutionaries and particularly the A-B League.

Be that as it may, the balance sheet was understandably running against the Central Soviet Area, and the liabilities were

staggering. The greatest trouble with the Central Soviet Area
was described to be the absence of a clear and definite class
line and the lack of adequate mass work. All this was attributed
to the influence of Li Li-sanism, and it was charged that the
comrades in the Soviet areas did not fully understand the defects
of the Li-san line as opposed to the correct line of the Comintern.

Specifically, the absence of class and mass lines was found
in: (1) the setting up of Soviet bases and the Red Army, (2) the
handling of the agrarian problem, (3) the relation of the governmental machine to the party and the masses, (4) the labor and
the anti-imperialist movements, and (5) the ideological struggle
and educational work.

Against the background of the weaknesses identified, a detailed list of six major tasks was assigned to the Central Soviet
Area: (1) consolidation of the Soviet bases, (2) solution of the
land problem, (3) expansion of the Red Army, (4) establishment
of a central government, (5) strengthening of the party, and (6)
the fight against the A-B League as well as all erroneous ideol-
ogies.

To all intents and purposes the present document was nothing
but a catalogue of grievous errors allegedly committed by the
Communist leaders in the Central Soviet Area. If taken at face
value, it would be so devastating and degrading to the leaders in
the Central Soviet Area that they would all look like monsters in
Chinese Communist annals. Accordingly, fifteen years later, on
April 20, 1945, the erstwhile leaders of the Central Soviet
Area, having achieved undisputed leadership of the party under
the banner of Mao, adopted the "Resolution on Some Historical
Problems" to rehabilitate themselves in revenge for the wrongs
done them by the Russian Returned Student group. A comparison
between that resolution and the present directive letter reveals
interesting differences as follows:

1. On the one hand, the Russian Returned Students saw the
complete bankruptcy of the Kuomintang rule in both internal and
external affairs and signs of its imminent collapse. (See directive letter, p. 9.) On the other, Mao's machine stated that the
Russian Returned Student group had exaggerated the crisis of
the Kuomintang rule and therefore made a total miscalculation
of the situation. (See resolution, contained in Mao Tse-tung,
Selected Works, Chinese edition, Vol. 3, p. 917; English edition, Vol. 4, p. 184; reprint of the resolution, p. 17.)

2. In the opinion of the Russian Returned Students, the Red

Army had suffered from lack of a settled Soviet base, so it should act to seize one or more big cities (directive letter, p. 12). In contrast, Mao's machine took the position that the main base of the Chinese revolution should be in the countryside rather than the city (see resolution, contained in Mao Tse-tung, *Selected Works,* Chinese edition, Vol. 3, p. 977; English edition, Vol. 4, p. 195; reprint of the resolution, p. 30), and that guerrilla warfare rather than positional warfare should be developed in the rural districts rather than in urban centers. *(Ibid.,* Chinese edition, Vol. 3, p. 976; English edition, Vol. 4, p. 194; reprint of the resolution, p. 29.)

3. The Russian Returned Student group was in favor of a harsh treatment of the rich peasants, removing their fertile land and giving them poor land instead (directive letter, pp. 4, 15). On the other hand, Mao's machine stood for equal redistribution treating them according to the principles of draw-on-the-plentiful-to-make-up-for-the-scarce and draw-on-the-fat-to-make-up-for-the-lean—principles to which the Russian Returned Students objected. (See resolution, contained in Mao Tse-tung, *Selected Works,* Chinese edition, Vol. 3, p. 974; English edition, Vol. 4, p. 191; reprint of the resolution, p. 25.)

4. The Russian Returned Student group charged that the Red Army had not yet abandoned the wrong idea of guerrilla warfare (directive letter, p. 16) and that its structure did not fit in a large-scale war organization (directive letter, p. 17). In contrast, Mao's machine stood for guerrilla warfare in the Chinese revolution (see resolution, Mao Tse-tung, *Selected Works,* Chinese edition, Vol. 3, p. 984; English edition, Vol. 4, p. 203; reprint, pp. 38-39) and objected to the exaggeration of the importance of converting the Red Army into a regularized military machine. *(Ibid.,* Chinese edition, Vol. 3, p. 978; English edition, Vol. 4, p. 196; reprint, p. 33.)

Of course, it was possible that the present directive letter was issued by the Central Politburo after it had moved from Shanghai to Kiangsi. This suggestion agrees with the views of Chang Kuo-t'ao and Kung Ch'u, both of whom declared during interviews in Hongkong in late October, 1959, that the central headquarters of the CCP moved to Kiangsi in the summer or early fall of 1931. Kung Ch'u stated categorically that the central office of the party arrived in Kiangsi before the proclamation of the Central Soviet Government in November, 1931.

According to Chang Kuo-t'ao, there was a top-ranking party meeting in Shanghai in April, 1931, of which no record was probably left behind. It was resolved that the Central Committee should be moved from the Shanghai underground to the Soviet areas owing to increasing difficulties imposed on CCP activities in Shanghai. In consequence, Shen Tse-min and Chang Kuo-t'ao himself left for the Oyuwan Soviet Area in western Anhwei, Jen Pi-shih for the Hsiangosi Soviet Area in western Hupeh, and Chou En-lai, Ch'in P'ang-hsien, and Chang Wen-t'ien for the Central Soviet Area in Kiangsi. In July Chang Kuo-t'ao received a notice saying that the Central Politburo was scheduled to start work in Juichin, Kiangsi, in August. In Shanghai there was left a newly formed agency called the Central Bureau headed by Liu Shao-ch'i. With the transfer of the Central Committee to Kiangsi, Chang added, Mao's power was greatly curtailed.

Reminded that he gave the fall of 1932 as the date of the transfer of the Central Committee during an interview with Robert North (see Robert North, *Moscow and Chinese Communists*, p. 158), and that the Mao leadership in 1945 dated the transfer in the early days of 1933 (see "Resolution on Some Historical Problems," contained in Mao Tse-tung, *Selected Works*, Chinese edition, Vol. 3, p. 968; English edition, Vol. 4, p. 185; reprint of the resolution, p. 18), Chang Kuo-t'ao stated that all these dates must be mistaken.

According to Charles B. McLane, 1931 given as the date of the transfer of the CCP Central Committee was supported by a KMT source, and 1932 supported by the ex-Communist Li Ang, while Russian sources even spoke of the CCP central organs as being located in the KMT area after the 1933 date. (See Charles B. McLane, *Soviet Policy and the Chinese Communists, 1931-1946*, pp. 39-40.)

Our Difficulties in the Policy Switch (我們在轉變中的困難 Wo-men tsai chuan-pien chung ti k'un-nan), leading article in *Red Flag Weekly*, No. 16, September 10, 1931, pp. 27-30, 052.1/809, BIC; approximately 1,500 words.

This leading article of the CCP organ ascribed the difficulties confronted during the policy switch following the Fourth Plenum to the negativism of the rightists and the dependent character of lower cadres. The principal difficulty lay in the fact that the political line could not be completely carried out in practical work.

The policy switch occurred, it was stated, in three respects:

(1) increased guidance over the party in the Soviet areas so as to make it in tune with the party line, (2) unity of the party through the defeat of Li Li-san and rightists, (3) change in mass work.

It was revealed that some comrades were still hankering after the good old days and saying the present situation in the party was not so good as in the past, while others even in the leading echelon went so far as to question the wisdom of the party decisions following the Fourth Plenum, stating that many of those decisions were simply impracticable.

14

Submission of the Local Party in Kiangsi

Political Resolution Adopted by the First Party Congress of the (Central) Soviet Area (蘇區黨第一次代表大會通過政治決議案 Su-ch'ü tang ti-i-tz'u tai-piao ta-hui t'ung-kuo cheng-chih chüeh-i-an), printed by the Central Bureau, Soviet Areas, in November, 1931; 008.235/1833 C.1-2, SSC; approximately 10,000 words.

By this resolution the first party congress of the Central Soviet Area formally accepted the directive of the Central dated September 1, 1931. This marked the successful penetration of Ch'in Pang-hsien's machine into the Central Soviet Area, where Mao had been the main leader. In retrospect, the Mao group pointed out that it was this conference that on the basis of the erroneous program of the Fourth Plenum smeared the correct line of the party in southern Kiangsi and western Fukien as representing the rich peasant line and Right opportunism and brought about changes in the correct leadership of both the party and the army there. (See "Resolution on Some Historical Problems," April 20, 1945, contained in Mao Tse-tung, *Selected Works*, Chinese edition, Vol. 3, p. 968; English edition, Vol. 4, p. 185; reprint of the resolution, p. 19.)

This resolution is virtually a reproduction of the Central directive of September 1, 1931. It admitted all the charges brought by the Central directive against the Soviet areas and pledged to carry out the tasks assigned them.

The text of this resolution is divided into three parts, namely, (1) two different lines in the Soviet movement—the Comintern versus Li Li-san, (2) a review of the record of the Central So-

viet Area, (3) the current political situation and the central
tasks of the party. As concerns the first point, it was stressed
that the party in the Soviet areas had made the mistake of following the Li-san line in the past year and that not until the
adoption by the Fourth Plenum of the Comintern line did the Soviet movement begin to tread a right path. Meanwhile, Mao's
land policy of draw-on-the-plentiful-to-make-up-for-the-
scarce and draw-on-the-fat-to-make-up-for-the-lean as adopted
by the February 7 (1930) conference was also condemned. This
land policy was also known as a policy of "distributing land to
all people." It was described as representing the rich peasant
line and confusing class relations in the rural districts.

The second part of the present document, which is devoted to
a review of the work of the Central Soviet Area, is a catalogue
of monstrous blunders committed. It points out that the Enlarged Meeting of the Central Bureau of the Soviet Areas, which
took place in late March, 1931, to liquidate the Li-san line, was
a turning point in the policy of the party in the Soviet areas. Before the enlarged meeting, it is stated, the Central Bureau had
followed the compromising line of the Third Plenum of September, 1930, while the local party units and even the party leadership in the Red Army had followed the Li-san line. Nevertheless, the enlarged meeting was guilty of the most serious error
made by the Central Soviet Area, as pointed out by the Central
directive of September 1, 1931, namely, the absence of a clear
and definite class line and the lack of adequate mass work.
Specifically, the Central Soviet Area was blamed for the following mistakes: The Soviet base was fluid and unsettled and had
no link with other bases; the Red Army had not freed itself from
the tradition of guerrilla tactics; the land program was infected
with Right and Left opportunism; the Soviet regime, as well as
the trade unions, was penetrated by class heretic elements; a
narrow empiricism prevailed within the party; there was no
adequate work of mass education in the fight against counterrevolution.

The third and last part of the present resolution contains a
six-point program for the Central Soviet Area, which was actually copied from the Central directive of September 1, 1931. In
conclusion, the Right deviation was stressed as the main danger
in the two-front struggle.

Resolution on the Question of Party Reconstruction Adopted

by the First Party Congress of the (Central) Soviet Area (蘇 區
黨 第 一 次 代 表 大 會 通 過 黨 的 建 設 問 題 決 議 案
Su-ch'ü tang ti-i-tz'u tai-piao ta-hui t'ung-kuo tang ti chien-she
wen-t'i chüeh-i-an), printed by the Central Bureau, Soviet
Areas, in November, 1931; 008.235/9021, SSC; approximately
10,000 words.

Along with its companion paper, the Political Resolution described previously, this piece represented an ambitious attempt
on the part of the Russian Returned Students, led by Ch'in Pang-
hsien, to seize control of the party in the Central Soviet Area,
where Mao had been the leading figure. Though both papers had
the same object in view, their points of emphasis were different. This was concerned with party reconstruction, while the
other dealt with the political question.

This document falls into four sections, namely, (1) the background and mission of the party in the Soviet areas, (2) the
present position of the party there, (3) the central task of party
reconstruction, and (4) the two-front struggle. Needless to say,
this paper is a whole list of mistakes caused by a lack of class
line and of adequate mass work, as charged by the Russian Returned Student leadership. Specifically, the mistakes included
narrow empiricism, pragmatical opportunism, a weak proletarian basis, ideological poverty, and what not.

Of course, many of the charges may have been exaggerated
and should therefore not be accepted at face value. But they do
provide clues to an understanding of party work in the Soviet
areas, and particularly the clash between Mao's machine and
Mif's protégés there.

Like all major documents on the party structure including the
constitution of the CCP, this paper contains the all-important
semantic quibble concerning the proletariat and their leadership
in the revolution. On the one hand, the Communist Party is defined as the vanguard of the proletariat. On the other, it is prescribed to be the paramount duty of the Communist Party to lead
the proletariat in the revolution (page 8). Accordingly, the word
"proletariat" had two different meanings: the working class and
the Communist Party. It may mean one or the other as the case
may be. When a Communist speaks of the proletarian leadership of the revolution, he almost always has the leadership of
the Communist Party in mind. For this reason, the revolution
in the hinterland in Kiangsi must be led by the proletariat as

well, even though there was practically no proletariat to speak
of there.

Chang Kuo-t'ao confirmed this explanation of the semantic
quibble when he in an interview in Hongkong in late October,
1959, declared that the expression "the agrarian revolution led
by the proletariat" actually meant the agrarian revolution led by
the Communist Party.

Resolution on the Problem of the Red Army Adopted
by the First Party Congress of the (Central) Soviet Area
(蘇區黨第一次代表大會通過紅軍問題決議案
Su-ch'ü tang ti-i-tz'u tai-piao ta-hui t'ung-kuo hung-chün wen-
t'i chüeh-i-an), printed by the Central Bureau, Soviet Areas, in
October, 1931; 008.5526/2137/C.1, SSC; approximately 3,500
words.

This document recognized the Red Army as the main force in
the revolution, whose immediate objective was to set up revolutionary bases and win preliminary successes in one or more
provinces. It was, therefore, essential to expand and consolidate the Red Army, which had suffered from what was called
guerrillaism as distinguished from guerrilla tactics. Accordingly, a list of malpractices should be eliminated, to wit, guerrillaism, party monopolism, routinism, and so forth.

Political Resolution Adopted by the Enlarged Conference of
the CCP Provincial Committee of the Kiangsi Soviet Area (中共
江西蘇區省委擴大會議政治決議案 Chung-
kung chiang-hsi su-ch'ü sheng-wei k'uo-ta hui-i cheng-chih
chüeh-i-an), December, 1931; lithographed; 008.236/5048-2/C.
1, SSC; also printed in *Documents of or concerning the Enlarged*
Conference of the Provincial Committee of the Kiangsi Soviet
Area, 008.236/5048-2/C.2, SSC; approximately 8,000 words.

This document followed in the footsteps of the resolutions of
the First Party Congress of the (Central) Soviet area of November, 1931, just as the latter followed in the footsteps of the directive letter of the Central to the Soviet areas dated September
1, 1931. Accordingly, the contents of this piece are in general
agreement with those of the said resolutions and directive let-

ter. Many of the specific items in the present document were even copied almost verbatim.

It is clear that the present document represented the formal acceptance by the party leadership of Kiangsi province of the resolutions and directive letter in question.

Verbose and stilted, this document is nothing but a repetition of the same old arguments contained in the statements accepted by this document.

A Letter from the CCP Central Bureau of the Soviet Areas to the CCP Kiangsi Provincial Committee (中共蘇區中央局致中共江西省委信 Chung-kung su-ch'ü chung-yang-chü chih chung-kung chiang-hsi sheng-wei hsin), January 19, 1932; lithographed by the CCP Kiangsi Provincial Committee, February 7, 1932, contained in *Documents of or concerning the Enlarged Conference of the Provincial Committee of the Kiangsi Soviet Area,* 008.236/5048-2/C.2, SSC, leaves 16-21; approximately 4,000 words.

This statement represented a flat refusal on the part of the Central Bureau to endorse the work of the party in Kiangsi province as manifested in the Enlarged Conference of the Provincial Committee of the Kiangsi Soviet Area convened in December, 1931, though the conference, as described previously, was supposed to be held along the new party line.

In spite of the fact that the Central Bureau found the resolution of the Kiangsi Provincial Enlarged Conference to be in general agreement with that of the First Party Congress of the (Central) Soviet Area held in the previous month, it nevertheless criticized and lessoned the party apparatus of Kiangsi province in the following terms:

1. There was no adequate reorientation toward the Comintern line, especially in the sphere of mass work. All this was attributed to commandism, narrow empiricism, routinism, and pragmatical opportunism, which were considered more rampant in Kiangsi than in other Soviet areas.

2. There was no adequate estimation of the new revolutionary situation, which was thought to be ripe for a Communist expansion. The expansion, it is stated, should be in the direction of the north and, in anticipation of this, the Soviet area in Kiangsi should be linked together with that on the Kiangsi-Hunan border.

3. Mass activism should be promoted to implement the redis-

tribution of landholdings and the expansion of the Red Army.

4. Both ideological struggle and political training should be emphasized in the work of combating counterrevolution.

5. The class basis of the party was weak and its class consciousness infirm. However, the backward peasant mentality had made itself felt. All such phenomena, it is said, should be overcome and those who held such ideas should be replaced by new cadres who followed the Comintern line.

Resolution of the (Kiangsi) Provincial Committee Accepting the Directive Letter from the Central Bureau (省委接受中央局指示信的決議 Sheng-wei chieh-shou chung-yang-chü chih-shih-hsin ti chüeh-i), February 11, 1932; lithographed; printed in *Documents of or concerning the Enlarged Conference of the Provincial Committee of the Kiangsi Soviet Area*, 008.236/5048-2/C.2, SSC, leaves 22-26; approximately 3,500 words.

By virtue of this resolution the Kiangsi Provincial Committee expressed its acceptance of the directive letter of the Central Bureau dated January 19, 1932. The content of this resolution is literally a repetition of that of the directive letter in question.

15

The First National Soviet Congress

The Central Soviet Area in Kiangsi (江西的中央蘇區
Chiang-hsi ti chung-yang su-ch'ü), dated September 3, 1931;
printed in *Red Flag Weekly,* No. 24, November 27, 1931, pp.
39-50, 052.1/809, BIC; approximately 5,600 words.

This is a news report on the general conditions in the Central
Soviet Area in which the Central Soviet Government was to be
proclaimed. The report is divided into six parts dealing with
(1) distribution of Soviet regimes, (2) economic conditions, (3)
land redistribution, (4) mass organization, (5) local armed
units, and (6) the Red Army.

Part 1 gives the size of the Central Soviet Area and the number of counties in it. It reports that the area was formed by
merging a number of scattered Communist-controlled regions
and that the Kiangsi Provincial Soviet Government was not set
up until after the capture of Kian in October, 1930.

Perhaps the most important part of this report is part 3 on
land redistribution, giving a brief account of the experiments of
several land redistribution programs, which had been introduced one after another. On February 7, 1930, it is stated, the
Southwest Kiangsi Soviet Government was created, which was
the first major step ever taken to draw the scattered tiny Soviet
areas together and unify the multifarious land redistribution
programs of the past. It was this government that implemented
the equal redistribution of land on the basis of the draw-on-the-
plentiful-to-make-up-for-the-scarce principle, which was later
supplemented by another principle known as draw-on-the-fat-to-
make-up-for-the-lean. Then followed the collectivization plan

of Li Li-san. But both these programs were dismissed as Right and Left deviations, and revisions were reported to have been introduced. This would suggest that the present correspondence reflected the attitude of the Russian Returned Student group then in power.

Celebrate the First National Soviet Congress (慶 祝 蘇 維 埃 第 一 次 全 國 代 表 大 會 Ch'ing-chu su-wei-ai ti-i-tz'u ch'üan-kuo tai-piao ta-hui), by Szu Mei (Chang Wen-t'ien); printed in *Red Flag Weekly*, No. 22, October 30, 1931, 052.1/ 809, BIC; approximately 1,100 words.

As its title indicates, this article offered its felicitations to the First National Soviet Congress scheduled to open at Juichin, Kiangsi, on November 7, 1931, the anniversary of the Bolshevik revolution in Russia.

Though published nine days before the opening of the congress, this article by a leading member of the Russian Returned Student group then in party leadership disclosed practically all the major decisions the congress was to make. This would suggest that the congress was a mere formality and that the Central Committee of the Chinese Communist Party had made the decisions for the congress beforehand.

Specifically, this article revealed that the congress was to adopt a labor law, a land law, economic policies, and so forth, and the basic contents of these laws and policies were given in brief. While determined to abolish unequal treaties and confiscate foreign properties in China, it was stated, the congress would grant freedoms to the toiling masses and uphold self-determination. Above all, the congress was to proclaim a central Soviet government on the basis of the democratic dictatorship of workers and peasants.

It should be noted that as soon as they achieved power in January, 1931, the Russian Returned Students lost no time in pointing out the importance of holding a Soviet congress. (See Resolution of the Enlarged Fourth Plenum, sec. 5, par. 5.) On September 1 they ordered the leaders of the Central Soviet Area to make up their mind to set up without delay a central Soviet government during the First National Soviet Congress scheduled to open on November 7, 1931. (See A Directive Letter of the Central Committee to the Soviet Areas, September 1, 1931, "central tasks," No. 4.)

Telegram from the Chinese Soviet Congress to the CCP Central (中華蘇維埃代表大會給中共中央電 Chung-hua su-wei-ai tai-piao ta-hui chi chung-kung chung-yang tien), dated November 18, 1931, signed by the Presidium of the Congress; printed in *Red Flag Weekly,* No. 25, December 4 (?), 1931, pp. 1-2, 052.1/809, BIC; approximately 280 words.

At long last the First National Soviet Congress opened at Juichin, Kiangsi, on November 7, 1931. To mark the occasion, according to this wire, a parade of the Red Army was held in the morning and a torchlight procession in the evening. Tens of thousands of people were said to have resounded jubilation.

There were present altogether 610 delegates, who represented the various Soviet areas, the Red Army units, the National Labor Federation, the Seamen's Union, and so forth. The Oyuwan Soviet, the second largest Soviet area situated in the borderland of Hupeh, Honan, and Anhwei, was not included in the list of the Soviet areas that had sent delegates to the congress. According to Chang Kuo-t'ao during an interview in Hongkong in late October, 1959, this omission was only due to the practical difficulties of transportation, since Oyuwan was cut off from Kiangsi by KMT troops.

The successful convocation of the congress was thought to represent the triumph of the Chinese revolution under the leadership of the CCP. It was made clear that the congress had discussed and unanimously adopted a constitution, a labor law, a land law, and resolutions on the Red Army and economic policies, all introduced by the CCP Central Committee.

By the time this wire was sent off, the congress was electing the personnel of the new government.

Robert North quotes Chang Kuo-t'ao to the effect that it was Chou En-lai who called the congress and who presently "squeezed Mao out" and saw to it that Mao was not elected to the party Central Committee. (See Robert North, *Moscow and Chinese Communists,* p. 158.)

For brief information concerning the opening of the congress, available in Western literature, see Robert North, *Moscow and Chinese Communists,* p. 152, and Victor Yakhontoff, *The Chinese Soviets,* p. 130.

Proclamation of the Central Executive Committee of the Chi-

nese Soviet Republic, No. 1 (中 華 蘇 維 埃 共 和 國) 中 央
執 行 委 員 會 佈 告 第 一 號 Chung-hua su-wei-ai kung-ho-
kuo chung-yang chih-hsing wei-yüan-hui pu-kao, ti-i hao), dated
December 1, 1931; an original official copy of the proclamation,
008.631/1084, SSC; also printed in *Red China,* No. 1, December 11, 1931, p. 2, 008.1052/2125/V.1, SSC; approximately
1,050 words.

This was the first official announcement of the establishment
of the Central Soviet Government in China.

It was stated that the First All-China Soviet Congress opening
on November 7 had adopted a political program, a constitution,
a land law, a labor law, resolutions on the Red Army and economic policies, and so forth. It formally proclaimed the Chinese
Soviet Republic.

A sixty-three-man Central Executive Committee of the new
government was elected, with Mao standing at the head of the
list. The Central Executive Committee held its first meeting on
November 27, electing Mao chairman and Hsiang Ying and Chang
Kuo-t'ao vice-chairmen.

The Central Executive Committee was the organ of supreme
political power in the intervals between national Soviet congresses. Under it was a Council of People's Commissars, which
was the equivalent of a cabinet. Also Mao was elected chairman
of the Council of People's Commissars, with Hsiang Ying and
Chang Kuo-t'ao as vice-chairmen. The cabinet was composed of
nine commissariats in charge of foreign, military, labor, financial, land, educational, interior, judicial, and inspectoral affairs. In addition, there was established a State Political Security Bureau under the cabinet.

With the proclamation of the Central Soviet Government, it
was stated, there were two diametrically opposed regimes in
existence on Chinese soil: the Chinese Republic and the Chinese
Soviet Republic. The latter would do what it could to win preliminary successes in one or more provinces with a view to the
ultimate triumph of the revolution all over the country. (See *A
Collection of Red Bandit Reactionary Documents,* Vol. 3, pp.
649-51).

Judging from the list of the members of the government, it is
hard to say that Mao's power had appreciably declined at that
time despite the fact that the Russian Returned Student group had
penetrated the government.

Ten Great Political Programs of the CCP (中國 共產 黨
十 大 政綱) Chung-kuo kung-ch'an-tang shih ta cheng-kang),
reproduced as a proclamation by the General Political Department, Third Army Corps, Red Army, n. d., n. p.; lithographed;
008. 221/4041, SSC; 167 words.

Though not indicated, this proclamation is taken verbatim
from part 2, section 4, of the Political Resolution of the CCP
Sixth National Congress held in Moscow in July, 1928. That it
was reissued as a proclamation in Kiangsi shows that the Political Resolution as well as other resolutions of the Sixth National
Congress of the CCP served as guiding principles for the Soviet
movement in Kiangsi.

The text of the ten items of this political platform can readily
be found in Communist literature as, for instance, in *Red
Documents*, p. 142, and *The International Line*, pp. 63-64. An
English version appears in *A Documentary History of Chinese
Communism* by Conrad Brandt, Benjamin Schwartz, and John
Fairbank, p. 132.

The Political Program of the Chinese Soviet Republic (中 華
蘇 維 埃 共 和 國) 政綱) Chung-hua su-wei-ai kung-ho-
kuo cheng-kang), adopted by the First National Soviet Congress
in November, 1931; reproduced in *A Collection of Red Bandit
Reactionary Documents*, Vol. 3, pp. 657-58, 008. 2129/4077/
V. 3, SSC; approximately 800 words.

This political program differs radically from the political
program adopted by the National Conference of Delegates from
Soviet Areas in May, 1930, notably in the sphere of land policy.
As described previously, the 1930 statement, like the provisional land law adopted simultaneously, forbids the sale, lease,
and mortgage of land and stands for land nationalization. By contrast, the present statement, like the land law adopted at one
and the same time, permits the sale, lease, and mortgage of
land and contains no provision of immediate land nationalization.

In enumerating the various enactments of the First National
Soviet Congress, as has been noted previously, the first official
proclamation of the Central Soviet Government placed the present statement before all other laws and resolutions adopted by
the First National Soviet Congress, including the constitution.
This gives the impression that the political program looked even

more fundamental in nature than the constitution, not to speak of other laws and resolutions. This can be seen from a comparison of all these laws and regulations as follows:

Political Program	Constitution	Labor Law	Land Law	Resolution on Special Treatment to Red Army	Resolution on Economic Policies
Articles 1-2	Article 8				
Article 3	Article 1				
Article 4	Article 14				
Article 5	Article 5	Articles 14, 15, 41, and articles relating to wages and female workers			
Article 6	Article 6		Articles 1, 12		
Article 7				All basic ideas	
Article 8	Article 9				
Article 1	Article 17				
Article 9	Article 7				All basic ideas

Moreover, the present statement differs from Li Li-san's political program of 1930 as follows:

1. Foreign relations. This statement promises to conclude equal treaties with imperialist countries after abolition of all old treaties and permits the continued operations of foreign capital under the laws of the Soviet Government after the confiscation of the imperialist banks and enterprises in China. In contrast, the 1930 statement contains no such provisions.

2. Labor. The 1930 statement fixes the minimum wage of a worker at forty Chinese dollars per month among other things, whereas the present document contains no such provision.

3. Land revolution. The two documents are poles apart in this respect, as described previously.

4. Economic policies. The present statement permits private enterprises and free trade, whereas the 1930 political program contains no such provision.

5. Freedoms. The present document contains no provisions for individual freedoms, whereas the 1930 statement provides for the freedoms of assembly, association, and speech and the right to strike.

General Principles of the Constitution of the Chinese Soviet Republic (中華蘇維埃共和國憲法大綱) Chung-

hua su-wei-ai kung-ho-kuo hsien-fa ta-kang), adopted by the
First National Soviet Congress on November 7, 1931; printed in
Red Flag Weekly, No. 25, December 4 (?), 1931, pp. 2-7,
052. 1/809, BIC; approximately 3,000 words.

This is the text of the constitution of the Chinese Soviet Republic, adopted by the First National Soviet Congress on November 7, 1931. The form of government was designated a revolutionary democratic dictatorship of the workers and peasants as
a transitional step to the ultimate dictatorship of the proletariat.
All the exploiting classes were deprived of political rights and
freedoms.

The governmental form of a democratic dictatorship of the
workers and peasants was nothing new. In China, it was first
adopted by Li Li-san's draft constitution of September, 1930. As
a matter of fact, there is little basic difference between this
text and the Li Li-san draft except in language and in the arrangement of clauses. This can be seen from the following comparison:

1930 Draft	1931 Text
Article 2, section 1	Article 10
Article 2, section 2	Article 4, section 1
Article 3	Article 4, section 2
Article 4, section 1	Article 11
Article 4, section 2	Article 12
Article 5	Article 14
Article 6	Articles 8, 17
Article 7	Articles 1, 2
Article 8	Articles 5, 6, 7

The Comintern impact on this constitution is obvious. By far
the greatest and most immediate authority on which this constitution was based was the Comintern directives of July 23, 1930,
and July, 1931. To a lesser degree, Moscow's influence dates
as far back as the Comintern resolution of November, 1926, on
the Chinese problem. It must be remembered that the governmental form of a revolutionary democratic dictatorship of the
workers and peasants, which was Lenin's formula of 1905, was
provided for in the Comintern directive of July 23, 1930 (sections 22 and 24) and that it was the very governmental form
postulated by Stalin for the Chinese revolution, as distinguished
from the governmental form of proletarian dictatorship advo-

cated by Trotsky. (See Ch'en Tu-hsiu's Reply to the Comintern, February 17, 1930.)

It was explained in the Comintern directive of July 23, 1930, that the democratic dictatorship of workers and peasants in China would be considerably different from the 1905 pattern of Russia. There were several reasons for this. On the one hand, there was the example of the Soviet Union, which had been successfully building up socialism. On the other, the Chinese Communist Party would form the majority of the new government, thereby assuring the leadership of the proletariat over the peasantry. Meanwhile, the Chinese democratic dictatorship would not tolerate the enterprises of Chinese and foreign capital; it would move in the direction of socialism. Accordingly, the element of socialism was the outstanding feature of the revolutionary democratic dictatorship of workers and peasants in China. Though the transition from capitalism to socialism in China would have to pass through many more phases than the Russian revolution of 1917, it would certainly be of a much shorter duration than would have been expected in Russia in 1905.

As its title indicates, this document is only a body of general principles of the constitution. Thus far we have not found a full-fledged constitution of the time in addition to the present document. But a secondary source makes mention of a more complete constitution and, more specifically, refers to articles 70-84 of that constitution. (See *A Collection of Red Bandit Reactionary Documents*, Vol. 3, pp. 812-16, 819, 825, 827-28.) Since the present document contains only seventeen articles, that constitution, if any, must be something else. However, in reporting on the constitution before the Second National Soviet Congress on January 31, 1934, Hsiang Ying declared that the brief constitution adopted by the First National Soviet Congress was basically sound but that it had not yet become a complete and technically satisfactory constitution. (See *Red China,* February 3, 1934, p. 3.) He did not mention, even by implication, the existence of a fundamental law other than the present one during or after the First National Soviet Congress of November, 1931.

As described previously, this constitution was introduced by the Central Committee of the CCP. (See Telegram from the Chinese Soviet Congress to the Central Committee of the CCP, dated November 18, 1931.) This would suggest that the present constitution was the work of the Russian Returned Student leadership.

An English version of this constitution appears in the Harvard publication *A Documentary History of Chinese Communism*, pp. 220-24. It was taken from the Yakhontoff study, *The Chinese Soviets*, p. 217, acknowledged as "courtesy of the International Publishers" (p. 500). The Harvard publication boasts a number of corrections in the faulty English translation. On examination, however, it still contains a number of textual errors which should be corrected. Examples:

Errors	*Corrections*
t'u-hao [village bosses], monks—all exploiting and counterrevolutionary elements (toward end of article 2)	capitalists, rich peasants, monks, and all exploiting and counterrevolutionary elements
promulgate orders and resolutions (end of article 3)	promulgate laws, orders, and resolutions
broad masses (toward end of article 4)	broad masses of workers, peasants, and toiling population
It shall be permissible (toward end of article 8)	It shall at present be permissible
Mongolians, Tibetans (article 14)	Mongolians, Moslems, Tibetans

Draft Land Law (土地法草案 T'u-ti fa ts'ao-an) prepared by the CCP Central Committee in 1931; printed in *Draft Resolutions Introduced by the CCP Central Committee to the First National Soviet Congress*, reproduced by the Political Department, Third Army Corps, First Route Army, Chinese Workers' and Peasants' Red Army, pp. 9-14, n. d., 008.631/8064-2, SSC; approximately 2,400 words.

As described in the collection *Draft Resolutions Introduced by the CCP Central Committee to the First National Soviet Congress*, referred to above, the Central Committee of the CCP prepared five draft resolutions for submission to the First National Soviet Congress, namely, (1) resolution on the problem of the Red Army, (2) land law, (3) labor law, (4) economic policies, (5) organization and function of the Workers' and Peasants' Inspectorate. The last-named resolution has not been seen mentioned in other available Chinese Communist documents, and the draft constitution as outlined in a previous item is not included in this collection of draft resolutions.

There is no doubt that the land law passed by the First National Soviet Congress was the final version of the draft land law introduced by the CCP Central Committee. There are indeed some verbal discrepancies between the two texts, but they are by no means of basic importance. The more significant changes are the ones relating to the alliance of the middle peasants and the opposition to the rich peasants.

The Communists in China, as in Russia, have made a point of allying themselves with the middle peasants. To that end, the first thing to do is not to violate the interests of the middle peasants. In regard to the equal redistribution of all land, the draft land law provides that it cannot be carried out unless the basic masses of the peasants are willing to lend direct support to it. This seems to mean that the support of the poor peasants and hired farm hands will be a requisite for the equal redistribution of land.

But the final text of the land law as adopted by the First National Soviet Congress included the additional clause that the middle peasants may not take part in equal redistribution if the majority of them do not want it. In this way the interests of the middle peasants are more carefully protected.

Moreover, the draft land law provides for a mixed system of land redistribution, that is, redistribution according to the number of people in each family and their labor power. By contrast, the land law as finally adopted adds an alternative provision to the effect that, apart from the mixed system referred to, land may also be equally redistributed according to the number of persons in each family in so far as the middle peasants, poor peasants, and hired farm hands are concerned, whereas, with respect to the rich peasants, their labor power will be the principal consideration to be supplemented only by the criterion of the number of members in their families. In addition, the spare houses, farming implements, and so forth of the rich peasants will be confiscated, a provision not so stern in the draft resolution submitted by the CCP Central Committee.

Thus, the rich peasants are more ruthlessly discriminated against in the final text of the land law than in the draft resolution.

Land Law of the Chinese Soviet Republic (中 華 蘇 維 埃 共

和國) 土 地 法 Chung-hua su-wei-ai kung-ho-kuo t'u-ti fa),
adopted by the First National Soviet Congress in November,
1931; an original copy of the proclamation issued jointly by the
Presidium of the Congress and the Central Executive Committee
of the Chinese Soviet Government on December 1, 1931,
008.742/4043, SSC; reproduced in (1) *The Soviet Code*, Vol. 2,
pp. 41-47, 008.542/V.2, SSC; (2) *A Collection of Red Bandit
Documents*, Vol. 1, pp. 2-9, 008.2129/4070/V.1, SSC; (3) *A
Collection of Red Bandit Reactionary Documents*, Vol. 3, pp.
922-27, 008.2129/4077/V.3, SSC; approximately 2,500 words.

This is the land law of the Chinese Soviet Government, introduced by the CCP Central Committee under the leadership of the
Russian Returned Students, and enforced right up to the end of
the Kiangsi regime in 1934. Leaving a more detailed discussion
of this law to another volume on the agrarian revolution, we
wish to point out the following for our present purposes:
    1. In contradistinction to the land law of the Li Li-san leader-
ship dated May, 1930, this law permits the lease and sale of
land, but not collectivization.
    2. Unlike the land law of the Chu-Mao group, the basic prin-
ciples of which were introduced or reaffirmed in the February 7
(1930) Conference, this law does not use the number of people as
the only criterion for land redistribution, but a mixed criterion
of labor power and the number of people.
    3. This law was the most Moscow-oriented of all land laws
enacted by Chinese Communists during the period under study.

    Draft Labor Law (勞 働 法 草 案 Lao-tung fa ts'ao-an),
prepared by the CCP Central Committee in 1931; printed in
*Draft Resolutions Introduced by the CCP Central Committee to
the First National Soviet Congress*, reproduced by the Political
Department, Third Army Corps, First Route Army, Chinese
Workers' and Peasants' Red Army, n.d., 008.631/8064-2, SSC,
pp. 15-25; also printed in *Red Flag of the North*, No. 15, October 25, 1932, pp. 63-73, 052.1/806, BIC; approximately 4,000
words.

In spirit, this draft labor law agrees with the final text of the
labor law adopted by the First National Soviet Congress in November, 1931. In form, a number of gaps in this draft have
been filled in the final text, as can be seen from chapters 1 and

11 of the latter dealing with the general principles and the handling of lawbreakers respectively.

There seems to be no essential difference between this draft labor law and Li Li-san's labor protection law of May, 1930.

It is clear that this draft resolution was inspired by Moscow. The latest evidence was the Comintern directive of July, 1931. Thus:

Comintern Directive	*Draft Labor Law*
Eight-hour work	Article 1
Equal work, equal pay	Article 12
Annual holidays	Article 9
Sunday rest	Article 9
Protection of child and juvenile labor	Articles 2, 27-33
Full pay during sickness	Article 46
Allowance for the wounded	Articles 46, 48
Social assurance at expense of employers	Note to chapter 6
Prior consent of labor union to dismissal of workers	Articles 34, 18, 55

The Labor Law (勞働法 Lao-tung fa), adopted by the First National Soviet Congress in November, 1931; reproduced in *A Collection of Red Bandit Reactionary Documents*, Vol. 5, pp. 1342-56, 008. 2129/4077/V. 5, SSC; approximately 6, 300 words.

As explained previously, the discrepancies between this labor law and its draft submitted by the CCP Central Committee lie in form rather than in spirit. These discrepancies outweigh those between the land law adopted by the First National Soviet Congress and its draft.

This law consists of twelve chapters and seventy-five articles, whereas its draft has only eight chapters and sixty-three articles. The draft contains no provision for the scope of application, whereas this law prescribes that it applies to all hired laborers in industrial enterprises, workshops, productive undertakings, public and private institutions (article 1). As to the cases of violations of the labor law, the draft law states that specific regulations should be enacted to deal with them (article 60). In contrast, this law provides that the People's Court shall decide such cases and give effect to the decisions made (articles 72, 73).

This labor law was promulgated on December 1, 1931, only to be replaced by another code on October 15, 1933. An English version of this law, which contains numerous errors of translation, appears in the Yakhontoff publication, *The Chinese Soviets*, pp. 224-75. The text of the 1933 code is printed in *The Soviet Code*, compiled by the People's Judicial Commissariat, July, 1934, Vol. 2, pp. 1-40 and reproduced in *A Collection of Red Bandit Reactionary Documents*, Vol. 5, pp. 1366-95.

Draft Resolution of the First National Soviet Congress on the Question of the Red Army (全國 蘇維埃第一次代表大 會紅軍問題決議案草案 Ch'üan-kuo su-wei-ai ti-i-tz'u tai-piao ta-hui hung-chün wen-t'i chüeh-i-an ts'ao-an), prepared by the CCP Central Committee in 1931; printed in *Draft Resolutions Introduced by the CCP Central Committee to the First National Soviet Congress*, reproduced by the Political Department, Third Army Corps, First Route Army, Chinese Workers' and Peasants' Red Army, n. d., 008.631/8064-2, SSC, pp. 1-7; approximately 2,100 words.

This draft resolution concerns itself primarily with the unification of the command and the reform of the quality of the Red Army. It hardly ever touches upon the question of military strategy. It contains the following specific proposals:

1. To set up a revolutionary military council as the supreme command of the Red Army.

2. To draw as many workers and hired farm hands as possible into the Red Army to "assure the proletarian leadership in the Red Army."

3. To ascertain and increase political work in the Red Army.

4. To appoint more workers, hired farm hands, and poor peasants as military commanders.

5. To establish a military academy.

6. To consolidate the supply departments in the Red Army.

7. To define the responsibility of Soviet agencies at all levels to assist in the operations of the Red Army.

8. To draw up plans of special treatment to Red Army men.

Resolution on the Problem of the Red Army (紅軍問題

決議案 Hung-chün wen-t'i chüeh-i-an), adopted by the First
National Soviet Congress; 008.5526/2137-2, SSC; approximately
2,100 words.

With the exception of one particular point, this resolution as
finally adopted by the First National Soviet Congress agrees entirely with its draft text as introduced by the CCP Central Committee, described previously. The exception is that a set of
regulations governing special treatment to Red Army men was
adopted by the Congress as an appendix to the present document,
whereas the text of the draft resolution contains only the idea of
enacting such regulations.

   Draft Resolution on Economic Policies (經濟政策草
案 Ching-chi cheng-ts'e ts'ao-an), prepared by the CCP Central Committee in 1931; printed in *Draft Resolutions Introduced
by the CCP Central Committee to the First National Soviet Congress,* reproduced by the Political Department, Third Army
Corps, Chinese Workers' and Peasants' Red Army, n.d.,
008.631/8064-2, SSC, pp. 27-30; approximately 1,300 words.

This draft resolution on economic policies covers industry,
commerce, finance, and municipal administration. Agriculture
is not included, probably because there was already a land law.
But the abolition of usury and the confiscation of the property of
landlords and gentry are recapitulated here.
    According to this statement, all key industries that were un-
der the control of the imperialists were to be nationalized. Foreign enterprises might continue production under new contracts.
Chinese enterprises remained in the hands of the old owners
provided that production was under the supervision of the workers.
    Free trade was provided—on paper. Cooperatives were encour-
aged.
    All old taxes and levies were abolished. A unified system of
progressive taxation was introduced at the expense of capitalists.
    A workers' and peasants' bank was to be established, and old
banks and banking houses were placed under supervision.
    By municipal administration was meant simply the disposal of
confiscated properties. Houses went to coolies and all other
properties to poor people.

The final text of this draft resolution as adopted by the First National Soviet Congress is thus far not available.

Draft Resolution on the Organization and Function of the Workers' and Peasants' Inspectorate (工 農 檢 查 處 的 組 織 系 統 與 任 務 草 案 Kung-nung chien-ch'a-ch'u ti tsu-chih hsi-t'ung yü jen-wu ts'ao-an), prepared by the CCP Central Committee in 1931; printed in *Draft Resolutions Introduced by the CCP Central Committee to the First National Soviet Congress,* reproduced by the Political Department, Third Army Corps, Chinese Workers' and Peasants' Red Army, n.d., 008.631/8064-2, SSC, pp. 31-36; approximately 2,100 words.

The Workers' and Peasants' Inspection Commissar was one of the nine cabinet ministers created by the First National Soviet Congress. He had his own chain of command right down to the county and district levels. The office of this new post was all part and parcel of the government structure.

The terms of reference of this new functionary were extensive. His power extended to virtually all aspects of political life except in the party and the Red Army. He had close connection with those party officials who had charge of intraparty control and supervision. Specifically, he had the following principal powers and functions:

1. To assure the carrying out of the policies of the land revolution in the interests of the toiling masses.

2. To supervise the implementation of economic policies.

3. To prepare and attend to Soviet elections to ensure the effective rule of workers and peasants.

It is not clear whether this draft resolution was adopted by the First National Soviet Congress. But the fact is that the institution of the workers' and peasants' inspection was established by that congress.

16

The Japanese Attack

Precipitates a Drive to Protect Russia

Resolution of the Central concerning the Incident of the Forcible Occupation of Manchuria by Japanese Imperialists (中 央 關 於 日 本 帝 國 主 義 強 佔 滿 洲 事 變 的 決 議 Chung-yang kuan-yü jih-pen ti-kuo chu-i ch'iang-chan man-chou shih-pien ti chüeh-i), September 22, 1931 (the date September 20 as printed in this mimeographed copy of the document seems to be a mistake, as can be seen from a check with other copies in clear print), 008.235/6050, SSC; contained in *A Guide to the Anti-Imperialist Struggle and the Armed Protection of the Soviet Union*, compiled and printed by the Propaganda Department, Central Bureau, Soviet Areas, CCP, October, 1932, 008.222/7106/C.1-2, SSC, pp. 3-10; approximately 3,500 words.

The Japanese invasion of Manchuria on September 18, 1931, called a halt to KMT anti-Communist operations for some time and helped the growth of the Communist movement in China.

As can be seen from this statement, the Russian Returned Students saw a twofold significance in the Japanese attack. On the one hand, they took it as a sign of the beginning of a concerted attack of the imperialists against the Soviet Union. On the other, they considered that the Japanese attack would intensify the internal crisis of the KMT, which in turn would help strengthen the unity of the various KMT cliques in an effort to fight the Communist revolution. Consequently, the CCP called upon the revolutionary masses to cooperate in armed protection of the Soviet Union and to create a united front from below with a view to the overthrow of the KMT rule.

In 1945 the Mao leadership listed a number of miscalculations on the part of the Russian Returned Students after the Japanese attack. They overstressed, it was charged, the possibility of a concerted imperialist attack against the Soviet Union. They overlooked the fact that the rising tide of nationalism had out-weighed class antagonisms in the country. They exaggerated the impending disintegration of the KMT and mistook middle-road-ers for enemies. They revived the slogan of the seizure of key cities with a view to preliminary successes in one or more provinces. (See "Resolution on Some Historical Problems, " April 20, 1945, printed in Mao Tse-tung, *Selected Works,* Chi-nese edition, Vol. 3, pp. 967-68; English edition, Vol. 4, p. 184; reprint of the resolution, p. 17.)

In attempting to explain the position of the Russian Returned Students, the Communist historian Ho Kan-chih states that there should have been a national defense government and an anti-Japanese united army to meet the situation created by the Japanese attack but that the party leadership rejected such an approach. With respect to the question of the protection of the Soviet Union in particular, Ho declares that exaggerating a com-mon attack of the imperialists against the Soviet Union had two unfavorable consequences. On the one hand, the Japanese inva-sion of China had been overlooked, with the result that the CCP had isolated itself from the great anti-Japanese movement of the time by failing to stress the importance of maintaining the terri-torial integrity of China. On the other, the underrating of the tensions among the imperialists had let slip a chance of utiliz-ing those tensions to the advantage of the struggle against Japan. (See Ho Kan-chih, *History of the Contemporary Chinese Revolu-tion,* 1958, pp. 156-61.)

It seems superfluous to point out that the slogan of the protec-tion of the Soviet Union as embodied in the present statement was based on the resolution of the Eleventh Plenum of the ECCI described previously. Earlier, that idea appeared in section 14 of the Comintern directive of July 23, 1930. It may be recalled that during the crisis of the Chinese Eastern Railway in 1929 Li Li-san also raised this slogan, to which Ch'en Tu-hsiu objected. (See Benjamin Schwartz, *Chinese Communism and the Rise of Mao,* pp. 145-46.)

The Peace Policy of the Soviet Union and the Anti-Soviet Struggle during the Japanese Invasion of Manchuria (滿洲事變中蘇聯的和平政策與反蘇聯的鬥爭 Man-

chou shih-pien chung su-lien ti ho-ping cheng-ts'e yü fan su-lien
ti tou-cheng), by Lo Fu (Chang Wen-t'ien), November 4, 1931;
printed in *Red Flag Weekly*, No. 23, November 20, 1931, pp.
53-58, 052.1/809, BIC; approximately 2,100 words.

The purpose of this article was to defend the slogan "Armed
Protection of the Soviet Union" raised by the CCP after the Japanese attack.

The writer listed three things as evidence of imperialist preparations for war against the Soviet Union:

1. All newspapers of imperialist countries after the Japanese
attack stressed that the Soviet Union would send troops to northern Manchuria.

2. France, Great Britain, and the United States in the League
of Nations urged Japan to advance northward instead of southward.

3. The forthcoming negotiations of France with the United
States and Germany would be focused on the question of establishing an economic blockade against the Soviet Union.

*A Letter from the CCP Central to Party Headquarters at All
Levels—regarding Leadership of and Participation in a Campaign
Week Dedicated to the Fight against Imperialists' Invasion of the Soviet Union and Their Partition of China As Well As to the Enlargement of the Revolutionary National War* (中共中央致各
級黨部一封信 —— 關於領導和參加反對
帝國主義進攻蘇聯瓜分中國與擴大革命民
族戰爭的運動週 Chung-kung chung-yang chih ko chi
tang-pu i-feng hsin—kuan-yü ling-tao han ts'an-chia fan-tui ti-kuo
chu-i chin-kung su-lien kua-fen chung-kuo yü k'uo-ta ko-ming
min-ch'u chan-cheng ti yün-tung-chou), dated March 30, 1932;
printed in *True Words (Shih-hua)*, No. 4, May 10, 1932, pp. 8-
9, 008.2105/3002, SSC; approximately 900 words.

As its subtitle indicates, this letter called upon the party
units at all levels to participate in and lead a propaganda and
agitation week dedicated to the fight against imperialists' invasion of the Soviet Union and their partition of China. The CY
was made to sponsor the week which was to last in Shanghai
from April 5 to 12 and in the various provinces from April 23
to 30.

As can be seen from a later entry, this letter formed one of
the bases of another statement, issued by the Central Bureau on
May 11, 1932, which was described by Mao's leadership in 1945
as one of the major statements representing the erroneous Left
line of the Russian Returned Student leadership.

*Declaration of War against Japan by the Provisional Central
Government of the Chinese Soviet Republic* (中華蘇維埃共
和國臨時中央政府宣佈對日戰爭宣言 Chung-
hua su-wei-ai kung-ho-kuo lin-shih chung-yang cheng-fu hsüan-
pu tui-jih chan-cheng hsüan-yen), dated April 15, 1932; printed
in *Red China,* No. 18, April 21, 1932, p. 2, 008. 1052/2125/V.
1, SSC; approximately 1,300 words.

Hereby the Central Soviet Government declared war on Japan.
This was a war on paper only; far away in the hinterland of
China, the Soviet regime and its Red Army had no actual fight-
ing against the Japanese at all.

In fact, what was uppermost in the Communist mind was not
a war against Japan but a fight against the KMT. The Communists made this unmistakably clear when they stressed that the
KMT rule must be removed before a real war of national revolution and a direct fight against Japan could be waged.

Accordingly, with the masses in the Soviet areas under its effective control, the Communist regime called upon the workers,
peasants, soldiers, students, and all toiling masses in the non-
Communist areas to take up arms against the KMT and the Japanese.

It should be noted that the text of this declaration also appears
in the *Red Flag Weekly,* published in Shanghai by the Central
Department of Propaganda, CCP, No. 40, May 15, 1932, pp. 1-
3, under a slightly different title, bearing the date and place
April 20, 1932, Juichin, Kiangsi. This text is divided into two
sections. A comparison of the two texts shows that there are as
many as twenty units of verbal discrepancies and many more
punctuation distinctions between them. Some of the textual discrepancies are of account. For example, the last thirty characters in the first section of the text in the *Red Flag Weekly* are
entirely different from the eighty-one characters of the corres-
ponding passage in the *Red China* text.

An English version of this statement appears in Victor Yakhontoff, *The Chinese Soviets,* 1934, pp. 236-38, originally pub-

lished by the Friends of the Chinese People, New York, 1934.
Obviously, this translation is based on a Chinese text like that in
the *Red Flag Weekly*, though bearing a different date, April 26,
1932.

*Letter from the CCP Central to the Party Headquarters in
the Various Soviet Areas, Objecting to Imperialists' Invasion of
Soviet Russia and Their Partition of China* (中共中央為反
對帝國主義進攻蘇聯瓜分中國給各蘇區黨部
信 Chung-kung chung-yang wei fan-tui ti-kuo chu-i chin-kung
su-lien kua-fen chung-kuo chi ko su-ch'ü tang-pu hsin), dated
April 14, 1932; printed in the small collection of documents entitled *A Guide to the Anti-Imperialist Struggle and the Armed
Protection of the Soviet Union,* compiled and printed by the
Propaganda Department, Central Bureau, Soviet Areas, September 18, 1932, pp. 13-21, 008. 222/7106/C. 1, 2, SSC; also
in *True Words (Shih-hua),* No. 4, May 10, 1932, pp. 5-8,
008. 2105/3002, SSC; approximately 4, 400 words.

This statement formed one of the bases of another document,
issued by the Central Bureau on May 11, 1932, which, as can
be seen from a later entry, was viewed by Mao's machine in
1945 as one of the major documents representing the erroneous
Left line of the Russian Returned Student leadership.

Proceeding on the assumption that international imperialism
was preparing war against the Soviet Union and contemplating
partition of China, this statement claimed that the imperialists
were actually behind the KMT Third Campaign and were aiding
and abetting the Nationalists for another military adventure.

Under the circumstances, this statement set five major tasks
for the party in the Soviet areas:

1. Consolidating and expanding the Soviet base, bringing the
various Soviet areas together, and achieving preliminary successes in one or more provinces.

2. Strengthening the Soviet regimes on the central and provincial levels.

3. Stepping up propaganda and agitation against imperialism.

4. Mobilizing and organizing the masses of workers and
peasants.

5. Linking the anti-imperialist campaign with support for the
Soviet Union.

In conclusion, the present document reaffirms the two-front

struggle with the Right deviation as the main danger, coupled
with an enumeration of the contents of Right and Left deviations.

Resolution of the Central Bureau, Soviet Areas, CCP, con-
cerning Leadership of and Participation in the Campaign Week
Dedicated to the Fight against Imperialists' Invasion of the So-
viet Union and Their Partition of China As Well As to the En-
largement of the Revolutionary War (中 共 蘇 區 中 央 局
關 於 領 導 和 參 加 反 對 帝 國 主 義 進 攻 蘇 聯
瓜 分 中 國 與 擴 大 革 命 戰 爭 運 動 週 的 決 議
Chung-kung su-ch'ü chung-yang-chü kuan-yü ling-tao han ts'an-
chia fan-tui ti-kuo chu-i chin-kung su-lien kua-fen chung-kuo yü
k'uo-ta ko-ming chan-cheng yün-tung-chou ti chüeh-i), dated
May 11, 1932; printed in *True Words (Shih-hua)*, No. 4, May
10, 1932, pp. 9-12, 008.2105/3002, SSC; approximately 5,300
words.

Listed in the Mao-sponsored "Resolution on Some Historical
Problems" of 1945 as one of the major statements representing
the erroneous Left line of the Russian Returned Student leadership, this document was based on three statements of the CCP
Central, two of which, dated March 30 and April 14 respectively, have been described previously, while a third one dealing with May demonstrations is unavailable. On examination,
this document is seen to have been drawn directly from a number of Comintern statements, such as the resolution of the ECCI
Eleventh Plenum of April, 1931, the resolution of the CCP concerning the conclusion of the ECCI Eleventh Plenum adopted in
August, 1931, and editorials of Communist International dated
November 11 and December 10, 1931, respectively. Among all
the sources of the present document the CCP Central resolution
of January 9, 1932, on winning preliminary successes in one or
more provinces, which will be discussed later in this study,
stood out as the most authoritative and comprehensive one.
In this statement the Central Bureau not only formally accepted the Central directives in question but also practiced self-
criticism in unmistakable terms. The Central Bureau confessed
that it had persistently committed errors of Right opportunism,
such as underestimating the revolutionary situation, overesti-
mating the contradictions of the imperialist powers, overlooking the imperialists' invasion of the Soviet Union and their partition of China, and so forth. It admitted that it began to make

the errors long before the party conference of November, 1931.

In consequence, the present resolution assigned a number of major tasks to the party in the Soviet areas, which were actually a repetition of the tasks assigned to the Soviet areas by the Central Committee in its directive of April 14, 1932, described previously. The most important of these tasks were to bring all Soviet areas together by force, to take key cities, such as Kanchow, Fuchou (Linch'üan), and Nanch'ang, and achieve preliminary successes in one or more provinces.

In conclusion, as in the Central directive of April 14, Right opportunism was characterized as the main danger.

17

The Oyuwan and Hsiangosi Soviets

The Soviet Movement in the Oyuwan Area (鄂 豫 皖 區
的 蘇 維 埃 運 動 O-yü-wan ch'ü ti su-wei-ai yün-tung),
printed in *Red Flag Weekly*, No. 25, November 27, 1931,
052.1/809, BIC; approximately 6,500 words.

This article falls into three parts: (1) circular wire of the
Second Soviet Conference of the Oyuwan Area, (2) declaration of
the said conference, and (3) strengthening and development of
the area. It gives an otherwise unavailable, though incomplete,
picture of the Oyuwan area which occupied the borderland of
Hupeh, Honan, and Anhwei and which was second only to the
Central Soviet Area in Kiangsi in strength. In brief, this article
brings out the following major points:

1. The Oyuwan Soviet Area started with a handful of poorly
equipped Communist refugees in Huangan in northeastern Hupeh
after the KMT-CCP split in 1927. Little by little it grew in size
and strength. The area actually comprised several scattered
small regions; it hardly ever became an integrated area.

2. A local branch of the CCP Central Committee, known as
the Central Sub-bureau of the Oyuwan Soviet Area, was established in June, 1931, holding its first meeting on June 28. It
was described as a milestone in the development of Communism
there. Before this, it was said, the Li-san line and the compromising line had successively prevailed. The Second Conference of Delegates of Workers, Peasants, and Soldiers opened on
July 1 and adopted a land law which was soon enforced in the
area.

3. It would seem that the Oyuwan Soviet area was an inde-

pendent regime having little to do with the Central Soviet Area
in Kiangsi. Thus, when the First National Soviet Congress
opened on November 7, 1931, the Oyuwan Soviet did not send a
delegation there. Rather it held a conference of its own, known
as the Second Soviet Conference of the Oyuwan Area opening on
November 7, 1931. Like the First National Soviet Congress held
in Kiangsi, this conference adopted a land law, a set of organic
principles of the Soviet Government, and a host of resolutions on
military, diplomatic, educational, economic, labor, youth, and
other questions. In addition, it elected a Soviet Government all
its own.

According to Chang Kuo-t'ao during an interview in Hongkong
in late October, 1959, the independent action of the Oyuwan Soviet was based on a resolution of the Central Politburo to the effect that the several Soviet areas could make their own decisions
to meet local requirements in view of the enormous difficulties
of transportation caused by the pressure of the KMT. Chang
Kuo-t'ao himself headed the Central Sub-bureau of the Oyuwan
Soviet Area, while Shen Tse-min, a member of the Russian Returned Student group, served as secretary of the local provincial
committee, which was placed under the jurisdiction of the Central Sub-bureau. Chang and Shen were close friends, and perhaps for that reason Shen had been picked by the Russian Returned Student leadership to work in Oyuwan.

As the conference of November 7, 1931, was the second of its
kind in the Oyuwan area, the question was put to Chang just when
the first conference took place. He said he did not know because
that had occurred before his return to China. Questioned
whether or not Oyuwan had any Russian aid, he said "no" and, in
addition, he did not hear of any Russian aid to Kiangsi, either.
On the contrary, he stated, Oyuwan sent money to KMT areas to
foment mass revolts.

*The Great Victory of Combating Counterrevolution in the
Oyuwan Soviet Area* (鄂 豫 皖 蘇 區 肅 反 的 偉 大 勝
利 O-yü-wan su-ch'ü su-fan ti wei-ta sheng-li), by (Ch'en)
Ch'ang-hao, November 22, 1931; printed in *Red Flag Weekly*,
No. 28, January 18, 1932, pp. 43-57, 052.1/809, BIC; approxi-
mately 7, 200 words.

This statement reveals a large-scale purge in the Red Army
in the Oyuwan area, which looked very much like the Fut'ien in-

cident of 1930 in Kiangsi. It was stated that the purge followed
the discovery of a military plot against the Communist authority
there, a plot which was allegedly scheduled to start on September 15, 1931, at Mapu, a town about twenty miles northeast of
Chinchiachai, the capital of the Oyuwan Soviet. Thanks to its
discovery at an early date, the plot was nipped in the bud.

As a counteraction against the plot, it was disclosed, a host
of drastic measures had been adopted: More than a thousand
military commanders and political workers at levels ranging
from the division to the platoon had been purged; all the cadres
in the party corps in the Red Army reshuffled; the party organization basically changed; and the military, political, and economic structures completely reorganized. It is significant to
note that among the causes of the purge was listed the correct
leadership of the Fourth Plenum held under the auspices of
Pavel Mif in January, 1931.

Like the Fut'ien incident, this alleged plot was attributed to
the A-B League, the Third Party, the Reorganizationists, and
the rich peasants. The ringleaders of these counterrevolutionary
groups, it was said, began to penetrate the Red Army in the
Oyuwan area as early as 1928. They had allegedly been sent to
Oyuwan from Shanghai, Hankow, and other places.

It was pointed out that the supreme command of these counterrevolutionary groups was a nine-man military council which had
its subordinate organizations at all levels in the army. The
chairman of the military council was a certain General Hsü Chi-
shen who was the commander of the first army appointed by the
Communist leadership. Among the suspected military rebels
discovered and arrested were two divisional commanders, a divisional political commissar, eight regiment commanders, and
five regiment political commissars. On the side of the regional
party units, as distinguished from the party units in the army,
virtually all the county party secretaries and the party corps
chiefs were implicated in the plot. It was estimated that more
than seven hundred of the thousand and odd men purged in the
Red Army were members of the CCP and that approximately
1,600 rich peasants were liquidated in addition.

Understandably it was concluded that the work of combating
counterrevolution was not finished yet and that it should continue
unabated.

The Truth about the Reorganizationists, The A-B League,

and the Third Party (改組派 A B 團 第三黨的真
面目 Kai-tsu-p'ai A-B t'uan ti-san tang ti chen mien-mu), issued by the Security Bureau, Northwest Anhwei, Special Soviet, January 17, 1932, 262/812, BIC; approximately 5,500
words.

This statement gives a brief account of the general activities
of the Reorganizationists, the A-B League, and the Third Party
in the Oyuwan Soviet Area. It was issued shortly after the publication of Ch'en Ch'ang-hao's article on the victory in the fight
against counterrevolution in Oyuwan described previously. The
leading spirits of the counterrevolutionary movement and their
general course of action as outlined in this statement are almost
the same as in Ch'en's article. The difference is that while this
is a general description of the operations of the counterrevolutionaries in the Oyuwan Soviet, the Ch'en article is primarily
concerned with the alleged plot occurring at Mapu, Anhwei.

Telegram from the Oyuwan Central Sub-bureau (鄂豫皖
中央分局來電 O-yü-wan chung-yang fen-chü lai tien),
dated October 9, 1932; printed in *Struggle* (Shanghai), No. 28,
October, 1932, p. 1, 052.1/809, BIC; mimeographed; approximately 130 words.

This telegram was signed by (Chang) Kuo-t'ao, (Shen) Tse-
min, (Ch'en) Ch'ang-hao, and (Hsü) Hsiang-ch'ien. This would
suggest that these four men were the Communist leaders in the
Oyuwan Soviet Area, at any rate in 1932.
In December, 1936, Mao attacked the strategic thinking of the
Oyuwan leaders, saying that they advocated an immediate attack
on Wuhan and that they made essentially the same mistake as
some leading comrades in Kiangsi at that time. (See Mao Tse-
tung, *Selected Works*, Vol. 1, Chinese edition, p. 189; English
edition, pp. 201-2.)

Correspondence from the Hsiangosi Soviet Area (湘鄂西
蘇區通信 Hsiang-o-si su-ch'ü t'ung-hsin), printed in *Red
Flag Weekly*, No. 17, September 15, 1931, pp. 34-37, 052.1/
809, BIC; approximately 1,400 words.

This correspondence attempts to compare the conditions in

the Hsiangosi Soviet during the Li-san line with those after the Fourth Plenum.

Hsiangosi, or western Hunan-Hupeh, covered an area lying across northern Hunan and western Hupeh with the Hunghu lake as the center. In the summer of 1930 the area comprised as many as eleven counties. At one time it shrank to two or three counties after the bulk of the Red garrison was transferred to other places in the heyday of the Li-san line. By the spring of 1931 it expanded again to include seven counties.

The influence of Li Li-san on the Communist movement in this area was described as twofold. On the one hand, he was castigated for having weakened the defense of the area by transferring most of the local garrison away. On the other, the rich peasants were said to have benefited from Li Li-sanism to the detriment of the poor peasants and hired farm hands.

After the Fourth Plenum, it was said, the Li-san line had been liquidated in this area. As a result, the damages done to this area had for the most part been repaired and the area was again growing in size and strength.

A Letter from the Central to the Hsiangosi Central Sub-bureau (中央給湘鄂西中央分局的信 Chung-yang chi hsiang-o-hsi chung-yang fen-chü ti hsin), dated November 17, 1931; mimeographed; 224. 2/804, BIC; approximately 4,300 words.

Like the CCP Central directive of September 1, 1931, to the Kiangsi Soviet, described previously, this letter is a catalogue of grievous mistakes ascribed by the Russian Returned Student leadership to the Hsiangosi Soviet. In respect to all the three Comintern assignments to the CCP, namely, the Red Army, the Soviet regime, and the agrarian revolution, the Hsiangosi Soviet was described as totally wrong. It was also thought wrong in the prosecution of intraparty work, such as lack of collective leadership, bureaucratism, and the two-front struggle. It seems clear that this letter represented a bold attempt of the Russian Returned Students to extend their control to the Hsiangosi area.

Central (Politburo) Resolution concerning the Party Central Sub-bureau in Hsiangosi (中央關於湘鄂西黨中央分局的決議 Chung-yang kuan-yü hsiang-o-hsi tang chung-

yang fen-chü ti chüeh-i), dated November 25, 1931; mimeographed; 224. 2/804, BIC; approximately 1, 600 words.

This resolution warned the Hsiangosi leaders that it was
wrong to give up the base at the Hunghu lake to flee north. The
veteran trade unionist Teng Chung-hsia, who had been in charge
of the local party after. his return from Russia in 1930, was ordered to be attacked for his opportunism. A two-front struggle
in the Hsiangosi Soviet was urged to give effect to the Comintern and CCP Central lines.

*Resolution of the Hsiangosi Provincial Committee Relating to
Comrade Teng Chung-hsia* (湘鄂西省委對鄧中夏同
志的決議 Hsiang-o-hsi sheng-wei tui teng-chung-hsia
t'ung-chih ti chüeh-i), dated December 9, 1931; printed in *Red
Flag Weekly*, No. 29, January 25, 1932, pp. 70-73, 052. 1/809,
BIC; approximately 1, 400 words.

It seems clear that this statement was inspired by the Central
Politburo resolution concerning the Hsiangosi Central Sub-bureau, dated November·25, 1931, described previously. The local party leader Teng Chung-hsia was singled out for attack on
charges of escape, retreat, pessimism, underestimation of
enemy strength, and so forth. It was resolved that the Central
Politburo be requested to remove him from all work and punish
him as a party member.

It will be recalled that Teng Chung-hsia was as old a member
of the party as the party itself. He joined Li Ta-chao's camp
at Peking in 1921 and ranked with Chang Kuo-t'ao, Lo Chang-
lung, and Ho Meng-hsiung as leading cadres. He was one of the
three persons who had to return to China from Moscow in the
fall of 1930 as a result of the factional struggle in the Sun Yat-
sen University at Moscow, the other two being Ch'ü Ch'iu-pai
and Yü Fei. Thus, he belonged to the camp of the old cadres
who were vying with the protégés of Pavel Mif in intraparty
politics.

*A Letter from the Central to the Hsiangosi Central Sub-bu-
reau and Provincial Committee* (中央給湘鄂西中央
分局與省委信 Chung-yang chi hsiang-o-hsi chung-yang

fen-chü yü sheng-wei hsin), dated December 14, 1931; mimeographed; 224.2/804, BIC; approximately 1,500 words.

   In reply to a letter of the Hsiangosi Soviet dated December 14,
1931, the Russian Returned Student leadership stated that some
achievements had been scored in the Hsiangosi area since the
establishment of the Central Sub-bureau but that the mistakes
committed were still numerous. It was revealed that rank-and-
file members and local party leaders attacked one another un-
scrupulously. Teng Chung-hsia was attacked as ever.

18

A Forward and Offensive Program

A Statement of the CCP Central Committee to Comrades on the Current Situation (中 國) 共 產 黨 中 央 委 員 會 為 日 前 時 局 告 同 志 書 Chung-kuo kung-ch'an-tang chung-yang wei-yüan-hui wei mu-ch'ien shih-chü kao t'ung-chih shu), dated December 11, 1931; printed in *Red Flag Weekly*, No. 27, December 17, 1931, 052.1/809, BIC; approximately 2,500 words.

Following the First National Soviet Congress of November, 1931, the CCP policy was growing tough. This statement antedated a number of CCP key statements which were characterized by the radicalism of the Russian Returned Student leadership. Examples of these key statements of the CCP were afforded by the statements of January 1 and 9, 1932, in which the fight against non-Communist groups and the winning of preliminary successes in one or more provinces were emphasized respectively.

Some of the basic ideas denounced by the Mao-sponsored "Resolution on Some Historical Problems" of 1945 can be found in this statement. For instance, this statement described the KMT as "disintegrating and shaky" and dismissed all non-Communist political groups as "the most dangerous thing in the revolution," while the Mao machine in 1945 charged the Russian Returned Student leadership with having exaggerated the disintegration of the ruling class and having sought to destroy all middle-of-the-road groups. In addition, when the struggle against the so-called Lo Ming line was waged in 1933-34, the basic ideas of that struggle could also be found in the present statement.

Statement of the CCP on the Current Situation (中 國 共 產 黨 對 於 時 局 的 主 張 Chung-kuo kung-ch'an-tang tui-yü shih-chü ti chu-chang), January 1, 1932; printed in a compendium of four documents entitled *A Fight for Leading the Masses in the Revolution and Establishing Their Soviet Regime,* published by the Central Bureau, Soviet Areas, CCP, April, 1932, 008.1010/8137, SSC, pp. 1-17; approximately 5,200 words.

Sounding like a New Year's message, this piece was as radical in tone as any other statements issued by the Russian Returned Student leadership of the time. It called upon the nation to rally around the standard of the CCP and its newly established Soviet regime in an effort to overthrow the rule of the KMT and imperialists in China. It stood for elimination of all non-Communist parties or groups in the country and urged the necessity of winning preliminary successes in one or more provinces.

CCP Central Resolution on Winning Preliminary Successes of the Revolution in One or More Provinces (中 共 中 央 關 於 爭 取 革 命 在 一 省 與 數 省 首 先 勝 利 的 決 議 Chung-kung chung-yang kuan-yü cheng-ch'ü ko-ming tsai i-sheng yü su-sheng shou-hsien sheng-li ti chüeh-i), January 9, 1932; printed in *True Words (Shih-hua),* No. 3, April 20, 1932, pp. 7-11; 008.2105/3002, SSC; approximately 7,200 words.

This document represented a milestone in the forward policy of the CCP. It signified the revival, to a lesser degree, of the Li Li-san policy of taking urban centers so as to achieve preliminary successes in one or more provinces.

In 1945 the Mao machine listed this document as one of the major statements representing the dangerous Left line of the Russian Returned Student leadership. (See "Resolution on Some Historical Problems," April 20, 1945, printed in Mao Tse-tung, *Selected Works,* Chinese version, Vol. 3, p. 968; English edition, Vol. 4, p. 185; reprint of the resolution, p. 18.) The Communist historian Ho Kan-chih explains that in advocating preliminary successes in one or more provinces, the party leadership wanted the broad masses of the entire nation to give support only to the Communist moves in Hunan, Hupeh, and Kiangsi but not to an over-all plan for the overthrow of the Nanking government. (See Ho Kan-chih, *History of the Contempo-*

rary Chinese Revolution, pp. 160, 161.) In contrast, Lo Fu
(Chang Wen-t'ien), a leading member of the Russian Returned
Student Faction, hailed this document on April 21, 1932, as a
sound policy, saying that only a Right opportunist would look
upon it as a manifestation of Li Li-sanite adventurism. (See Lo
Fu, "Victories in Attacks of the Chinese Workers' and Peas-
ants' Red Army," published in the *Red Flag Weekly,* No. 40,
May 15, 1930, relevant passages appearing on pp. 9-11.)

This document has three basic arguments regarding the situation in China, namely, (1) impending economic collapse, (2)
failure of the KMT Third Campaign, and (3) Japanese invasion
of Manchuria. All these arguments were drawn from an editorial of the Comintern organ *Communist International* of November 11, 1931, under the title of "The Revolutionary Crisis in
China and the Responsibility of a Member of the CCP" (reproduced in *True Words (Shih-hua),* No. 3, April 20, 1932, pp. 1-
7). Even the figures showing Red Army successes in Kiangsi as
contained in this document were taken from the Comintern editorial.

The present resolution saw a new situation in China favorable
to the development of the revolution. A policy switch put the
Chinese Communists again on the offensive. The idea of taking
key cities for the purpose of achieving preliminary successes in
one or more provinces was revived. Quite apart from Comintern postulations, the withdrawal of large numbers of Nationalist troops from the hinterland to deal with the Japanese attack
gave, in fact, the Communists a good chance to advance.

In the present resolution the Communist leadership talked
seriously of linking the various Soviet areas together by force.
This would be brought about in two units: one unit south of the
Yangtse River with Kiangsi as the center and the other to the
north of it.

The cities uppermost in the Communist mind, as revealed in
this document, were those situated along the Kan River in Kiangsi, such as Nanch'ang, Kian, and Fuchou (Linch'üan).

*The Danger of a Great Imperialist War and the Urgent Task
of the Party at Present* (帝國主義大戰的危機與黨
的目前緊急任務 Ti-kuo chu-i ta-chan ti wei-chi yü tang
ti mu-ch'ien chin-chi jen-wu), by Chou En-lai, February 9,
1932; printed in *True Words (Shih-hua),* No. 1, February 14,
1932, pp. 1-4, 008.2105/3002, SSC; approximately 6,500 words.

Based on the CCP Central resolution of January 9, this article was written against the background of the Japanese attack on Shanghai on January 28, 1932. The writer urged a national anti-Japanese movement and a swift Communist expansion through seizure of key cities with a view to achieving preliminary successes in one or more provinces.

Chou En-lai dismissed all neutralist groups as the most dangerous enemies and stressed the Right deviation as the main danger in the two-front struggle. He pointed out that there were feverish war preparations against the USSR on the part of the imperialists among whom contradictions had grown to great dimensions.

Chang Kuo-t'ao declared during an interview in Hongkong in late October, 1959, that Chou En-lai played a very important role within the Chinese Communist hierarchy in Kiangsi. This was largely due to his superior personal ability relative to other party leaders such as Ch'in Pang-hsien.

According to an ex-Communist source, the Japanese attack on Shanghai was followed by important policy decisions of the CCP. The party leadership in Kiangsi called an emergency meeting in which both political and military resolutions were adopted. Politically, the party should urge a national anti-Japanese campaign, thereby relieving KMT pressure on the Communists and facilitating the Communist expansion. Militarily, steps must be taken to occupy key cities among which Kanchow should first be taken in order to bring the separated Soviet areas on both sides of the Kan River together. During discussion of strategic and tactical questions relative to the taking of Kanchow in a subsequent military conference, this source added, Mao came to loggerheads with Chou En-lai, who had the support of the Russian Returned Student group. Mao stood persistently for mobile and guerrilla tactics, maneuvering the enemy into Communist areas only to beat him under favorable conditions. In contrast, Chou En-lai advocated positional warfare aimed at taking cities and carrying the fight to enemy territory. In the end, Chou's views prevailed. This marked a turning point in Communist strategy and tactics: the general trend thenceforth was toward positional warfare coupled with a mania for the taking of cities. (See Kung Ch'u, *The Red Army and I*, pp. 310-14.)

Struggle for the More Complete Bolshevization of the Chinese Communist Party (為中共更加布爾塞維克化而鬥爭

Wei chung-kung keng-chia pu-erh-se-wei-k'e-hua erh tou-
cheng), by Ch'en Shao-yü; first edition, Shanghai, February,
1931, under the title of "Two Lines"; second edition, Moscow,
March, 1932; third edition, Yenan, July, 1940, under the present title; 224.07/372, BIC; approximately 100,000 words.

The importance of this book in Chinese Communist annals can
be seen from the fact that the Mao machine in 1945 liquidated
it as the one document which the Fourth Plenum of January,
1931, approved as the general program of the Russian Returned
Student leadership. (See "Resolution on Some Historical Problems," April 20, 1945, printed in Mao Tse-tung, *Selected
Works*, Chinese edition, Vol. 3, p. 966; English edition, Vol.
4, p. 182; reprint of the resolution, p. 15.)

In making the above comment, the Mao machine was obviously
not free from confusion or distortion. The fact was that this
book was published in February, 1931, and that it was apparently
not approved by the Fourth Plenum, which had taken place one
month earlier. More important, the authority on which the
Fourth Plenum was based was the Comintern directive received
on November 16, 1930, but not the present book by Ch'en Shao-
yü, though this book as it first appeared in 1931 was based on
that directive as well as the Comintern letter of July 23, 1930.

Be that as it may, the importance of this book cannot be overestimated. But the importance lies in the part of the book called
postscript inserted in the second edition published in Moscow in
1932, but not the first edition published in Shanghai in 1931 as
the Mao machine would have us believe. The postscript contains
virtually all the major points which Mao and his group in the
1945 "Resolution on Some Historical Problems" severely attacked.

As it is, this book is divided into two parts plus forewords
and appendixes. The first part, dealing with the Li-san line and
the Third Plenum, was the text of the first edition published in
Shanghai in 1931. The second part, labeled postscript, was included when the second edition of the book was published in
Moscow in March, 1932. This second part contains descriptions
of the fight against Lo Chang-lung and the two-front struggle
over and above some fresh light thrown on the Li-san line.

Apart from repetitions of the general arguments of the Comintern directives of July 23 and November 16, 1930, the first
edition of this book raises an interesting theoretical question in
regard to the position of the capitalists and intermediate classes

in the revolution. The author criticized the Li Li-san leadership for having failed to grasp the counterrevolutionary character of the capitalists and bourgeois reformists, mistaking them for a "third group" or an "intermediate camp." He took the position that the present stage of the Chinese revolution was a struggle against imperialists, feudal remnants, and capitalists and that the revolution could not hope to succeed without a determined struggle against the imperialists (chapter 2, sections 2-3).

Should the Chinese Communists in the present stage combat capitalists apart from imperialists and feudal remnants? Mao and his group said no. In 1945 Mao's machine complained that all the Left lines in CCP history had failed to understand the necessity of cooperating with or neutralizing the various intermediate groups and that they had advocated unqualified opposition to the capitalists and even the upper echelon of the petty bourgeoisie. With reference to the third Left line led by the Ch'en Shao-yü group in particular, Mao's machine charged that this group had overstressed the weight of capitalism in China's economy and exaggerated the fight against capitalists in the present stage of the Chinese revolution. (See "Resolution on Some Historical Problems," contained in Mao Tse-tung, *Selected Works*, Chinese edition, Vol. 3, p. 965; English edition, Vol. 4, p. 181; reprint of the resolution, p. 13.) It was further charged that this group had placed the struggle against capitalists on an equal footing with the struggle against imperialists and feudalists and denied the existence of an intermediate camp or a third group. *(Ibid.*, Chinese edition, Vol. 3, p. 974; English edition, Vol. 4, p. 191; reprint of the resolution, p. 26.)

More than a year had elapsed before the second edition of this book appeared at Moscow in March, 1932. In this interval a great deal of change had taken place in the power relationships within the Chinese Communist hierarchy. Against the background of the new intraparty developments, Ch'en Shao-yü put forward positive standpoints of his own in the second edition of his publication as distinguished from mere criticisms in the first edition. The following points are particularly worthy of note:

1. Workers versus peasants. In dealing with the uneven development of the Chinese revolution (postscript, chapter 1, section A-3), Ch'en Shao-yü placed particular emphasis on the leading role of the proletariat. He denounced the theory then prevailing among certain comrades that the peasants in China had a greater revolutionary character than the workers or, in

other words, that the workers had lagged behind the peasants, and that the Soviet movement then in progress was purely a peasant revolutionary movement without the participation and leadership of the working class. He pointed out that there were individual comrades who had overlooked the strength of the Chinese working class and unduly overstressed the independent political role of the peasantry. These people, he emphasized, had sought to create "a theory of the unusual revolutionary character of the peasantry in colonial and semi-colonial countries," according to which the peasantry was assigned a top role in the revolutionary cause while the proletariat was reduced to the status of an assistant to the peasantry. In fact, he stated, these people had overlooked the basic fact that the peasants had no independent political thought and role of their own and that they must always be led by the working class in order to carry out a successful revolution.

In contrast, Mao had steadfastly insisted that the bourgeois-democratic revolution was essentially a peasant revolution. (See "Resolution on Some Historical Problems," April 20, 1945, contained in Mao Tse-tung, *Selected Works*, Chinese edition, Vol. 3, p. 973; English edition, Vol. 4, p. 190; reprint of the resolution, p. 25.) He had taken the position, as has been noted previously, that "The revolution in semi-colonial China will fail only if the peasant struggle does not have the leadership of the workers, but in no case will it be disadvantageous to the revolution itself if the development of the peasant struggle goes beyond the influence of the workers." (See "A Single Spark Can Start a Prairie Fire," by Mao Tse-tung, January 5, 1930.) All the Left lines in CCP history, Mao observed, had underestimated the decisive role of the peasantry in the Chinese revolution. In particular the third Left line, he pointed out, had made the mistake of objecting to the so-called "unusual revolutionary character of the peasantry." (See "Resolution on Some Historical Problems," April 20, 1945, contained in Mao Tse-tung, *Selected Works*, Chinese edition, Vol. 3, p. 974; English edition, Vol. 4, p. 192; reprint of the resolution, p. 26.)

2. Consequences of the Fourth Plenum line. The author struck a triumphant note when he recalled the sweeping transformation of party work in the Soviet areas following the Fourth Plenum: establishment of agencies of the Central, convocation of party conferences at all levels, reorganization of the party leadership at all levels, reform of the Red Army, re-election of the Soviet regimes, and so forth. He flattered himself that all these re-

forms had made it possible to beat back the KMT Fourth Campaign in the spring of 1933 (postscript, chapter 1, section A-4).

On the contrary, the Mao machine held a different view. It claimed that the erroneous policy of the party leadership after the Fourth Plenum had transformed the whole system of the party and of the Red Army in the Soviet areas. If it had not been for the far-reaching influence of Mao's strategic thinking on the Red Army, it was stated, it would have been impossible to repulse the KMT Fourth Campaign. (See "Resolution on Some Historical Problems," April 20, 1945, Mao Tse-tung, *Selected Works*, Chinese edition, Vol. 3, pp. 968-69; English edition, Vol. 4, pp. 185-86; reprint of the resolution, p. 19.)

3. The taking of big cities. In the first edition of this publication, Li Li-san's capture of Changsha was viewed as a turning point in the transformation of his policy from Right opportunism to Left putschism. Because of that event, he was criticized for having adopted a political line in opposition to Marxism-Leninism (chapter 2, section 4).

In the second edition, however, the author had changed his opinion. He had come to hail the historical significance of Changsha. From the mistakes made in Changsha, he stated, the conclusion must not be drawn that "key cities should not be taken anyway." Accordingly, he was of the opinion that the Red Army should be made strong enough to take key cities (postscript, chapter 1, section B-2).

In view of the foregoing, Mao's machine commented in 1945 that the Russian Returned Students, like Li Li-san, were still primarily interested in the big cities rather than in the rural districts. The principal difference lay, it was said, in the fact that while Li Li-san only called for the cooperation of the Red Army in the seizure of big cities, the Russian Returned Students wanted the Red Army to seize them directly. (See "Resolution on Some Historical Problems," April 20, 1945, Mao Tse-tung, *Selected Works*, Chinese edition, Vol. 3, p. 978; English edition, Vol. 4, pp. 195-96; reprint of the resolution, p. 31.)

4. The two-front struggle. In the last part of the postscript, the author dealt with the two-front struggle with particular reference to the Right deviation as the main danger. According to him, a section of people in certain Soviet areas had shown glaring signs of Right deviation: (1) misinterpreting the policy of consolidating the bases as a "retreat line" or "conservatism"; (2) misinterpreting the taking of cities under certain conditions to mean that cities must not be seized at any time; and (3) re-

sorting to "flight, " "escape" or "retreat" in the event of an enemy attack. As can be seen later, all these abusive appellations came to the fore when the struggle against the so-called Lo Ming line was waged at the expense of the Mao group in 1933-34.

Furthermore, the author exposed what he believed to be the subtle devices of the saboteurs of the two-front struggle. These saboteurs comprised: (1) compromisers, who pretended to have little or no interest in intraparty struggles, taking pride in standing aloof; (2) double-faced men, who nominally obeyed the decisions of the party leadership but actually sought to sabotage them; and (3) "smugglers, " who brought opportunism into the party clandestinely.

In contrast, Mao's machine commented in 1945 that though the third Left line led by Ch'en Shao-yü criticized the Left deviation of Li Li-san, its chief characteristic was its attack on the "Right" aspect of the Li-san line. (See "Resolution on Some Historical Problems, " contained in Mao Tse-tung, *Selected Works*, Chinese edition, Vol. 3, p. 964; English edition, Vol. 4, p. 181; reprint of the resolution, p. 13.) Ch'en Shao-yü and his group, it was charged, indiscriminately discredited all those who found the third Left line impracticable and doubted its wisdom or supported and executed it half-heartedly. They called them by all objectionable names such as "Right opportunism, " "the rich peasant line, " "the Lo Ming line, " "the compromising line, " "double-faced persons. " They attacked and fought them ruthlessly as they did criminals and enemies. *(Ibid.,* Chinese edition, Vol. 3, pp. 986-87; English edition, Vol. 4, p. 206; reprint of the resolution, p. 42.)

Uphold the Victory of the Red Army in the Nation, Execute the Positive and Offensive Line Resolutely (擁護全國紅軍的勝利，堅決執行積極進攻的路線 Yung-hu ch'üan-kuo hung-chün ti sheng-li, chien-chüeh chih-hsing chi-chi chin-kung ti lu-hsien), by Chou En-lai; printed in *True Words (Shih-hua),* No. 5, May 30, 1932, pp. 1-4, 008.2105/ 3002, SSC; approximately 5,700 words.

This article presents Chou En-lai's strategic thinking in unmistakable terms.

According to Kung Ch'u, a top-ranking ex-Communist eyewitness, the failure of the Communist attack on Kanchow in late February and early March, 1932, caused more friction between

Mao and Chou En-lai than ever before, while the plan to link the Soviet areas on both sides of the Kan River continued unabated. (See Kung Ch'u, *The Red Army and I*, pp. 318-22.)

Based on both the editorial of the *Communist International* of November 11, 1931, and the CCP Central resolution of January 9, 1932, this article charged that the Central Soviet area, unlike the Oyuwan and Hsiangosi Soviet areas, had committed opportunistic errors of procrastination and wait-and-see on account of a lack of understanding of what was called the positively forward and offensive line. No attempt had, it was charged, been made to take key cities after the party conference of November, 1931. Though things had improved since January, 1932, an underestimation of the political situation led nevertheless to dismal failure at Kanchow. It was pointed out that the time-honored strategy and tactics of maneuvering the enemy into Communist territory, though sound and effective during the first three KMT campaigns, was no longer valid in 1932, when the party's policy was directed toward expanding Soviet territory and knocking the enemy in non-Communist areas. The military defeat at Kanchow meant that the Kiangsi Soviet had failed in the taking of a key city, thus losing the chance of achieving preliminary successes in Kiangsi and its neighboring provinces.

Under the circumstances, Chou En-lai reaffirmed the so-called positively forward and offensive line in unmistakable terms. Specifically, this line would mean: expanding Soviet territory swiftly, engaging the enemy on KMT territory, bringing Kiangsi and its neighboring Soviet areas together with force, taking key cities in the Kan valley such as Nanch'ang, Fuchou (Linch'üan), Kian, Kanchow, and P'inghsiang, so as to achieve preliminary successes in one or more provinces.

Any departure from the foregoing was termed an error of Right opportunism, to which Chou En-lai objected.

It is noteworthy that about a year later Pavel Mif expressed his opinion on the strategy and tactics of the Chinese Red Army, which did not seem to harmonize with Chou En-lai's thinking. Mif said that the primary purpose of the Chinese Red Army was to preserve Communist territory, particularly the Central Soviet Area, and that, to that end, the Red Army must maintain its mobile character and avoid a clash with the main forces of the enemy. It was essential to maneuver a part of enemy forces into Communist areas and employ guerrilla tactics and revolutionary masses against them. Of course, he added, it was important to take urban centers, but considering the superior strength of the enemy, it was necessary to encircle rather than occupy them under the circumstances. (See *Struggle* [Kiangsi], probably Juichin, Organ of the Central Bureau of the Soviet Areas of the CCP, published by the Party Press Committee, Central Bureau, Soviet Areas, CCP, No. 23, August 22, 1933, pp. 13-17, in which appears the last part of the Chinese version of Mif's article entitled "A New Phase of the Revolutionary Crisis in China, " published in *Communist International,* April, 1933.)

Directive Telegram of the Central and Resolution of the Central Bureau regarding Winning and Achieving Preliminary Successes in Kiangsi and Its Neighboring Provinces (中央指示電與中央局關於爭取和完成江西及其鄰近省區革命首先勝利的決議 Chung-yang chih-shih tien yü chung-yang-chü kuan-yü cheng-ch'ü han wan-ch'eng chiang-hsi chi ch'i lin-chin sheng-ch'ü ko-ming shou-hsien sheng-li ti chüeh-i), dated May 21 and June 16, 1932, respectively; reprinted by the Political Department, Third Army Corps, Red Army, July 14, 1932, 008. 222/2012, SSC; mimeographed; directive approximately 1,000 words, resolution approximately 11,000 words.

As its title indicates, this item consists of two documents: a Central directive issued on May 21, 1932, and a Central Bureau resolution of June 16, 1932, accepting the directive. The directive is brief and, to make matters worse, its last part is missing. The resolution is quite a tirade in which the Central Bureau made an abject self-criticism in regard to the question of winning preliminary successes in one or more provinces.

On the basis of the directive, the Central Bureau reasoned that the antagonism of the two worlds, capitalist and communist, had led to a bifurcation of political power in China and that the political developments had been favorable to the cause of the revolution. Under such circumstances, the new responsibility of the CCP was to take a few key cities in order to achieve preliminary successes in one or more provinces.

However, the Central Bureau admitted that it had failed to fulfil its responsibility in spite of the achievements made. It had, for example, been guilty of Right opportunism and bad leadership.

The Central Bureau recalled that its errors dated from its

October, 1931, statement on the current situation, which was based on an underestimation of the political situation. Next came the November, 1931, party congress of the Central Soviet Area, which, despite its reorientation, could not rid itself of grievous errors of opportunism. Since January, 1932, the Central Bureau admitted, it had had a better understanding of the party policy of taking key cities and achieving initial successes in one or more provinces, but this understanding was still not adequate.

Accordingly, the Central Bureau called for the elimination of the errors of Right opportunism so as to make possible the taking of key cities and the winning of preliminary successes in one or more provinces. This was called the positively forward and offensive policy under which the several scattered Soviet areas surrounding Kiangsi should be brought together and the major cities along the Kan River such as Nanch'ang, Fuchou, Kian, Kanchow, and Kiukiang should be occupied.

In order to attain this objective the Central Bureau laid down a ten-point program for the party in the Central Soviet Area to follow. The major points were: (1) strengthening the leadership of the proletariat in the Soviets and in the Red Army, (2) solving the land problem by correcting the error of equal redistribution, (3) establishing a firm Soviet regime by reforming the leadership of lower echelons of the Soviet hierarchy, and so forth.

A Working Program for Party Development and Party Reform (發展黨和改造黨的工作大綱 Fa-chan tang han kai-tsao tang ti kung-tso ta-kang), adopted by the CCP Central Bureau, Soviet Areas, June 12, 1932; printed in *Reconstruction of the Party* (Kiangsi), No. 2, June 15, 1932, pp. 1-30, 008.2126/9021, SSC; approximately 11,300 words.

According to an official statement of the Mao machine in 1945, the central party leadership held a conference at Ningtu in southern Kiangsi in August, 1932, which, like the Party Congress of November, 1931, brought about a sweeping change in the leadership of both the party and the army at the expense of Mao. (See "Resolution on Some Historical Problems," April 20, 1945, Mao Tse-tung, *Selected Works*, Chinese edition, Vol. 3, p. 968; English edition, Vol. 4, p. 185; reprint, p. 19.) A non-Communist source says that after the Ningtu Conference,

Mao left his position in the army on the plea of illness to give
place to Chou En-lai, who soon took over control of the Red
Army. (See *A Collection of Red Bandit Reactionary Documents*,
Vol. 2, pp. 449-50.) In 1936, Mao told Edgar Snow that from
October, 1932, until the beginning of the Long March he devoted
his time almost exclusively to work with the Soviet government,
leaving the military command to Chu Teh and others. (See Edgar Snow, *Red Star over China*, p. 185.)

By piecing together bits of information outlined above, one
has good reason to believe that Mao probably lost his military
power as a result of the Ningtu Conference of August, 1932,
though his personal influence in the Red Army apparently continued. It is, indeed, impossible to exaggerate the importance
of the Ningtu Conference in Chinese Communist annals. But
unfortunately no documentations of the conference are available.

The present statement was an over-all party reform program
to be carried out in Kiangsi from July through September, 1932.
It was sponsored by the Russian Returned Student group. It applied not only to the party units of the whole civilian region but
also to those of the Red Army. There can be little doubt that the
Ningtu Conference was held under the influence of this general
party reform plan, though this plan was not intended for the
conference exclusively.

In a classic Communist way this party reform program complained of the inadequacies of the party congress of November,
1931. It was charged that the accomplishments of that conference were confined to the top level of the party and had never
reached the bottom. Accordingly, a thorough transformation in
the manner of work of the entire party in the Soviet areas was
called for. There should, for instance, be collective leadership
within the party and a general re-election from the bottom upward.

Significantly, it was pointed out that this party reform plan
was introduced in the context of a new aggressive program of
the party: carrying the revolutionary war outward in a positive
way and seizing key cities with a view to preliminary successes
in the province of Kiangsi—a program which the party conference
of November, 1931, was said to have neglected.

*Resolution of the Central on the Imperialist-KMT Fourth
"Campaign" and Our Tasks* (中央關於帝國主義國民
黨四次"圍剿"與我們的任務的決議 Chung-

yang kuan-yü ti-kuo chu-i kuo-min-tang szu-tz'u "wei-chiao"
yü wo-men ti jen-wu ti chüeh-i), adopted June 21, 1932;
printed in *Revolution and War*, No. 1, August 1, 1932,
008.105/4487-2, No. 1, leaves 1-10, SSC; approximately
9,500 words.

Drafted at the beginning of the KMT Fourth Campaign in
June, 1932, this tirade was a passionate comparison of the
relative strength of the two opposing sides, with the conclusion
that victory would belong to the Communists. This served as a
guide to the Communist course of action in the face of the KMT
Fourth Campaign.

The most important part of this document is the eighth and
last section, which contains a ten-point program for the party
in both Soviet and non-Soviet areas. Essentially this program
contained almost the same old points of view as the CCP statements issued since January, 1932. The most important items
intended for the Soviet areas were as follows:

1. To mobilize the masses and to bring home to them the
significance of the watchwords: "Lose no inch of Soviet territory
to the enemy," "Achieve preliminary successes in Hunan, Hupeh, and Kiangsi," and so forth.

2. To take positive, offensive steps to smash the main forces
of the enemy, and to create a situation for taking Nanch'ang and
encircling Wuhan. But these, it was added, should not be interpreted as military adventurism or desperationism.

3. To begin military maneuvers against cities, forts, and so
forth and carry out guerrilla warfare behind the lines of the
enemy.

*Letter from the Central to the Central Bureau, Soviet Areas,
and to Both the Fukien and Kiangsi Provincial Committees*
(中央給蘇區中央局及閩贛兩省委信 Chung-
yang chi su-ch'ü chung-yang-chü chi min kan liang sheng-wei
hsin), dated July 21, 1932; printed in *True Words (Shih-hua)*,
No. 8, September 20, 1932, pp. 1-9, 008.2105/3002, SSC; approximately 15,000 words.

A general directive for party work in Kiangsi and western
Fukien, shedding considerable light on CCP policies during
1932.

After paying a routine tribute to the achievements made in the

Central Soviet Area, the Central pointed out a number of major mistakes made in that area, which must be corrected in the light of the party line of the time. The mistakes were as follows:

1. There was no adequate understanding of the fact that the direct peril to the proletariat in the world was not the war among the imperialists, as the party leadership in the Central Soviet area had conceived, but their war against the Soviet Union.

2. There was no understanding that the imperialists were the direct organizers and commanders of the KMT campaigns.

3. There was no real understanding of the serious antagonism between the two different regimes in the nation, and at the same time there was an exaggeration of the internal conflict of the enemy. Accordingly, the seriousness of the enemy attack was overlooked, so much so that people were playing with what was, in effect, guerrilla warfare.

4. The leadership of the proletariat had been overlooked in the agrarian revolution, as well as in other respects, under the pretext that there was no proletariat in the Soviet areas at all or that the proletariat there lacked the revolutionary activism of the peasantry. Therefore, there was very little labor union work for more than half a year before the party congress of November, 1931.

In the circumstances, the Central assigned a number of what were called historic tasks to the party in the Central Soviet Area, all meant for the war then in progress. The historic tasks, being all Communist platitudes, were as follows:

1. To strengthen the Soviet regimes, both central and local; to enable them to become the real organizers and leaders of the revolution in the nation.

2. To expand and consolidate the Red Army.

3. To carry on revolutionary work in the KMT areas resolutely, a work in which the Central Soviet Area had lagged behind.

4. To improve work in mass organizations, notably in labor unions and poor peasant corps.

5. To step up self-criticism.

Resolution of the Central Bureau on the Red Army Expansion —a Review of the Red Army Expansion in July and August (中央局關於擴大紅軍的決議 —— 七八兩月擴

大红军的檢閱) Chung-yang-chü kuan-yü k'uo-ta hung-
chün ti chüeh-i-ch'i pa liang yüeh k'uo-ta hung-chün ti chien-
yüeh), adopted on September 7, 1932; printed in *True Words*
(Shih-hua), No. 8, September 20, 1932, pp. 9-12, 008.2105/
3002, SSC; approximately 5,000 words.

This document reveals that the Red Army expansion drive
was in full swing in May and again in the three months from
July to September, 1932, but that the record was far from satisfactory. In July and August only half the number of recruits
under the original plan was reported in Kiangsi, while not more
than one-thirteenth reported in Fukien. This was attributed to
the failure of the party to bring home to the population the significance of the forward policy of the time, which was described
as a manifestation of opportunism.

It was resolved that one-tenth of the party members in the key
districts in Kiangsi and western Fukien must be made to join
the army in September and October, so as to set an example for
the masses and strengthen the leadership of the party in the
army. This was to be done in conjunction with the party reform
work aimed at the elimination of Right opportunism.

*The First Anniversary of the Founding of the Soviet Central
Government and the Soviet Movement in China* (蘇維埃中央
政府成立一週年與中國蘇維埃運動 Su-wei-
ai chung-yang cheng-fu ch'eng-li i chou-nien yü chung-kuo su-
wei-ai yün-tung), by Po T'ai (Liang Po-t'ai), printed in *True
Words (Shih-hua)*, No. 9, October 25, 1932, pp. 9-11,
008.2105/3002, SSC; approximately 2,500 words.

Contains a brief ten-point record of the Central Soviet Government since its founding on November 7, 1931. Of particular
interest from the angle of power relations within the Communist
hierarchy is the revelation, in item 2, that a complete reshuffle
had been effected in the Soviet regimes ranging from the town-
ship to provincial levels, carrying with it a relentless elimination of corrupt bureaucrats and class heretical elements.

In a decree of the Central Soviet Government, dated September 20, 1932, a sweeping reorganization of the local Soviet regimes was ordered on charges of incompetence. It is noteworthy that this decree was issued in the name of Mao as chairman of the Central Soviet Government and countersigned by

two vice-chairmen. (See *Red China,* September 27, 1932.)

Incidentally, it may be recalled that twelve days before this statement was published, that is, on October 14, the Noulens, an Austrian couple identified as Comintern agents, were sentenced to life imprisonment by KMT authorities.

Resolution of the Central Bureau, Reviewing the Emergency Mobilization Work of Local Party Headquarters to Crush the Massive Attack of the Enemy (中央局關於粉碎敵人大舉進攻地方黨部緊急動員工作檢閱的決議 Chung-yang-chü kuan-yü fen-sui ti-jen ta-chü chin-kung ti-fang tang-pu chin-chi tung-yüan kung-tso chien-yüeh ti chüeh-i), adopted November 21, 1932; printed in *True Words (Shih-hua),* No. 10, November 30, 1932, pp. 4-7, 008.2105/3002, SSC; approximately 3,200 words.

In the face of the KMT Fourth Campaign, the Central Soviet Government issued an emergency mobilization order on October 13, 1932, calling upon all people in the Soviet areas to give everything they had and everything they were to the fight against the enemy. It was made clear that anything short of the requirement of the order, such as hesitation or escape, would be dealt with according to revolutionary discipline. This emergency mobilization order was published in *Red China* of October 16, 1932.

In the lapse of more than a month, the CCP Central Bureau of the Soviet Areas reviewed the progress of mobilization as set forth in reports sent in by local party units which took the lead in revolutionary activities. It was found that the record of mobilization was far from satisfactory. This was found in a number of things, the most important of which were these: in the first place, a complacent feeling of peace had prevailed in the heart of the Soviet region, while people in the peripheral areas had lived in fear, vacillation, and escapism. Second, the plan of recruiting one-tenth of CP and CY members for the army in September and October had not achieved the desired result, so this plan had been stopped. Third, work in the sphere of peasant and guerrilla forces had not been adequately done, resulting in serious mistakes of vacillation, fear, conservatism, procrastination, and pure defense.

The above phenomena were ascribed to an underestimation of the massive attack of the enemy, coupled with a number of opportunistic errors, including formalism, commandism, bureaucratism, peasant pacifism, and conservatism, and the so-called "solid-breastwork-and-empty-field" tactics which were reputedly a great favorite of Mao.

Under the circumstances, a four-point program was laid down to step up mobilization in the Central Soviet Area in keeping with the forward and offensive policy of the party. In the first place, the two-front struggle should be promoted with emphasis on the fight against Right opportunism, which had allegedly converted the positively forward and offensive line into a purely retreat and defensive line. Second, guerrilla warfare should be stepped up in KMT areas. Third, there should be a general political mobilization through coordination of the government and mass organizations, such as poor peasant corps and labor unions. Fourth, the manner of work in the mass mobilization should be changed in such a way that bureaucratism, commandism, and so forth would be removed.

Combat All Erroneous Ideas about the Massive Attack of the Enemy (反 對 對 於 敵 人 大 舉 進 攻 的 一 切 錯 誤 認 識 Fan-tui tui-yü ti-jen ta-chü chin-kung ti i-ch'ieh ts'o-wu jen-shih), editorial of *Red China*, No. 42, November 28, 1932, 008.1052/2125/V.2, SSC; approximately 1,550 words.

This editorial was essentially in agreement with the November 21 resolution of the Central Bureau, described previously. It was meant to combat all forces which stood in the way of war mobilization. The first thing attacked was the idea that mobilization was just a military measure, having nothing to do with other aspects of social life. The second misconception was that there was nothing to be feared until war was fought at one's door. In the peripheral areas, the situation was even worse. People simply thought of flight in a panic before the enemy. All these seem to have set the stage for what came to be known as the Lo Ming line in the year following.

Emergency Resolution of the Central Council of People's Commissars—concerning War Mobilization and Working Manner (中 央 人 民 委 員 會 緊 急 決 議 —— 關 於 戰 爭 動 員 和 工 作 方 式 Chung-yang jen-min wei-yüan-hui chin-chi chüeh-i—kuan-yü chan-cheng tung-yüan han kung-tso fang-shih), adopted November 29, 1932; printed in *Red China*,

No. 43, December 5, 1932, pp. 1-2, 008.1052/2125/V.2, SSC; approximately 2,700 words.

In reviewing the execution of the emergency mobilization order of October 13, 1932, the Central Council of People's Commissars, which was actually the cabinet with Mao as chairman, found that the record was far from satisfactory. This was ascribed to the following political misconceptions:

1. The seriousness of the massive attack of the enemy had generally been overlooked, and therefore a general complacency and pacifism had prevailed among the masses.

2. In the peripheral districts the hard reality of enemy harassment had seized the people with a panic which had, in turn, led to despair and defeatism.

3. The forward and offensive policy had been misunderstood as though it were the business of the Red Army alone, so the civilians were there to wait and see.

In addition, the cabinet complained of the lack of a mass line and listed the necessary steps to make up this gap.

It is noteworthy that the three political misconceptions mentioned above, stressed in large characters, were the very things that were the target of attack during the subsequent denunciation of the Lo Ming line in 1933.

Resolution of the CCP Central concerning the Imperialist-KMT Fifth "Campaign" and the Task of Our Party (中 共 中 央 關 於 帝 國 主 義 國 民 黨 五 次 "圍 剿" 與 我 們 黨 的 任 務 的 決 議 *Chung-kung chung-yang kuan-yü ti-kuo chu-i kuo-min-tang wu-tz'u "wei-chiao" yü wo-men tang ti jen-wu ti chüeh-i*), adopted July 24, 1933; printed in *Struggle* (Kiangsi), No. 21, August 12, 1933, pp. 1-7, 008.2105/7720/V.2, SSC; approximately 6,400 words.

This document represented the basic, vigorous policy of the CCP with respect to the KMT Fifth Campaign then in preparation. It should be read in conjunction with two other papers: one is a lengthy statement made by Po Ku, which will be discussed in the next entry, while the other is a diagram of the present document prepared early in September, 1933, for the cadets of the Red Army Academy, which is available in SSC under the call number 008.222/5059.

In retrospect, Mao's machine in 1945 ascribed the Commu-

nist defeat in the KMT Fifth Campaign to the erroneous strategic policy of the then party leadership, which found expression
in watchwords like these: "A decisive war between two routes
for China, " "Abandon no inch of territory of the bases. " (See
"Resolution on Some Historical Problems, " April 20, 1945,
printed in Mao Tse-tung, *Selected Works,* Chinese edition,
Vol. 3, p. 978; English edition, Vol. 4, p. 196; reprint of the
resolution, pp. 31-32; see Hu Hua, *History of the Chinese
Revolution of New Democracy,* first draft, revised edition,
Peking, 1952, pp. 144-45.) Indeed, the present document contains the very strategic thinking that was the target of attack
by the Mao group after they had achieved control of the party.

This document begins by citing the resolution of the Comintern's Twelfth Plenum, held in Moscow during September,
1932, to confirm the intensification of the revolutionary situation in China, which was evident from three things: the mounting struggle with imperialism, the collapse of the national
economy, and the failure of the KMT Fourth Campaign. In reviewing the KMT Fourth Campaign, this document gives a balance sheet on the Communist side, asserting that the assets
that had contributed to the Communist victory were the product
of the correct leadership of the party. Of particular interest
for our present purposes is perhaps the idea of the struggle between the two different routes with which China was allegedly
confronted. The one was the colonial route under the sway of
imperialism, while the other was a Soviet China which enjoyed
independence, freedom, and territorial integrity. The Communist struggle against the impending KMT Fifth Campaign aimed,
it was pointed out, at the attainment of the latter objective. But
this was no easy task, it was warned; it would require the entire party to fulfil what was called its urgent task—a task which
would make it necessary to wage a struggle against Right and
Left deviations including the Lo Ming line and to carry out the
directives of the Comintern and the CCP Central faithfully.

*Struggle for Smashing the Enemy's Fifth "Campaign" and
for Winning an Independent, Free Soviet China* (為 粉碎敵
人 的 五 次 「圍剿」 與 爭取 獨立 自由的 蘇維埃
中國 而 鬥爭 Wei fen-sui ti-jen ti wu-tz'u "wei-chiao" yü
cheng-ch'ü tu-li tzu-yu ti su-wei-ai chung-kuo erh tou-cheng),
a speech delivered by Po Ku (Ch'in Pang-hsien) before a meeting of the party's active elements of the Central level on July

24, 1933; printed in *Red China,* No. 99, August 4, 1933, pp. 1-
6, 008. 1052/2125/V. 4, SSC; approximately 15, 000 words.

As described previously, this tirade was an explanatory
statement on the CCP Central resolution adopted on the same
day in connection with the KMT Fifth Campaign. Recommended
by the editor of *Red China* as a most important document, it
represented the vigorous position of the party chief on the impending KMT offensive, calling upon the comrades to do what
they could to contribute to the aggressive program of the party.

Being explanatory in character, this statement naturally repeats the essentials of the CCP Central resolution in question.
However, this is a much more detailed statement and contains
particulars which throw more light on the power relations
within the Chinese Communist hierarchy than does the CCP
Central resolution. Thus:

1. This statement takes a clearer and more definite stand on
China's struggle between the so-called two opposing routes,
imperialist and colonial or Soviet and independent.

2. In discussing the intensification of the revolutionary situation in China, this statement stressed what was known as the
direct revolutionary situation—a term which applied to the Li
Li-san type of adventurism.

3. The success in repulsing the KMT Fourth Campaign was
attributed to the correct leadership of the party, which consisted of the relentless fight against Right opportunism and the
Lo Ming line.

4. Communist weaknesses as manifested in the KMT Fourth
Campaign were believed to be more political than military in
character. They consisted primarily in inadequacy in exposing
the reformist groups and overcoming opportunist tendencies.
By contrast, the position of the Mao machine as set forth in the
1945 "Resolution on Some Historical Problems" was the other
way around.

*Urgent Tasks of the Red Army of the Central Area in
Smashing the Fifth "Campaign" of the Enemy* (粉 碎 敵 人
五 次 "圍 剿" 中 央 區 紅 軍 的 緊 急 任務   Fen-sui
ti-jen wu-tz'u "wei-chiao" chung-yang-ch'ü hung-chün ti chin-
chi jen-wu), by Chou En-lai; printed in *Red Star Journal*, No.
4, August 27, 1933, p. 1, 008. 1052/2160, SSC; also in *Struggle*

(Kiangsi), No. 24, August 29, 1933, pp. 1-4, 008. 2105/7720/
V. 2, Nos. 16-25, SSC; approximately 2, 800 words.

In this statement Chou En-lai reaffirmed the importance of
the CCP Central resolution on the KMT Fifth Campaign adopted
on July 24, 1933, described previously. It is understandable
that his points of view were along the general lines of that resolution.

This statement was the fifth part of a speech delivered by
Chou En-lai before a meeting of political cadres of the Red
Army. On the basis of the CCP Central resolution, he assigned
six tasks to political workers: (1) continuing the expansion of
the Red Army, (2) strengthening political training and military
technique, (3) coordinating regular and guerrilla warfare, (4)
following the general strategy of the army, (5) helping the
masses in the land investigation drive then in progress, and (6)
stepping up the mass movement in the KMT areas.

In conclusion, Chou En-lai emphasized the importance of
eliminating all deviatory tendencies that went beyond the scope
of the leadership of the CCP. He called upon all comrades and
Red Army activists to carry on a ruthless struggle against all
sorts of opportunism such as vacillation, pessimism, passiv-
ity, despair, and weariness of work.

As can be seen from the two preceding entries, the basic
spirit of this statement was opposed to the Mao-sponsored
"Resolution on Some Historical Problems" of 1945.

It should be noted that this was the first available statement
made by Chou En-lai after he had become political commissar
of the Red Army on May 8, 1933. By a government decision that
day Chou was appointed political commissar of the Red Army
and concurrently of the First Front Army, while Chu Teh continued to be commander-in-chief of both. (See *Red China*, No.
78, May 11, 1933, p. 1.) It will be recalled that the First Front
Army grew out of the Fourth Army of the Chingkangshan period,
with Chu Teh as commander and Mao as political commissar.
This First Front Army constituted almost the entire body of the
Red Army in the Kiangsi-Fukien area, the rest of the Red Army
being scattered in other provinces. (See Miao Ch'u-huang, *A
Short History of the Chinese Communist Party* [first draft], Peking, 1956, p. 80.) By becoming political commissar, Chou En-
lai gained control of the Red Army in general and the First
Front Army in particular. As has been noted previously, Mao
had probably lost his military power after the Ningtu Conference

of August, 1932. No matter what had become of him immediately after the conference, his hold on the Red Army was now
definitely taken over by Chou En-lai as a result of the government decision made on May 8, 1933. (For powers and functions
of a political commissar in the Red Army, see Kung Ch'u, *The
Red Army and I*, pp. 273-75.)

Incidentally, it may be recalled that during the later period of
the Kiangsi regime a German Communist worked with the Chinese Communists under the assumed name of Li T'e. According to Kung Ch'u, this German was one of three military agents
sent by the Comintern to Kiangsi, the other two having failed to
reach the destination owing to KMT interception en route. Kung
Ch'u said that this German actually pulled wires behind the
scenes in Kiangsi. (See Kung Ch'u, *The Red Army and I*, pp.
400-3; see Robert North, *Moscow and Chinese Communists*, p.
164.) According to Chang Kuo-t'ao during an interview in Hongkong in late October, 1959, however, Li T'e did not have much
power under the Kiangsi Soviet.

*Smashing the (KMT) Fifth "Campaign" and the Task of Soviet
Economic Reconstruction* (粉碎五次 "圍" "剿" 與 蘇維
埃經濟建設任務 Fen-sui wu-tz'u "wei-chiao" yü su-
wei-ai ching-chi chien-she jen-wu), a speech delivered by Mao
Tse-tung on August 12, 1933, before the Seventeen-County Economic Reconstruction Conference in southern Kiangsi; printed
in *Red China*, No. 102, August 16, 1933, pp. 2-4, 008.1052/
2125/V.4, SSC; approximately 7,500 words.

In the middle of August, 1933, two economic reconstruction
conferences were held in the Central Soviet Area, one held in
Juichin with an attendance of seventeen counties' delegates in
the south and another in Posheng attended by eleven counties'
delegates in the north. (For information regarding the conference in the south, see *Red China*, August 19, 1933.) These conferences, like the land investigation drive then in progress,
were "a gigantic class struggle," designed to apply mass activism to the economic front (quotation taken from proceedings of
the forty-fifth session of the cabinet known as Council of People's Commissars, section 2, published in *Red China*, July 23,
1933, p. 1).

The present statement was an opening speech of Mao before
the Juichin conference, dealing primarily with the importance

of economic reconstruction under the KMT blockade. Occasionally, it touched upon the power relations within the Chinese Communist hierarchy of that time. Mao attributed the Communist success in repulsing the KMT Fourth Campaign to three major factors: (1) gallantry of the army, (2) activism of the masses, (3) the correct line of the party leadership. As a corollary, he reckoned on the same factors of success for the CCP in the impending KMT Fifth Campaign, namely, (1) the Red Army, (2) the masses, (3) implementation of the CCP forward and offensive line.

Obviously, Mao's position as outlined in this statement harmonized with his stand in his article "A New Situation and A New Task," published in *Red China* for July 29, 1933, but not with the CCP "Resolution on Some Historical Problems," adopted on April 20, 1945, under Mao's sponsorship. For a discussion of this question, see the entry "A New Situation and A New Task" in the section on the fight against the Lo Ming line.

The significance of this statement cannot be fully understood if one overlooks the fact that KMT troops employed blockhouse tactics and an economic blockade against the Communists during the Fifth Campaign. Blockhouses were built in such a fashion that they formed an encirclement of the Communist areas and the encirclement gradually narrowed until the Communists were so hard pressed that they had to evacuate Kiangsi at last.

Intimately connected with the blockhouse tactics was the economic blockade. There was a terrible scarcity of salt, kerosene, cloth, and other supplies in Kiangsi. With the progress of the fighting, the scarcity of such supplies became increasingly acute, so much so that no salt was available toward the end of the campaign. To counteract this economic pressure the Communists had to redouble their efforts to increase production. That was why the two economic conferences in question were held and Mao emphasized the importance of economic reconstruction in the present speech.

19

The United Front from Below

The International Situation and the Tasks of the Various Comintern Branches—Resolution of the Comintern Twelfth Plenum on the Report of Comrade Kuusinen (國) 際 情 勢 和 共 産 國) 際 各 支 部 的 任 務 —— 國) 際 第 十 二 次 全 會 關 於 庫 西 寧 同 志 報 告 的 決 議 Kuo-chi ch'ing-shih han kung-ch'an kuo-chi ko chih-pu ti jen-wu-kuo-chi ti-shih-erh-tz'u ch'üan-hui kuan-yü kuu-si-nen t'ung-chih pao-kao ti chüeh-i), adopted in September, 1932; Chinese version appearing in *Struggle* (Shanghai), No. 31, December 5, 1932, pp. 2-8, 052.1/809, BIC, and in *Red Flag Weekly*, No. 53, December 10, 1932, pp. 2-21, 052.1/809, BIC; approximately 9,200 words.

This ECCI resolution proceeded on the assumption that the relative stability of capitalism was coming to an end and that the world was moving toward a transitional period leading to another war and revolution. It was pointed out that the Far East would be the main theater of the impending war and that a revolutionary situation existed in China, where the Soviet movement had been crowned with success in a large area.

The Comintern reached the conclusion above after a reappraisal of the international situation which had developed during the sixteen months following the Eleventh ECCI Plenum held in April, 1931.

In assigning different tasks to the Communist parties in different countries, the Kremlin entrusted the CCP with a six-point program as follows:

1. To mobilize the masses under the slogan of striving for

China's independence and unity in the national revolutionary struggle against the Japanese and other imperialists.

2. To develop and unite the Soviet areas and strengthen the Red Army.

3. To overthrow the KMT regime.

4. To turn Red labor unions into mass organizations and win over the workers in KMT labor unions.

5. To spread guerrilla activities and to organize peasant committees in Manchuria.

6. To give publicity both to the successes in the Soviet areas and to the slogan of an alliance of the Chinese and Russian workers and peasants.

The present statement reaffirmed a number of Comintern-made policies for the CCP: the united front from below, the fight against reformism, rightism, and so forth. It should be remembered that not until after this ECCI resolution did the CCP policy of a united front from below transcend the scope of ordinary mass movements to become a powerful political movement for winning over the armed forces of the nation to the side of the Communist cause, as manifested in the CCP declaration of January 17, 1933. (Cf. Robert North, *Moscow and Chinese Communists*, pp. 160-61.)

For a better understanding of this document, two other pieces should be read, namely, (1) editorial of *Pravda* October 2, 1932, entitled "The Conclusion of the ECCI Twelfth Plenum," reproduced in the *Red Flag Weekly* of January 31, 1933, pp. 21-26, and (2) a circular concerning the ECCI Twelfth Plenum, issued by the ECCI Political Secretariat, reproduced in *Struggle* (Shanghai), Organ of the CCP, December 5, 1932, p. 1, and in the *Red Flag Weekly* of December 10, 1932, pp. 1-2.

The importance of this statement can be seen from the fact that it provided the ideological background of the fight against the Lo Ming line in 1933-34 and of the Fifth Plenum of the CCP Central Committee held in January, 1934.

Declaration of the Chinese Soviet Provisional Central Government and the Revolutionary Military Council of the Workers' and Peasants' Red Army (中華蘇維埃臨時中央政府工農紅軍革命軍事委員會宣言 Chung-hua su-wei-ai lin-shih chung-yang cheng-fu kung-nung hung-chün ko-ming chün-shih wei-yüan-hui hsüan-yen), dated January 17, 1933;

printed in *Red China,* No. 48, January 28, 1933, p. 1, 008.1052/
2125/V. 2, SSC; approximately 900 words.

This appeal was directed to the mass of the Chinese people
including the soldiers. What the Communists openly sought was
an armistice with armed forces.

The actual target of attack under the terms of this statement
was the KMT rather than the Japanese. The Communists made
it abundantly clear that they wanted to fuse the anti-imperialist
and anti-KMT struggles into one revolutionary war.

Mao Tse-tung, Hsiang Ying, Chang Kuo-t'ao, and Chu Teh
jointly signed this appeal and put forward three conditions for
armistice as follows:

1. Immediate cessation of the offensive against the Soviet
areas.

2. Immediate guarantee of popular democratic rights (freedoms of assembly, association, speech, strike, publication,
and so forth).

3. Immediate arming of the mass of people and formation of
armed volunteer troops for the defense of China and for the
fight for her independence, unity, and territorial integrity.

On the basis of the three conditions listed above, the Chinese
Communists entered into a military alliance with KMT rebels
in Fukien late in 1933. The military alliance with the Fukien
rebels represented the apogee of the united front from below
under the Kiangsi Soviet. As this question constitutes the subject of discussion in a later separate section, it is not necessary to enlarge on it here.

In 1945 Mao's machine endorsed the present statement. (See
"Resolution on Some Historical Problems, " printed in Mao
Tse-tung, *Selected Works,* Chinese edition, Vol. 3, p. 975;
English edition, Vol. 4, p. 192; reprint of the resolution, p.
27.)

An English version of this statement appears in *International
Press Correspondence* for January 26, 1933, pp. 91-92, which
is extensively quoted in Robert North, *Moscow and Chinese
Communists,* p. 161. There are some discrepancies between
the Chinese and English texts.

*Declaration of the Provisional Central Government of the
Chinese Soviet Republic and the Revolutionary Military Council
of the Workers' and Peasants' Red Army* (中華蘇維埃共

和國臨時中央政府與工農紅軍革命軍事委員會的宣言 Chung-hua su-wei-ai kung-ho-kuo lin-shih chung-yang cheng-fu yü kung-nung hung-chün ko-ming chün-shih wei-yüan-hui ti hsüan-yen), dated April 15, 1933; printed in *Struggle* (Shanghai), No. 40, April 21, 1933, pp. 6-7, 052.1/809, BIC; mimeographed; approximately 1,900 words.

This statement reaffirmed the three conditions for a cessation of civil war as contained in the January 17, 1933, declaration. The three conditions remained unchanged with two exceptions:

First, the freedom of strike had been changed to that of dem-onstration among the specified democratic rights.

Second, the release of political prisoners had been added to the list of the specified democratic rights.

A Statement of the CCP Central Committee to the People of the Whole Country on the Japanese Imperialists' Invasion of North China and Their Threat of Conquest of the Entire Nation (中國共產黨中央委員會為日本帝國主義強佔華北併吞中國告全國民眾書 Chung-kuo kung-ch'an-tang chung-yang wei-yüan-hui wei jih-pen ti-kuo chu-i ch'iang-chan hua-pei ping-t'un chung-kuo kao ch'üan-kuo min-chung shu), dated April 10, 1934; printed in *Struggle* (Kiangsi), No. 59, May 15, 1934, pp. 1-6, 008.2105/7720/V.5, SSC; ap-proximately 4,200 words.

This statement says: "All Chinese who are really willing to combat imperialism and not content to see their country go to pieces must unite in an anti-imperialist united front, irrespec-tive of political inclination, occupation, or sex, to fight Japan and other imperialists."

Thus, it looks as though this statement did not exclude the KMT from the proposed united front. But, at the same time, this statement still raises the slogan of overthrowing the KMT. Accordingly, the united front program of the CCP at this time was still a united front from below.

Then a seven-point program was put forward as follows:

1. Opposing the KMT policy of surrender and betrayal; aban-doning all illusions about the League of Nations and the United States.

2. Defending the independence and territorial integrity of China.

3. Calling upon the people to join the anti-Japanese war and guerrilla operations.

4. Confiscating properties of the Japanese and traitors.

5. Removing all influence of the Japanese and other imperialists.

6. Immediate cessation of hostilities against the Soviet areas as well as among the warlords.

7. Opposing the Sino-Japanese Tangku truce of May, 1933, and all direct negotiation with Japan.

Some sources give the above seven points as five and the date of this statement as the fifteenth or twentieth of April, 1934. Fortunately there is little difference in substance. (See *Struggle* [Kiangsi], No. 65, June 23, 1934, p. 7, and No. 69, August 10, 1934, p. 18.)

It is significant to note that this piece paved the way for two subsequent statements in favor of a united front in Kiangsi: (1) the fundamental anti-Japanese war program of the Chinese people, signed by Madame Sun Yat-sen and others, May 3, 1934; and (2) declaration on the march of the Chinese Workers' and Peasants' Red Army to the north to resist Japan, July 15, 1934.

In commenting on CCP policy after the Japanese invasion of Manchuria, as has already been noted, the Communist historian Ho Kan-chih declares that a national defense government and anti-Japanese united army should have been formed to meet the situation created by the Japanese attack but that the party leadership of the time rejected such an approach. (See Ho Kan-chih, *History of the Contemporary Chinese Revolution*, pp. 159-61.)

Actually, it was not until August 1, 1935, when Mao had already achieved control of the party leadership, that the CCP formally proposed the formation of a national defense government and an anti-Japanese united army. (See "Resolution on Some Historical Problems," printed in Mao Tse-tung, *Selected Works*, Chinese edition, Vol. 3, p. 975; English edition, Vol. 4, p. 193; reprint of the resolution, p. 27; cf. Robert North, *Moscow and Chinese Communists*, pp. 176-77; Conrad Brandt, Benjamin Schwartz, and John Fairbank, *A Documentary History of Chinese Communism*, pp. 240, 488-89.) Ho Kan-chih's thesis that the idea of an interparty united front had already been brewing in Kiangsi is baseless.

Fundamental Anti-Japanese War Program of the Chinese People (中國人民對日作戰的基本綱領) Chung-

kuo jen-min tui-jih tso-chan ti chi-pen kang-ling), issued on
May 3, 1934; printed in *Red China*, No. 236, September 21,
1934, pp. 1-2, 008. 1052/2125/V. 8, SSC; approximately 3, 100
words.

Though issued under a different name to appeal to the people,
this statement was actually a near reproduction of the CCP
statement of April 10, 1934 on Japanese aggression. It was professedly signed by a total of 1, 779 persons, with the name of
Madame Sun Yat-sen at the head of the list. It was issued under
the name of a preparatory board of the committee on armed
self-defense of the Chinese nation.

Proceeding on the assumption that it was impossible to pin
any hope on the KMT to resist Japan and look to the League of
Nations and the United States for help, the only alternative was
for all the Chinese people to rise in arms for self-defense. To
that end, a six-point program for common action was formulated as follows:

1. A general mobilization of all land, sea, and air forces for
war against Japan.

2. A general mobilization of all the people.

3. Arming all the people.

4. Confiscating properties of Japanese nationals in China and
Chinese traitors to meet the expenses of war.

5. Setting up a committee on armed self-defense of the Chinese nation to be elected by representatives of workers, peasants, soldiers, students, and businessmen.

6. Cooperating with all enemies of Japan.

Twelve years later, Mao's machine listed this statement as
one of the sound policy pronouncements of the CCP in the early
thirties. (See "Resolution on Some Historical Problems, "
April 20, 1945, printed in Mao Tse-tung, *Selected Works*, Chinese edition, Vol. 3, p. 975, p. 1001, note 17, cf. Vol. 1, p.
159, note 15; English edition, Vol. 4, pp. 192-93, p. 342, note
18, cf. Vol. 1, p. 314, note 16; reprint of the resolution, p.
27, p. 63, note 19.)

*Manifesto on the Anti-Japanese War by the Committee on
Armed Self-Defense of the Chinese Nation* (中國民族武裝
自衛委員會為對日作戰宣言 Chung-kuo min-tsu
wu-chuang tzu-wei wei-yüan-hui wei tui-jih tso-chan hsüan-
yen), issued June 20, 1934; printed in *Red China*, No. 236,

September 21, 1934, pp. 2-3, 008.1052/2125/V.8, SSC; approximately 5,000 words.

The object of this statement was to publicize the fundamental anti-Japanese program of May 3, 1934, described previously. The main points of view are identical; only the structure of the language in the document is different.

20

The Fight against the Lo Ming Line

The Urgent Task of the Party in a Decisive Fight against the Enemy's Fourth "Campaign" (關) 於 在 粉 碎 敵 人 四 次 "圍 剿" 的 決 戰 前 面 量 的 緊 急 任 務 **Kuan-yü tsai fen-sui ti-jen szu-tz'u "wei-chiao" ti chüeh-chan ch'ien-mien tang ti chin-chi jen-wu),** by the Central Bureau, CCP, Feburary 8, 1933; printed in *Struggle* (Kiangsi), No. 2, February 4, 1933, pp. 1-3, 008.2105/7720/V.1, SSC; approximately 2,100 words.

In the first days of February, 1933, the Communists in Kiangsi were beginning to bear the brunt of the attack of the Fourth Campaign of government troops. As that was a life-or-death struggle for the Communists, it was but natural that they would throw everything behind the fighting and would not tolerate any letdown.

Meanwhile, the Twelfth Plenum of the ECCI, held in Moscow during September, 1932, called upon the Communists in the various countries to step up their revolutionary struggle at a time when a new stage favorable to the revolution was supposedly in sight. This Comintern position plus the KMT Fourth Campaign provided the background against which the present statement of the CCP was drafted. (See Po Ku, "Support the Bolshevik Forward and Offensive Line of the Party," February 16, 1933, printed in *Struggle* [Kiangsi], No. 3, February 23, 1933, pp. 4-10; reproduced in *A Collection of Red Bandit Documents,* Vol. 7, pp. 225-46.)

Evidence of Comintern influence on the present statement is further provided by an ex-Communist source which says that

the Communists in Kiangsi were seriously expanding the Red
Army on a large scale in February, 1933, under Comintern instructions. (See Kung Ch'u, *The Red Army and I,* pp. 359-60.)
This Communist move in the Red Army expansion coincides
with the first item of the program contained in the present
statement.

The present statement contains eight points which may be
summed up as follows:

1. To increase the strength of the Red Army to a million men.

2. To call upon workers and peasants to be up in arms by
joining the Red Guards, the Youth Vanguards. . . .

3. To call upon the Independent Divisions and Regiments
(i.e., local peasant armed organizations, *ibid.,* pp. 369-70) as
well as guerrilla forces to carry on a vigorous mobile defensive
fight in the peripheral region in southern Kiangsi and western
Fukien.

4. To lead the nation against the Japanese and other imperialists.

5. To mobilize all economic resources for the sake of war.

6. To complete the spring farming work earlier than usual
and thus increase the production of land.

7. To expand and strengthen the Soviet areas by all means.

8. To improve transportation for the convenience of the fighting.

In conclusion, it was stressed that Right opportunism in the
form of retreat or escape in a panic before the enemy was for-
bidden and that any wavering defensive line as opposed to the
party's offensive line was to be condemned.

*Decision of the Central Bureau on the Minyüehkan (Fukien-
Kwangtung-Kiangsi) Provincial Committee* (中 央 局 關) 於
閩 粵 贛 省 委 的 決 定 Chung-yang-chü kuan-yü min-
yüeh-kan sheng-wei ti chüeh-ting), February 15, 1933; printed
in *Struggle* (Kiangsi), No. 3, February 23, 1933, pp. 1-2;
008.2105/7720/V.1, SSC; approximately 800 words.

The object of this document was to launch a party-wide drive
in support of the Central Bureau statement of February 8, 1933,
described previously. This marked the beginning of the struggle
against what was known as the Lo Ming line. As a result, Mao's
followers were hard hit.

It was pointed out that a grave crisis had developed within

the Fukien Provincial Committee since Lo Ming, acting secretary of the committee, had formed an opportunistic line with a
small number of comrades rallying around him, filled with pessimism and despair, inclined toward retreat and escape, isolated from the masses, and addicted openly to liquidationism.
Though there were isolated cases of resistance to Lo Ming
within the Provincial Committee, it had not assumed the pro-
portions of a widespread campaign, and consequently opportunism was still a stumbling block to party work.

In consequence, a seven-point program was adopted with particular reference to the following:

1. A drive should immediately be launched within the party to
fight the opportunistic line represented by Lo Ming.

2. The Fukien Provincial Committee should be condemned for
its attitude of corrupt liberalism toward the Lo Ming line—an attitude according to which no attempt was made to take a determined stand against the line.

3. With the removal of Lo Ming, a new provincial committee
was established to take over the party in Fukien.

In retrospect, the Mao machine recorded in 1945 that Lo
Ming was attacked because he considered that party work in the
peripheral region in western Fukien should be different from
that in the heart of the Soviet base in southern Kiangsi in view of
the difficult situation in Fukien. The Left deviationists wrongly
exaggerated his position to be an escape-and-retreat line characterized by pessimism, opportunism, and liquidationism.
Thereupon, a party-wide drive against the so-called Lo Ming line
was set in motion. (See "Resolution on Some Historical Problems," April 20, 1945, note 33, contained in Mao Tse-tung, *Selected Works*, Chinese edition, Vol. 3, pp. 1001-2; reprint of
the resolution, note 35, p. 64.) It was emphasized that the Left
party leadership of the time failed to draw a line between the
heart of the base and the peripheral region *(ibid.,* Chinese edition, Vol. 3, p. 982; English edition, Vol. 4, p. 201; reprint of
the resolution, p. 36), and that it took advantage of the Lo Ming
line as well as all other lines to eliminate dissenters in ruthless
"intraparty struggles" *(ibid.,* Chinese edition, Vol. 3, pp. 986-
87; English edition, Vol. 4, p. 206; reprint of the resolution,
pp. 42-43.)

According to a hostile source, the question of the Lo Ming
line emerged from a controversy over the military strategy between Mao and Chou En-lai. Mao stood for mobile and guerrilla
tactics, maneuvering the enemy into Communist areas only to

beat him under favorable circumstances. On the contrary, Chou
favored engaging the enemy on enemy soil. Ch'in Pang-hsien
and his group supported Chou and referred the case to the Comintern delegation in Shanghai. At last, the Comintern delegate
(sic) decided in favor of Chou. Stationed in western Fukien, Lo
Ming knew nothing about the case. In the face of the overwhelming KMT offensive there, he went in for the traditional Communist guerrilla tactics. Contrary to his expectation, that provided Ch'in Pang-hsien and company with a pretext for eliminating Mao's men in southern Kiangsi and western Fukien under the
name of the Lo Ming line. (See *A Collection of Red Bandit Reactionary Documents*, Vol. 2, pp. 448-89.)

One cannot fail to note how the above story of the Mao-Chou
controversy over the military strategy harmonizes with a more
detailed account given by the ex-Communist leader Kung Ch'u
who was on the spot when the controversy broke out. As described elsewhere in this study, the controversy occurred early
in 1932 with the result that Chou got the upper hand of Mao.
That had a far-reaching effect on subsequent Communist strategy in Kiangsi. (See Kung Ch'u, *The Red Army and I*, pp. 312
ff.)

*Support the Bolshevik Forward and Offensive Line of the
Party* (擁護黨的布爾塞維克的進攻路線
Yung-hu tang ti pu-erh-se-wei-k'e ti chin-kung lu-hsien), by Po
Ku (Ch'in Pang-hsien), February 16, 1933; printed in *Struggle*
(Kiangsi), No. 3, February 23, 1933, pp. 4-10, 008. 2105/7720/
V. 1, SSC; reproduced in *A Collection of Red Bandit Documents*,
Vol. 7, pp. 225-46, 008. 2129/4070/V. 7, SSC; approximately
6, 000 words.

Among all source materials on the Lo Ming line this is perhaps the most specific and informative statement ever seen. It
is actually the last part of a speech delivered by the party
leader in the Red Army Academy, containing a clear-cut comparison between what was known as the forward and offensive
line of the party and the retreat and defensive line allegedly
represented by Lo Ming.

To begin with, Po Ku defined the party line of the time as a
"forward and offensive line. " He claimed that this line was decided by both the Comintern and the Chinese Communist Party.
As a matter of fact, however, the contents of the line as em-

bodied in the present statement were drawn almost verbatim
from the paragraph dealing with the task of the Chinese Communist Party in section 5 of the resolution of the Twelfth Plenum
of the ECCI held in September, 1932. There are only a few additions in the present statement to emphasize the aggressive
character of the line. (For full text of the Chinese version of
the resolution of the ECCI Twelfth Plenum, see *Struggle* (Shanghai), No. 31, December 5, 1932, leaves 2-8.)

Po Ku pointed out that the CCP was required to carry out the
new party line, which contained the following items:

1. To mobilize the masses against the Japanese and other
imperialists as well as the Kuomintang.

2. To mobilize the workers and toiling masses to resist the
KMT offensive against the Soviet areas; to expand and strengthen
the Soviet areas and the Red Army.

3. To step up economic and political struggle in non-Communist areas.

4. To win over the broad masses of workers.

5. To promote guerrilla warfare among the peasants, particularly in Manchuria.

6. To propagandize successes achieved in the Soviet areas as
well as in Russia.

How should, then, the CCP carry out the new party line in the
Soviet areas? Po Ku cited the Central Bureau's eight-point resolution of February 8 as a guide for action, emphasizing that it
was the main substance of the line for the moment.

However, he found that a group of wavering elements in the
party were following a retreat and escape line characterized by
pessimism, opportunism, and liquidationism. They set themselves against the party line, thus undermining the party structure. He singled out Lo Ming and a county party secretary in
western Fukien by the name of Yang Wen-chung as spokesmen
of this group and took them to task as symbols of the pernicious
line they were supposed to represent. Specifically, Lo Ming was
quoted as saying among other things:

I don't think we can thoroughly change the mood of the masses
even if we ask our best leader Chairman Mao or Chairman Hsiang
Ying (of the Military Council), Comrade Chou En-lai, Comrade Jen
Pi-shih, or go to the Soviet Union to ask Comrade Stalin or bring
Lenin back to life and ask them all to come to Upper or Lower
Ch'inan or some other place to address the masses three days and
nights to step up political propaganda.

Meanwhile, Yang Wen-chung was said to have addressed a

letter, under the influence of Lo Ming, to the Fukien Provincial Committee couched in terms like those of a political program. The letter allegedly contained the following four points:

1. The second and fourth army corps should be sent back to Anhwei and Hupeh to pin down KMT forces there. . . .

2. The party has taken the place of the government in formulating all major (political) plans (for example, expansion of the Red Army, local armed organizations, the land problem) with the result that the party's attention has been diverted from the task of leading the mass struggle. It is therefore suggested that all administrative work, expansion of the Red Army and local armed forces, and so forth be planned by the government . . . and that the party give more attention to the study of the ways of the mass struggle. . . .

3. There are too many and varied mass organizations in existence, which are at once confusing and hollow. They should be cut down or amalgamated as far as possible.

4. The quality of local armed forces should be improved. Attention should be paid to work in the peripheral region where the expansion of the Red Army should differ from that in the heart of the Soviet stronghold.

Po Ku compared the party line and the so-called Lo Ming line point for point and concluded that the forward and offensive line of the party must prevail and that any attempt at compromise was out of the question.

Significantly, Po Ku remarked with profound regret that adherents to the Lo Ming line were even found among the "leading comrades of the party."

Resolution Adopted by the Conference of CP and CY Members, Fourth Class Graduates and Cadres Ranking with and above Company Commanders, Workers', and Peasants' Red Army Academy (工 農 紅 軍 學 校 第 四 期 畢 業 學 生 中 全 體 黨 員 團 員 及 連 一 級 以 上 幹 部 的 黨 員 團 員 大 會 決 議 Kung-nung hung-chün hsüeh-chiao ti-szu-ch'i pi-yeh hsüeh-sheng chung ch'üan-t'i tang-yüan t'uan-yüan chi lien i chi i-shang kan-pu ti tang-yüan t'uan-yüan ta-hui chüeh-i), February 16, 1933; printed in *Struggle* (Kiangsi), No. 3, February 23, 1933, p. 3, 008. 2105/7720/V. 1, SSC; approximately 300 words.

After having heard the speech of Po Ku, described previously, the members of the audience formally expressed their endorsement of the speech in the present statement. Though short and brief, this piece covers practically all the main points of view involved in the present question. It lays emphasis on Lo Ming's disobedience to the resolution of the Twelfth Plenum of the ECCI and calls for an ideological struggle to set the party in the right path. It brings out the interesting point that the Lo Ming group wanted to convert the party into a "research" institution.

What Is the Opportunistic Line of Comrade Lo Ming? (什十麼是羅明同志的機會主義路線? Shih-mo shih lo-ming t'ung-chih ti chi-hui chu-i lu-hsien?), by Lo Fu (Chang Wen-t'ien), February 18, 1933; printed in *Struggle* (Kiangsi), No. 3, February 23, 1933, pp. 10-15, 008.2105/7720/V.1, SSC; reproduced in *A Collection of Red Bandit Documents*, Vol. 7, pp. 246-63, 008.2129/4070/V.7, SSC; approximately 5,000 words.

Written by one of the top-ranking Russian Returned Students, this article quotes extensively from Lo Ming in order to prove him wrong. Allowing for possible misrepresentations and distortions, Lo Ming can be seen here more clearly than anywhere else.

To judge from his own words quoted here, Lo Ming believed that guerrilla and mobile warfare was the only effective way to save the desperate situation in western Fukien in the face of the overwhelming KMT offensive. He little thought that this time-honored Communist tactic was the very thing that got him into trouble. Said he:

> Since we did not in the past have the experience of such an intense fighting in this area, particularly in Lungyen and Shanghang, and since, above all, during the course of the onslaught of the enemy we did not go in for positive guerrilla warfare and for well-organized mobile defense in order to give the enemy a blow and extend our position outward, we are literally seized with a panic and at a loss how to act. . . .

Interestingly, the writer of this article picks up only the words "literally seized with a panic and at a loss how to act" as evidence of the opportunistic line of Lo Ming and leaves untouched his other words in the passage quoted above.

Again, Lo Ming stated:

We must realize that the most important of all factors (making for pessimism and despair among the masses) is that our military mobilization is far from adequate or, more concretely, that the party has not quite artistically led the armed struggle.

Strangely enough, on the basis of the foregoing passage the writer blames Lo Ming for his plot to separate military mobilization from all other things, such as party leadership, political mobilization, and class struggle.

The above are just two of the numerous instances cited to attack Lo Ming with his own words. To give additional evidence of the charge, the letter of Yang Wen-chung, described in a previous entry, is also cited.

As is disclosed in this article, Lo Ming apparently operated in western Fukien from the very beginning of Communist penetration there. He was branded a Li Li-sanist. He had allegedly committed a series of grievous errors since the Fourth Plenum of the Central Committee held in January, 1931. During the long period of his leadership in western Fukien, it is stressed, the masses had been estranged from the party.

On examination, this article seems to suggest that if there was a Lo Ming line at all, it was his position in favor of guerrilla and mobile warfare. Once involved in intraparty struggles, the article was distorted.

What Is the Forward and Offensive Line? (什 麼 是 進 攻 路 線 ? Shih-mo shih chin-kung lu-hsien?), by Jen Pi-shih, February 19, 1933; printed in *Struggle* (Kiangsi), No. 3, February 23, 1933, pp. 15-18, 008. 2105/7720/V. 1, SSC; reproduced in *A Collection of Red Bandit Documents*, Vol. 7, pp. 263-73, 008. 2129/4070/V. 7, SSC; approximately 3,000 words.

According to this article, the ideas of the Lo Ming line were not confined to western Fukien but were prevalent in Kiangsi also, though conditions in Kiangsi had begun to change for the better while the situation in western Fukien continued to deteriorate.

The peripheral counties in Kiangsi, such as Nanfeng, Kuanch'ang, Ihuang, Loan, Yungfeng, Chishui, T'aiho, Huich'ang, Hsünwu, and Anyüan had allegedly long been bogged down in tactics of simple defense, and it was not until recently that the situation began to improve there. In the heart of the Communist

stronghold in southern Kiangsi, it was charged, the morale was
not good either.

Conditions in western Fukien were even worse, it was stated.
The Soviet area in the southern part of western Fukien had
shrunk, while the newly expanded Soviet area in the northern
part was far from secure. Worst of all, a section of the Fukien
party leadership had rallied around the standard of Lo Ming,
while the other section saw fit to compromise with him.

In addition to the stereotyped arguments, it was pointed out
that the forward and offensive line was not restricted to the
military, as was generally imagined. It was stressed that it
covered the entire scope of the Soviet struggle, though the military was always an important factor.

It was added that the forward and offensive line had been successful only in certain aspects of the struggle even in the most
advanced parts of the Soviet areas. Examples of these aspects
are: expansion of the Red Army, subscription for public bonds,
mobilization of coolies, and so forth. It was therefore suggested
that an all out effort be made to consummate the party line.

*Resolution of the CY Central Bureau, Soviet Areas, regard-
ing the Unfolding of the Struggle against the Lo Ming Line* (少
共蘇區中央局關於開展反羅明路線鬥爭
的決議 Shao-kung su-ch'ü chung-yang-chü kuan-yü k'ai-
chan fan lo-ming lu-hsien tou-cheng ti chüeh-i), February 20,
1933; printed in *Struggle* (Kiangsi), No. 3, February 23, 1933,
pp. 2-3, 008.2105/7720/V. 1, SSC; approximately 900 words.

Aside from a routine approbation of the CP decision to liquidate the Lo Ming line, this resolution disclosed a sweeping reshuffle in the Fukien branch of the CY, including the removal of
its chief. This was done under the plea of the Lo Ming line
which, it was said, dated from the latter half of 1931, when a
trend toward relying on military force and distrusting the
masses had developed under the regime of the West Fukien Special Committee. It was suggested that the campaign against the
Lo Ming line and any compromise with it be extended to the entire organization of the CY in the Soviet areas.

Combat Corrupt Liberalism (反對腐朽的自由主
義 Fan-tui fu-hsiu ti tzu-yu chu-i), by Shang K'un; printed in

Struggle (Kiangsi), No. 3, February 23, 1933, pp. 18-20,
008. 2105/7720/V. 1, SSC; approximately 2, 200 words.

In denouncing the Lo Ming line, the CCP stigmatized any attempt at compromise as corrupt liberalism. This abusive term
can be found in virtually all the major statements in regard to
the line, but it is never so clearly expounded as in the present
article.

Assuming that the Lo Ming line was untenable, this writer
charges that the majority of the members of the Fukien Provincial Committee did not take a firm stand against it, but chose to
compromise with or surrender to it. This attitude, as the
writer puts it, was guilty of corrupt liberalism which, in turn,
contributed to the development of the Lo Ming line.

Furthermore, it is stated, the error inherent in this compromising attitude could not be explained away by merely pleading
ignorance or inexperience. To a Bolshevik, it is emphasized,
the important thing is not his repentance, as with a religious
man, but his self-criticism through which he must not only confess to errors but also understand and combat them in the interests of the party line.

Why was it that people in Fukien did not combat the Lo Ming
line resolutely but took the position of compromise and liberalism? It was because they suffered from opportunism and looked
upon the forward and offensive line of the party with suspicion
and hesitation. The writer therefore concludes that the fight
against corrupt liberalism must be regarded as an integral part
of the fight against the retreat-and-escape line, and that it follows that it would not be easy to do away with the retreat-and-
escape line if the effort was not accompanied by a removal of
the oscillating and compromising liberalism.

The bulk of this article is a repetition of the same old arguments in favor of the party's forward and offensive line.

*Struggle for the Strengthening of Party Leadership in the
Revolutionary War* (為加強黨對革命戰爭的領
導而鬥爭 Wei chia-ch'iang tang tui ko-ming chan-cheng ti
ling-tao erh tou-cheng), by Shou Ch'ang; printed in *Struggle*
(Kiangsi), No. 18, July 15, 1933, pp. 5-8, 008. 2105/7720/V. 2,
SSC; approximately 3,000 words.

This article discloses the significant fact that after the KMT

Fourth Campaign the tentacles of the anti-Lo Ming campaign were extending to the Red Army in western Fukien.

T'an Chen-lin, who had charge of the party in the army in the military area in Fukien, was found to have identified himself with the Lo Ming line. He became the target of attack in a provincial party conference held on June 12, 1933. Practically all the charges against Lo Ming applied to him.

T'an Chen-lin, vice minister of Rural Work under the present Peiping regime, served as an army political commissar in western Fukien for quite a while. After the Communist evacuation of Kiangsi late in 1934, he was left behind with Ch'en Yi, now Chinese Communist foreign minister, to continue underground work in the once familiar Central Soviet Area. As a top GPU man in this area, he was responsible for the reportedly unprecedented intraparty mass execution on the eve of the Long March. (See Kung Ch'u, *The Red Army and I,* pp. 242, 245, 267, 271, 406, 435, 436.)

According to the present article, T'an's attitude toward the Lo Ming line and the small faction responsible for the line in Kiangsi was never clear. This small faction consisted of four men named Teng, Mao, Ku, and Hsieh. Teng was identified as Teng Hsiao-p'ing, a confederate of Mao. (See *ibid.,* pp. 198, 208.) Though the names of the other three were not given in full, the contexts of relevant documents show that they were Mao's brother Mao Tse-t'an, Mao's henchman Ku Po who was active during the Fut'ien incident of 1930, and a certain Hsieh Wei-chün who, as described elsewhere in this study, also identified himself with the Mao group. The charges against this four-man group and, for that matter, against T'an Chen-lin centered on two points: (1) land policy—equal redistribution, draw-on-the-fat-to-make-up-for-the-lean, and so forth; (2) military strategy—maneuvering the enemy deep into Communist areas and no fighting on enemy soil. As is generally known, these two theories were Mao's favorites.

It was revealed in this article that Li Shao-chiu who played an important role in the Fut'ien incident of 1930 on behalf of Mao was expelled from the party during the course of the anti-Lo Ming campaign. According to a news report in *Red China* of July 8, 1933, p. 6, Mao Tse-t'an was also hard hit.

A New Situation and a New Task (新 的 形 勢 與 新 的 任 務 Hsin ti hsing-shih yü hsin ti jen-wu), by Mao Tse-tung;

printed in *Red China*, No. 97, July 29, 1933, p. 3, 008. 1052/
2125/V. 4, SSC; approximately 1, 700 words.

This article, published between the KMT Fourth and Fifth
Campaigns, is Mao's only available statement which can be said
to have a bearing on the controversy over the Lo Ming line.

The subject matter of this article was Mao's personal survey
of the factors making for the Communist victory over the KMT
Fourth Campaign as well as his hope for a greater Communist
effort in the face of the forthcoming Fifth Campaign. Among
other things, he urged an increase of 50, 000 Red Army men in
three months from August to October, 1933.

The interesting thing is that the basic ideas of this article of
Mao contradict those of the relevant sections of the 1945 "Resolution on Some Historical Problems, " which was also sponsored
by Mao. The contradictions of his two statements can be seen
from the following:

1. The 1945 resolution attributes the Communist victory over
the KMT Fourth Campaign to Mao's strategic thinking which
consisted in guerrilla and mobile warfare. (See Mao Tse-tung,
Selected Works, Chinese edition, Vol. 3, pp. 969, 984; English
edition, Vol. 4, pp. 186, 203; reprint of the resolution, pp. 19,
38-39.) In contrast, the present article ascribes the Communist
victory over the KMT Fourth Campaign to a number of factors
among which the forward and offensive line of the party as formulated by the Russian Returned Student leadership ranks first.
"Owing to the correct forward and offensive line of the party
and the positive leadership of the Soviet . . ." this article
states, "we have basically smashed the Fourth Campaign of the
enemy. "

2. The 1945 resolution attacks the Russian Returned Students
for their exaggeration of the weaknesses of the enemy, described as "completely shaky, " "extremely panic-struck, " "final death, " "accelerated collapse, " "general collapse, " and so
forth. *(Ibid.,* Chinese edition, Vol. 3, p. 982; English edition,
Vol. 4, p. 200; reprint of the resolution, p. 36.) Interestingly,
Mao in the present article portrays the enemy of that time in
almost the same terms as the Russian Returned Students: "a fatal blow, " "unprecedented debacle and collapse, " "fundamentally shaky, " "general collapse, " "frightened out of their wits, "
and so forth.

3. The 1945 resolution accuses the Russian Returned Students
of their objection to what was called the "doctrine of retreat

and escape. " *(Ibid.,* Chinese edition, Vol. 3, pp. 984-85; English edition, Vol. 4, p. 204; reprint of the resolution, p. 40.) Mao's position outlined in the present article is no different from the Russian Returned Students. "We must set ourselves, " said Mao, "against any underestimation of the new revolutionary situation today, against all war weariness, particularly against those opportunists who would retreat and escape in a panic before the Fifth Campaign of the enemy. "

Combat Right Opportunism That Submits to Difficulties (反 對 向 坦 難 投 降 的 右 傾 機 會 主 義 Fan-tui hsiang k'un-nan tou-hsiang ti yu-ch'ing chi-hui chu-i), by Liang P'ing, August 4, 1933; printed in *Struggle* (Kiangsi), No. 23, August 22, 1933, pp. 17-20, 008. 2105/7720/V. 2, SSC; *Red Flag Weekly,* No. 36, January 1, 1934, pp. 76-83, 052. 1/809, BIC; approximately 3, 500 words.

This article was directed against the finance minister of the Central Soviet Government, Teng Tzu-hui, who was censured for his Right opportunism, wavering and oscillating in the face of difficulties. According to *Red China* for July 23, 1933, the author was vice-minister of national economy.

Proceeding on the assumption that the drive against the Lo Ming line was one of the major factors in the defeat of the KMT Fourth Campaign, the present writer saw an impact of that drive on the forthcoming Fifth Campaign that threatened to rage on a larger scale. To that end, Teng Tzu-hui was singled out for attack.

Like Lo Ming, Teng Tzu-hui was said to have committed a whole host of errors: incorrect assessment of the living conditions of the peasantry, lack of confidence in the masses, exaggeration of financial difficulties, submission to necessity, increase in taxation and in the issue of banknotes. All these were allegedly the product of opportunism and bore no resemblance to the financial policies of Lenin. In conclusion, this writer stated that one of the basic conditions for beating back the forthcoming KMT Fifth Campaign would be an inexorable struggle against the wavering and vacillating Right opportunism, without neglecting the peril of Left opportunism.

Barely five days after the publication of this article, on August 9, the Central Soviet Government in a cabinet resolution demoted Teng Tzu-hui to the post of vice-minister of finance.

The reasons given for his demotion were essentially the same
as the charges against him as outlined above. (See *Red China,*
August 25, 1933, p. 1.)

*Regarding "General Conclusions of the Party Congresses in
the Various Counties of the Province" of Kiangsi* (關) 於 江
西 "全 省 各 縣 代 表 大 會 的 總 結" kuan-yü chiang-
hsi "ch'üan-sheng ko hsien tai-piao ta-hui ti tsung-chieh"), by
Lo Mai (Li Wei-han), September 18, 1933; printed in *Struggle*
(Kiangsi), No. 27, September 25, 1933, pp. 8-10, 008.2105/
7720/V.3, SSC; approximately 2,000 words.

During August, 1933, the party units of the various counties
of Kiangsi called separate conferences to review their work and
to accept the new tasks assigned them by the Central and provincial leadership in anticipation of the imminent KMT Fifth
Campaign. A general report on these conferences was issued by
the Kiangsi Provincial Party Headquarters, published in *Red
China* for September 18, 1933, p. 6 (as indicated in this article,
also published in *Provincial Committee Correspondence,* issued
by the Kiangsi Provincial Committee of the CCP, 1933-34, No.
3, which is not available). This report came to the conclusion
that "The party congresses of the various counties have in general been fairly successful. "
The present article challenges the conclusion of the above report, saying that the favorable comment of the report did not
apply at least to one congress, that is, the one called by the three
counties of Ihuang, Anlo, and Ch'ungjen, where there was no
real fight against the Lo Ming line as requested by the Central
Bureau. It was therefore requested that the said congress of the
three counties be declared null and void and that a new conference be held instead.
As to the other counties, the record was considered to be
generally good, except that the fight against Left opportunism
had been inadequate and that the idols of the local leaders of the
Lo Ming line, identified as Mao Tse-t'an, Hsieh Wei-chün and
Yü Tse-hung, had not been destroyed.
In addition, it is stated, there were inadequacies in the execution of decisions of the central leadership and in the two-front
fight against Right and Left deviations. The hope was expressed
that these inadequacies would be made up in the provincial party

conference which was to be held on September 27, 1933. (See
Red China, October 6, 1933, p. 1.)

   *How Should the Party in Fukien Effect a Complete Change in
Work under Its New Mission?* (在 新 的 任務 下 福建
黨 應 如 何 爭 取 工 作 的 澈 底 轉 變 ? Tsai hsin ti
jen-wu hsia fu-chien tang ying ju-ho cheng-ch'ü kung-tso ti
ch'e-ti chuan-pien?), by Shou Ch'ang; printed in *Struggle* (Kiangsi), No. 27, September 25, 1933, pp. 10-13, 008. 2105/7720/
V. 3, SSC; approximately 3, 300 words.

   On the eve of the KMT Fifth Campaign, the Communists were
confronted with a new situation and a new task. This necessi-
tated eliminating what influence of the Lo Ming line remained in
the Soviet areas.
   The present writer states that the party in Fukien scored a
success in the fight against the Lo Ming line but that the success
was far from adequate. This, according to him, could be seen
from these things: weak leadership made for tailism; looking
down upon organizational work led to estrangement of the
masses; formalism prevailed.
   In order to bring about an improvement in party work in Fukien, therefore, the following suggestions were made:
   1. To eliminate all influence of the Lo Ming line and counteract what was called liberalism.
   2. To improve and strengthen party leadership in the masses.
   3. To wage a relentless fight against bureaucratism and
formalism.

   Before the First Party Congress of Yüehkan Province (在
粵贛 省 第 一 次 黨 代 表 會 議 的 前 面 Tsai
yüeh-kan sheng ti-i-tz'u tang tai-piao hui-i ti ch'ien-mien), by
Lo Mai (Li Wei-han), November 4, 1933; printed in *Struggle*
(Kiangsi), No. 34, November 12, 1933, pp. 1-5, 008. 2105/
7720/V. 3, SSC; approximately 4, 500 words.

   As the area of the Kiangsi Provincial Soviet was too large for
efficient administration in times of crisis, seven counties in the
extreme south were set aside to form a separate province
named Yüehkan (abbreviation of Kwangtung-Kiangsi) in accordance with a cabinet decision of August 16, 1933. (See *Red China,*

August 31, 1933, p. 5.) Two months later, the first party congress of the new province was held when the KMT Fifth Campaign had just begun. The southern front facing the KMT attack
from Kwangtung was never a major one, so the Communist tactics there were predominantly mobile and guerrilla in nature.

As pointed out in this article, Yüehkan province had lagged
behind in party work. A section of leading cadres demonstrated
"extreme vacillation of opportunism" while more than two-
thirds of the 20,000 CY and CP members of that province
showed no enthusiasm for work. The guerrilla forces were not
strong enough, while the land investigation drive then in progress was not as effective as it should be. The situation was described as very serious, indeed.

All the above phenomena were attributed to the Lo Ming line,
and therefore the paramount task of the party in Yüehkan province was directed at once toward getting rid of what had flowed
from that line and carrying out scrupulously the aggressive program of the central leadership. To that end, it was emphasized,
what was needed was action, not words.

In addition, a change in the leadership on all levels was
stressed with a view to eliminating opportunistic and double-
faced elements. This change, to be effective, called for a party
action in organization, not just in ideology.

*Oppose the Lo Ming Line in the Red Army As Represented by
Hsiao Ching-kuang* (反對紅軍中以肅勁光為代
表的羅明路線 Fan-tui hung-chün chung i hsiao-ching-
kuang wei tai-piao ti lo-ming lu-hsien), by Chou En-lai, November 25, 1933; printed in *Struggle* (Kiangsi), No. 38, December
12, 1933, pp. 3-5, 008.2105/7720/V.3, SSC; approximately
2,000 words.

By the time this article was published, Chou En-lai had long
been political commissar of the Red Army with powers to coun-
tersign all orders of the commander-in-chief, thereby controlling the military machine. (See *Red China*, March 6, 1933, p.
2, May 11, 1933, p. 1; Kung Ch'u, *The Red Army and I*, pp.
270-75.) As described previously, his strategic thinking was
radically different from that of Mao and a controversy between
them occurred early in 1932. This controversy over the military
strategy was reported to have led to the liquidation of the Lo
Ming line.

In the present article Chou En-lai called for a swift elimination of the Lo Ming line in the Red Army in the face of the KMT Fifth Campaign and singled out Hsiao Ching-kuang, the deposed military commander in the Minkan (Fukien-Kiangsi) area, as a symbol for attack. Hsiao as garrison commander was held responsible for the fall of Lich'uan, a strategic county seat in western Kiangsi bordering on Fukien, in September, 1933. To many it must have seemed that this event had a far-reaching effect on the Communist strategy. It probably frustrated the Communist plan to wage a big decisive war in northern Fukien in order to keep southern Kiangsi intact. (See *History of the Fifth Campaign by the Third Route Bandit-Suppression Army*, compiled by the Department of Staff, Third Route Army, Vol. 1, chap. 2, pp. 1-2; *A Collection of Red Bandit Reactionary Documents*, Vol. 6, p. 1710.)

Defeated and deposed, Hsiao was blamed for all the errors inherent in the Lo Ming line: retreat, escape, vacillation, Right opportunism, and what not. He was described as the executer, leader, and promoter of the Lo Ming line in the Red Army.

According to the present article, the case of Hsiao was not an accidental and isolated one. It must have had its roots deep down in the Red Army, especially in the troops under his command. Thus, a general campaign against the Lo Ming line in the Red Army was called for. As the anti-Lo Ming drive assured the success in beating back the KMT Fourth Campaign, the present move against Hsiao as a symbol of the Lo Ming line in the Red Army would prove a basic factor of the ultimate victory in the fight against the KMT Fifth Campaign then in progress.

Let Fire Be Aimed at Those Who Waver Opportunistically in Face of the Urgent Task of the Party! (火 力 向 着 在 黨 的 緊 急 任 務 前 面 表 示 機 會 主 義 動 搖 的 份 子! Huo-li hsiang-cho tsai tang ti chin-chi jen-wu ch'ien-mien piao-shih chi-hui chu-i tung-yao ti fen-tzu), by Lo Mai (Li Wei-han), January 8, 1934; printed in *Struggle* (Kiangsi), No. 43, January 19, 1934, pp. 4-7, 008.21025/7720/V.4, SSC; approximately 3,000 words.

This article was directed against those who were considered not to have done a good job in the so-called Red Army expansion surprise drive in December, 1933, a month which was dedicated to that drive in the face of the KMT Fifth Campaign then in progress.

Four ranking cadres were punished by the central party leadership on charges of wavering opportunism during the drive. Two of them got a reprimand. Ch'en T'an-ch'iu, party chief of Fukien, who published his widely cited "Reminiscences of the First Congress of the Communist Party of China" in the October, 1936, issue of *Communist International,* was removed from office. Ku Po, who played an important role in the Fut'ien incident of 1930 on behalf of Mao, faced the serious question of losing his party membership. He was described as a typical double-faced man and one of the leaders of the anti-party faction of the Lo Ming line in Kiangsi. It was suggested that the drive against opportunism as manifested in the Red Army expansion campaign be made to range over the length and breadth of the party.

21

The Revolt in Fukien

The Anti-Japanese, Anti-Chiang Preliminary Agreement
(反 日 反蔣 的 初 步 協 定   Fan-jih fan-chiang ti ch'u-
pu hsieh-ting), dated October 26, 1933; printed in *Red China*,
No. 149, February 14, 1934, p. 4, 008.1052/2125/V.5, SSC;
approximately 700 words.

The revolt in Fukien took place on November 20, 1933, when
Ch'en Ming-shu and his group, supported by the Nationalist
Nineteenth Route Army, called a "provisional conference of delegates of the Chinese people" in Foochow, the capital of Fukien
province, as a result of which an independent government was
proclaimed the next day. The revolt was quelled in less than
two months. Before its discomfiture it posed no less a problem
to the Communists than to the National Government. (For a
story of the revolt, see Lei Hsiao-ch'en *Thirty Years of Turmoil in China*, Hongkong, The Asia Press Ltd., 1955, Vol. 1,
pp. 212-16.)
The revolt resulted from a military alliance between the rebels and the Communists, concluded on October 26, 1933. The
present document is the full text of the alliance, released by the
Central Soviet Government in January, 1934, following a report
of Chang Wen-t'ien in regard to the matter. (See *Red China*,
February 14, 1933, p. 4.) It was concluded by the Central Soviet
Government and the Red Army on the one side and the Fukien
Provincial Government and the Nineteenth Route Army on the
other. It was called a preliminary agreement because a defini-
tive arrangement was to be made after the carrying out of the
terms of this agreement. In 1945, Mao's machine expressed

itself satisfied with the signing of this agreement. (See "Resolution on Some Historical Problems, " April 20, 1945, printed in Mao Tse-tung, *Selected Works*, Chinese edition, Vol. 3, p. 975; English edition, Vol. 4, p. 192; reprint of the resolution, p. 27.)

This preliminary agreement consists of eleven articles, the most important of which are as follows:

1. Both sides shall immediately stop military action and draw a provisional demarcation line in which both sides shall not station their respective main forces.

2. Both sides shall restore their trade relations according to the principle of mutual help and cooperation.

3. Fukien shall release all political criminals held in prison.

4. Fukien shall give support to all organized revolutionary activities within its borders and grant freedoms of publication, speech, assembly, association, and strike.

5. After the conclusion of the present preliminary agreement, Fukien shall immediately issue an anti-Chiang declaration and make preparations for military action against Chiang and Japan.

According to a non-Communist source, Ch'en Ming-shu came into contact with a Communist agent in Shanghai in the spring of 1933, who suggested to him the formation of a united front against both Japan and the National government. Through this agent Ch'en got in touch with the Communist regime in Kiangsi. After arriving in Fukien in October, Ch'en sent an emissary to Shanghai to negotiate an agreement with the Communists there. The Communists sought instructions from Moscow, which decided in favor of cooperation in a military form but not on a party basis. In consequence, the military pact was signed. (See Lei Hsiao-ch'en, *Thirty Years of Turmoil in China*, pp. 213-15.)

Communist and ex-Communist sources indicate that the Fukien rebels took the initiative in approaching the Communists for a united front by sending a representative named Hsü Ming-hung to Juichin, Kiangsi, to negotiate the matter. This man finally signed the military agreement on behalf of Fukien, the Communist representative being P'an Chien-hsing (alias P'an Han-nien). (See *Red China*, February 14, 1934, p. 3; Kung Ch'u, *The Red Army and I*, pp. 363-64.)

Statement of the CCP Central Committee to the People of the Whole Nation with Respect to the Fukien Incident (中 國) 共 産

黨 中央委員會為福建事變告全國民眾
Chung-kuo kung-ch'an-tang chung-yang wei-yüan-hui wei fu-
chien shih-pien kao ch'üan-kuo min-chung), dated December 5,
1933; printed in *Struggle* (Kiangsi), No. 38, December 12, 1933,
pp. 1-3, 008. 2104/7720/V. 3, SSC; reprinted by the Minkan Provincial Committee, CCP, 008. 234/3115, SSC; approximately
2, 100 words.

Two weeks after the birth of the rebel government in Fukien,
the CCP Central Committee under the leadership of the Russian
Returned Students issued this public statement in denunciation
of that regime. It was charged that the rebels had not kept their
promises as provided in the preliminary military agreement.
This charge was followed by a campaign of invectives against
the rebels, which did not come to a stop until after the total collapse of the Fukien regime.

In 1936, Mao told Edgar Snow that the Chinese Communists
made two major mistakes in Kiangsi: failure to unite with the
rebels in Fukien and adoption of positional warfare instead of
guerrilla tactics. (See Edgar Snow, *Red Star over China*, 1944,
p. 186.) About the same time Mao discussed at greater length
the strategic blunder of failing to give support to Fukien in a
treatise on the strategic problems of China's revolutionary war.
(See Mao Tse-tung, *Selected Works*, Chinese edition, Vol. 1,
pp. 230-31; English edition, Vol. 1, p. 251.) In 1945, Mao's
machine reiterated essentially the same idea in an official statement. (See "Resolution on Some Historical Problems, " April
20, 1945, printed in Mao Tse-tung, *Selected Works*, Chinese
edition, Vol. 3, p. 982; English edition, Vol. 4, p. 20; reprint
of the resolution, p. 36.) Thus, it has been generally understood that Mao held the Russian Returned Student leadership responsible for non-cooperation with the Fukien rebels, which led
to the Communist debacle in Kiangsi. (cf. Robert North, *Moscow and Chinese Communists*, p. 166.)

However, a top-ranking colleague of Mao in Kiangsi tells a
different story. Kung Ch'u, former chief-of-staff of the Chinese
Central Red Army, says that it was Mao who stood for a cautious approach to the Fukien problem and was actually responsible for failure to cooperate with the rebel regime. (See Kung
Ch'u, *The Red Army and I*, pp. 362-67, 395-400.)

Whatever the inside story, this much is certain: the Communist leaders were divided over the Fukien rebellion and some of
them refused to give it effective support, which fact contributed

to the Communist defeat in Kiangsi late in 1934. Pavel Mif, the Comintern delegate to China in 1930, also testified to this effect. (See Pavel Mif, *Heroic China: Fifteen Years of the Communist Party of China*, Chinese edition, 1936, p. 105.)

Since this is the first statement of its kind, it seems useful to sum up its salient contents here. For convenience in discussion, this document may be divided into three parts: (1) causes of the revolt, (2) nature of the rebel government, and (3) tasks of the CCP in Fukien.

Since the Japanese attack on Mukden on September 18, 1931, this paper states in part 1, the entire nation has become disillusioned over the KMT's announced policy of resistance to Japan and other imperialists. The masses have come to realize that only a Soviet program can save China from imperialism. This has caused so much confusion in the KMT ranks that a group of them has gone the length of setting up a rival regime in Fukien.

However, this statement charges in part 2 that the Fukien regime has rendered only lip service. It suppresses the very freedoms it has promised the people. It has done nothing to improve the lot of the toiling masses. Its per capita land redistribution program is designed to destroy the will of the peasantry in their fight against the landlords, and so forth.

So long as it does not back up its words with deeds, the Fukien regime represents just another group of the old KMT politicians, deceiving the people with new methods and under a new name. At bottom, they have no intention to remove the old reactionary rule but to preserve it.

Accordingly, the CCP Central Committee in the third and last part of this statement calls upon the toiling masses in Fukien to perform a list of urgent tasks. The masses should, for instance, organize themselves into labor unions, peasant associations, armed forces, and so forth. They should ask the newly established Fukien government to help arm them for the purpose of driving KMT and Japanese forces from Fukien. Workers are to stage strikes and peasants are to overturn landlords. Meanwhile, the masses should bring pressure to bear upon the rebels to present an effective united front with the Communists.

In conclusion, this paper reaffirms the theory of two alternative roads for China—Soviet or colonial—leaving no room for a third road.

The Fukien Incident and Our Tasks (福建的事變與

我們的任務 Fu-chien ti shih-pien yü wo-men ti jen-wu),
editorial of *Red Flag Weekly,* No. 63, January 1, 1934, Shanghai, pp. 1-11, 051. 2/809/N. 63, BIC; approximately 5, 800
words.

This editorial of the Communist organ agrees essentially with
the CCP Central Committee statement of December 5, 1933, on
the Fukien incident, described previously. The difference lies
in details, not in substance. Being a longer but less authoritative one, this paper may be consulted to help understand the
Central Committee statement in question.

At the end of this editorial is a list of five specific tasks of the
CCP to meet the new situation created by the revolt in Fukien.
These tasks may be summed up as follows:

1. To strengthen the Bolshevik consciousness of the party,
expose the conspiracy of the Nineteenth Route Army, and make
no mistake about the deceptiveness of reformism.

2. To unmask the humbug of the Fukien regime and spread the
anti-imperialist movement.

3. To mobilize the masses to oppose the KMT Fifth Campaign
and support the Soviet regime and its anti-Japanese program.

4. To mobilize the masses to fight for their democratic rights
and expose the sham democracy in Fukien.

5. To take advantage of the promises made by Fukien to expand the party organization of the CCP.

In reading this editorial, one gains the impression that the
Communists demanded more than the Fukien regime could accept without causing its own destruction.

The Question of the Fukien Incident (福建事變問題
Fu-chien shih-pien wen-t'i), n. d. , n. p. , indicated as reference
material for discussion in party cells, 008. 236/3115, SSC;
mimeographed; approximately 1, 900 words.

A little more than an outline of the CCP Central Committee
statement of December 5, 1933, on the Fukien incident, prepared for the training of party members. It may be consulted to
help in the understanding of the Central Committee statement in
question. (For a Western view of the Fukien rebellion, see
Franz Michael and George Taylor, *The Far East in the Modern
World,* pp. 417-18.)

The First Telegram from the Chinese Soviet Provisional Central Government to the People's Revolutionary Government in Fukien and the Nineteenth Route Army (中華蘇維埃臨時中央政府致福建人民革命政府與十九路軍的第一電 Chung-hua su-wei-ai lin-shih chung-yang cheng-fu chih fu-chien jen-min ko-ming cheng-fu yü shih-chiu-lu-chün ti ti-i tien), dated December 20, 1933; printed in *Red China,* No. 149, February 14, 1934, p. 4, 008.1052/2125/ V.5, SSC; approximately 520 words.

This wire, signed by Mao Tse-tung and Chu Teh, was released in January, 1934, together with the Communist-Fukien military agreement of October 26, 1933. The two Communist leaders complained that the Fukien regime had taken no positive action against Japan and Chiang Kai-shek since the conclusion of the said agreement, but that Chiang Kai-shek had dispatched large numbers of troops to Fukien while Japan had completed preparations for taking Amoy and Foochow in support of him. Cautioning against any negative attitude and hesitation, Mao and Chu expressed the hope that positive steps would be taken to fight Chiang and Japan along the lines agreed upon and that the masses would be really armed and granted all kinds of freedoms. Stating that they were ready to unite with the Fukien regime and conclude a military agreement with it for fighting purposes, Mao and Chu requested an early reply as to the decision that might be made.

The Second Telegram from the Chinese Soviet Provisional Central Government to the People's Revolutionary Government and the People's Revolutionary Army in Fukien (中華蘇維埃臨時中央政府致福建人民革命政府及人民革命軍第二電 Chung-hua su-wei-ai lin-shih chung-yang cheng-fu chi fu-chien jen-min ko-ming cheng-fu chi jen-min ko-ming chün ti-erh tien), dated January 13, 1934, printed in *Red China,* No. 149, February 14, 1934, p. 4, 008.1052/2125/V.5, SSC; approximately 560 words.

Released simultaneously with the Communist-Fukien preliminary military agreement and the first Communist telegram described previously, this wire was addressed to the Fukien rebels when Foochow was about to fall and their days were numbered. At this critical moment Mao and Chu made the following six urgent proposals:

1. The Fukien government should immediately grant rights to the people as promised.

2. The Fukien government should immediately arm the masses in defense of Foochow and other strategic cities.

3. The masses should be helped to organize themselves against Chiang and Japan, and they should not be stopped from doing so.

4. Practical steps should be taken to support mass organizations in the rear of the enemy.

5. Unreliable elements should be removed from among the rebels themselves.

6. It should be proclaimed to the Nineteenth Route Army that the only way to fight Japan and Chiang would be to cooperate throughout with the Soviet Government and the Red Army, supported by a concerted military action.

It was stressed that an armed mass front was a prerequisite of success. If such a front could be formed Foochow might not fall and, even if Foochow fell, the enemy might not hold out long. The Fukien regime was therefore requested to consider the matter seriously and make an early reply.

The Second Statement of the CCP Central Committee on the Fukien Incident (中 國) 共 產 黨 中 央 委 員 會 為 福 建 事 變 第 二 次 宣 言 Chung-kuo kung-ch'an-tang chung-yang wei-yüan-hui wei fu-chien shih-pien ti-erh-tz'u hsüan-yen), dated January 26, 1934; printed in (1) *Red China*, Special Edition during the Second National Soviet Congress, No. 4, January, 1934, p. 2, 008.1052/2125/V.5, SSC; (2) *Struggle* (Kiangsi), No. 45, February 2, 1934, pp. 1-3, 008.2105/7720/V.4, SSC; (3) in a leaflet, 008.222/3115, SSC; approximately 2,600 words.

This statement of the CCP Central Committee was issued after the Fukien regime had been defeated by the forces of the National Government. The CCP felt no sympathy for the short-lived regime. On the contrary, it castigated the rebels in unmistakable terms and used the case as evidence to reaffirm its professedly tenable position as set forth in its December 5, 1933, statement to the effect that there were only two alterna-

tive roads for China to choose—colonial or Soviet—leaving no
room for a third road.

The Fukien rebellion was described as being an intermediate,
reformist regime which by its very nature was opposed to a revolutionary cause initiated and carried out by the masses themselves. Its true motive was not to lead a revolution of the workers and peasants as it claimed, but to prevent and destroy it.

The failure of the Fukien regime was said to be due to these
causes: (1) military procrastination and inactivity; (2) political
collaboration with the imperialists; (3) no unfeigned arming of
the masses; (4) no improvement of the lot of workers and peasants, plus actual obstruction to workers' strikes and peasants'
land struggle.

It was stressed that there was no hope for the liberation of
China from the KMT-imperialist rule unless the masses rose
on their own and carried on the revolution along the Soviet road.

*Declaration of the Central Government of the Chinese Soviet
Republic on the Fukien Incident* (中 華 蘇 維 埃 共 和 國)
中 央 政 府 為 福 建 事 變 宣 言   Chung-hua su-wei-ai
kung-ho-kuo chung-yang cheng-fu wei fu-chien shih-pien hsüan-
yen), issued February 11, 1934; printed in *Red China*, No. 149,
February 14, 1934, p. 3, 008.1052/2125/V.5, SSC; approximately 2, 200 words.

This declaration was issued after the debacle of the short-
lived revolt in Fukien. For convenience in discussion, it may be
divided into three parts, namely, (1) background of the preliminary agreement, (2) Fukien's failure to fulfill the agreement,
and (3) the Soviet position.

It was revealed that the Fukien rebels first dispatched a delegate by the name of Hsü Ming-hung to Juichin with the word that
they were willing to reach a rapprochement with the Soviets on
the basis of the three-point program for a united front enunci-
ated by the latter on January 17, 1933. As described in the item
on that program, the Communists thereby offered to conclude an
armistice with any hostile armed forces on three conditions,
namely, (1) immediate cessation of the offensive against the Soviet areas, (2) immediate guarantee of freedoms to the people,
and (3) immediate arming of the mass of people and formation
of armed volunteer troops for the defense of China. (For the

text of the three-point program, see *Red China*, January 28, 1933, p. 1.) On the basis of these three points, the Central Soviet Government entered into the preliminary military agreement with the rebels in Fukien.

After the conclusion of the agreement, according to this statement, the Fukien rebels declared themselves independent of the KMT and adopted a political program of a reformist nature. But in fact, it was charged, they made little effort to live up to their words. They continued collusion with the Japanese and American imperialists. They failed to grant democratic rights to the masses on the pretext of wartime security. They not only did nothing to improve the lot of the toiling masses but stood in the way of the mass struggle. Being military defeatists, they stooped to taking shelter in an imperialist (Japanese) legation *(sic)* and its gunboat. Despite repeated Communist warnings, the Fukien regime resented the masses and thus collapsed after a brief existence of more than fifty days.

It was stressed that from the preliminary military agreement and related telegrams released, one could see the firm position of the Soviet Government against Japan and Chiang Kai-shek. The Soviet Government wanted, therefore, to make it clear that its three-point united front program of 1933 remained unchanged, the Fukien incident notwithstanding. The important thing was action, not words. Any reformist clique, which was apt to make promises but not to keep them, would be eliminated as ever. The only way to achieve national liberation was the Bolshevik road, this declaration concluded.

On the Agreement with the Nineteenth Route Army As Released by the Chinese Soviet Central Government (論 中 華 蘇 維 埃 中 央 政 府 所 公 佈 的 對 十 九 路 軍 的 協 定 Lun chung-hua su-wei-ai chung-yang cheng-fu so kung-pu ti tui shih-chiu-lu-chün ti hsieh-ting), by K'ai Feng, February 15, 1934; printed in *Struggle* (Kiangsi), No. 48, February 23, 1934, pp. 6-13, 008.2105/7720/V.4, SSC; approximately 6,800 words.

Judging by its content and date, this article was doubtless intended to give an explanation of the declaration of the Central Soviet Government on the Fukien incident, issued on February 11, 1934. It is illuminating and reasonably informative. It must be read in conjunction with the Soviet government declaration in question.

This article is divided into three parts dealing with (1) the Soviet struggle for the formation of anti-Japanese arrangements, (2) compromises in Marxism-Leninism, and (3) some lessons learned.

The first part begins with a recognition of the 1933 three-point program as a historic event. It was on the basis of that program that the military agreement of October 26, 1933, with the rebels in Fukien was concluded. Here the author makes a textual comparison between the relevant articles of those two instruments, which shows a striking parallel between them.

The author claimed that the military agreement was made possible by three factors: (1) growth of the revolutionary undercurrent in Fukien, (2) contradictions within the KMT, and (3) the invincibility of the Red Army.

Although the military agreement came to an end after the discomfiture of the Fukien regime, it was stressed, the 1933 program for a united front remained unchanged. The Soviet Government and the Red Army were ready to negotiate a similar military agreement with any armed forces that might accept the three principles of the 1933 program.

As some comrades expressed doubts as to the desirability of concluding the military agreement with the Fukien rebels, it was emphasized in part 2 of this article that Marxism-Leninism did not exclude the possibility of compromise in case of necessity. On the contrary, a compromise with another political party or faction at the right moment was a prerequisite of success. Both Lenin and Stalin were quoted as supporting this theory.

Part 3 of this article is devoted to a listing of five lessons the CCP is alleged to have learned from the rapprochement with the Fukien regime. The five lessons are:

1. It was desirable to exploit the contradictions of the enemy in the interests of the CCP. A good example was afforded by the present case in which the KMT economic blockade of the Kiangsi Soviet was broken in at least one important sector, and a part of the KMT forces in Kiangsi had to be transferred to Fukien to deal with the rebels, thus weakening the KMT strength built up for the Fifth Campaign.

2. Despite the risks involved in coming to terms with reformism, the CCP had carefully made use of the chance to increase its influence in Fukien.

3. The military agreement with the Fukien rebels had shown that only the Chinese Soviet Government was really engaged in a struggle for national liberation.

4. It was possible to form a united front against Japan, only if the matter was approached along the Communist line.

4. The swift action of the CCP was absolutely necessary at a moment of emergency. This was all the more true in Fukien, where party work was weak.

The Rise and Fall of the People's Revolutionary Government in Fukien (福建人民政府的產生及其覆滅 Fu-chien jen-min cheng-fu ti ch'an-sheng chi ch'i fu-mieh), by Po Ku (Ch'in Pang-hsien), July 8, 1934; printed in *Struggle* (Kiangsi), No. 69, August 4, 1934, pp. 13-17, 008.2105/7720/V. 6, SSC; approximately 2,500 words.

This is a section of a long address delivered by the party chief before the Society for the Study of Marxism on July 8, 1934, described elsewhere in this study. After more than half a year, Po Ku set forth his personal views on the Fukien rebellion in unmistakable terms.

In the fall of 1933, Po Ku said, the Fukien rebels left the KMT to form a reformist faction of their own. But they were not any different from the KMT on that account, except that a section of masses looking for a third road were rallying around them. In dealing with these KMT rebels, according to Po Ku, the CCP adopted the following three basic policies:

1. To win allies among the masses by exploiting the contradictions of the ruling class.

2. To expose the reactionary character of the Fukien regime and to emphasize that only the Soviet road was the correct revolutionary road.

3. To conclude a preliminary military agreement with the Fukien rebels in accordance with the three conditions laid down by the CCP on January 17, 1933, and at the same time to condemn their hesitation and procrastination in carrying out the agreement.

The above basic policies were said to be based on the teachings of Lenin and Stalin. To give effect to those policies, Po Ku pointed out, the following five steps were taken by the CCP:

1. To lay bare the untruths of the political program of the

Fukien regime as shown in watchwords like "per capita land redistribution" and "the producing people."

2. To promote the mass movement by taking advantage of the anti-Japanese and anti-Chiang slogans of Fukien.

3. To strengthen work among workers, peasants, and toiling masses.

4. To conclude a preliminary military agreement with the rebels and condemn their sabotage.

5. To incite the soldiers of the Nineteenth Route Army to sedition.

These steps and others, according to Po Ku, had combined to bring about the downfall of the Fukien regime. This proved that not only the KMT but any third road could not hope to succeed.

In this connection, it is interesting to note that Mao said practically the same thing before the Second National Soviet Congress in January, 1934. The emergence of the People's Revolutionary Government, Mao stated, signified a further disruption of the KMT. Because of the great success of the Soviet movement and the bankruptcy of the KMT before the eyes of the people, he went on, a part of the reactionary ruling class had to adopt new methods to attempt a third road in order to save themselves from dying. But their attempt was bound to fail. The broad masses would not, Mao concluded, distinguish them from the KMT if they did not base themselves on the real interests of workers and peasants and toiling masses, or follow the same basic policies as those of the Chinese Soviet Government, or recognize the three conditions put forward by the CCP in April, 1933, for the conclusion and implementation of an anti-Japanese and anti-KMT agreement. (See Mao's report to the Second National Soviet Conference, end of section 3, printed in *Red China*, January 26, 1934, p. 3.)

Again, in his concluding remarks following the discussion of the said report, Mao reiterated that the emergence of the People's Revolutionary Government represented a new trick to deceive the people on the part of a section of the reactionary ruling class who wanted to save themselves from dying. In the feeling that the CCP was their enemy while the KMT was out of date, they devised a third road under the name of the People's Revolutionary Government in order to deceive the masses. They had, Mao concluded, no revolutionary significance at all, as was now shown by facts. (See Mao's "Concluding Remarks on the Report of the Central Executive Committee," printed in *Red China*, January 31, 1934, p. 1.)

As indicated elsewhere in this study, the foregoing two passages of Mao's statements are not included in the texts of the two statements hitherto available to the outside world. The passage in Mao's report to the Second National Soviet Congress is omitted in the text in the Yakhontoff book, *The Chinese Soviets*, 1934, p. 255, though other passages of section 3 of that statement, in which the present passage appears, are retained. The same passage does not appear in the Harvard publication, *A Documentary History of Chinese Communism*, either, for the whole section 3 of the statement is omitted. As to the passage in Mao's concluding remarks on his report, it is also omitted in the text printed in Mao Tse tung, *Selected Works*, Vol. 1, Chinese version, pp. 131-36; English version, Vol. 1, pp. 147-52.

The omissions seem to be significant. They have concealed Mao's own words on the Fukien rebellion.

22

The Fifth Plenum

Notice of the CCP Central Politburo (中 國 共 産 黨 中 央 政 治 局 通 知 Chung-kuo kung-ch'an-tang chung-yang cheng-ch'ih-chü t'ung-chih), dated February 10, 1934; printed in *Struggle* (Kiangsi), No. 47, February 16, 1934, p. 1, 008. 2101/7720/V. 4, SSC; approximately 260 words.

This notice declared that the Fifth Plenum had been held at Juichin in January, 1934, during which the following three reports had been made:

1. The current situation and the tasks of the party, by Po Ku.
2. The economic struggle of laborers and the work of labor unions in KMT areas, by Ch'en Yün.
3. The Chinese Soviet movement and its tasks, by Lo Fu.

It should be remembered that the three reports mentioned above were adopted as official resolutions of the Fifth Plenum. (Cf. *History of the Chinese Communist Party 1934*, p. 5, compiled under the auspices of the Intelligence Department, Foreign Office, Tokyo.)

Besides, it was stated, additional members of the Central Committee and members of the Politburo were elected.

Resolution on the Current Situation and the Tasks of the Party (目 前 的 形 勢 與 黨 的 任 務 決 議 Mu-ch'ien ti hsing-shih yü tang ti jen-wu chüeh-i), adopted by the Fifth Plenum of the Central Committee on January 18, 1934; printed in *Struggle* (Kiangsi), No. 47, February 16, 1934, pp. 1-16, 008. 2101/7720/V. 4, SSC; approximately 12, 700 words.

This tirade represented the line of the Fifth Plenum of the CCP Central Committee, held in January at Juichin. As described previously, it was originally a report made by the party chief Po Ku before that plenum.

Mao's machine in 1945 described the Fifth Plenum as the apogee of the third Left line under the Russian Returned Student leadership. The specific charges: (1) The Fifth Plenum saw the existence of a direct revolutionary situation in China; (2) it repeated the standpoint of the Li-san line; (3) it further promoted (intraparty) struggles and attacks of a sectarian nature. (See "Resolution on Some Historical Problems, " printed in Mao Tsetung, *Selected Works,* Chinese edition, Vol. 3, p. 969; English edition, Vol. 4, p. 186; reprint of the resolution, pp. 19-20.)

The substance of practically all the above charges can be found in the present document.

Based on the postulations of the Twelfth Plenum of the Comintern, held in September, 1932, this document proceeded on the assumption that China was heading for "a transitional period leading to a new stage of revolution and war. " It followed that China's revolutionary crisis had reached a new acute stage—a direct revolutionary situation in China. It was stated that this was evident from the rapid growth of the Soviet movement, which had become a keystone of the Chinese revolution. This movement had led to the emergence of two antagonistic regimes in China, which were fighting each other for power and survival. Under the circumstances, China had only two alternatives before her, a colonial status or a Soviet revolution—and there was no third road left. Accordingly, the party should do what it could to crush the KMT Fifth Campaign and combat all middle-of-the-road, reformist groups. This was the urgent task of the party at the time.

The present resolution spoke highly of the Fourth Plenum of January, 1931, which the Mao leadership in 1945 attacked in unmistakable terms, as described previously.

It was emphasized that the acute revolutionary situation that existed at the moment called for a greater effort of the party than ever before to lead the masses to crush the KMT Fifth Campaign, through which the imperialist-KMT combination was leading the nation down the road to becoming a colony.

In an effort to accomplish the party's urgent task, there should be no hesitation in expanding the Red Army positively and implementing land policy correctly in the Soviet areas. Meanwhile, strikes must be stepped up in KMT areas.

In order to make the revolutionary struggle successful, it was important to adhere to the Bolshevik line of the party and to achieve harmony between behavior and ideology. Accordingly, it would be imperative to promote the two-front struggle with Right opportunism as the main danger and to frustrate attempts at compromise and double-dealing.

In conclusion, the present document cites again the abovementioned postulations of the Comintern Twelfth Plenum to prove that the fight against the KMT Fifth Campaign would decide China's destiny between a Soviet regime and a colony.

Conclusion of the CCP Central Committee Fifth Plenum
(中 國) 共 產 黨 中 央 委 員 會 第 五 次 全 會 總 結
Chung-kuo kung-ch'an-tang chung-yang wei-yüan-hui ti-wu-tz'u ch'üan-hui tsung-chieh), by Po Ku (Ch'in Pang-hsien), printed in *Struggle* (Kiangsi), No. 48, February 23, 1934, pp. 1-6, 008. 2105/7720/V. 4, SSC; approximately 4, 200 words.

The purpose of this article was to give an explanation of the "Resolution on the Current Situation and the Tasks of the Party" adopted by the Fifth Plenum on January 18, 1934. As described previously, that resolution was originally drafted by Po Ku; so he was in a unique position to throw light on it in the present article.

Naturally, this article is in agreement with the resolution in question in all essential points. However, this article is a much more concise one; it looks like a condensation, brief but comprehensive. More important, this article contains several outstanding points which can help in the understanding of the letter and spirit of the resolution.

In the first place, this article lauds the Fifth Plenum and its resolution as "having tremendous significance to the revolutionary movement in China. " In contrast, the Mao-sponsored 1945 "Resolution on Some Historical Problems" takes an opposite view.

Second, this article, like the resolution of the Fifth Plenum, proceeds on the assumption that China was then heading for "a transitional period leading to a new stage of revolution and war, " as postulated by the Twelfth Plenum of the Comintern. It may or may not be significant that the present article and the resolution in question add the word "acute" to the expression "revolutionary situation"—a word which is not contained in the

statement of the Comintern Twelfth Plenum. More important,
this article points out that the Fourth Plenum of the CCP Central Committee, held in January, 1931, was "in a crucial moment of the rising tide of the revolution, " and that in the lapse
of three years the Fifth Plenum of January, 1934, had moved
forward into "a stage of revolutionary crisis" or a stage in
which "a revolutionary situation exists in China. "

Third, the urgent task of the party as decided by the Fifth
Plenum was to crush the KMT Fifth Campaign. To that end, the
party was called upon to strengthen its work in both Soviet and
KMT areas. In this connection, the present article stresses
that "whoever overlooks work in labor unions cannot be regarded as a member of the CCP and that the greatest trouble
with the party is the weakness of its work with respect to labor. "

Fourth, the present article as well as the resolution of the
Fifth Plenum holds the Right deviation responsible for the Communist setbacks in the KMT Fifth Campaign. By contrast, the
Mao group laid the blame on the third Left line, as is evident
from the 1945 "Resolution on Some Historical Problems. "

*Resolution of the Fifth Plenum concerning the Economic
Struggle and the Work of Labor Unions in White Areas* (五 中 全
會 關 於 白 色 區 域 中 經 濟 鬥 爭 與 工 會 工 作
的 決 議 Wu-chung ch'üan-hui kuan-yü pai-se ch'ü-yü
chung ching-chi tou-cheng yü kung-hui kung-tso ti ch'üeh-i),
printed in *Struggle* (Kiangsi), No. 50, March 11, 1934, pp. 1-
12, 008. 2105/7720/V. 4, SSC; approximately 14,600 words.

As its title indicates, this statement concerns the economic
struggle and the work of labor unions in the KMT-ruled areas.
It was designed to dovetail with the over-all Communist efforts
to pin down the KMT Fifth Campaign then in progress. As described previously, this piece was originally a report made by
Ch'en Yün during the plenary session.

*Instructions of the Fifth Plenum to the Party Corps of the
Second National Soviet Congress* (五 中 全 會 給 二 次 全
蘇 大 會 黨 團 的 指 令 Wu-chung ch'üan-hui chi erh-
tz'u ch'üan-su ta-hui tang-t'uan ti chih-ling), printed in *Struggle*
(Kiangsi), No. 47, February 16, 1934, pp. 16-20, 008. 2105/

7720/V. 4, SSC; also in *Documents of the Second National Soviet Congress of the Chinese Soviet Republic,* pp. 9-22, 008.61029/ 5049, SSC; approximately 4, 700 words.

As described previously, this document was originally a report made by Lo Fu before the Fifth Plenum.

The importance of this document can be seen from the fact that it embodies the guiding principles for the work of the Second National Soviet Congress, which was to be held soon afterwards. The guiding principles:

1. Since there were two alternatives for China to choose—a Soviet road or a colonial road—only the Soviet road could save China from ruination by the KMT and imperialists.

2. To concentrate all efforts on protecting Soviet areas as well as taking new urban centers.

3. To increase the strength of the Red Army to a million men.

4. To solve the agrarian problem thoroughly and improve the livelihood of the workers.

5. To lay stress on economic reconstruction in order to break the economic blockade of the KMT.

6. To promote guerrilla warfare around the Soviet areas.

7. To consolidate the Soviet bases, old and new.

8. To improve Soviet work so as to establish a close link with the workers and peasants.

It should be emphasized once again that this document provided the basis for the work of the Second National Soviet Congress, which was to be held after the Fifth Plenum. The state-of-the-union message of Chairman Mao which featured that congress was, for instance, drafted on the basis of the present document.

23

The Second National Soviet Congress

Resolution of the Central Executive Committee Relative to the Convocation of the Second National Soviet Congress (中央執行委員會關於召集第二次全蘇大會的決議 Chung-yang chih-hsing wei-yüan-hui kuan-yü chao-chi ti-erh-tz'u ch'üan-su ta-hui ti chüeh-i), dated June 8, 1933; printed in *Red China*, No. 86, June 17, 1933, p. 2, 008.1052/2125/V.3, SSC; approximately 760 words.

According to article 4 of the organic law of the Central Soviet, which will be discussed later, the National Soviet Congress shall be called by the Central Executive Committee of the Chinese Soviet Government every two years. As the First National Soviet Congress opened on November 7, 1931, the two-year period would expire on November 7, 1933.

Against this background, the Central Executive Committee of the Chinese Soviet Government adopted the present resolution which consisted of the following points, *inter alia:*

1. The Second National Soviet Congress was scheduled to convene in the Central Soviet Area on December 11, 1933.

2. The Council of the People's Commissars, which was the equivalent of a cabinet, should prepare a report on governmental work of the past two years to be submitted to the congress.

3. New local Soviets at all levels, and delegates to the projected congress should be elected well in advance.

4. Delegates from KMT-ruled areas and neighboring countries were welcome to attend.

A Communist source says that the convocation of the congress was once delayed until New Year's Day of 1934. (See *Red*

Star Journal, No. 12, October 22, 1933, p. 3; cf. *History of the Chinese Communist Party 1934,* pp. 68-70, compiled under the auspices of the Intelligence Department, Foreign Office, Tokyo.) As it finally turned out, the congress was called for January 22-February 7, 1934.

Working Plan for Preparations of the Second National Soviet Congress (準備第二次全蘇大會的工作計畫) Chun-pei ti-erh-tz'u ch'üan-su ta-hui ti kung-tso chi-hua), dated June 10, 1933; printed in *Red China,* No. 88, June 23, 1933, p. 1, 008.1052/2125/V.3, SSC; approximately 700 words.

As is evident from this statement, a Central Government Preparatory Commission for the Second National Soviet Congress was set up as a consequence of the June 8 decision to call the congress. This document is an outline of the working plan prepared by that commission. It contains these items:
1. Documents to be drafted.
2. Regulations to be revised.
3. Preparatory work to be done in the Central Soviet Area.
4. Preparatory work to be done in other Soviet areas.
5. Delegates from the White areas.
6. Government report on its two-year work.
7. Administrative work in connection with the congress.
8. A committee on draft resolutions.

How the Election of Delegates to the Second National Soviet Congress Will Be Held in the Red Army (二次全蘇大會在紅軍中怎樣進行選舉 Erh-tz'u ch'üan-su ta-hui tsai hung-chün chung tsen-yang chin-hsing hsüan-chü), printed in *Red Star Journal,* No. 12, October 22, 1933, p. 3, 008.1052/2160, SSC; approximately 1,600 words.

This is a set of provisions governing the election of Red Army delegates to the Second National Soviet Congress. It was revealed that the opening of the congress had been postponed until the New Year's Day of 1934.

Greet the Great Revolution of the Chinese Soviet Victory (迎

接中國蘇維埃勝利的大革命 Ying-chieh
chung-kuo su-wei-ai sheng-li ti ta ko-ming), editorial of *Red
China*, Special Edition during the Second National Soviet Congress, No. 7, January 22, 1934, p. 1, 008.1052/2125/V.5,
SSC; approximately 2,200 words.

After several months of preparation the Second National Soviet Congress opened at Juichin, Kiangsi, on January 22, 1934.

The congress was greeted by the official organ of the Central
Soviet Government, *Red China*, with a series of special issues
of the paper running from January 22 through February 3. This
editorial represented the paper's first official congratulations
on the congress.

The paper attached great historic significance to the congress, which was held to size up past experiences at a time
when a great victory, it was claimed, was in store for the Soviet government. In the two years following the First National
Soviet Congress, a good deal of progress was said to have been
made, notably in the military field. Nevertheless, the paper
expressed the hope that the congress would take steps to give
effect to the following, *inter alia:*

1. To increase the strength of the Red Army to 1,000,000
men.

2. To stir up class struggle.

3. To improve the work of leadership.

According to news items appearing in the *Red China* of January 24, p. 2, more than seven hundred delegates attended the
congress with a total of about fifteen hundred visitors present.
It was Mao who announced the opening of the congress at 2:00
p.m. when a salute of three guns was fired. A seventy-five-
man presidium was elected with Mao and Po Ku standing at the
head of the list. At the suggestion of Po Ku, such international
Communist leaders as Stalin, Kalinin, Molotov, Thälmann, and
Okano were elected members of an honorary presidium by de-
fault.

To the Second National Soviet Congress(獻給第二次
全國蘇維埃代表大會 Hsien chi ti-erh-tz'u ch'üan-
kuo su-wei-ai tai-piao ta-hui), by Hung Yi; printed in *Struggle*
(Kiangsi), No. 44, January 26, 1934, pp. 4-8, 008.2105/7720/
V.4, SSC; approximately 7,000 words.

On the occasion of the Second National Soviet Congress, the writer sent his personal greetings and expressed the hope that the Soviet movement would be successful in China. He cited the resolution of the ECCI Eleventh Plenum and the CCP resolution accepting that ECCI resolution for support.

The Opening of the Second National Soviet Congress and the Collapse of the "People's" Government in Fukien (二 次 全 蘇 大 會 的 開 幕 與 福 建 "人 民" 政 府 的 破 產 Erh-tz'u ch'üan-su ta-hui ti k'ai-mo yü fu-chien "jen-min" cheng-fu ti p'o-ch'an), by K'ai Feng, January 25, 1934, printed in *Struggle* (Kiangsi), No. 45, February 2, 1934, pp. 4-7, 008.2105/7720/V.4, SSC; approximately 7,000 words.

In attempting to compare and contrast the opening of the Second National Soviet Congress with the failure of the Fukien rebellion, this article decided that the presence or lack of popular support made the difference. This case was taken as proof that the Soviet road provided the only way out for China and that any third road of a reformist nature was out of the question.

A Stenographic Copy of the Opening Speech of Chairman Mao (毛 主 席 講 詞 的 速 寫 Mao chu-hsi chiang-tz'u ti su-hsieh), printed in *Red China*, Special Edition during the Second National Soviet Congress, No. 2, January 24, 1934, p. 1, 008.1052/2125/V.5, SSC; approximately 1,000 words.

As its title indicates, this is a stenographic copy of the opening speech of Chairman Mao on behalf of the Central Soviet Government before the Second National Soviet Congress. It is brief; nothing in it has gone beyond the scope of the editorial of *Red China* for January 22, 1934, described previously. It stresses the point that the responsibility of the congress was to smash the KMT Fifth Campaign then in progress and to spread the Soviet movement to all other parts of the country.

Extract of the Speech of Comrade Po Ku (博 古 同 志 致 詞 的 節 錄 Po-ku t'ung-chih chih-tz'u ti chieh-lu),

printed in *Red China,* Special Edition during the Second National
Soviet Congress, No. 2, January 24, 1934, p. 1, 008.1052/
2125/V.5, SSC; approximately 1,000 words.

This is the opening speech of Po Ku on behalf of the CCP
Central Committee before the Second National Soviet Congress.
Like the speech of Mao, it has not gone beyond the scope of the
editorial of the *Red China* of January 22, 1934, on the subject.

Speech of Comrade Chu Teh (朱 德 同 志 致 詞 Chu-
te t'ung-chih chih-tz'u), printed in *Red China,* Special Edition
during the Second National Soviet Congress, No. 2, January 24,
1934, p. 2, 008.1052/2125/V.5, SSC; approximately 850 words.

This is the opening speech of Chu Teh on behalf of the Red
Army. Understandably it is concerned primarily with military
accomplishments. Like other opening speeches, it is brief and
formal.

*Report of the Central Executive Committee and the Council
of People's Commissars of the Chinese Soviet Republic to the
Second National Soviet Congress* (中華蘇維埃共和國
中央執行委員會與人民委員會對二次全國
蘇維埃代表大會的報告 Chung-hua su-wei-ai kung-
ho-kuo chung-yang chih-hsing wei-yüan-hui yü jen-min wei-
yüan-hui tui erh-tz'u ch'üan-kuo su-wei-ai tai-piao ta-hui ti
pao-kao), by Mao Tse-tung; printed in *Documents of the Second
National Soviet Congress of the Chinese Soviet Republic,* pp.
122-24, 008.61029/5044, SSC; also in *Red China,* Special Edition during the Second National Soviet Congress, No. 3, January
26, 1934, pp. 1-12 (pp. 5-8 missing), 008.1052/2125/V.5,
SSC; approximately 39,000 words.

This was the state-of-the-union message of Chairman Mao
Tse-tung to the Second National Soviet Congress opening at Juichin on January 22, 1934. It was delivered by Mao to the congress on the afternoon of January 24 and the morning of January
25. (For information of the congress, see *Red China* from January 22 through February 3, 1934; also *Red Star Journal,* February 4, 1934.)
An English version of this statement appears in the Yakhontoff

book, *The Chinese Soviets,* pp. 249-83, acknowledged as a reproduction from the Communist organ *Chinese Workers' Correspondence,* Shanghai, March 31, 1934, without any corrections or changes, by courtesy of Miss Agnes Smedley. As indicated in the introductory remarks, this version is an extract from the text in *Red China,* January 26, 1934. A check with the Chinese original shows that the errors of commission and omission in this translation are too many to be enumerated here, though the general framework of the document is about the same.

From the incomplete Yakhontoff text a further extract was made by Harvard scholars for inclusion in *A Documentary History of Chinese Communism,* pp. 226-39. They stated that they checked the English translation with a Japanese and a Chinese text and that the Chinese text which enabled them to correct the faulty English translation was taken, as the original Chinese source claimed, from the organ of the Soviet Areas, *Struggle* (Kiangsi), No. 66 (see pp. 500-1). Unfortunately, we have looked over *Struggle* (Kiangsi), No. 66, June 30, 1934, but have not found the text of Mao's speech in question.

As indicated on page 501, the Harvard publication omits many sections of the Yakhontoff text. It should be no derogation of the Harvard publication to say that it has made still more incomplete the already incomplete address of Mao as presented by Yakhontoff, though the translation technique of the Harvard text is on the whole an improvement.

Needless to say, omissions have done the text an injustice. As pointed out elsewhere in this work, for instance, Mao's comment on the Fukien rebellion at the end of section 3 of this address is omitted in both the Yakhontoff and Harvard publications. This would be significant in view of the fact that the Fukien rebellion has become a subject of debate in Chinese Communist history.

A close study of the Chinese text of Mao's speech shows that some of his basic conceptions of the Chinese revolution as set forth in this speech conflict with the standpoints of the 1945 "Resolution on Some Historical Problems" sponsored by him. These conflicts of views are especially significant in the light of intraparty struggle. Examples:

First, the 1945 statement attacks the resolution of the Fifth Plenum of January, 1934, for its "blind judgment" (see Mao Tse-tung, *Selected Works,* Chinese edition, Vol. 3, p. 969; English edition, Vol. 4, p. 186; reprint of the resolution, p. 19) which is to the effect that the revolutionary crisis in China had reached a new, acute stage as postulated by the Twelfth Plenum of the Comintern. The present document in its second paragraph echoes the resolution of the Fifth Plenum by saying that "the period in which we live today is one when the revolutionary situation in China has taken a more acute turn and when the whole world is entering upon a transitionary period leading to a new stage of war and revolution."

Second, the 1945 statement, which was primarily directed against the Russian Returned Students, accuses them of overlooking the wishes of the intermediate classes by deciding arbitrarily that the crux of the matter in the Chinese revolution was the desperate struggle between revolution and counterrevolution. (*Ibid.*, Chinese edition, Vol. 3, p. 968; English edition, Vol. 4, p. 184; reprint of the resolution, p. 17.) Interestingly, the present document takes the same position with the Russian Returned Students when it states that "the crucial factor in the present Chinese situation is . . . a life-and-death struggle between revolution and counterrevolution. . . ."

Third, the 1945 statement blames the Russian Returned Students for overstressing the KMT Fifth Campaign as a decisive factor shaping the destiny of China as a colony or a Soviet nation. (*Ibid.*, Chinese edition, Vol. 3, p. 969; English edition, Vol. 4, p. 186; reprint of the resolution, pp. 19-20.) The present document shares this view of the Russian Returned Students in unmistakable terms.

Fourth, the 1945 statement ascribes the Communist victory over the KMT Fourth Campaign to Mao's strategic thinking rather than to the party line (*ibid.*). By contrast, the present document gives credit to the party line of the time.

However, there are also a number of differences between the present speech delivered by Mao and the resolution of the Fifth Plenum sponsored by the Russian Returned Students. For instance, the Fifth Plenum resolution pins the hope for a successful Chinese revolution on the leadership of the party exclusively, while the present speech bases its hope on the combined strength of the party, the government, the army, and the masses. Again, the Fifth Plenum resolution goes in for a socialist revolution when the democratic revolution of the workers and peasants is carried out in important parts of the nation. In contrast, the present statement takes the position that a socialist revolution will not take place until after the completion of the bourgeois-democratic revolution all over the country.

Pavel Mif described this statement as the central task of the

Second National Soviet Congress when he gave a brief account of
the congress in his 1936 publication *Heroic China.*

As described previously, this statement was drafted on the
basis of the Instructions of the Fifth Plenum to the Party Corps
of the Second National Soviet Congress.

Concluding Remarks on the Report of the Central Executive
Committee (關) 於 中 央 執 行 委 員 會 報 告 的 結
論 Kuan-yü chung-yang chih-hsing wei-yüan-hui pao-kao ti
chieh-lun), by Mao Tse-tung; printed in *Red China*, Special Edition during the Second National Soviet Congress, No. 5, January 31, 1934, pp. 1-2, 008.1052/2125/V.5, SSC; also in *Documents of the Second National Soviet Congress of the Chinese Soviet Republic,* pp. 125-39, 008.61029/5044, SSC; approximately
5,800 words.

Chairman Mao's state-of-the-union message to the Second Na-
National Soviet Congress was discussed by the delegates in several committees on January 26 and again by them in a body next
day. The present statement constituted Mao's concluding remarks after the discussion. Judging by its tone, it was probably
made on January 27, 1934. (For views expressed by delegates
during the discussion, see *Red China* of January 31, 1934, pp.
3-4.)

The text of this statement is included in Mao Tse-tung, *Selected Works,* volume one, under the title "Take Care of the
Living Conditions of the Masses and Attend to the Methods of
Work," dated January 27, 1934. (See *ibid.,* Vol. 1, Chinese
version, pp. 131-36; English version, pp. 147-52.) The first
part of this statement is omitted in Mao Tse-tung, *Selected
Works.* This part constitutes almost one-fourth of the full text
as published in *Red China.* Besides, there are many omissions
and changes of individual words in the text contained in Mao's
Selected Works.

Some of the omissions are significant. As described elsewhere in this study, Mao's comment on the Fukien rebellion of
November, 1933-January, 1934, as contained in the statement,
was omitted.

Resolution on the Report of the Central Executive Committee
(關) 於 中 央 執 行 委 員 會 報 告 的 決 議 Kuan-

yü chung-yang chih-hsing wei-yüan-hui pao-kao ti chüeh-i), adopted by the Second National Soviet Congress; printed in *Documents of the Second National Soviet Congress of the Chinese Soviet Republic,* pp. 140-43, 008.61029/5044, SSC; approximately 1,100 words.

Hereby, the Second National Soviet Congress expressed itself satisfied with Chairman Mao's state-of-the-union message, listing a series of tasks to be performed for the purpose of smashing the KMT Fifth Campaign in accordance with the resolution of the congress. It concluded by reaffirming the belief that the ultimate success of the revolution was assured.

General Principles of the Constitution of the Chinese Soviet Republic (中華蘇維埃共和國憲法大綱 Chung-hua su-wei-ai kung-ho-kuo hsien-fa ta-kang), adopted by the Second National Soviet Congress in January, 1934; printed in *Documents of the Second National Soviet Congress of the Chinese Soviet Republic,* pp. 144-51, 008.61029/5044, SSC; also in *A Collection of Red Bandit Reactionary Documents,* Vol. 3, pp. 672-78, 008.2129/4077, SSC; approximately 2,800 words.

With the exception of a small number of individual words and expressions, the text of this constitution agrees entirely with that of the 1931 constitution. Examples of the discrepancies follow:

	1931 Text	*1934 Text*
Preamble	two paragraphs	one paragraph
Article 1	fundamental law; national economic reconstruction	basic law; soviet economic reconstruction; to unite with the middle peasantry (supplied)
Articles 2, 4	Red Army soldiers	Red warriors
Article 3	congress of workers', peasants', and soldiers' council (soviet)	congress of workers', peasants', and soldiers' Soviet
Article 6	feudal system; distribute (land) to poor	feudal exploitation; distribute (land) to hired

	1931 Text	*1934 Text*
	peasants and middle peasants	farm hands, poor peasants and middle peasants
Article 7	toiling masses	laboring masses
Articles 9, 12	class war	revolutionary war
Article 15	Chinese masses	Chinese nation
Article 11	protect the fair sex	protect women
Article 17	close alliance	close allies

It is hard to see any real significance in the above discrepancies, excepting perhaps (1) the addition of the words "unite closely with the middle peasantry" to article 1, and (2) the addition of the hired farm hands to the beneficiaries of land redistribution in article 6.

Speaking before the congress on the afternoon of January 31, Hsiang Ying said that the 1931 constitution was basically sound though some shortcomings had made it not quite suitable for execution and propaganda and that the present constitution, remaining unchanged in principle, seemed much better than the old one after close examination. He mentioned a draft constitution prepared by the CCP Central Committee, which had not arrived in time for discussion. (See *Red China*, February 3, 1934, p. 3.)

Organic Law of the Central Soviet of the Chinese Soviet Republic (中 華 蘇 維 埃 共 和 國 中 央 蘇 維 埃 組 織 法 Chung-hua su-wei-ai kung-ho-kuo chung-yang su-wei-ai tsu-chih fa), promulgated on February 17, 1934; printed in *Documents of the Second National Soviet Congress of the Chinese Soviet Republic*, pp. 152-66, 008.61029/5044, SSC; approximately 3,400 words.

This organic law of the Central Soviet was enacted in accordance with the general principles of the constitution of the Chinese Soviet Republic, annotated previously. It consists of fifty-one articles, divided into ten chapters dealing with, *inter alia*, (1) the National Soviet Congress, (2) the Central Soviet Congress, (3) powers of the above-mentioned two organs, (4) presidium of the Central Executive Committee, (5) Council of People's Commissars. An important document, indeed, for the study of the organization and functions of the Central Soviet.

Three Important Reports: Discussions and Conclusions (三個重要報告： 討論與結論 San-ko chung-yao pao-kao: t'ao-lun yü chieh-lun), dated January 28-31, 1934; printed in *Red China*, Special Edition during the Second National Soviet Congress, No. 6, February 1, 1934, p. 2, 008.1052/ 2125/V. 5, SSC; approximately 3,000 words.

From January 28 to 31 the congress heard three different reports on Red Army reconstruction, economic reconstruction, and Soviet reconstruction respectively. This paper gives the gist of all the three reports.

The importance of these three reports should not be underestimated, as can be seen from the fact that they constituted three of the six items on the agenda of the congress, the other three being Mao's state-of-the-union message, adoption of the constitution and other laws, and election of a new government. The three speakers were Chu Teh, Lin Po-ch'ü (Lin Tsu-han), and Wu Liang-p'ing who was to become the People's Commissar of National Economy in the new government.

Resolution on the Problem of the Red Army (關於紅工軍問題的決議 Kuan-yü hung-chün wen-t'i ti chüeh-i), adopted by the Second National Soviet Congress, January, 1934; printed in *Documents of the Second National Soviet Congress of the Chinese Republic*, pp. 167-75, 008.61029/5044, SSC; approximately 3,000 words.

Proceeding on the assumption that the resolution on the Red Army adopted by the First National Soviet Congress had been satisfactorily carried out, this statement reaffirmed the traditional policy to expand and strengthen the Red Army.

Resolution on Soviet Economic Reconstruction (關於蘇維埃經濟建設的決議 Kuan-yü su-wei-ai ching-chi chien-she ti chüeh-i), adopted by the Second National Soviet Congress, January, 1934; printed in *Documents of the Second National Soviet Congress of the Chinese Soviet Republic*, pp. 176-87, 008.61029/5044, SSC; approximately 5,000 words.

As its title indicates, this document aimed at the promotion of economic reconstruction, which had become growingly urgent in the face of the KMT blockade. Practically all the economic policies carried out in the Communist-controlled Kiangsi-Fukien area in 1934 were based on this document. For instance, the exportation of timber, paper, rice, and so forth was encouraged in exchange for the importation of salt, cloth, kerosene, and so forth, which were far from adequate to meet the needs of the local population.

Resolution on Soviet Reconstruction(蘇維埃建設
決議案 Su-wei-ai chien-she chüeh-i-an), adopted by the Second National Soviet Congress, January, 1934; printed in *Documents of the Second National Soviet Congress of the Chinese Soviet Republic,* pp. 188-98, 008.61029/5044, SSC; approximately 4,300 words.

This document concerns itself with the organization and work of the various levels of the Soviet government with particular reference to local government. It praised the past record and encouraged future improvement.

Labor Law of the Chinese Soviet Republic (中華蘇維
埃共和國勞動法 Chung-hua su-wei-ai kung-ho-kuo lao-tung fa), adopted and promulgated by the Central Executive Committee of the Chinese Soviet Republic, October 15, 1933; printed in *The Soviet Code,* Vol. 2, pp. 3-40, 008.542/4424/ V.2, SSC; approximately 17,000 words.

Adopted a little more than three months before the convocation of the Second National Soviet Congress, this document was primarily intended to fill the gap left by the labor law of December 1, 1931, that did not provide for an exceptional treatment for the middle peasants, poor peasants, and handicraftsmen who hired auxiliary labor. To consolidate the alliance between workers and peasants, it was stated, the middle peasants, poor peasants, and handicraftsmen who hired auxiliary labor must be more favorably treated than other classes of people who hired auxiliary labor. Specifically, this new group of people could be exempted from certain punishments provided in this law if they hired auxiliary labor contrary to this law but with the consent of both the laborers concerned and the labor union. This new law was made necessary, it was said, by the experience gained since 1931. With the adoption of this law the labor law of December 1, 1931, became null and void.

Outline for Discussion in Regard to the Conclusions of the Second National Soviet Congress (二 蘇 大 會 總 結 討 論 提 綱 Erh-su ta-hui tsung-chieh tao-lun t'i-kang), printed in *Documents of the Second National Soviet Congress of the Chinese Soviet Republic,* pp. 199-214, 008.61029/5044, SSC; approximately 5,500 words.

This outline served as a guide for the training of cadres in regard to the Second National Soviet Congress. It gives a general idea of what the Communist leaders wanted the rank and file to understand about the circumstances and achievements of the congress.

Decisions of the Second National Soviet Congress on the National Emblem, the National Flag, and the Army Flag (第 二 次 全 蘇 大 會 關 於 國 徽 國 旗 及 軍 旗 的 決 定 Ti-erh-tz'u chüan-su ta-hui kuan-yü kuo-hui kuo-ch'i chi chün-ch'i ti chüeh-t'ing), printed in *Red China,* Special Edition during the Second National Soviet Congress, No. 7, February 3, 1934, p. 3, 008.1052/2125/V.5, SSC; also in *Documents of the Second National Soviet Congress of the Chinese Republic,* pp. 215-16, 008.61029/5044, SSC; approximately 200 words.

This piece contains a design of the national emblem, a design of the national flag, and a design of the army flag.

Report on Urgent Mobilization (關 於 緊 急 動 員 的 報 告 Kuan-yü chin-chi tung-yüan ti pao-kao), by Mao Tsetung, January 29, 1934; printed in *Red China,* Special Edition during the Second National Soviet Congress, No. 6, February 1, 1934, p. 1, 008.1052/2125/V.5, SSC; approximately 1,400 words.

On the afternoon of January 29, Mao in behalf of the presidium of the congress moved surprisingly that the congress be closed on February 1, six days earlier than originally scheduled. This move was due to the fact that the Fukien rebellion had been suppressed and that KMT forces were quickly closing in on the Communist base with overwhelming superiority. Mao coupled the move with an urgent appeal for redoubled efforts to resist the enemy. The move was accepted without any sign of hesitation.

Telegram of the Second National Soviet Congress to the Officers and Soldiers of the Red Army (二 蘇 大 會 致 紅 軍 指 戰 員 電 Erh-su ta-hui chih hung-chün chih-chan-yuan tien), dated January 24, 1934; printed in *Red Star Journal*, No. 27, February 4, 1934, p. 1, 008.1052, 2160, SSC; approximately 700 words.

In this telegram the Second National Soviet Congress sent its greetings to the officers and soldiers of the Red Army in recognition of their services performed. The text of this telegram is followed by a news report in the *Red Star Journal* on the progress and close of the congress.

Declaration of the Second National Soviet Congress (第 二 次 全 國 蘇 維 埃 代 表 大 會 宣 言 Ti-erh-tz'u ch'üan-kuo su-wei-ai tai-piao ta-hui hsüan-yen), dated February 1, 1934; printed in *Red China*, Special Edition during the Second National Soviet Congress, No. 7, February 3, 1934, p. 2, 008.1052/2125/V.5, SSC; also in *Documents of the Second National Soviet Congress of the Chinese Soviet Republic*, pp. 1-8, 008.61029/5044, SSC; approximately 2,000 words.

Over and above the usual Communist expressions of revolutionary ambition and exuberant assurance, this declaration contains the following major points:

1. There are two different roads lying ahead for China to choose—the Soviet road and the colonial road—and it is impossible for them to compromise. That is to say, there is no possibility of "peaceful cohabitation" (not to be confused with peaceful coexistence, a term which has hardly ever been used in Chinese documents) between the KMT regime and the Soviet regime.

2. The Soviet regime is willing to conclude an armistice with any armed forces which would stop attacking the Soviet areas and the Red Army and would grant freedoms to the broad masses.

3. Any illusion of a third road of a reformist nature is doomed to failure, as can be seen from the debacle of the Fukien rebellion.

Mao Tse-tung's Speech at the Close of the Congress (毛 澤 東 大 會 閉 幕 詞 Mao-tse-tung ta-hui pi-mo tz'u), printed in *Red China*, Special Edition during the Second National Soviet Congress, No. 7, February 3, 1934, p. 1, 008.1052/2125/V.5, SSC; approximately 800 words.

Just as he announced the opening of the congress, Mao delivered the final official speech at the close of the congress. With great emotion and force, Mao urged the delegates not only to bring about the democratic dictatorship of workers and peasants in a bourgeois-democratic revolution but also ultimately to realize the proletarian dictatorship in a socialist revolution. He closed his speech amid the applause of the audience.

Proclamation of the Central Executive Committee of the Chinese Soviet Republic, No. 1 (中 華 蘇 維 埃 共 和 國) 中 央 執 行 委 員 會 佈 告 , 第 一 號 Chung-hua su-wei-ai kung-ho-kuo chung-yang chih-hsing wei-yüan-hui pu-kao, ti-i hao), dated February 5, 1934; an original official copy of the proclamation, 008.631/1084-2, SSC; also printed in *Red China*, No. 148, February 12, 1934, p. 1 (document dated February 3, 1934 here), 008.1052/2125/V.5, SSC; approximately 1,200 words.

At the last session of the congress, held on the morning of February 1, a total of 175 members of the Central Executive Committee of the Central Soviet Government was elected together with 36 alternates. The list was ready-made. Only one candidate was reported to have failed in the election, but his name was not disclosed. (See *Red China*, February 3, 1934, p. 1.)

The new Central Committee of the government held its first session on the morning of February 3, during which a seventeen-man presidium of the Central Committee and a Council of People's Commissars (equivalent to a cabinet) were elected. Mao was elected chairman of the presidium with Hsiang Ying and Chang Kuo-t'ao as vice-chairmen. Chang Wen-t'ien was elected chairman of the cabinet composed of eleven people's commissars. (See *Red China,* February 6, 1934, p. 1.)

The present document was the official announcement of the result of the elections, that is, the complete list of the personnel of the new government. A comparison of this government with the 1931 line-up reveals the following interesting points:

1. Thirty-two of the sixty-three members of the 1931 CEC (Central Executive Committee) were re-elected in 1934.

2. One hundred and forty-three members of the new CEC were not included in the old government.

3. The 1931 CEC was headed by a single chairman, while the 1934 CEC was led by a presidium of seventeen persons with one of them serving as chairman.

4. Mao headed both the CEC and CPC (Council of People's Commissars) with Hsiang Ying and Chang Kuo-t'ao as vice-chairmen of both organs in the 1931 line-up. In 1934 Mao remained as chairman of the CEC with the same old two vice-chairmen, but Chang Wen-t'ien, a leading member of the Russian Returned Student group, became chairman of the CPC (equivalent to the premier) with no deputies.

5. The 1931 CEC was composed of only 63 members while the 1934 CEC consisted of 175 members and 36 alternates.

6. In the 1934 cabinet there were two new departments for national economy and for food.

7. The chairman and vice-chairmen of the military council were appointed by the CEC in 1931 while they were elected by the CEC in 1934.

8. Of the nine people's commissars in the 1931 cabinet only three remained on their posts in 1934, namely, Wang Chia-ch'iang (a member of the Russian Returned Student group) as commissar of foreign affairs, Chu Teh as commissar of military affairs, and Ch'ü Ch'iu-pai as commissar of education.

9. Powerful Russian Returned Students Po Ku and Chang Wen-t'ien and their supporters Chou En-lai and Hsiang Ying were among the members of the CEC presidium which was apparently created to keep Mao in check.

24

The Retreat

Fascism, Danger of War, and the Tasks of the Communist Parties in the Various Nations—Resolution of the ECCI Thirteenth Plenum on the Report of Comrade Kuusinen (法西主義，戰爭危險與各國共產黨的任務 —— 共產國際執委第十三次全會關於庫西寧同底報告所通過的提綱 Fa-hsi-chu-i, chan-cheng wei-hsien, yü ko-kuo kung-ch'an-tang ti jen-wu-kung-ch'an kuo-chi chih-wei ti shih-san tz'u ch'üan-hui kuan-yü kuu-si-nin t'ung-chih pao-kao so t'ung-kuo ti t'i-kang), adopted in December, 1933; Chinese version appearing in *Struggle* (Kiangsi), No. 55, April 10, 1934, pp. 2-15, 008. 2105/7720/V.5, SSC; approximately 4,500 words.

Though adopted in December, 1933, this Comintern resolution was not accepted by Chinese Communists until April 12, 1934 (see *Struggle* [Kiangsi], No. 56, April 21, 1934, pp. 13-16), or cited by their official organs until an editorial of the April 28, 1934, issue of *Struggle* of Kiangsi. But by the last-mentioned date, as will be seen later, the military situation had already become so desperate to the Chinese Communists that they had to face the vital problem of retreat. So, it remains to be seen just how much this Comintern resolution had influenced the thinking and action of the Chinese Communists.

Proceeding on the assumption that the world was approaching a new cycle of revolution and war, the present resolution of the ECCI Thirteenth Plenum, held in December, 1933, assigned the following five major tasks to the Communist parties in the various nations:

1. Opposing the fascist ideology.
2. Opposing the fascistization of bourgeois regimes.
3. Opposing the Social Democrats and supporting the united front from below.
4. Improving mass work and strengthening the party structure.
5. Striving for the revolutionary cause and the Soviet regime.

This resolution touches upon China briefly, but the weight it attaches to her is by no means small. On the one hand, for instance, it says: "In China—there are war, intervention and revolution." On the other, it declares: "The Chinese revolution has become a great factor in the world revolution."

It should not be forgotten that the Comintern policy of combating fascism was nothing new. It was provided, for instance, in the resolutions of the Eleventh and Twelfth Plenums of the ECCI, held in April, 1931, and September, 1932, respectively.

The issue of the CCP organ *Struggle* (Kiangsi) in which the present resolution appears contains three other statements concerning the ECCI Thirteenth Plenum, which should be read together with the present one. The three statements are an ECCI report on the Thirteenth Plenum, a decision on the convocation of the Comintern Seventh World Congress, and a financial statement of the ECCI.

In addition, the April 7, 1934, issue of the *Struggle* of Kiangsi contains the declaration of the ECCI Thirteenth Plenum, calling upon the workers and Communists all over the world to combat the White Terror in capitalist countries, notably Germany and China.

[CCP] Resolution on the Resolution of the ECCI Thirteenth Plenum (關於國際十三次全會提綱的決定 Kuan-yü kuo-chi shih-san-tz'u ch'üan-hui ti-kang ti chüeh-ting), adopted by the CCP Central Committee on April 12, 1934; printed in *Struggle* (Kiangsi), No. 56, April 21, 1934, pp. 13-16, 008.2105/7720/V.5, SSC; approximately 2,100 words.

By this statement the CCP indicated its complete agreement with the resolution of the Thirteenth Plenum of the ECCI.

Our Victory in the Fifth Campaign—on Prolonged War (1) (上

次 戰 役 中 我 們 的 勝 利 —— 論 持 久 戰

[-] Wu-tz'u chan-i chung wo-men ti sheng-li–lun ch'ih-chiu-chan [1]), by Chou En-lai, March 13, 1934; printed in *Red Star Journal*, No. 33, March 18, 1934, pp. 1-3, 008.1052/2160, SSC; approximately 10,000 words.

Following the debacle of the Fukien rebellion, things had taken a dramatic turn to the detriment of the Communists. The Nationalist troops which had been sent to Fukien to combat the rebels had now been employed to fight the Communists from the east, filling an important gap in the Nationalist strategy of encirclement. By the time of this writing, Chou En-lai admitted, the east route column of the Nationalist troops, coming from Fukien, had combined with the north route column to form the principal body of the KMT blockading troops, the south and west route armies being secondary in importance. After five and a half months of war, it was pointed out, the immediate target of KMT attack was Kuangch'ang, a strategic city about eighty miles north of Juichin.

Chou En-lai recognized that in the Fifth Campaign, as distinct from the four previous campaigns, the Nationalists were waging a prolonged war based on blockhouse tactics. They were, for instance, in the cities, controlling superior material supply and transportation facilities, and could rely on the support of the imperialists. The Communists, however, were in the rural districts, devoid of such material advantages, and, to make matters worse, were cut off from the Soviet Union and the Communist movements in other countries. Accordingly, as Chou put it, the Nationalists had simply wanted to prosecute a prolonged war to starve the Communists to death.

But the Communists had nothing to fear, Chou declared. They had the support of the combined strength of the masses and the Red Army, which was believed to be invincible. Chou, then, gave a variety of figures of Communist successes in support of his thesis.

The present statement is, indeed, a most interesting and informative comparison of the relative strengths of the CCP and KMT armed forces engaged in the Fifth Campaign, dealing extensively with strategical and tactical problems. This comparison seems all the more important in view of the fact that it was Chou's belief that the outcome of the Fifth Campaign would determine the future course of China: a colonial or Soviet road.

This piece is indicated as the first of a series of articles by

Chou En-lai. Unfortunately, the other installments are not available.

The Workers' and Peasants' Red Army and the Masses of the Soviet Areas Must All Mobilize for War in Defense of Kuangch'ang!!! (工農紅軍和全蘇區群眾一致動員起來為保衛廣昌而戰 !!! Kung-nung hung-chün han ch'üan-su-ch'ü ch'ün-chung i-chih tung-yüan ch'i-lai wei pao-wei kuang-ch'ang erh chan!!!), by Chou En-lai, April 18, 1934; printed in *Red Star Journal*, No. 38, April 22, 1934, p. 1, 008.1052/2126, SSC; approximately 1,500 words.

As its title indicates, this statement stressed the importance of defending the strategic city of Kuangch'ang, on which the Nationalist troops were rapidly closing in. They were now reported only ten miles from the city which had become an important target of their attack after the defeat of the Fukien rebellion.

A Directive Letter from the CCP Central Committee and the Central Council of People's Commissars to the Party and Soviets in the War Zone (中共中央委員會中央人民委員會給戰地黨和蘇維埃的指示信 Chung-kung chung-yang wei-yüan-hui chung-yang jen-min wei-yüan-hui chi chan-ti tang han su-wei-ai ti chih-shih-hsin), dated April 24, 1934; printed in *Struggle* (Kiangsi), No. 58, May 5, 1934, pp. 1-7, 008.1052/2125/V.7, SSC; approximately 6,000 words.

When Kuangch'ang was about to fall, the Communist leadership issued this directive to both the party and Soviet rank and file, outlining the guiding principles of work for them to follow. The principles given are as follows:

1. Mobilizing and arming the masses to join the revolutionary war and to develop extensive guerrilla tactics. This was considered essential to counteract the blockhouse and blockade tactics of the KMT troops.

2. Introducing a reign of Red Terror in which the broad masses should be made to join the struggle against counterrevolution.

3. Laying great practical stress on the work of disintegrating the KMT troops.

4. Readjusting the organization of the party, government, and mass bodies to the rapidly changing requirements of the war.

Fight to the End for Territory, for Freedom, and for the Soviet Regime! (為 土 地, 為 自 由, 為 蘇 維 埃 政 權 戰 鬥 到 底 ! Wei t'u-ti, wei tzu-yu, wei su-wei-ai cheng-ch'üan chan-tou tao ti!), by Chou En-lai, April 27, 1934; printed in *Red Star Journal*, No. 39, April 29, 1934, p. 1, 008.1052/2160, SSC; approximately 2,300 words.

At this writing, the fall of Kuangch'ang was imminent, and farther east, south, and west the encircling KMT forces were advancing rapidly. In calling upon the people to do what they could to help fight the enemy, Chou En-lai reiterated the Communist determination that no inch of territory should be abandoned to the enemy.

According to an ex-Communist source, Communist policy-makers held an important conference to discuss strategic and tactical problems before the fall of Kuangch'ang. Among other things, the following two points were decided:

1. Communist forces under the command of Fang Chih-min in the Fukien-Chekiang-Kiangsi border area should break through the enemy in the northeast to deploy to the region bordering Chekiang and southern Anhwei. For political purposes, this detachment should bear the title of a Red Army vanguard marching north to fight the Japanese.

2. The defense line running from Kuangch'ang to Posheng (Ningtu) and Shengli (Lungkanghsü) was made a line for a decisive war. Should this line be broken, the main body of the Red Army should break through by surprise the KMT encirclement in the southwestern sector bordering Kwangtung. (See Kung Ch'u, *The Red Army and I,* pp. 393-94.)

"Death or Victory" (死 亡 或 者 勝 利 Szu-wang huo-che sheng-li), by Chang Wen-t'ien; printed in *Red China*, No. 181, April 28, 1934, p. 1, 008.1052/2125/V.7, approximately 1,400 words.

In this article the premier of the Central Soviet Government

called upon all fellow Communists to go to the front to lead the
operations against the KMT forces closing in upon Kuangch'ang.

In so doing, the premier reiterated the watchwords characteristic of the strategic thinking of the Russian Returned Student
leadership during the KMT Fifth Campaign, such as: "Don't let
the enemy occupy an inch of our Soviet territory, " "Smash the
imperialist-KMT Fifth Campaign. " These watchwords were
later dismissed by Mao and his group as erroneous. (See Mao
Tse-tung, "Strategic Problems of China's Revolutionary War, "
contained in Mao Tse-tung, *Selected Works,* Chinese edition,
Vol. 1, p. 200; English edition, Vol. 1, p. 214; "Resolution on
Some Historical Problems, " contained in the same, Chinese
edition, Vol. 3, pp. 978, 985; English edition, Vol. 4, pp. 196,
204; reprint of the resolution, pp. 32, 40.)

The title of this article was attributed to Lenin who was said
to have used it for encouragement of the comrades of the
Sverdlov University who were being sent to the front during the
civil war in Russia.

Kuangch'ang fell to KMT troops the day this article was published. (See *Red China,* No. 184, May 4, 1934, p. 2.)

The Crucial Moment for a Decisive War in the Second Phase .
of the Fifth Campaign and Our Tasks (五 次 戰 役 第 二 步
的 決 戰 關 頭 和 我 們 的 任 務 Wu-tz'u chan-i ti-
erh-pu ti chüeh-chan kuan-t'ou han wo-men ti jen-wu), dated
April 28, 1934; printed in *Struggle* (Kiangsi), No. 58, May 5,
1934, pp. 7-14, 008.1052/2125/V.7, SSC; approximately 6,300
words.

Though published a week later, this editorial was written the
day Kuangch'ang fell to KMT troops.

It was stated that the civil war that was going on did not concern the Chinese Soviets alone but had a global significance as
well. In support of this thesis, the resolution of the Thirteenth
ECCI Plenum was cited, which declared that the world was approaching a new cycle of revolution and war.

Like a previous statement by Chou En-lai, this article pointed
out that the KMT Fifth Campaign was a prolonged war based on
blockhouse tactics. The KMT troops adopted these tactics, it
was pointed out, because they knew the Communist weaknesses:
no big cities, no economic centers, no ports, no big mines, no
large factories—in a word, the CCP had not yet seized big cities

where the proletarians assembled, but still found itself in the rural districts which had grown from the agrarian revolution.

Accordingly, the central watchword remained: "Smash the enemy's Fifth Campaign completely." Out of this central watchword came a number of war slogans such as, "Everything for war," "Victory at all costs," and so forth.

Although Kuangch'ang Has Fallen, We Must Smash the Enemy at All Costs! (廣昌雖然陷落了，我們無論如何要粉碎敵人！ Kuang-ch'ang sui-jan hsien-lo liao, wo-men wu-lun ju-ho yao fen-sui ti-jen!), by Chou En-lai, April 30, 1934; printed in *Red Star Journal*, No. 40, May 5, 1934, pp. 1-2, 008.1052/2160, SSC; approximately 2,000 words.

In this leading article, Chou En-lai openly recognized the fall of Kuangch'ang as a major step forward on the part of the encircling KMT troops and characterized the military situation as extremely serious. In doing so, he intended to heighten the Communist morale rather than frustrate it. He attacked all sorts of vacillation of Right opportunism and concluded by quoting Stalin as saying: We "have only one will, one thought, that is to say, we must triumph and smash the enemy at all costs!"

We Must Triumph at All Costs! (我們無論如何要勝利！ Wo-men wu-lun ju-ho yao sheng-li!); by Chang Wen-t'ien; printed in *Red China*, No. 183, May 1, 1934, pp. 1-2, 008.1052/2125/V.7, SSC; approximately 4,400 words.

In attempting to bolster the Communist morale in the face of the mounting pressure of the KMT troops, the Communist premier in this article still withheld the news of the fall of Kuangch'ang from the public. It was but natural that the Communist premier attacked all sorts of letdown at such a critical moment. The remarkable thing was that he singled out the so-called "solid-breastwork-and-empty-field" tactic for attack as a manifestation of Right opportunism. That tactic, as described previously, was Mao's favorite.

"My Position Is over There, on the Front, Standing on the

Forefront of the Battle Line!" ("我的位置在那邊，在前線上，站在戰線的最前面！" "Wo-ti wei-chih tsai na-pien, tsai ch'ien-hsien shang, chan-tsai chan-hsien ti tsui-ch'ien mien!"), by Po Ku, May 12, 1934; printed in *Red China*, No. 189, May 16, 1934, p. 1, 008.1052/2125/V.7, SSC; approximately 2,450 words.

By the time this leading article was written, the military situation was becoming more than ever serious to the Communists. The party leader frankly admitted that the KMT troops were daily narrowing their encirclement of the heart of the Central Soviet Area and that victory or death was to be determined in a few months. He therefore called upon all party members, workers, and peasants to join the Red Army to fight on the front to the last man. He urged them to give everything they had and everything they were to the defense of Soviet territory.

The title of this article was borrowed from Lenin.

Let's Arm and Join the Red Army! (武裝起來，到紅軍中去！ Wu-chuang ch'i-lai, tao hung-chün chung ch'ü!), issued as a declaration of the Central Revolutionary Military Council, May 14, 1934; printed in *Red China*, No. 190, May 18, 1934, p. 1, 008.1052/2125/V.7, SSC; approximately 1,400 words.

The content and wording of this declaration agree in general with the May 12 article of Po Ku, described previously. Specifically, Chu Teh, chairman of the Central Revolutionary Military Council, who signed the present declaration, disclosed that a total of 50,000 men would be collected for the Red Army within three months from May through July. He stressed frankly that the Communists were already confronted with the question of "victory or death."

Meanwhile, it was announced that 50,000 troops should be recruited for the month of May alone. (See *Red Star Journal*, May 10 and 15, 1934.)

As has been noted previously, the shortage of man power was coupled with the lack of food, cloth, salt, and so forth. Communist publications such as *Red China* and the *Red Star Journal* contained a good deal of data on measures taken by the Communists to meet this desperate situation, particularly during the last months of the Kiangsi regime.

The CCP Is the Only Leader in the Anti-Imperialist and Agrarian Revolution in China (中 國 共 產 黨 是 中 國 反 帝 與 土 地 革 命 中 的 唯 一 領 袖 Chung-kuo kung-ch'an-tang shih chung-kuo fan-ti yü t'u-ti ko-ming chung ti wei-i ti ling-hsiu), by Wang Ming (Ch'en Shao-yü); printed in *Struggle* (Kiangsi), No. 66, June 30, 1934, pp. 1-12, 008.2105/ 7720/V.6, SSC; approximately 9,100 words.

Judging from the fact that it made mention of the anti-Japanese program adopted by the CCP in April, 1934, this article was doubtless written after the fall of Kuangch'ang. Nevertheless, it did not betray the slightest idea of a retreat. On the contrary, the writer, leader of the Russian Returned Students, felt sure of the success of the CCP.

Among the three Left lines of 1927-35 which were the target of attack by Mao's machine in 1945, the hardest hit was the third Left line under the leadership of the Russian Returned Student group headed by Wang Ming. In contrast, Wang Ming in this article extolled the third Left line to the skies. Except for minor flaws, in his opinion, that line left nothing to be desired.

Wang Ming claimed that the Chinese revolution had achieved great successes in the few years that had just passed and that those successes had been due to what he called the further Bolshevization of the party. According to him, this was evident from the following:

1. The resolute and unwavering execution of the general political line determined by the Central Committee under the leadership of the Comintern.

2. The raising of basic tactical slogans at the right moment in accordance with particular circumstances and class relations.

3. The tactics and practical steps for the implementation of party policy based on the above-mentioned slogans.

4. The strengthening and development of party organization as shown in the increase in the number of party members, supported by significant figures.

In addition, successes in the two-front struggle against Right and Left deviations were also claimed, so much so that the party had allegedly achieved an unprecedented unity of ideology and organization.

Nevertheless, a number of inadequacies were mentioned at the end of the article, as was common in Communist literature.

*What Has the CCP Done or Will It Do to Prosecute the Na-
tional Revolutionary War of the Armed Masses?* (為著實
現武裝民眾的民族革命戰爭, 中國共產黨
做了些什麼和將做些什麼 ?   Wei-cho shih-
hsien wu-chuang min-chung ti min-tsu ko-ming chan-cheng
chung-kuo kung-ch'an-tang tso-liao hsieh shih-mo han chiang
tso hsieh shih-mo), by Po Ku (Ch'in Pang-hsien), July 8, 1934;
printed in *Struggle* (Kiangsi), No. 69, August 4, 1934, pp. 1-
20, 008. 2105/7720/V. 6, SSC; approximately 16,000 words.

This speech delivered by the party leader before the Society
for the Study of Marxism on July 8, 1934 was a summing up of
the achievements of the CCP in the period 1931-34 with particular reference to the campaign against Japan. It disclosed for the
first time that a section of the Red Army could be sent to fight
the Japanese.

The content of this speech is generally like that of Wang
Ming's article entitled "The CCP is the leader in the anti-imperialist and agrarian revolution in China, " described previously. As is natural in a eulogy of this nature, this address
contrasts sharply with the criticism leveled by Mao's machine
against Po Ku and his group in the "Resolution on Some Historical Problems, " adopted on April 20, 1945.

To begin with, Po Ku discussed briefly the basic principles,
slogans and stratagems of the CCP in the fight against imperialism. All these are essentially a repetition of the viewpoints
of Wang Ming in the aforesaid article.

Po Ku gave a relatively detailed account of the anti-imperi-
alist record of the party in the 1931-34 period. He divided the
record into four phases: first, from the Japanese invasion of
Manchuria on September 18, 1931, to the Nanking demonstra-
tions on November, 1931; second, from the Japanese attack on
Shanghai on January 28, 1931, to the united front program of
January 17, 1933; third, the Fukien revolt, November, 1933-
January, 1934; fourth, fresh Japanese aggression in 1934.

The first period was described as the most confusing, characterized by severe struggles among all parties and cliques.
During this period the CCP followed four tactics, among others,
(1) to fight for a quasi-lawful position for the party in public affairs, (2) to manipulate mass meetings sponsored by counterrevolutionaries, (3) to initiate mass demonstrations, and (4) to
form anti-Japanese mass organizations.

The second period was marked by a series of timely and flexible tactics that had proved successful. The most important events during this period were the declaration of war on Japan on April 15, 1932, the anti-Japanese three-point program of January 17, 1933, and the united front policy set forth in the Central Committee letter to the Manchurian Provincial Committee in September, 1933.

The revolt in Fukien characterized the whole third period in which the CCP allied itself with the Fukien rebels though laying bare their counterrevolutionary character at the same time.

In the fourth and last period the most important development was the anti-Japanese united front program of April 20, 1934. But events had marched so fast that a mere program coupled with empty talk would not do. The time was ripe for the Red Army to send a part of its troops to fight the Japanese imperialists, and it was revealed that the central government and the military council had already reached some decision on this score. All the Red Army men were therefore called upon to make ready for action to lead the entire nation to prosecute a holy war against Japan at any moment.

It is important to note that this statement of the party leader heralded the July 15 declaration of the central government and the military council, announcing the dispatch of a vanguard of the Red Army to fight the Japanese.

In Celebrating "August 1, " We Must Annihilate the Enemies within the Doors of the Soviet Areas and Destroy Them behind Their Backs! (紀念 八一 ， 我們要消滅敵人 在蘇區門內, 要瓦解 敵人 在 他 們 的 背 後 Chi-nien "pa-i, " wo-men yao hsiao-mieh ti-jen tsai su-ch'ü men-nei, yao wa-chiai ti-jen tsai ta-men ti pei-hou!), by Chou En-lai, July 10, 1934; printed in *Red Star Journal*, No. 53, July 15, 1934, p. 1, 008. 1052/2160, SSC; approximately 2, 700 words.

As its title indicates, this leading article aimed to encourage the fighting spirit of the Communist soldiers on the occasion of the Red Army Day. It was revealed that the two strategic cities of Chienning and Liench'eng in western Fukien had fallen and that it was relatively quiet at all fronts in June. If there was any hint of a general retreat in this article, it was not clear.

Declaration of the Central Government of the Chinese Soviet Republic and the Revolutionary Military Council of the Chinese Workers' and Peasants' Red Army on the March of the Chinese Workers' and Peasants' Red Army to the North to Resist Japan

(中華蘇維埃共和國中央政府中國工農紅軍 革命軍事委員會為中國工農紅軍北上抗日 宣言) Chung-hua su-wei-ai kung-ho-kuo chung-yang cheng-fu chung-kuo kung-nung hung-chün ko-ming chün-shih wei-yüan-hui wei chung-kuo kung-nung hung-chün pei-shang k'ang-jih hsüan-yen), issued July 15, 1934; printed in *Red China,* No. 221, August 1, 1934, p. 1, 008. 1052/2125/V. 8, SSC; approximately 2, 200 words.

Issued under the name of Chairmen Mao Tse-tung and Chu Teh together with their deputies, this declaration announced, as Po Ku had hinted a week before, that a vanguard of the Red Army was being ordered to march north to fight the Japanese aggressors. It was stated that all the remainder of the Red Army would follow suit if the KMT troops accepted the three cease-fire conditions put forward by the CCP on January 17, 1933.

This declaration contained a five-point program against Japan, which was based on the CCP statement of April 10, 1934.

The Communist historian Ho Kan-chih records that the CCP organized a vanguard of anti-Japanese troops in July, 1934, to march north to resist the Japanese. This vanguard cut its way through the enemy in Fukien, Chekiang, Anhwei, and Kiangsi and reached the Huaiyü mountains in northeastern Kiangsi toward the end of the year. In August, Ho adds, another column of Communist troops, identified as the Sixth Army Corps, was ordered to withdraw from its base on the Hunan-Kiangsi border to pave the way for a general retreat of the main body of the Red Army. In September, still another column in the Oyuwan area accomplished a breakthrough by surprise and won a base in southwestern Shensi soon afterwards. All these military movements, Ho adds, had been made to dovetail with the Red Army's plan of an over-all shift of strategy which was carried out in October, 1934. (See Ho Kan-chih, *History of the Contemporary Chinese Revolution,* pp. 171-72; cf. Kung Ch'u, *The Red Army and I,* p. 404.)

Thus, it has become apparent that the organization of the

anti-Japanese vanguard in July, 1934, was the first practical
step the Chinese Communists had taken in their general plan
for the Long March. This should be all the clearer in view of
the fact that the present declaration, as mentioned above,
points out that all the remainder of the Red Army would follow
suit if the January 17, 1933, cease-fire offer was accepted. In
1937, the Communist historian Hsü Meng-ch'iu declared that he
was transferred to Lin Piao's army in July, 1934, in preparation for the Long March. (See Helen F. Snow [Nym Wales], *Red
Dust*, Stanford, Stanford University Press, 1952, p. 64.)

It is not clear precisely when and how the decision on the
Communist withdrawal from the Kiangsi-Fukien area was made.
On the basis of an interview with Chang Kuo-t'ao, Robert North
states that the Chinese Communists referred that matter to
Moscow, which, in the next to the last radiogram received in
the autumn of 1934, advised the Chinese Communists to pull out
and seek safety somewhere—as far as Outer Mongolia, if neces-
sary. Chang Kuo-t'ao was quoted as saying that Po Ku and Chou
En-lai made the local decision to evacuate. (See Robert North,
Moscow and Chinese Communists, p. 164.)

According to Dr. Hu Shih, it was reliably reported that leading Communists attributed the success of the Long March to
what Stalin had taught as "the strategy of retreat." It was this
Lenin-Stalin doctrine of "correct retreat," he adds, that had influenced the military thinking at Juichin in 1934 and had resulted
in the Long March and the survival of the Red Army. (See Hu
Shih, "China in Stalin's Grand Strategy," toward the end of section 3, published in *Foreign Affairs,* an American quarterly review, October, 1950.)

Whatever the discussions in Juichin and possibly in Moscow
with regard to the question of evacuation, subsequent Russian
and Chinese sources are agreed that the Communist evacuation
of the Kiangsi-Fukien area was a decision of strategy. In 1936,
Pavel Mif declared that the main body of the Red Army evacuated Kiangsi and set out for the Long March in order to "conserve its strength." (See Pavel Mif, *Heroic China,* Chinese
version, p. 106.) In the same year, Mao referred more than
once to the Long March as a strategic retreat or a shift of
strategy. (See Mao Tse-tung, *Selected Works,* Chinese edition,
Vol. 1, p. 188; English edition, Vol. 1, p. 200.) Mao explained: "A strategic retreat is a planned strategic step which
an inferior force, unable to smash quickly the offensive of a
superior force, adopts in order to conserve its strength and

wait for an opportune moment for beating the enemy. " *(Ibid.,* Chinese edition, Vol. 1, p. 167; English edition, Vol. 1, p. 210.) One cannot fail to note how Mao's explanation harmonized with the strategic thinking of Stalin, who, in expounding the strategy of retreat, quoted Lenin for support. (See J. Stalin, *Problems of Leninism,* English edition, Moscow, Foreign Language Publishing House, 1954, p. 88; a slightly different translation of Stalin's passage on the strategy of retreat, as quoted by Hu Shih, is contained in William C. Bullitt, *The Great Globe Itself, A Preface to World Affairs,* New York, Charles Scribner's Sons, 1946, Appendix III, p. 299. As pointed out by Dr. Hu, this passage was quoted *in toto* in Chang Hao (Lin Yü-ying), *The Tactical Line of the Chinese Communist Party,* probably 1937, p. 31.)

Use a Six-Point Program to Destroy the Enemy (用 六 大 政 綱 來 瓦 解 敵 人 Yung liu-ta kang-ling lai wa-chiai ti-jen), by Chou En-lai; printed in *Red Star Journal,* No. 54, July 20, 1934, p. 1, 008. 1052/2160, SSC; approximately 1, 000 words.

On the basis of the anti-Japanese five-point program embod-ied in the July 15 declaration, Chou En-lai in this article put forward six points for consumption of the White troops. The six points:

1. Go north to fight the Japanese and stop attacking the Soviet areas forthwith. The Chinese should not fight the Chinese.

2. Demand the freedom of assembly, association, speech, and action to fight the Japanese.

3. Improve the livelihood and raise the pay of the soldiers.

4. Conclude an armistice and an anti-Japanese alliance with the Red Army.

5. Kill the (KMT) officers who would not allow their troops to fight the Japanese, and then desert to the Red Army.

6. Do no harm to workers and peasants in the Soviet areas and object to KMT suppression of the anti-Japanese movement.

This statement was made on the occasion of the dispatch of a vanguard of the Red Army to march north to fight the Japanese. For instructions of the General Political Department in explana-tion of the nature and purpose of the anti-Japanese vanguard, see *Red Star Journal,* No. 57, August 5, 1934, p. 2.

An Interview with Comrade Mao Tse-tung: The Current Situation and the Red Army's Anti-Japanese Vanguard (毛澤東同志談：目前時局與紅軍抗日先遣部隊 Mao tse-tung t'ung-chih t'an: mu-chien shih-chü yü hung-chün k'ang-jih hsien-ch'ien pu-tui), printed in *Red China*, No. 221, August 1, 1934, p. 2, 008. 1052/2125/V. 8, SSC; approximately 3, 600 words.

Interviewed, Chairman Mao told a *Red China* reporter that the Red Army's anti-Japanese vanguard was sent off on August 1, 1934. However, a news dispatch appearing on the same page of the official organ of the Soviet Government states that the vanguard set out in July. The marshaling of all available evidence suggests that the latter date seems to be the correct one.

Mao declared that the Red Army in all parts of the country had been ordered to make ready for departure at any time in the wake of the vanguard. Unlike the official declaration of July 15, described previously, Mao did not mention the three cease-fire conditions put forward by the CCP on January 17, 1933.

Up to this moment, there was no official public indication of the idea of a general retreat of the Red Army. The dispatch of the so-called vanguard in question was still wrapped in the mystery of the anti-Japanese slogan.

More important, Mao's own status at this time was also a mystery. Kung Ch'u, former chief-of-staff of the Chinese Central Red Army, reports that Mao was then placed on probation as a party member by order of Moscow in connection with the Fukien rebellion. Mao was denied access, Kung says, to all party meetings and was not present at the meeting in which the decision on the Long March was made. During his probationary period beginning in or before August, 1934, Mao was allegedly not even in Juichin, having been virtually exiled to Yuitu, a county seat about fifty miles west of Juichin. Not until the eve of the Long March did Mao return to Juichin to join the exodus. Mao was quoted to the effect that he had been discharged as a member of the CCP Central Committee three times and reprimanded eight times since he joined the Chinese Communist Party.

According to Chang Kuo-t'ao during an interview in Hongkong in late October, 1959, it was probably true that Mao had been expelled as a member of the CCP Central Committee or Politburo three times and reprimanded eight times. This was what

Mao often told people including Chang himself. But only the expulsion decided by the Politburo enlarged meeting of November,
1927, had been made public, while the time and nature of the
other seven punishments remained unknown. Chang Kuo-t'ao
was not sure whether Mao was placed on probation in connection
with the Fukien rebellion. Whatever the true story about Communist non-cooperation with the Fukien rebels, Chang declared, the fact was that Mao had been deprived of virtually all
authority by that time and that therefore he had no power to
make the decision. (See Kung Ch'u, *The Red Army and I*, pp.
395-400.)

With reference to the Fukien rebellion, Kung Ch'u tells another sensational story to the effect that the Soviet Union sent
a sizable amount of military aid to the Chinese Communists,
which was stopped at Vladivostock owing to the quick collapse
of the Fukien regime, and that only a sum of financial aid managed to reach Kiangsi and provided the Chinese Communists
with necessary funds for the Long March. *(Ibid.*, pp. 362-67.)
Questioned about the reliability of this story of Russian aid,
Chang Kuo-t'ao was disinclined to believe that the story was
true. He said that gossip of one sort or another was common in
Communist circles.

*Let the Move of the Anti-Japanese Vanguard of the Red Army
Mark the Beginning of a Real, Extensive National Revolutionary
War of the Armed People* (使紅軍抗日先遣隊的出
動成為真正的廣大的武裝民眾民族革命戰
爭的開始 Shih hung-chün k'ang-jih hsien-ch'ien-tui ti ch'u-
tung ch'eng-wei chen-cheng ti kuang-ta ti wu-chuang min-chung min-
tsu ko-ming chan-cheng ti k'ai-shih), editorial of *Struggle* (Kiangsi),
No. 70, August 16, 1934, pp. 1-6, 008.2105/7720/V.6, SSC;
approximately 4,200 words.

This editorial characterized the dispatch of the vanguard of
the Red Army to fight the Japanese as a historic event. It suggested that the time was fast approaching when the Red Army
would fight face to face with the Japanese.

This statement contained the same six points that Chou En-
lai raised in his article dated July 20, 1934. It may or may not
be significant to note that Chou's article antedated this editorial
of the party organ by almost four weeks.

Incidentally, the *Struggle* of Kiangsi for June 24, 1934,

carried an editorial, urging the necessity of bringing home to the people the CCP anti-Japanese program of April 10, 1934. That editorial may be useful for reference, though it does not touch the question of the vanguard of the Red Army.

A New Situation and a New Victory (新 的 形 勢 與 新 的 勝 利 Hsin ti hsing-shih yü hsin ti sheng-li), by Chou En-lai, August 18, 1934; printed in *Red Star Journal*, No. 60, August 20, 1934, pp. 1-2, 008.1052/2160, SSC; approximately 3,800 words.

For the first time since the start of the KMT Fifth Campaign in the fall of 1933, Chou En-lai in this article hinted at a general Communist retreat, though it was not so clear to outsiders at the moment. Said Chou:

We must resolutely thrust our way into the rear of the enemy, straight into the remote rear of the enemy, in order to settle down and to develop. . . . [We must] create a new situation and not turn back to the old Soviet areas again. . . . This is our guide for war at the present moment.

Chou En-lai, who as political commissar of the Red Army supervised military policy-making at the time, made the above observations amidst a number of factors:

1. A new KMT offensive was launched during the latter half of July with Shihch'eng, a strategic city located about midway between Kuangch'ang and Juichin, as the immediate target.

2. A breakthrough had already been initially accomplished by the anti-Japanese vanguard of the Red Army in the direction of Fukien and Chekiang.

3. Another column of Red Army forces had just evacuated the Communist position west of the Kan River in Kiangsi. This column, as described previously, had actually meant to prepare the way for the retreat of the main body of the Red Army.

Chou En-lai made no secret of the fact that the enemy was now aiming at Juichin and that the crucial moment for a decisive war would be in September or October.

Everything Is for the Defense of the Soviet! (一 切 為 了 保 衛 蘇 維 埃 ! I-ch'ieh wei-liao pao-wei su-wei-ai!), by Chang Wen-t'ien, September 26, 1934, printed in *Rea China,*

No. 239, September 29, 1934, pp. 1-2, 008. 1052/2125/V. 8, SSC; approximately 4, 400 words.

This was the first official indication that the strategic thinking of the Russian Returned Student leadership was coming to an end, strategic thinking which was reflected in slogans: "Don't let the enemy occupy an inch of Soviet territory!" "Fight the enemy on Soviet soil to the last man!" and so forth.

After a brief reference to the anti-Japanese vanguard and the Sixth Army Corps which accomplished a breakthrough from the Hunan-Kiangsi border area, described previously, the Chinese premier outlined the various forms of fight which the Communist forces had had to take in view of the changing conditions in different localities of the country. The various forms of fight: mobile operations, blockhouse or positional warfare, guerrilla tactics, and even strategic or tactical retreat.

As the battle had spread to the whole country, Chang Wen-t'ien pointed out, tactics would have to differ with the varying conditions of the different battlefields. Under the present circumstances, he stressed, the general forward and offensive line of the party should in no way be interpreted to mean that offensives alone could lead to victory. Other forms of warfare would have to be adopted so that the party might not suffer from the dogmatic rationalization that revolution was a straight, uninterrupted, and always upward process leading to victory. Accordingly, all the different forms of struggle, such as offensive, counteroffensive, defensive, and retreat, would have to be employed according to circumstances in order to bring the revolution to a complete victory. The revolution, he emphasized, would be a long-range struggle which could not be expected to be completed in a matter of days, months, or even years.

Interestingly, Chang Wen-t'ien reversed his former position by saying that all arguments in favor of defending every inch of Soviet territory or engaging the enemy on Soviet territory to the last man were opportunistic.

[An Appeal] from the Central Government of the Chinese Soviet Republic and the Central Committee of the CCP to All the People of the Soviet Areas for Unfolding Mass Guerrilla Warfare (中華蘇維埃共和國) 中央政府 中國共産黨中央委員會 為發展群眾的游擊戰爭告全蘇區民眾 Chung-hua su-wei-ai kung-ho-kuo

chung-yang cheng-fu chung-kuo kung-ch'an-tung chung-yang
wei-yüan-hui wei fa-chan ch'ün-chung ti yu-chi chan-cheng kao
ch'üan-su-ch'ü min-chung), dated October 3, 1934; printed in
Red China, No. 240, October 3, 1934, p. 1, 008.1052/2125/
V.8, SSC; approximately 1,900 words.

As its title indicates, this document appealed to the masses
for launching all-out guerrilla warfare to protect themselves
and harass the enemy at a moment described as most critical
and urgent. Obviously, the guerrilla operations in contemplation were intended to serve two purposes: On the one hand, they
were to cover the projected evacuation of the main body of the
Red Army, which would be carried out at any moment. On the
other, they were to be employed to pin down a large body of
KMT troops in the Central Soviet Area where a small column of
Communist troops was to be left behind to carry on guerrilla
activities in collaboration with local armed units organized by
the Communists.

According to an ex-Communist source, a sweeping reshuffle
was effected in the Red Army to prepare for the Long March.
Chou En-lai was named chairman of the Military Council in
place of Chu Teh, who was appointed commander-in-chief of
the whole body of the Red Army which was to undertake the
Long March. The government and party headquarters were to
move with this body of the Red Army. Hsiang Ying, one of the
two vice-chairmen of the Central Soviet Government, was left
behind as commander of all the guerrilla forces in the Kiangsi-
Fukien area with Ch'en Yi, now foreign minister at Peiping, as
political commissar. (See Kung Ch'u, *The Red Army and I*, pp.
404-6.)

*Unfold Extensive Mass Guerrilla Warfare to Protect the
Central Soviet Area* (開展廣泛的群眾游擊戰爭
保衛中央蘇區 K'ai-chan kuang-fan ti ch'ün-chung yu-
chi chan-cheng pao-wei chung-yang su-ch'ü), by Hsiang Ying,
October 18, 1934; printed in *Red China*, No. 243, October 20,
1934, p. 1, 008.1052/2125/V.8, SSC; approximately 2,600
words.

On the basis of the joint appeal of the Central Soviet Government and the CCP Central Committee under date of October 3,
1934, Hsiang Ying, Vice-Chairman of the Central Soviet Gov-

ernment, hereby called upon the mass of people to unfold all-out guerrilla warfare to protect the Central Soviet Area. This was only natural because Hsiang was going to direct all guerrilla activities in the Kiangsi-Fukien area after the evacuation of the main body of the Red Army.

The interesting thing is that up to this late date preparations for the evacuation were still kept secret from the people. By the time the present statement was published, the Red Army must have already started on the Long March a week or so before. But Hsiang Ying did not give the slightest hint at the matter in the present statement except to the few highest authorities who knew about it beforehand.

Nym Wales quoted Hsü Meng-ch'iu to the effect that the first public indication of the idea of the Long March was in an article by Lo Fu in the newspaper *Red China* on October 1. Unfortunately, this issue of the paper is not available. Hsü was quoted as saying that one week was given for mobilizing to leave and that the people who regarded the Red Army as invincible knew the Red Army was mobilizing to move somewhere but did not know where. Hsü and his company left Juichin on October 15, 1934. (See Helen F. Snow [Nym Wales], *Red Dust*, pp. 64-65.)

The October 20, 1934, issue of the *Red China* in which the present statement appears is the last issue available. In all probability this was actually the last issue, No. 243, since the founding of the paper on December 11, 1931.

25

Mao Rewrites History

Resolution on Some Historical Problems (關) 於 若 干 歷
史 問 題 的 決 議 Kuan-yü jo-kan li-shih wen-t'i ti
chüeh-i), adopted by the Seventh Enlarged Plenary Session of
the CCP Sixth Central Committee (since the Sixth National Congress of 1928), on April 20, 1945; printed in Mao Tse-Tung,
Selected Works, Chinese edition, Vol. 3, pp. 955-1002; English edition, Vol. 4, pp. 171-218; also a one-volume reprint in
circulation; approximately 30,000 words.

This document is extremely important to the study of the Chinese Communist movement in 1930-34, which is the subject of
this volume. It reflects Mao's position in relation to the three
Left lines led respectively by Ch'ü Ch'iu-pai, Li Li-san, and
the Russian Returned Students during 1927-35. It tells the story
with particular reference to the 1931-34 period, which remains
largely a myth, if not a blank, in our knowledge of the history
of the CCP to date.

Moreover, this document, though actually reflecting Mao's
position, is technically not a statement of his personal opinion.
It has been officially adopted by the party as the party ideology.
It represents the official position of the Mao leadership as to
the three Left lines in question, especially the third Left line
led by the Russian Returned Students, whom Mao and his group
regarded as their bitterest and most formidable enemy.

Inasmuch as the text of this document is available almost
everywhere in the world and as it has been extensively cited in
this study, it should not be necessary to recapitulate its contents here. Suffice it to say that this document is primarily a

record, though one-sided, of the tension between the Mao group
and the Russian Returned Students during 1931-34. First of all,
it gives a general account of the development of the three Left
lines with particular reference to the 1931-34 period. Then it
makes a fairly detailed comparison of the points of view of both
sides in the political, military, organizational, and ideological
fields. Practically all the major divergences of policy between
the Mao group and the Russian Returned Students can be found
in this statement.

Being one-sided, of course, this statement cannot be accepted
at face value in all respects. As has already been noted, Mao's
own words uttered on several occasions in Kiangsi did not agree
with the present statement. For example, Mao had expressed
different views from the present statement on the Lo Ming line,
on the Fukien rebellion, and during the Second National Soviet
Congress.

It has not been generally known to the outside world, but Mao
and his group made clear in this statement that their conflict
with the Russian Returned Students developed to such an extent
that Mao's leadership in various places in Kiangsi was eventually replaced by the Russian Returned Students or their agents.
It would appear that Mao retained virtually nothing but the titu-
lar chairmanship of the Central Soviet Government on the eve
of the Long March.

One cannot fully understand the significance of this document
if one overlooks the fact that this document was a product of the
so-called *cheng-feng* movement in Yenan in 1942-44 for the cor-
rection of unorthodox tendencies in party ideology and activity.
Significantly, Chang Kuo-t'ao declared during an interview in
Hongkong in late October, 1959, that it was not until Yenan that
the impact of Pavel Mif on the Kiangsi Soviet was liquidated.

According to an official account, the CCP Central Politburo
met to discuss party history several times in 1942-43. All senior cadres of the party were made to join the discussion in
1943-44. The result was the preparation of a draft statement
which was adopted by the party as the "Resolution on Some Historical Problems." It was made clear that after Mao's achieve-
ment of the party leadership in the Tsunyi Conference of January, 1935, many a party cadre still did not understand the nature of the erroneous party lines of the past. In order to achieve
ideological conformity, the history of the party with particular
reference to the 1931-34 period was tailored like the present

statement. (See Mao Tse-tung, *Selected Works*, Chinese edition, Vol. 3, p. 942; English edition, Vol. 4, p. 157.)

Thus, this statement was directly connected with the first part of Mao's speech before a meeting of senior party cadres at Yenan on April 12, 1944, dealing with "Our Study and the Current Situation." *(Ibid.,* Chinese edition, Vol. 3, pp. 941 ff.; English edition, Vol. 4, pp. 157 ff.) Also linked with it were other *cheng-feng* documents such as "Reform Our Study," dated May, 1941, and "Rectify the Party's Style of Work," dated February 1, 1942. *(Ibid.,* Chinese edition, Vol. 3, pp. 795 ff., 813 ff.; English edition, Vol. 4, pp. 12 ff., 28 ff.)

More remotely, this statement was indebted to Mao's article "Strategic Problems of China's Revolutionary War," dated December, 1936, in which the 1931-34 Left line was attacked in unmistakable terms. *(Ibid.,* Vol. 1, Chinese edition, pp. 178, 185, 189, 199-200; English edition, pp. 190-91, 187-88, 201-2, 213-14.) To a lesser degree, it was connected with Mao's statement "On the Tactics of Fighting Japanese Imperialism," dated December 27, 1935. If we trace the line of thought of this document to Mao's ideas of a still earlier period, we would do well to include a number of other statements made by him. Examples:

1. "Why Can China's Red Political Power Exist?" (October 5, 1928).

2. "On the Rectification of Incorrect Ideas in the Party" (December, 1929).

3. "A Single Spark Can Start a Prairie Fire" (January 5, 1930). (All the above statements are contained in Mao Tse-tung, *Selected Works,* volume one.)

In addition to the text of this document appearing in Mao Tse-tung, *Selected Works,* as indicated above, there is a single-volume reprint of the document in circulation. Though the two texts agree with each other, the notes in them differ slightly. While the original text contains forty-three notes, the reprint contains forty-six notes.

It is understandable that the English version of this document is not so clear and forcible as the Chinese original and that therefore it does not make easy and fascinating reading. It is perhaps primarily for this reason that this key statement, despite its basic importance and easy accessibility, has hardly ever been cited or mentioned in Western literature to date. Inevitably there are some textual errors in the English version though great efforts havé obviously been made to make it as faithful to the original as possible. Examples:

Errors	*Corrections*
1. a "situation of immediate revolution" would soon prevail in one or several important provinces, including their major cities (Mao Tse-tung, *Selected Works*, English edition, Vol. 4, p. 181, lines 28-30).	the so-called "direct revolutionary situation" would soon engulf one or several important provinces in which there were key cities.
2. With a few exceptions the same was true of the Red Army forces in other revolutionary bases. Many comrades engaged in practical work also voiced their opposition to Li's line through organizational channels *(ibid.,* p. 179, lines 30-34).	The Red Army in other revolutionary bases, except individual scattered regions, had also achieved generally identical results. In the White areas many comrades engaged in practical work also rose against the Li-san line through the channel of the party structure.
3. surround the cities from the countryside *(ibid.,* p. 178, line 29).	surround the cities with the countryside.

Chronology

1930

January 5.   Mao enunciates the Chu-Mao type of policies, placing emphasis on establishing a base in Kiangsi including Western Fukien.

January.   Chu-Mao group establishes a base in the Kiangsi-Fukien border area, setting the stage for subsequent development.

January or February.   Second party conference of Kiangsu province.

February 7.   Mao sponsors a party conference in southern Kiangsi, in which land policies are formulated.

Southwest Kiangsi Soviet Government is set up.

February 8.   Enlarged ECCI Presidium meeting opens in Moscow.

February 17.   Ch'en Tu-hsiu rejects a Comintern request for a trip to Moscow to discuss his expulsion from the CCP.

Spring.   Chou En-lai arrives at Moscow at the request of Pavel Mif, head of the Chinese Section of the Eastern Department of the Comintern, and reportedly takes over charge of the Chinese delegation to the Comintern.

March 26.   Li Li-san urges the establishment of a revolutionary regime in one or more provinces first in view of the approach of a nationwide high tide of the revolution.

April 3.   Li Li-san leadership orders the Fourth Army under the Chu-Mao leadership in Kiangsi to march north instead of south in anticipation of an imminent storm and urges Mao to attend a projected conference of delegates of Soviet areas in Shanghai.

April 26.   CCP leadership sends another note to Mao urging him to attend the projected Shanghai conference.

May 31.   National Conference of Delegates from the Soviet Areas takes place in Shanghai, adopting a political program, a labor protection law and a provisional land law, and urging the formation of a national Soviet government.

May or early June.   Pavel Mif arrives in China as Comintern delegate, bringing with him a group of his protégés popularly known as the Russian Returned Students including Ch'en Shao-yü, Ch'in Pang-hsien, Chang Wen-t'ien, Shen Tse-min, and Wang Chia-ch'iang.

June 11.   Politburo adopts a resolution on the present political tasks, generally known as the Li-san line.

June or early July.   Ch'en Shao-yü, Wang Chia-ch'iang, Ho Tzu-shu, and Ch'in Pang-hsien are punished for criticizing the Li-san line.

July.   Second plenum of the Southwest Kiangsi Special Committee raises objections to the land policies adopted by the February 7 Conference.

July 23.   ECCI Political Secretariat issues a directive to the CCP, setting forth different policies from the Li-san line.

July 28.   Ch'angsha falls to Communist forces.

August 1 or 6.   Central Action Committee formed.

August 3.   Speaking before a Politburo meeting, Li Li-san declares defiantly that Moscow does not understand the Chinese situation and that it would be different to talk to Moscow after the capture of Wuhan.

September 8.   Ho Meng-hsiung expresses himself against the Li-san line.

September 12.   Standing Committee of the Central Preparatory Commission for the National Soviet Congress meets in session, preparing a draft constitution, reaffirming the labor protection law, and revising the provisional land law.

September 24.   Third Plenum of the CCP Central Committee opens. As a consequence, it is resolved that the Li-san line was an error of tactics but not of line.

September.   A second Red Army attack on Changsha fails.

October.   Kiangsi Provincial Soviet Government is created.

October or November.   Li Li-san is sent to Moscow at Comintern request.

November 16.   CCP receives an ECCI directive, rejecting the Third Plenum verdict that the Li-san line was an error of tactics rather than line.

November 22.   An enlarged Politburo meeting decides that the Third Plenum, though adopting a compromising attitude, has operated within the scope of the Moscow line.

December.   First KMT campaign begins.

December 8.   Fut'ien incident occurs, during which Mao suppresses opponents identified as Li Li-sanists.

December 16.   Ch'en Shao-yü and associates, who were punished for criticizing the Li-san line, are rehabilitated. Meanwhile, Ho Meng-hsiung, who was removed by the Kiangsu Provincial Action Committee in September, is also rehabilitated.

December 23.   The Central issues circular no. 96, allegedly representing a turning point of CCP policy toward accepting the Comintern line.

1931

Early January.   Fourth Plenum of the CCP Central Committee convenes under Mif's sponsorship at Shanghai. On the basis of the Comintern directive received November 16, 1930, the Plenum formally
liquidates the Li-san line. The Russian Returned Students are set up
in party leadership despite the opposition of the Lo Chang-lung–Ho
Meng-hsiung group who subsequently withdraw from the plenum. Li
Li-san, Ch'ü Ch'iu-pai, and a few others are removed from party
leadership while Chou En-lai is re-elected.

January.   Ch'en Tu-hsiu sponsors a conference of various opposition groups in Shanghai which set up a Central Committee of their
own, it is reported.

January 15.   Central Bureau of the Soviet Areas is created with
Chou En-lai, Hsiang Ying, Mao Tse-tung, Chu Teh, and five others
as members.

                     The Action Committee and the General Front Commit-
tee are abolished.

January 17.   Wang K'e-ch'üan withdraws from the Kiangsu Provincial Committee and threatens to form an independent provincial
setup.

                     Ho Meng-hsiung and associates are arrested in Shang-
hai and executed by the KMT three weeks later.

January 27.   Wang K'e-ch'üan and Lo Chang-lung are removed
from the party leadership. In addition, Lo Chang-lung is discharged
as a party member.

January 30.   Wang K'e-ch'üan is dismissed from the party.

February 20.   Politburo adopts a resolution on the action of the
Chinese delegation to the Comintern during 1929-30.

Late March.   First Enlarged Meeting of the Central Bureau of Soviet Areas convenes to liquidate the Li-san line.

April.   ECCI Eleventh Plenum is held in Moscow.

                     Chang Kuo-t'ao returns to Shanghai from Moscow.

June.   Second KMT campaign begins.

June 24.   Hsiang Chung-fa, CCP secretary-general, is executed by
the KMT.

June 28.   Central Sub-bureau of the Oyuwan Soviet Area holds its
first meeting after coming into being.

July 1.   Second Conference of Workers', Peasants', and Soldiers'
Delegates in Oyuwan opens.

Early fall.   Third KMT Campaign begins.

September 1.   The Provisional Central, formed under the leadership of Ch'in Pang-hsien, issues a directive to the Soviet areas,
marking the beginning of power struggle between Ch'in and Mao,
with the former victorious.

September 18.   Japanese attack on Manchuria.

November.   First Party Congress of the (Central) Soviet Area
held.

November 7.   First National Soviet Congress opens at Juichin. As a result, it adopts a political program, a constitution, a land law, a labor law, and resolutions on the Red Army and economic policies. The Chinese Soviet Republic is proclaimed.

Second Soviet Congress of the Oyuwan Area opens in Anhwei.

November 27.   Central Executive Committee of the Soviet Government holds its first meeting, electing Mao chairman and Hsiang Ying and Chang Kuo-t'ao vice-chairmen.

December 1.   Provisional Central Government of the Chinese Soviet Republic is proclaimed. (Some sources say November 7 when the Soviet Republic as distinguished from the Soviet Government is proclaimed.)

1932

January 9.   Politburo adopts a resolution on winning preliminary successes in one or more provinces, representing a milestone in CCP forward policy.

January 28.   Japanese attack on Shanghai.

February.   Communists fail to take Kanchow, Kiangsi, which reportedly leads to a conflict between Mao and Chou En-lai on military strategy.

March.   The revised edition of the 1931 Ch'en Shao-yü book *Struggle for the More Complete Bolshevization of the Chinese Communist Party* is published at Moscow. The book is viewed by the Mao group as representing the Third Left line (1931-35).

April 15.   Central Soviet Government declares war on Japan (some sources say April 20).

June.   KMT Fourth Campaign begins.

August.   A party conference convenes at Ningtu, Kiangsi, after which Mao begins to lose military power.

September.   ECCI Twelfth Plenum held in Moscow.

October.   Oyuwan and Hsiangosi Soviet areas evacuated.

October 13.   Central Soviet government orders an urgent war mobilization.

October 14.   The Noulens, an Austrian couple, are sentenced to life imprisonment.

October 15.   Ch'en Tu-hsiu arrested in Shanghai.

1933

January.   According to the official version of Mao's machine, the CCP central headquarters moves from Shanghai to Kiangsi. Some sources say late summer of 1931 or early fall of 1932.

January 17.   The CCP Central declares for an armistice under three conditions: (1) cessation of attack, (2) guarantee of popular democratic rights, (3) arming the people and organizing armed volunteers for defense of China.

February 15.   Fight against the Lo Ming line begins.

March 3.   Central Soviet Government declares against Japanese occupation of Jehol and invasion of Peiping and Tientsin.

Spring.   Fourth KMT Campaign begins.

May 8.   Chou En-lai is appointed general political commissar of
the Red Army and concurrently of the First Front Army.

June 1.   Land investigation drive is decreed.

June 30.   August 1, anniversary of the Nanch'ang Uprising, is
made the Red Army Day.

August.   Two economic reconstruction conferences held in Kiangsi.

September 27.   Lich'uan, a strategic city in eastern Kiangsi, falls
to KMT forces.

October.   Fifth KMT Campaign begins.

October 15.   A new labor law promulgated.

October 26.   A military alliance is concluded between Communists
and the prospective Fukien rebels.

November 20.   Fukien revolts and an independent regime is proclaimed next day.

December.   ECCI Thirteenth Plenum held in Moscow.

Sometime in this year.   Li T'e, a German Comintern military
agent under an assumed Chinese name, arrives in Kiangsi.

1934

January 18.   Fifth Plenum of the CCP Central Committee convenes
at Juichin.

January 22.   Second National Soviet Congress opens at Juichin,
during which a constitution, an organic law of the central government, resolutions on the Red Army, economic reconstruction, Soviet reconstruction, and so forth are adopted.

January 24.   Mao begins addressing the Second National Soviet
Congress.

February 1.   Under KMT military pressure, the Second National
Soviet Congress closes six days ahead of schedule.

February 3.   During the first session of the new government Central Committee, Mao is elected chairman of its presidium while
Chang Wen-t'ien is elected premier.

March.   Land investigation drive re-opened.

April 10.   CCP issues a seven-point anti-Japanese statement.

April 28.   Kuangch'ang, a strategic city north of Juichin, falls to
KMT troops.

May 3.   An anti-Japanese war program is issued under the name
of 1779 persons.

July 8.   Po Ku hints at the idea of dispatching a Red Army vanguard
to fight the Japanese.

July 15.   A Red Army vanguard is ordered to march north to fight
the Japanese. This is intended to set the stage for a retreat.

August 20.   Chou En-lai hints at a general retreat.

October 3.   Central leadership appeals to the masses for unfolding
all-out guerrilla warfare, which is presumably intended to cover a
general retreat.

October 18.   Hsiang Ying, who is left behind to harass the enemy,
    appeals to the masses for unleashing all-out guerrilla tactics in de-
    fense of the Central Soviet area.
October.   General retreat from the Kiangsi-Fukien area.

Glossary

English	Chinese	Romanization
A-B League (Anti-Bolshevik League)	A-B團(鴨比團)	A-B t'uan
"Abandon no inch of territory of the bases."	不放棄根據地一寸土地	"Pu fang-ch'i ken-chü-ti i-ts'un t'u-ti."
Accelerated collapse	加速崩潰	Chia-su peng-k'uei
Action Committee	行委(行動委員會)	Hsing-wei (Hsing-tung wei-yüan-hui)
Activism of the masses	群衆的積極性	Ch'ün-chung ti chi-chi-hsing
Activists, active elements	活動份子 積極份子	Huo-tung fen-tzu, chi-chi fen-tzu
Acute revolutionary situation	尖銳的革命形勢	Chien-jui ti ko-ming hsing-shih
Adequate mass work	充分的群衆工作	Ch'ung-fen ti ch'ün-chung kung-tso
Adventurism	冒險主義	Mao-hsien chu-i
Agrarian revolution, land revolution	土地革命	T'u-ti ko-ming
All-China (or National) Federation of Labor	全總(中華全國總工會)	Ch'üan-tsung (Chung-hua Ch'üan-kuo tsung-kung-hui)
Alternate Member(s) of the Central Committee	候補中(央)委(員)	Hou-pu chung(-yang) wei(-yüan)
Antagonism between two different regimes	兩個政權的對立	Liang-ko cheng-ch'üan ti tui-li

313

Anti-Comintern	反國際	Fan kuo-chi
Anti-imperialism, anti-imperialist	反帝	Fan-ti
Anti-Japanese united army	抗日聯軍	K'ang-jih lien-chün
Anti-Japanese united front program	反日統一戰線綱領	Fan-jih t'ung-i chan-hsien kang-ling
Anti-Party tendencies	反黨傾向	Fan tang ch'ing-hsiang
Anti-rich peasant policy	反富農政策	Fan fu-nung cheng-ts'e
Anyüan	安遠	
Appointivism, appointive system	委派主義, 委派制度	Wei-p'ai chu-i, wei-p'ai chih-tu
Areas under reactionary rule	反動統治區域	Fan-tung t'ung-chih ch'ü-yü
Armed protection of the Soviet Union	武裝保護蘇聯	Wu-chuang pao-hu su-lien
Armed uprising, insurrection	武裝暴動, 武裝起義	Wu-chuang pao-tung, wu-chuang ch'i-i
Armed volunteer troops	武裝的義勇軍	Wu-chuang ti i-yung-chün
Army Corps	軍團	Chün-t'uan
Ascend-mountainism	上山主義	Shang-shan chu-i
August 7 (1927) Conference, August 7 Emergency Conference	八七會議, 八七緊急會議	Pa-ch'i hui-i, pa-ch'i chin-chi hui-i
Auxiliary labor	輔助勞動力	Fu-chu lao-tung-li
Backward peasant mentality	落後的農民意識	Lo-hou ti nung-min i-shih
Basic law (Constitution)	基本法(憲法)	Chi-pen fa (hsien-fa)
Basic masses	基本群眾	Chi-pen ch'ün-chung
Basic tactical slogans	基本策略口號	Chi-pen ts'e-lüeh k'ou-hao
Bela Kun	句臘昆	
BIC, Bureau of Investigation Collection	調查局資料	T'iao-ch'a-chü tzu-liao

Blind-actionism, putschism	盲動主義	Mang-tung chu-i
Blind judgment	盲動判斷	Mang-tung p'an-tuan
Blind obedience	盲從	Mang-ts'ung
Blockhouse tactics	堡壘政策	Pao-lei cheng-ts'e
Bolshevik consciousness of the party	黨的布爾塞(什)維克的意識	Tang ti pu-erh-se (-shih)-wei-k'e ti i-shih
Bolshevik forward and offensive line of the party	黨的布爾塞(什)維克的進攻路線	Tang ti pu-erh-se (-shih)-wei-k'e ti chin-kung lu-hsien
Bolshevik line of the party	黨的布爾塞(什)維克路線	Tang ti pu-erh-se (-shih)-wei-k'e lu-hsien
Bolshevization of the party	黨的布爾塞(什)維克化	Tang ti pu-erh-se (-shih)-wei-k'e-hua
Borodin, Michael	鮑羅庭	
Bourgeois-democratic revolution	資產階級民主革命	Tzu-ch'an chieh-chi min-chu ko-ming
Broad masses	廣大群眾	Kuang-ta ch'ün-chung
Bukharin	布哈林	
Bureaucratism	官僚主義	Kuan-liao chu-i
Cadres	幹部	Kan-pu
Campaign	圍勦	Wei-chiao
Canton Commune	廣州公社	Kuang-chou kung-she
Capitalism	資本主義	Tzu-pen chu-i
Capitalist(s)	資本家	Tzu-pen-chia
Central Action Committee	中央行動委員會	Chung-yang hsing-tung wei-yüan-hui
Central Bureau of the CY	團中央局	T'uan chung-yang-chü
Central Bureau of the Soviet Areas	蘇區中央局	Su-ch'ü chung-yang-chü

Central Committee, the Central, CC	中央，中央委員會	Chung-yang, chung-yang wei-yüan-hui
Central Committee Secretariat	中央秘書處	Chung-yang pi-shu-ch'u
Central Emergency Committee	中央非常委員會	Chung-yang fei-ch'ang wei-yüan-hui
Central Executive Committee, CEC	中央執行委員會	Chung-yang chih-hsing wei-yüan-hui
Central inspectors	中央巡視員	Chung-yang hsün-shih-yüan
(Central) Politburo	(中央)政治局	(Chung-yang) Cheng-chih-chü
Central Preparatory Commission for the National Soviet Congress	全國蘇維埃大會中央準備委員會	Ch'üan-kuo su-wei-ai ta-hui chung-yang chun-pei wei-yüan-hui
Central Revolutionary Military Council	中央革命軍事委員會	Chung-yang ko-ming chün-shih wei-yüan-hui
Central slogan	中心口號	Chung-hsin k'ou-hao
Central Soviet	中央蘇維埃	Chung-yang su-wei-ai
Central Soviet Area	中央蘇區	Chung-yang su-ch'ü
(Central) Soviet Area First Party Congress	(中央)蘇區黨第一次代表大會	(Chung-yang) Su-ch'ü tang ti-i-tz'u tai-piao ta-hui
Central Sub-bureau	中央分局	Chung-yang fen-chü
Central tasks	中心任務	Chung-hsin jen-wu
Chang Hao (Alias of Lin Yü-ying)	張浩	
Chang Kuo-t'ao	張國燾	
Chang Wen-t'ien	張聞天	
Ch'angsha	長沙	
Ch'angting	長汀	
Chapei	閘北	

Ch'en Ch'ang-hao	陳昌浩	
Ch'en Ming-shu	陳銘樞	
Ch'en Shao-yü	陳紹禹 (陳韶玉)	
Ch'en T'an-ch'iu	陳潭秋	
Ch'en Tu-hsiu	陳獨秀	
Ch'en Tu-hsiu group	陳獨秀派	Ch'en-tu-hsiu p'ai
Ch'en Yi	陳毅	
Ch'en Yu	陳友	
Ch'en Yüan-tao	陳原道	
Ch'en Yün	陳雲 (陳云)	
Cheng-feng documents	整風文獻	Cheng-feng wen-hsien
Cheng-feng movement	整風運動	Cheng-feng yün-tung
Chiai-fang she	解放社	
Chiang Han-po	江漢波	
Chiang Kai-shek	蔣介石	
Chienning	建寧	
Chih Fu (Alias of Ch'ü Ch'iu-pai)	之夫	
Chin Wan-pang	金萬邦	
Ch'in Pang-hsien	秦邦憲	
Chinchiachai	金家寨	
Chinese Communist Party, CCP	中國共產黨, 中共	Chung-kuo kung-ch'an-tang, Chung-kung
Chinese Communist Youth Corps, CY	中國共產青年團, 少共	Chung-kuo kung-ch'an ch'ing-nien-t'uan, Shao-kung
Chinese Eastern Railway	中東路	Chung-tung-lu

Chinese Left-Wing Communist Opposition	中國左派共產主義反對派	Chung-kuo tso-p'ai kung-ch'an chu-i fan-tui-p'ai
Chinese Revolutionary Military Council	中國革命軍事委員會	Chung-kuo ko-ming chün-shih wei-yüan-hui
Chinese Soviet movement	中國蘇維埃運動	Chung-kuo su-wei-ai yün-tung
Chinese Soviet Republic	中華蘇維埃共和國	Chung-hua su-wei-ai kung-ho-kuo
Chingkangshan	井崗山	
Chishui	吉水	
Chou En-lai	周恩來	
Chu Teh	朱德	
Chu Teh-Mao Tse-tung type of policies	朱德毛澤東式的政策	Chu-te Mao-tse-tung shih ti cheng-ts'e
Ch'ü Ch'iu-pai	瞿秋白	
Ch'ungjen	崇仁	
Circular	通告	T'ung-kao
Circular to All Party Members	告全黨同志書	Kao ch'üan-tang t'ung-chih shu
Civil strife of warlords	軍閥戰爭	Chün-fa chan-cheng
Class antagonism	階級矛盾, 階級對立	Chieh-chi mao-tun, chieh-chi tui-li
Class basis of the party	黨的階級基礎	Tang ti chieh-chi chi-ch'u
Class consciousness within the party	黨內階級意識	Tang nei chieh-chi i-shih
Class differentiation	階級分化	Chieh-chi fen-hua
Class heretical elements	階級異己分子	Chieh-chi i-chi fen-tzu
Class line	階級路線	Chieh-chi lu-hsien
Class struggle	階級鬥爭	Chieh-chi tou-cheng
Class war	階級戰爭	Chieh-chi chan-cheng

Clear and definite class line	明確的階級路線	Ming-ch'ueh ti chieh-chi lu-hsien
Collective farm	集體農場	Chi-t'i nung-ch'ang
Colonial road (route)	殖民地道路	Chih-min-ti tao-lu
Combat counterrevolution	肅反	Su fan
Comintern delegate	國際代表	Kuo-chi tai-piao
Comintern Eastern Department	共產國際東方部	Kung-ch'an kuo-chi tung-fang-pu
Comintern line	國際路線	Kuo-chi lu-hsien
Comintern Resolution on the Chinese Problem	共產國際關於中國問題議決案	Kung-ch'an kuo-chi kuan-yü chung-kuo wen-t'i i-chüeh-an
Commandism	命令主義, 命令制度	Ming-ling chu-i, Ming-ling chih-tu
Committee for the Amendment of the Resolution of the Fourth Plenum	四中全會決議案修改委員會	Szu-chung ch'üan-hui chüeh-i-an hsiu-kai wei-yüan-hui
Committee on Armed Self-Defense of the Chinese Nation	中國民族武裝自衛委員會	Chung-kuo min-tsu wu-chuang tzu-wei wei-yüan-hui
Communism	共產主義	Kung-ch'an chu-i
Communist International, Comintern, CI	共產國際, 國際	Kung-ch'an kuo-chi, kuo-chi
Communist movement	共產運動	Kung-ch'an yün-tung
Communist Party of the Soviet Union, CPSU	蘇聯共產黨, 聯共	Su-lien kung-ch'an-tang, lien-kung
Completely shaky	十分動搖	Shih-fen tung-yao
Compromise-ism	調和主義	T'iao-ho chu-i
Compromising attitude	調和態度	T'iao-ho t'ai-tu
Compromising line	調和路線	T'iao-ho lu-hsien
Comrade(s)	同志	T'ung-chih

Conclusion	結論, 總結	Chieh-lun, tsung-chieh
Conclusion by Chih Fu	之夫結論	Chih-fu chieh-lun
Conservatism	保守主義	Pao-shou chu-i
Consolidation of the Soviet bases	鞏固蘇維埃根據地	Kung-ku su-wei-ai ken-chü-ti
Contradictions of the systems of capitalism and socialism	資本主義制度與社會主義制度間的矛盾	Tzu-pen chu-i chih-tu yü she-hui chu-i chih-tu chien ti mao-tun
Control Commission	監察委員會	Chien-ch'a wei-yüan-hui
Correct line	正確路線	Cheng-ch'üeh lu-hsien
Corrupt liberalism	腐朽的自由主義	Fu-hsiu ti tzu-yu chu-i
Council of People's Commissars	人民委員會	Jen-min wei-yüan-hui
Counterrevolutionary activities	反革命活動	Fan ko-ming huo-tung
Counterrevolutionary character	反革命性	Fan ko-ming hsing
County	縣	Hsien
County Soviet Government	縣蘇	Hsien-su
Coward, corrupt opportunism	懦怯的腐朽的機會主義	No-ch'ieh ti fu-hsiu ti chi-hui chu-i
Crisis of the party	黨的危機	Tang ti wei-chi
Crucial moment of the revolutionary upsurge	革命高漲的緊要關頭	Ko-ming kao-chang ti chin-yao kuan-t'ou
CSS, China Stalin's Section	中國斯大林派	Chung-kuo szu-ta-lin p'ai
Dalburo	遠東局	Yüan-tung-chü
Decisive role of the peasantry in the Chinese revolution	農民在中國革命中的決定作用	Nung-min tsai chung-kuo ko-ming chung ti chüeh-ting tso-yung

Decisive war between the Soviet road (route) and the colonial road (route)	蘇維埃道路與殖民地道路的決戰	Su-wei-ai tao-lu yü chih-min-ti tao-lu ti chüeh-chan
"A decisive war between two routes for China"	中國兩條道路的決戰	"Chung-kuo liang-t'iao tao-lu ti chüeh-chan"
Defeatism	失敗主義	Shih-pai chu-i
Defensive line	防禦路線	Fang-yü lu-hsien
Delegation of the CCP Central Committee to the Comintern	中共中央駐國際代表團	Chung-kung chung-yang chu kuo-chi tai-piao-t'uan
Democratic centralism	民主集中制	Min-chu chi-chung chih
Democratic dictatorship of the workers and peasants	工農民主專政	Kung nung min-chu chuan-cheng
Democratic revolution of the workers and peasants	工農民主革命	Kung nung min-chu ko-ming
Deserter(s) of the revolution	革命叛徒	Ko-ming p'an-t'u
Desperationism	拼命主義	P'in-ming chu-i
Directive	指示	Chih-shih
Direct revolutionary action	直接革命行動	Chih-chieh ko-ming hsing-tung
Direct revolutionary situation	直接革命形勢	Chih-chieh ko-ming hsing-shih
Disintegration of the reactionary rule	反動統治的崩潰	Fan-tung t'ung-chih ti peng-k'uei
District	區	Ch'ü
District Committee	區委	Ch'ü-wei
"Doctrine of retreat and escape"	退卻逃跑主義	"T'ui-ch'ueh t'ao-p'ao chu-i"
Double-faced clique(s) (groups, or men)	兩面派	Liang-mien-p'ai
Draft program of the labor movement	職工運動提綱草案	Chih-kung yün-tung t'i-kang ts'ao-an
Draw-on-the-fat-to-make-up-for-the-lean	抽肥補瘦	Ch'ou-fei pu-sou

Draw-on-the-plentiful-to-make-up-for-the-scarce	抽多補少	Ch'ou-to pu-shao
Eastern Department of the Communist International, Comintern Eastern Department	共産國際東方部	Kung-ch'an kuo-chi tung-fang-pu
ECCI. *See* Executive Committee of the Communist International.		
ECCI Political Secretariat	共産國際執委政治秘書處	Kung-ch'an kuo-chi chih-wei cheng-chih pi-shu-ch'u
Economic strike(s)	經濟罷工	Ching-chi pa-kung
Economic struggle(s)	經濟鬥爭	Ching-chi tou-cheng
Egalitarian formula	平均主義的方式	P'ing-chün chu-i ti fang-shih
Egalitarianism	平均主義	P'ing-chün chu-i
Emergency Conference	緊急會議	Chin-chi hui-i
Emergency mobilization work	緊急動員工作	Chin-chi tung-yüan kung-tso
Empiricism	經驗主義	Ching-yen chu-i
Encircle the city with the countryside	鄉村包圍城市	Hsiang-ts'un pao-wei ch'eng-shih
Enlarged Fourth Plenum	擴大的四中全會	K'uo-ta ti szu-chung ch'üan-hui
Enlarged meeting, enlarged session	擴大會議	K'uo-ta hui-i
Enlargement of the revolutionary national war	擴大革命民族戰爭	K'uo-ta ko-ming min-tsu chan-cheng
Equal redistribution of land	土地平均分配，平分土地	T'u-ti p'ing-chün fen-p'ei, p'ing-fen t'u-ti
Error of line	路線錯誤	Lu-hsien ts'o-wu
Escape-and-retreat line	逃跑退却路線	T'ao-p'ao t'ui-ch'üeh lu-hsien
Escapism	逃跑主義	T'ao-p'ao chu-i

English	Chinese	Romanization
Estimation of the revolutionary situation	革命形勢的估量 (估計)	Ko-ming hsing-shih ti ku-liang (ku-chi)
Estrangement of the masses	脫離群眾	T'o-li ch'ün-chung
Everyday economic struggle	日常經濟鬥爭	Jih-ch'ang ching-chi tou-cheng
Excesses, excessive	過火	Kuo-huo
Executive Committee of the Communist International, ECCI	國際執委,共產國際執行委員會	Kuo-chi chih-wei, kung-ch'an kuo-chi chih-hsing wei-yüan-hui
Expansion of the Red Army	擴大紅軍	K'uo-ta hung-chün
Exploiting classes	剝削階級	Po-hsüeh chieh-chi
Extreme democratization	極端民主化	Chi-tuan min-chu-hua
Extremely panic-struck	恐慌萬狀	K'ung-huang wan-chuang
Extremism	極端主義	Chi-tuan chu-i
Factional activities	小組織(小團體)活動,派別活動	Hsiao-tsu-chih (hsiao-t'uan-t'i) huo-tung, p'ai-pieh huo-tung
Factional struggle	小組織(小團體)鬥爭,派別鬥爭	Hsiao-tsu-chih (hsiao-t'uan-t'i) tou-cheng, p'ai-pieh tou-cheng
Factionalism	小組織(小團體)觀念,派別觀念	Hsiao-tsu-chih (hsiao-t'uan-t'i) kuan-nien, p'ai-pieh kuan-nien
Fang Chih-min	方志敏	
Fascism	法西主義(法西斯主義)	Fa-hsi chu-i (fa-hsi-szu chu-i)
Fascist	法西斯蒂(法西斯)	Fa-hsi-szu-ti (fa-hsi-szu)
Fascist ideology	法西斯意識形態	Fa-hsi-szu i-shih hsing-t'ai

Fascistization of bourgeois regimes	資産階級政權的法西斯化	Tzu-ch'an chieh-chi cheng-ch'üan ti fa-hsi-szu-hua
Fatal blow	致命的打擊	Chih-ming ti ta-chi
February 7 (1930) Conference	二七會議	Erh-ch'i hui-i
Federation of Maritime Workers	海總	Hai-tsung
Fertile land	肥田	Fei-t'ien
Feudal exploitation	封建剝削	Feng-chien po-hsüeh
Feudal forces	封建勢力	Feng-chien shih-li
Feudal remnants	封建殘餘	Feng-chien ts'an-yü
Feudal system	封建制度	Feng-chien chih-tu
Fifth Campaign	第五次圍勦	Ti-wu-tz'u wei-chao
Fifth Plenum	五中全會	Wu-chung ch'üan-hui
Fight (struggle) against Li-sanism	反立三主義	Fan li-san chu-i
Fight (struggle) against the Li-san line	反立三路線	Fan li-san lu-hsien
Fight (struggle) against the Lo Ming line	反羅明路線鬥爭	Fan lo-ming lu-hsien tou-cheng
Fight against the "Right deviation" as the "main danger"	反對「主要危險」的「右傾」	Fan-tui "chu-yao wei-hsien" ti "yu-ch'ing"
Final death	最後死亡	Tsui-hou szu-wang
First Campaign	第一次圍勦	Ti-i-tz'u wei-chao
First Enlarged Session of the Central Bureau, Soviet Areas	蘇區中央局第一次擴大會議	Su-ch'ü chung-yang-chü ti-i-tz'u k'uo-ta hui-i
First "Left" line	第一次「左」傾路線	Ti-i-tz'u "tso"-ch'ing lu-hsien

First National Congress of the Chinese Workers', Peasants', and Soldiers' Council (Soviet) — 中國工農兵會議(蘇維埃)第一次全國代表大會 — Chung-kuo kung nung ping hui-i (su-wei-ai) ti-i-tz'u ch'üan-kuo tai-piao ta-hui

Foochow — 福州

Formalism — 形式主義 — Hsing-shih chu-i

Forward and offensive line — 進攻路線 — Chin-kung lu-hsien

Fourth Campaign — 第四次圍勦 — Ti-szu-tz'u wei-chao

Fourth Plenum — 四中全會 — Szu-chung ch'üan-hui

Front Committee — 前委(前敵委員會) — Ch'ien-wei (Ch'ien-ti wei-yüan-hui)

Fuchou (Linch'üan) — 撫州 (臨川)

Fukien-Chekiang-Kiangsi Border Area — 閩浙贛邊區 — Min-che-kan pien-ch'ü

Fukien incident, Fukien rebellion — 福建事變(閩變) — Fu-chien shih-pien (min-pien)

Fukien-Kwangtung-Kiangsi (Min-yüeh-kan) Border Special Area — 閩粵贛邊特區 — Min-yüeh-kan-pien t'e-ch'ü

Fundamental anti-Japanese war program of the Chinese people — 中國人民對日作戰的基本綱領 — Chung-kuo jen-min tui-jih tso-chan ti chi-pen kang-ling

Fundamental law (constitution) — 根本法(憲法) — Ken-pen fa (hsien-fa)

Fundamentally shaky — 根本動搖 — Ken-pen tung-yao

Fut'ien incident — 富田事變 — Fu-t'ien shih-pien

General Action Committee — 總行委 — Tsung hsing-wei

General collapse — 總崩潰 — Tsung peng-k'uei

General Front Committee — 總前委 — Tsung ch'ien-wei

General line of the party strategy — 黨的戰略總方針 — Tang ti chan-lüeh tsung fang-chen

General party line — 黨的總路線 — Tang ti tsung lu-hsien

General political department	總政治部	Tsung cheng-chih-pu
General political line	政治總路線	Cheng-chih tsung lu-hsien
General tasks of the Party	黨的總任務	Tang ti tsung jen-wu
Gigantic class struggle	偉大的階級鬥爭	Wei-ta ti chieh-chi tou-cheng
Growth of the revolutionary movement	革命運動向上生長	Ko-ming yün-tung hsiang-shang sheng-chang
Guerrilla concept	游擊觀念	Yu-chi kuan-nien
Guerrillaism	游擊主義	Yu-chi chu-i
Guerrilla and mobile warfare	游擊運動戰	Yu-chi yün-tung chan
Guerrilla warfare	游擊戰	Yu-chi chan
Heroism	英雄主義	Ying-hsiung chu-i
High flow, rising tide	高漲	Kao chang
High tide	高潮	Kao ch'ao
Hired farm hand association(s)	雇農工會	Ku-nung kung-hui
Hired farm hands	雇農	Ku-nung
Ho Ch'ang	賀昌	
Ho Kan-chih	何幹之	
Ho K'e-ch'üan	何克全	
Ho Meng-hsiung	何孟雄	
Ho Meng-hsiung-Lo Chang-lung group	何孟雄羅章龍派	Ho-meng-hsiung lo-chang-lung p'ai
Ho Tzu-shu	何子述	
Home-grown Party Workers	國內工作者	Kuo-nei kung-tso-che
Hsiang Chung-fa	向忠發	
Hsiang Ying	項英	

Hsiangosi Central Sub-bureau	湘鄂西中央分局	Hsiang-o-hsi chung-yang fen-chü
Hsiangosi Soviet Area	湘鄂西蘇區	Hsiang-o-hsi su-ch'ü
Hsiao Ching-kuang	蕭勁光	
Hsiao Kuan (Alias of Kuan Hsiang-ying)	小關	
Hsieh Han-ch'ang	謝漢昌	
Hsieh Wei-chün	謝唯俊	
Hsinfeng	信豐	
Hsinkuo	興國	
Hsü Chi-shen	許繼慎	
Hsü Hsi-ken	徐錫根	
Hsü Hsiang-ch'ien	徐向前	
Hsü Meng-ch'iu	徐夢秋	
Hsü Ming-hung	徐名鴻	
Hsünwu	尋鄔	
Hu Chiao-mu	胡喬木	
Hu Hua	胡華	
Hu Shih group	胡適派	Hu-shih-p'ai
Huang Kung-lüeh	黃公略	
Huang P'ing	黃平	
Huangan	黃安	
Huangp'i	黃陂	
Huich'ang	會昌	
Hunan-Hupeh (Hsi-ang-o) Border Special Area	湘鄂邊特區	Hsiang-o-pien t'e-ch'ü

Hunan-Hupeh-Kiangsi (Hsiang-o-kan) Border Special Area	湘鄂贛邊特區	Hsiang-o-kan-pien t'e-ch'ü
Hung Yi (Cheng Hung-yi)	洪易 (鄭洪易)	
Hunghu	洪湖	
Hupeh-Honan-Anhwei (Oyuwan) Border Special Area	鄂豫皖邊特區	O-yü-wan-pien t'e-ch'ü
I T'ien (Alias of Ch'ü ch'iu-pai)	一天	
Ideological struggle	思想鬥爭	Szu-hsiang tou-cheng
Ihuang	宜黃	
Imperialism	帝國主義	Ti-kuo chu-i
Independent Divisions and Regiments	獨立師團	Tu-li shih t'uan
Independent political role of the peasants	農民的獨立政治作用	Nung-min ti tu-li cheng-chih tso-yung
Industrial centers	產業中心	Ch'an-yeh chung-hsin
Industrial Committees	產業委員會	Ch'an-yeh wei-yüan-hui
Intellectuals	知識份子	Chih-shih fen-tzu
Intensification of the revolutionary situation	革命形勢的尖銳化	Ko-ming hsing-shih ti chien-jui-hua
Intermediate camps	中間營壘	Chung-chien ying-lei
Intermediate classes	中間階級	Chung-chien chieh-chi
Intraparty factions	黨內小團體(小組織)	Tang-nei hsiao-t'uan-t'i (hsiao-tsu-chih)
Intraparty struggle, intraparty conflict	黨內鬥爭	Tang-nei tou-cheng
Jen Pi-shih	任弼時	
Juichin	瑞金(瑞京)	
K'ai Feng (Alias of Ho K'e-ch'üan)	凱豐	

Kalinin	加里寧	
Kan River	贛江	Kan-chiang
Kanchow	贛州	
Key cities	中心城市	Chung-hsin ch'eng-shih
Kian	吉安	
Kiangsi-Fukien-Anhwei (Kan-min-wan) Border Special Area	贛閩皖邊特區	Kan-min-wan-pien t'e-ch'ü
Kiangsi Provincial Action Committee	江西省行委	Chiang-hsi sheng hsing-wei
Kiangsu Provincial Committee	江蘇省委	Chiang-su sheng-wei
Kiukiang	九江	
KMT-CCP collaboration	國共合作	Kuo kung ho-tso
Ku Po	古柏	
Ku Shun-chang	顧順章	
Kuan Hsiang-ying	關向應	
Kuangch'ang	廣昌	
Kuchumov	苦秋莫夫	
Kung Ch'u	龔楚	
Kuo Miao-ken	郭妙根	
Kuomintang, KMT, Nationalists	國民黨	Kuo-min-tang
Kuusinen, Otto	苦烏西寧, 庫西寧	
Labor law	勞動法	Lao-tung fa
Labor mentality	工人意識	Kung-jen i-shih
Labor movement	工人運動	Kung-jen yün-tung
Labor power	勞動力	Lao-tung li

Labor Protection Law	勞動保護法	Lao-tung pao-hu fa
Labor union	工會	Kung-hui
Laboring masses	勞動群眾	Lao-tung ch'ün-chung
Laissez-faire	放任主義	Fang-jen chu-i
Land investigation	查田	Ch'a-t'ien
Land investigation drive	查田運動	Ch'a-t'ien yün-tung
Land Law	土地法	T'u-ti fa
Land nationalization	土地國有	T'u-ti kuo-yu
Landlord(s)	地主	Ti-chu
Leadership	領導, 領導機關	Ling-tao, ling-tao chi-kuan
Leadership of the workers	工人的領導	Kung-jen ti ling-tao
Leading role of the proletariat	無產階級的領導作用	Wu-ch'an chieh-chi ti ling-tao tso-yung
Left deviation	左傾	Tso-ch'ing
Left deviationists, leftists	左傾份子	Tso-ch'ing fen-tzu
"Left" line	「左」傾路線	"Tso"-ch'ing lu-hsien
Left opportunism	左傾機會主義	Tso-ch'ing chi-hui chu-i
Left wing, leftist faction, or leftists	左派	Tso-p'ai
Lei Hsiao-ch'en	雷嘯岑	
Lenin	列寧(列寧)	
Leninism	列寧主義	
Li Ang	李昂	
Li Chien-ju	李劍如	
Li Chien-ju-Yü Tu-san group	李劍如余篤三派	Li-chien-ju yü-tu-san p'ai
Li Ch'iu-shih	李求實	

Li Li-san 李立三

Li Po-fang 李伯芳

Li-san line 立三路線 Li-san lu-hsien

Li Shao-chiu 李韶九

Li Ta-chao 李大釗

Li T'e (Alias Albert) 李特

Li Wei-han 李維漢

Li Wen-lin 李文林

Liang P'ing (Wu 亮平(吳亮平)
Liang-p'ing)

Liang Po-t'ai 梁柏台

Liao Ch'eng-yün 廖程雲

Liao Mu-ch'ün (Alias 廖慕群
of Ho Meng-hsiung)

Liberalism 自由主義 Tzu-yu chu-i

Lich'uan 黎川

Liench'eng 連城

Life-and-death strug- 革命與反革命的決死 Ko-ming yü fan-ko-
gle between revolu- 鬥爭 ming ti chüeh-szu
tion and counterrevo- tou-cheng
lution

Lin Piao 林彪

Lin Po-ch'ü (Lin Tsu- 林伯渠(林祖涵)
han)

Lin Yü-ying (Alias 林毓英
Chang Hao)

Liquidationism 取消主義 Ch'ü-hsiao chu-i

Liquidationist(s) 取消派 Ch'ü-hsiao-p'ai

Liquidationist agent 取消派的暗探 Ch'ü-hsiao-p'ai ti
an-t'an

Liquidationist line 取消路線 Ch'ü-hsiao lu-hsien

Liu Shao-ch'i	劉少奇	
Liu Shih-chi	劉士奇	
Liu Ti	劉敵	
Liu T'ieh-ch'ao	劉鉄超	
Liu T'ien-yo	劉天岳	
Lo Chang-lung	羅章龍	
Lo Fu (Alias of Chang Wen-t'ien)	洛甫	
Lo Mai (Alias of Li Wei-han)	羅邁	
Lo Ming	羅明	
Lo Ming line	羅明路線	Lo ming-lu-hsien
Lo Shou-nan	羅壽南	
Loan (Lo-an)	樂安	
Lominadze, Besso	羅明納茲	
Long March	長征	Chang-cheng
Lu Ch'iang	盧強	
Lu Hsün	魯迅	
Lungyen	龍岩	
Lushan	盧山	
Ma Yü-fu	馬玉夫	
Madyar, L.	馬其亞爾	
Main content of the Chinese revolution	中國革命的主要內容	Chung-kuo ko-ming ti chu-yao nei-jung
Main (principal) danger	主要危險	Chu-yao wei-hsien
Manchurian Provincial Committee	滿洲省委	Man-chou sheng-wei

Manuilsky, Dimitri	馬努伊斯基(馬魯伊里斯基)	
Mao Tse-t'an	毛澤覃	
Mao Tse-tung	毛澤東	
Mapu	麻埠	
Marxism	馬克思主義	Ma-k'e-szu chu-i
Marxism-Leninism	馬克斯列寧主義, 馬列主義	Ma-k'e-szu lieh-ning chu-i, ma-lieh chu-i
Mass Daily	群眾日報	Ch'ün-chung jih-pao
Mass demonstrations	群眾示威	Ch'ün-chung shih-wei
Mass line	群眾路線	Ch'ün-chung lu-hsien
Mass movement	群眾運動	Ch'ün-chung yün-tung
Mass organization(s)	群眾組織, 群眾團體	Ch'ün-chung tsu-chih, ch'ün-chung t'uan-t'i
Mass work	群眾工作	Ch'ün-chung kung-tso
Member(s) of the Central Committee	中央委員, 中委	Chung-yang wei-yüan, chung-wei
Middle-of-the-road groups, intermediate groups	中間派別	Chung-chien p'ai-pieh
Middle peasants	中農	Chung-nung
Mif, Pavel	米夫	
Minkan area	閩贛區	Min-kan ch'ü
Minyüehkan Soviet Area	閩粵贛蘇區	Min-yüeh-kan su-ch'ü
Minyüehkan Soviet Area Provincial Committee	閩粵贛蘇區省委	Min-yüeh-kan su-ch'ü sheng-wei
Mistakes of principle	原則的錯誤	Yüan-tse ti ts'o-wu

Mobile guerrilla tactics	流動游擊政策	Liu-tung yu-chi cheng-ts'e
Molotov	莫洛扎夫	
Monopolize the revolution	包辦革命	Pao-pan ko-ming
Municipal Committee	市委	Shih-wei
Nanch'ang	南昌	
Nanfeng	南豐	
Nanking demonstrations	南京大示威	Nan ching ta shih-wei
Narrow empiricism	狹隘的經驗主義	Hsia-ai ti ching-yen chu-i
National Conference of Delegates from the Soviet Areas	全國蘇維埃區域代表會議	Ch'üan-kuo su-wei-ai ch'ü-yü tai-piao hui-i
National Congress	全國代表大會	Ch'üan-kuo tai-piao ta-hui
National defense government	國防政府	Kuo-fang cheng-fu
National government	國民政府	Kuo-min cheng-fu
National revolutionary war	民族革命戰爭	Min-tsu ko-ming chan-cheng
Nationwide armed uprising	全國武裝暴動	Ch'üan-kuo wu-chuang pao-tung
Nationwide revolutionary upsurge	全國革命高潮	Ch'üan-kuo ko-ming kao-ch'ao
Negativism	消極主義	Hsiao-chi chu-i
New cadres	新幹部	Hsin kan-pu
New cycle of revolution and war	革命與戰爭的新週期	Ko-ming yü chan-cheng ti hsin chou-ch'i
New Democracy	新民主主義	Hsin min-chu chu-i
New revolutionary high tide, new revolutionary upsurge	新的革命高潮	Hsin ti ko-ming kao-ch'ao
New revolutionary rising tide	新的革命高漲	Hsin ti ko-ming kao-chang

New stage of revolution and war	革命與戰爭的新階段	Ko-ming yü chan-cheng ti hsin chieh-tuan
Nineteenth Route Army	十九路軍	Shih-chiu-lu-chün
Ningtu (Posheng)	寧都(博生)	
Ningtu Conference	寧都會議	Ning-tu hui-i
Non-Soviet areas	非蘇區	Fei su-ch'ü
North Bureau	北方局	Pei-fang chü
Objective revolutionary situation	客觀革命形勢	K'e-kuan ko-ming hsing-shih
Objective revolutionary situation on a national scale	全國的客觀革命形勢	Ch'üan-kuo ti k'e-kuan ko-ming hsing-shih
Offensive line	進攻路線	Chin-kung lu-hsien
Okano	長岡	
Old cadres, veteran cadres	老幹部	Lao kan-pu
Opportunism	機會主義	Chi-hui chu-i
Opportunist(s)	機會主義者	Chi-hui chu-i-che
Opportunistic line	機會主義路線	Chi-hui chu-i lu-hsien
Organizational opportunism	組織上的機會主義	Tsu-chih-shang ti chi-hui chu-i
Organizational preparation for armed uprisings	武裝暴動組織上的準備	Wu-chuang pao-tung tsu-chih-shang ti chun-pei
Organizational tasks	組織任務	Tsu-chi jen-wu
Organize political strikes	組織政治罷工	Tsu-chih cheng-chih pa-kung
Overestimation	過份估量(估計)	Kuo-fen ku-liang (ku-chi)
Overestimation of the speed and degree of the revolutionary movement	過份估量革命發展的速度與程度	Kuo-fen ku-liang ko-ming fa-chan ti su-tu yü ch'eng-tu
Overlook of the uneven development of the revolution	忽視革命的不平衡發展	Hu-shih ko-ming ti pu-p'ing-heng fa-chan

Oyuwan Central Sub-bureau	鄂豫皖中央分局	O-yü-wan chung-yang fen-chü
Oyuwan Soviet Area	鄂豫皖蘇區	O-yü-wan su-ch'ü
Pacifism	和平主義	Ho-p'ing chu-i
P'an Chien-hsing (Alias of P'an Han-nien)	潘健行	
P'an Han-nien	潘漢年	
Party Constitution	黨章	Tang-chang
Party Corps	黨團	Tang-t'uan
Party Corps of the National Labor Federation	全總黨團	Ch'üan-tsung tang-t'uan
Party discipline	黨的紀律	Tang ti chi-lü
Party headquarters at all levels	各級黨部	Ko chi tang-pu
Party leadership	黨的領導,黨的領導機關	Tang ti ling-tao, tang ti ling-tao chi-kuan
Party line	黨的路線	Tang-ti lu-hsien
Party monopolism	黨的包辦主義	Tang ti pao-pan chu-i
Party organ	黨的機關報	Tang ti chi-kuan-pao
Patriarchal repression	家長制度的壓迫	Chia-chang chih-tu ti ya-p'o
Patriarchism, patriarchal system	家長制度	Chia-chang chih-tu
Peaceful coexistence	和平共存	Ho-p'ing kung-ts'un
Peaceful cohabitation	和平共居	Ho-p'ing kung-chü
Peasant association(s)	農民協會	Nung-min hsieh-hui
Peasant committee(s)	農民委員會	Nung-min wei-yüan-hui
Peasant mentality	農民意識	Nung-min i-shih
Peasant revolution	農民革命	Nung-min ko-ming

Peasant revolutionary struggle	農民革命鬥爭	Nung-min ko-ming tou-cheng
Peasant struggle	農民鬥爭	Nung-min tou-cheng
Peasant warfare	農民戰爭	Nung-min chan-cheng
P'eng Shu-chih	彭述之	
P'eng Teh-huai	彭德懷	
P'eng Tse-hsiang	彭澤湘	
People's Court	人民法庭	Jen-min fa-t'ing
People's Revolutionary Army	人民革命軍	Jen-min ko-ming chün
People's Revolutionary Government in Fukien	福建人民革命政府	Fu-chien jen-min cheng-fu
Per capita land redistribution	計口授田	Chi-k'ou shou-t'ien
Peripheral region	邊緣地區	Pien-yüan ti-ch'ü
Pessimism	悲觀主義	Pei-kuan chu-i
Petty bourgeois intellectuals	小資產階級知識份子	Hsiao tzu-ch'an chieh-chi chih-shih fen-tzu
Petty bourgeoisie	小資產階級	Hsiao tzu-ch'an chieh-chi
P'ingchuan	平川	
P'inghsiang	萍鄉	
Playing at insurrection	玩弄暴動	Wan-lung pao-tung
Plenum, plenary session	全會, 全體會議	Ch'üan-hui, chüan-t'i hui-i
Po Ku (Alias of Ch'in Pang-hsien)	博古	
Po Shan (Alias of Li Li-san)	伯山	
Politburo	政治局	Cheng-chih-chü
Political Commissar	政治指導員	Cheng-chih chih-tao-yüan

Political demonstra-tions	政治示威	Cheng-chih shih-wei
Political department	政治部	Cheng-chih pu
Political leadership	政治領導	Cheng-chih ling-tao
Political line(s)	政治路線	Cheng-chih lu-hsien
Political mobiliza-tion of the broad masses	廣大群眾政治上的動員	Kuang-ta ch'ün-chung cheng-chih-shang ti tung-yüan
Political program	政綱	Cheng-kang
Political resolution	政治決議案	Cheng-chih chüeh-i-an
Political Resolution of the CCP Sixth National Congress	中共第六次全國代表大會政治決議案	Chung-kung ti-liu-tz'u ch'üan-kuo tai-piao ta-hui cheng-chih chüeh-i-an
Political strike(s)	政治罷工	Cheng-chih pa-kung
Political struggle(s)	政治鬥爭	Cheng-chih tou-cheng
Poor land	壞田	Huai-t'ien
Poor peasant(s)	貧農	P'in-nung
Poor peasant as-sociation(s)	貧農會	P'in-nung hui
Poor peasant corps	貧農團	P'in-nung t'uan
Popular democratic rights	民眾的民主權利	Min-chung ti min-chu ch'üan-li
Posheng (Ningtu)	博生(寧都)	
Positional warfare	陣地戰	Chen-ti chan
Positive experience	積極經驗	Chi-chi ching-yen
Positive guerrilla warfare	積極的游擊戰爭	Chi-chi ti yu-chi chan-cheng
Positively forward and offensive line	積極進攻路線	Chi-chi chin-kung lu-hsien
Pragmatical oppor-tunism	實際工作機會主義	Shih-chi kung-tso chi-hui chu-i
Pragmatists	實行家	Shih-hsing-chia

Preliminary agreement	初步協定	Ch'u-pu hsieh-ting
Preliminary success in one or more provinces	一省或幾省首先勝利	I-sheng huo chi-sheng shou-hsien sheng-li
Premature measures	過早辦法	Kuo-tsao pan-fa
Prepare armed uprisings	準備武裝暴動	Chun-pei wu-chuang pao-tung
Presidium	主席團	Chu-hsi-t'uan
Presidium of the ECCI	國際執委主席團	Kuo-chi chih-wei chu-hsi-t'uan
Private landownership	土地私有制	T'u-ti szu-yu-chih
Pro-Comintern cadres	擁護國際路線的幹部	Yung-hu kuo-chi lu-hsien ti kan-pu
Producing people	生產人民	Sheng-ch'an jen-min
Program for Pressing an Emergency Conference in Opposition to the Fourth Plenum	力爭緊急會議反對四中全會報告大綱	Li-cheng chin-chi hui-i fan-tui szu-chung ch'üan-hui pao-kao ta-kang
Program of action	行動綱領	Hsing-tung kang-ling
Le Proletaire	無產者	Wu-ch'an-che
Proletarian dictatorship	無產階級專政	Wu-ch'an chieh-chi chuan-cheng
Proletarian leadership	無產階級領導	Wu-ch'an chieh-chi ling-tao
Proletarian revolution	無產階級革命	Wu-ch'an chieh-chi ko-ming
Prolonged war	持久戰	Ch'ih-chiu-chan
Prospect of a high tide	高潮的前途	Kao-ch'ao ti ch'ien-t'u
Provincial Action Committee	省行委(行動委員會)	Sheng hsing-wei (hsing-tung wei-yüan-hui)
Provincial committee	省委	Sheng-wei
Provincialism, regionalism	地方主義	Ti-fang chu-i

Provisional Central Government of the Chinese Soviet Republic	中華蘇維埃共和國臨時中央政府	Chung-hua su-wei-ai kung-ho-kuo lin-shih chung-yang cheng-fu
Provisional Land Law	土地暫行法	T'u-ti tsan-hsing fa
P'u Ch'ing	蒲青	
Public trial	公審	Kung-shen
Punitivism, puni-tive system	處罰(懲辦)庄義處罰(懲辦)制度	Ch'u-fa (ch'eng-pan) chu-i, ch'u-fa (ch'eng pan) chih-tu
Pure defense	純粹防禦	Shun-ts'ui fang-yü
Purely defensive line	純粹防禦路線	Shun-ts'ui fang-yü lu-hsien
Putschism. See Blind-actionism		
Quasi-lawful position for the party	黨的半公開地位	Tang ti pan kung-k'ai ti-wei
Question of cadres	幹部問題	Kan-pu wen-t'i
Question of party re-construction	黨的建設問題	Tang ti chien-she wen-t'i
Reactionary forces	反動勢力	Fan-tung shih-li
Reactionary rule	反動統治	Fan-tung t'ung-chih
Reactionary ruling class	反動統治階級	Fan-tung t'ung-chih chieh-chi
Reconstruction of the party	黨的建設	Tang ti chien-she
Red Army	紅軍	Hung-chün
Red Army Academy	紅軍學校	Hung-chün hsüeh-hsiao
Red Army Academy Party Committee	紅軍學校校委	Hung-chün hsüeh-hsiao hsiao-wei
Red Army expansion drive	擴大紅軍運動,擴紅運動	K'uo-ta hung-chün yün-tung, k'uo-hung yün-tung
Red Army expansion surprise drive	擴紅突擊運動	K'uo-hung t'u-chi yün-tung
Red Army's Anti-Japanese Vanguard	紅軍抗日先遣部隊	Hung-chün kang-jih hsien-ch'ien pu-tui

English	Chinese	Romanization
Red Guards	赤衛軍(隊)	Ch'ih-wei-chün (-tui)
Red labor union(s)	赤色工會	Ch'ih-se kung-hui
Red regime	紅色政權	Hung-se cheng-ch'üan
Red terror	赤色恐怖	Ch'ih-se k'ung-pu
Red warriors	紅色戰士	Hung-se chan-shih
Redistribution of land	土地分配	T'u-ti fen-p'ei
Redistribution of land according to labor power	以勞動力為標準分田	I lao-tung-li wei piao-chun fen-t'ien
Redistribution of land according to the number of people	以人口為標準分田	I jen-k'ou wei piao-chun fen-t'ien
Reformism	改良主義	Kai-liang chu-i
Reformist cliques (factions or groups)	改良主義派別	Kai-liang chu-i p'ai-pieh
Regular warfare	正規戰	Cheng-kuei chan
Reorganization and replenishment of the party leadership at all levels	改造充實各級領導機關	Kai-tsao ch'ung-shih ko chi ling-tao chi-kuan
Reorganizationists	改組派	Kai-tsu-p'ai
Resolution on the organizational question	組織問題決議案	Tsu-chih wen-t'i chüeh-i-an
Resolution on the peasant movement	農民運動決議案	Nung-min yün-tung chüeh-i-an
Resolution on the Soviet question	蘇維埃問題決議案	Su-wei-ai wen-t'i chüeh-i-an
Resolution on the Work of the Central Committee	中央工作決議案	Chung-yang kung-tso chüeh-i-an
Retreat and defensive line	退守路線	T'ui-shou lu-hsien
Retreat line	退卻路線	T'ui-ch'üeh lu-hsien
Revolutionary activism	革命的積極性	Ko-ming ti chi-chi-hsing

Revolutionary base(s)	革命根據地	Ko-ming ken-chü-ti
Revolutionary character of the peasants	農民的革命性	Nung-min ti ko-ming hsing
Revolutionary democratic dictatorship of the workers and peasants	工農革命民主專政 (工農革命民權獨裁)	Kung nung ko-ming min-chu chuan-cheng (kung nung ko-ming min-ch'üan tu-ts'ai)
Revolutionary forces	革命勢力	Ko-ming shih-li
Revolutionary Military Council of the Workers' and Peasants' Red Army	工農紅軍革命軍事委員會	Kung nung hung-chün ko-ming chün-shih wei-yüan-hui
Revolutionary organizations	革命團體	Ko-ming t'uan-t'i
Revolutionary situation	革命形勢	Ko-ming hsing-shih
Revolutionary upsurge	革命高潮	Ko-ming kao-ch'ao
Revolutionary vanguard	革命先鋒隊	Ko-ming hsien-feng-tui
Revolutionary war	革命戰爭	Ko-ming chan-cheng
Rich peasant(s)	富農	Fu-nung
Rich peasant line	富農路線	Fu-nung lu-hsien
Right and Left River Soviet Special Area of Kwangsi	廣西左右江蘇維埃特區	Kuang-hsi tso-yu-chiang su-wei-ai t'e-ch'ü
Right deviation	右傾	Yu-ch'ing
Right opportunism	右傾機會主義	Yu-ch'ing chi-hui chu-i
Right wing, rightist faction or rights	右派	Yu-p'ai
Rising tide. See High flow		
Routinism	事務主義	Shih-wu chu-i
Ruling class	統治階級	T'ung-chih chieh-chi
Rural districts	鄉村	Hsiang-ts'un
Rural revolutionary base(s)	農村革命根據地	Nung-ts'un ko-ming ken-chü-ti

Russian Returned Student Faction (or Group)	留俄派	Liu-o p'ai
Safarov	薩活洛夫	
Second Campaign	第二次圍剿	Ti-erh-tz'u wei-chao
Second (Chapei) District Committee	(閘北)第二區委	(Cha-pei) ti-erh ch'ü-wei
Second "Left" line	第二次左傾路線	Ti-erh-tz'u "tso"-ch'ing lu-hsien
Second National Soviet Congress	第二次全國蘇維埃代表大會, 第二次全蘇大會	Ti-erh-tz'u ch'üan-kuo su-wei-ai tai-piao ta-hui, Ti-erh-tz'u ch'üan-su ta-hui
Second Party Congress of Kiangsu Province	江蘇省第二次代表大會	Chiang-su-sheng ti-erh-tz'u tai-piao ta-hui
Second Party Corps of the Labor Union	第二工會黨團	Ti-erh kung-hui tang-t'uan
Second Plenum	二中全會	Erh-chung ch'üan-hui
Second Plenum of the Southwest Kiangsi Special Committee	贛西南特委二全會議	Kan-hsi nan t'e-wei erh-ch'üan hui-i
Second (Kiangsu) Provincial Committee	(江蘇)第二省委	(Chiang-su) ti-erh sheng-wei
Secretary	書記	Shu-chi
Secretary-General	總書記	Tsung-shu-chi
Sectarianism	宗派主義	Tsung-p'ai chu-i
Sectarians	宗派主義者	Tsung-p'ai chu-i-che
Self-criticism	自我批評	Tzu-wo p'i-p'ing
Self-determination	自決	Tzu-chüeh
Semi-colonial	半殖民地	Pan chih-min-ti
Semi-proletariat	半無產階級	Pan wu-ch'an chieh-chi
Semi-Trotskyist line	半托洛斯基主義的路線	Pan t'o-lo-szu-chi chu-i ti lu-hsien

Separatist movement, or Separatist activities	分裂行動	Fen-lieh hsing-tung
Seventeen-County Economic Reconstruction Conference in Southern Kiangsi	江西南部十七縣經濟建設大會	Chiang-hsi nan-pu shih-ch'i hsien ching-chi chien-she ta-hui
Shaky	動搖	Tung-yao
Shang K'un (Yang Shang-k'un)	尚昆	
Shanghai Central District	滬中區	Hu-chung-ch'ü
Shanghai Eastern District	滬東區	Hu-tung-ch'ü
Shanghang	上杭	
Shao Shan (Alias of Chou En-lai)	少山	
Shao Shan Report	少山報告	Shao-shan pao-kao
Shen Tse-min	沈澤民	
Shengli (Lung-kanghsü)	勝利(龍崗墟)	
Shihch'eng	石城	
Shou Ch'ang	壽昌	
Shunchih (Chihli, Hopei)	順直	
Sino-Japanese T'angku truce	中日塘沽停戰協定	Chung-jih t'ang-ku t'ing-chan hsieh-ting
Sixth National Congress of the CCP	中共六次大會	Chung-kung liu-tz'u ta-hui
Social Democratic Party, Social Democrats	社會民主黨	She-hui min-chu tang
Socialist revolution	社會主義革命	She-hui chu-i ko-ming
Society for the Study of Marxism	馬克思主義研究會	Ma-k'e-szu chu-i yen-chiu-hui
"Solid breastwork and empty field"	堅壁清野	Chien-pi ch'ing-yeh
South Bureau	南方局	Nan-fang chü

Southwest Kiangsi Special Area	贛西南特區	Kan-hsi-nan t'e-ch'ü
Southwest Kiangsi Special Area Committee	贛西南特區委	Kan-hsi-nan t'e-ch'ü-wei
Southwest Kiangsi Special Regional Committee of the CY	少共贛西南特區委	Shao-kung kan-hsi-nan t'e-ch'ü-wei
South Wind Publishing Co.	南風出版社	Nan-feng ch'u-pan-she
Soviet areas	蘇維埃區域，蘇區	Su-wei-ai ch'ü-yü, su-ch'ü
Soviet government	蘇維埃政府	Su-wei-ai cheng-fu
Soviet Provisional Central Government	蘇維埃臨時中央政府	Su-wei-ai lin-shih chung-yang cheng-fu
Soviet regime	蘇維埃政權	Su-wei-ai cheng-ch'üan
Soviet road (route)	蘇維埃道路	Su-wei-ai tao-lu
Special Committee	特委	T'e-wei
Speed and degree of the revolutionary movement	革命發展的速度與程度	Ko-ming fan-chan ti su-tu yü ch'eng-tu
Speed of transformation	轉變速度	Chuan-pien su-tu
Sporadic tactical mistakes	個別的策略錯誤	Ko-pieh ti ts'e-lüeh ts'o-wu
SSC (Shih Sou Collection)	石叟資料室	Shih-sou tzu-liao shih
Stability of capitalism	資本主義的穩定	Tzu-pen chu-i ti wen-ting
Stage of revolutionary crisis	革命危機的階段	Ko-ming wei-chi ti chieh-tuan
Stalin	斯大林（斯達林，史達林）	
Standing Committee	常委	Ch'ang-wei
State farm	國有農場	Kuo-yu nung-ch'ang
Statement of views	意見書	I-chien-shu
State Political Security Bureau	國家政治保衛局	Kuo-chia cheng-ch'ih pao-wei-chü

Strengthening of the Party	鞏固黨	Kung-ku tang
Strengthening the alliance with the middle peasantry	鞏固中農聯盟	Kung-ku chung-nung lien-meng
Struggle against the Li-san line	反對立三路線的鬥爭	Fan-tui li-san lu-hsien ti tou-cheng
Struggle between two roads (routes)	兩條道路的鬥爭	Liang-t'iao tao-lu ti tou-cheng
Subjective powers	主觀力量	Chu-kuan li-liang
Sun Yat-sen University	中山大學(中大)	Chung-shan ta-hsüeh (Chung-ta)
Sun Yat-sen University Case	中大事件	Chung-ta shih-chien
Superficial unevenness of the revolutionary development in the cities and the countryside	城市與鄉村革命發展的表面不平衡	Cheng-shih yü hsiang-ts'un ko-ming fa-chan ti piao-mien pu-p'ing-heng
Supervisory Committee	審查委員會	Shen-ch'a wei-yüan-hui
Szu Mei (Alias of Chang Wen-t'ien)	思美	
Tactical error	策略錯誤	Ts'e-lüeh ts'o-wu
Tactical line	策略路線	Ts'e-lüeh lu-hsien
Tactics	策略	Ts'e-lüeh
T'aiho	泰和	
Tailism	尾巴主義	Wei-pa chu-i
Taiping Rebellion	太平天國運動	T'ai-p'ing t'ien-kuo yün-tung
T'an Chen-lin	譚震林	
T'an P'ing-shan	譚平山	
T'angku	塘沽	
Task(s)	任務	Jen-wu
Tayü	大庾	

Technical preparation for armed uprisings	武裝暴動技術上的準備	Wu-chuang pao-tung chi-shu-shang ti chun-pei
T'e Sheng (Yang T'e-sheng, alias of Hsiang Chung-fa)	特生	
T'e Sheng Report	特生報告	T'e-sheng pao-kao
Ten Great Political Programs	十大政綱	Shih ta cheng-kang
Teng Chung-hsia	鄧中夏	
Teng Hsiao-p'ing	鄧小平	
Teng Tzu-hui	鄧子恢	
T'eng Tai-yüan	滕代遠	
Thälmann	台爾曼	
Theory of the unusual revolutionary character of the peasantry in colonial and semi-colonial countries	殖民地半殖民地國家內農民特殊革命性的理論	Chih-min-ti pan-chih-min-ti kuo-chia nei nung-min t'e-shu ko-ming-hsing ti li-lun
Third Campaign	第三次圍勦	Ti-san-tz'u wei-chao
Third Enlarged Plenum of the CCP Central Committee	中國共產黨中央委員會擴大的第三次全體會議	Chung-kuo kung-ch'an-tang chung-yang wei-yüan-hui k'uo-ta ti ti-san-tz'u ch'üan-ti hui-i
Third group	第三派	Ti-san p'ai
Third "Left" line	第三次左傾路線	Ti-san-tz'u "tso"-ch'ing lu-hsien
Third Party	第三黨	Ti-san-tang
Third Period (third period of postwar capitalism)	第三期(戰後資本主義第三期)	Ti-san-ch'i (chan-hou tzu-pen chu-i ti-san-ch'i)
Third Plenum	三中全會	San-chung ch'üan-hui
Third road (route)	第三條道路	Ti-san-t'iao tao-lu

Toiling masses	勞苦群眾	Lao-k'u ch'ün-chung
Total collapse	完全破產	Wan-ch'üan p'o-chan
Total miscalculation	完全錯誤的估計	Wan-ch'üan ts'o-wu ti ku-chi
Township	鄉	Hsiang
Transformation of the revolution	革命的轉變	Ko-ming ti chuan-pien
Transitional period	過渡時期	Kuo-tu shih-ch'i
Transitional period leading to a new stage of revolution and war	走向革命與戰爭的新階段的過渡時期	Tsou-hsiang ko-ming yü chan-cheng ti hsin-chieh-tuan ti kuo-tu shih-ch'i
Transitional stage(s)	過渡階段	Kuo-tu chieh-tuan
Tribal insurrection	部落式的暴動	Pu-lo-shih ti pao-tung
Trotsky—Ch'en Tu-hsiu group	托陳派	T'o-Ch'en-p'ai
Trotskyite(s), Trotskyite group	托派(托洛斯基派)	T'o-p'ai (T'o-lo-szu-chi p'ai)
Ts'ai Chen-te	蔡振德	
Ts'ai Ho-shen	蔡和森	
Ts'ai Po-chen	蔡博真	
Ts'eng Ping-ch'ün	曾炳春	
Tseng Shan	曾山	
Tsunyi	遵義	
Tsunyi Conference	遵義會議	Tsun-i hui-i
Ts'ung Yün-chung	叢允中	
Tuan Liang-pi	段良弼	
Tuan Hsi-p'eng	段錫朋	
Tungku	東固	

Two-front struggle	兩條戰線鬥爭	Liang-t'iao chan-hsien tou-cheng
Under cover of the leftist language	在左傾詞句掩蓋下	Tsai tso-ch'ing tz'u-chü yen-kai-hsia
Underestimation	估量(計)不足	Ku-liang (-chi) pu-tsu
Underestimation of the revolutionary situation	革命形勢估量(計)不足	Ko-ming hsing-shih ku-liang (-chi) pu-tsu
Uneven development	不平衡發展	Pu-p'ing-heng fa-chan
Uneven development of the revolutionary movement	革命發展不平衡	Ko-ming fa-chan pu-p'ing-heng
United front	統一戰線	T'ung-i chan-hsien
United front from below	下層統一戰線	Hsia-ts'eng t'ung-i chan-hsien
Unprecedented debacle and collapse	空前慘敗與崩潰	K'ung-ch'ien ts'an-pai yü peng-k'uei
Unprincipled intra-party factional struggle	無原則的小組織鬥爭	Wu yüan-tse ti hsiao-tsu-chi tou-cheng
Unprincipled struggle	無原則的鬥爭	Wu yüan-tse ti tou-cheng
Unusual acuteness of the struggle of the workers	工人鬥爭的異常尖銳化	Kung-jen tou-cheng ti i-ch'ang chien-jui-hua
Unusual revolutionary character of the peasantry	農民特殊革命性	Nung-min t'e-shu ko-ming-hsing
Upper echelon of the petty bourgeoisie	上層小資產階級	Shang-ts'eng hsiao-tzu-ch'an chieh-chi
Upper or Lower Ch'inan	上下漢南	
Urban centers	中心城市	Chung-hsin ch'eng-shih
Urgent mobilization	緊急動員	Chin-chi tung-yüan
Urgent tasks	緊急任務	Chin-chi jen-wu
Vacillation	動搖	Tung-yao
Valuable assets of the party	黨的寶貴資本	Tang ti pao-kuei tzu-pen
Vanguard of the proletariat	無產階級先鋒隊	Wu-ch'an chieh-chi hsien-feng-tui

The Various Questions Prior to the Rising Tide of the Chinese Revolution	中國革命高漲前諸問題	Chung-kuo ko-ming kao-chang ch'ien chu-wen-t'i
Village bosses	土豪	T'u-hao
Wan-t'ai	萬(安)泰(和)	
Wan-t'ai Ho-tung Committee [of the CY]	少共萬泰河東委員會	[Shao-kung] wan-t'ai ho-tung wei-yüan-hui
Wan-t'ai-tung Committee	萬泰東委	Wan-t'ai-tung wei
Wang Chia-ch'iang (Wang Chia-hsiang)	王稼薔(王稼祥)	
Wang Chung-i	王仲一	
Wang Fan-i (Alias of Wang Feng-fei)	王凡一	
Wang Feng-fei	王鳳飛	
Wang K'e-ch'üan	王克全	
Wang Ming (Alias of Ch'en Shao-yü)	王明	
Wang Ming line	王明路線	
Wang T'ieh-chiang	王鉄江	
Wang Tse-chieh	汪澤楷	
Wavering elements	動搖份子	Tung-yao fen-tzu
Waves of the labor and peasant movements	工人運動和農民運動的浪潮	Kung-jen yün-tung han nung-min yün-tung ti lang-ch'ao
Weekly Service Program in Memory of Comrade Hsiang Chung-fa	向忠發同志紀念週工作大綱	Hsiang-chung-fa t'ung-chih chi-nien-chou kung-tso ta-kang
Wei Jen	爲人	
Wei T'o (Alias of Ch'ü Ch'iu-pai)	維它	

Weight of capitalism in China's economy	資本主義在中國經濟中的比重	Tzu-pen chu-i tsai chung-kuo ching-chi chung ti pi-chung
Wen Hu (Alias of Lo Chang-lung)	文虎	
Western Hupeh Soviet area	鄂西蘇區	O-hsi su-ch'ü
White areas	白區	Pai ch'ü
White terror	白色恐怖	Pai-se k'ung-pu
Workers' and Peasants' Inspection Commissar	工農檢查人民委員	Kung-nung chien-ch'a jen-min wei-yüan
Workers' and Peasants' Inspectorate	工農檢查處	Kung-nung chien-ch'a-ch'u
World Congress of the Comintern	共產國際世界大會	Kung-ch'an kuo-chi shih-chieh ta-hui
World revolution	世界革命	Shih-chieh ko-ming
Wu Hao (Alias of Chou En-lai)	伍豪	
Wu Hsiu-ch'üan	伍修權	
Wu Liang-p'ing	吳亮平	
Yang Wen-chung	揚文仲	
Yangtse Bureau	長江局	Ch'ang-chiang-chü
Yeh Chien-ying	葉劍英	
Yellow labor unions(s)	黃色工會	Huang-se kung-hui
Yenan	延安	
Youth Vanguards	少先隊，少年先鋒隊	Shao-hsien-tui, shao-nien hsien-feng-tui
Yü Fei	余飛	
Yü Tse-hung	余澤鴻	
Yü Tu-san	余篤三	

Yüehkan Province	粵贛省	Yüeh-kan sheng
Yün Tai-ying	惲代英	
Yung-chi-t'ai Special Committee	永吉泰特委	Yung-chi-t'ai t'e-wei
Yungfeng	永豐	
Yungyang	永陽	
Yütu	雩都	

Bibliography

The Anti-Japanese, Anti-Chiang Preliminary Agreement (反日反蔣的初步協定 Fan-jih fan-chiang ti ch'u-pu hsieh-ting), October 26, 1933; printed in *Red China*, No. 149, February 14, 1934, p. 4.

Bolshevik (布爾塞維克 Pu-erh-se-wei-k'e) (Shanghai), organ of the Central Committee, CCP, published in Shanghai. On file in BIC, 300.805/804; Vol. 4, No. 3, bearing the date of May 10, 1931. Generally known as *Pu-pao* 布報.

Bolshevik (布爾塞維克 Pu-erh-se-wei-k'e) (Kiangsi), organ of the CCP Central, published by the CCP Central Bureau, n. p., probably in Juichin; No. 1 bears the date of July, 1934, 008.105/4013, SSC.

Brandt, Conrad, Benjamin Schwartz, and John K. Fairbank, *A Documentary History of Chinese Communism*, Cambridge, Harvard University Press, 1952.

Bullitt, William C., *The Great Globe Itself, A Preface to World Affairs*, New York, Charles Scribner's Sons, 1946.

CCP Central (Politburo) Resolution on Winning Preliminary Successes of the Revolution in One or More Provinces (中共中央關於爭取革命在一省與數省首先勝利的決議 Chung-kung chung-yang kuan-yü cheng-ch'ü ko-ming tsai i-sheng yü su-sheng shou-hsien sheng-li ti chüeh-i), January 9, 1932; printed in *True Words (Shih-hua)*, No. 3, April 20, 1932, pp. 7-11.

Central (Politburo) Resolution concerning the Party Central Sub-bureau in Hsiangosi (中央關於湘鄂西黨中央分局的決議 Chung-yang kuan-yü hsiang-o-hsi tang chung-yang fen-chü ti chüeh-i), November 25, 1931; mimeographed, 224.2/804, BIC.

Chang Hao 張浩 (Lin Yü-ying 林毓英), *The Tactical Line of the Chinese Communist Party* (中共的策略路線 Chung-kung ti ts'e-lüeh lu-hsien), n. d., probably 1937; n. p.; also entitled "The Tactical Line of the Party" (黨的策略路線); 008.13/1134/C.1-2, SSC.

[Ch'en] Ch'ang-hao [陳] 昌浩, *The Great Victory of Combating Counterrevolution in the Oyuwan Soviet Area* (鄂豫皖蘇區肅反的偉大勝利 O-yü-wan su-ch'ü su-fan ti wei-ta sheng-li), November 22, 1931; printed in *Red Flag Weekly*, No. 28, January 18, 1932, pp. 43-57.

Ch'en Shao-yü 陳紹禹 *The Counterrevolutionary Activities of Lo Chang-*

353

lung & Co. after the Fourth Plenum (四中全會後羅章龍派的反
革命活動 Szu-chung ch'üan-hui hou lo-chang-lung-p'ai ti fan-ko-
ming huo-tung), contained in *Struggle for the More Complete Bolshe-
vization of the CCP,* pt. 4, sec. 2, chap. 2.
――――. *Struggle for the More Complete Bolshevization of the Chinese
Communist Party* (為中共更加布爾塞維克化而鬥爭 Wei chung-
kung keng-chia pu-erh-se-wei-k'e hua erh tou-cheng), 1st ed.,
Shanghai, February, 1931, 2d ed., Moscow, March, 1932, 3d ed.,
Yenan, July, 1940; 224.07/372, BIC.
Ch'en T'an-ch'iu 陳潭秋, *Reminiscences of the First Congress of
the Communist Party of China,* published in *Communist International,*
October, 1936.
Ch'en Tu-hsiu 陳獨秀, *Letter to All Comrades of the Party* (告全
黨同志書 Kao ch'üan-tang t'ung-chih shu), December 10, 1929;
262.3/372, BIC.
――――. *A Reply to the Communist International* (答國際的信 Ta kuo-
chi ti hsin), February 17, 1930; printed in *Le Proletaire* (無產者
Wu-ch'an-che), July 1, 1930, pp. 101-8, on file in the Hoover Li-
brary, Stanford University.
The Chinese Soviet Political Program (中國蘇維埃的政綱 Chung-
kuo su-wei-ai ti cheng-kang), taken from Political Resolution of the
Conference of Delegates from the Soviet Areas; reproduced in *A Collection of Red Bandit Secret Documents,* Vol. 2, leaves 1-2, also in
A Collection of Red Bandit Reactionary Documents, Vol. 3, pp. 655-56.
The Chinese Soviets, Vol. 1 (中國蘇維埃. 第一集 Chung-kuo su-
wei-ai, ti-i-chi), compiled and printed by the Central Preparatory
Commission for the National Soviet Congress (蘇維埃全國大會中央
準備委員會), November 7, 1930, n.p., probably Shanghai; mimeographed; 052.2/804, BIC. A collection of documents adopted by the
Central Preparatory Commission or prepared by it for adoption by
the National Soviet Congress originally scheduled to be held in November, 1930.
Chou En-lai, *Use a Six-point Program to Destroy the Enemy* (用六大
綱領來瓦解敵人 Yung liu-ta kang-ling lai wa-chiai ti-jen),
printed in *Red Star Journal,* No. 54, July 20, 1934, p. 1.
*Circular Letter of the CCP "August 7" Conference to All Party Mem-
bers* (中共「八七」會議告全黨黨員書 Chung-kung "pa-ch'i" hui-i kao
ch'üan-tang tang-yüan shu), August 7, 1927; reprinted in *The International Line,* Vol. 3, pp. 53-95, and *Red Documents,* pp. 93-135.
*Circular Note No. 2 of the Central Bureau—Resolution on the Fut'ien
Incident* (中央局通告第二號 — 對富田事變的決議 Chung-yang-
chü t'ung-kao ti-erh hao—tui fu-t'ien shih-pien ti chüeh-i), January
16, 1931; reprinted by the CCP Branch of the Fourth Army, January
23, 1931, mimeographed, 008.2127/5044, SSC.
*A Circular of the ECCI Thirteenth Plenum regarding the ECCI Thir-
teenth Plenum* (共產國際執委十三次全會關於共產國際執委
十三次全會的通知 Kung-ch'an kuo-chi chih-wei shih-san tz'u
ch'üan-hui kuan-yü kung-ch'an kuo-chi chih-wei shih-san tz'u ch'üan-

hui ti t'ung-chih), issued by the ECCI Political Secretariat; Chinese
version printed in *Struggle* (Kiangsi), No. 55, April 14, 1934, pp.
1-2.

A Circular of the ECCI Twelfth Plenum (共產國際執委十二次全會
的通知 Kung-ch'an kuo-chi chih-wei shih-erh-tz'u ch'üan-hui ti
t'ung-chih), issued by the ECCI Political Secretariat; Chinese version reprinted in *Struggle* (Shanghai), December 5, 1932, and *Red
Flag Weekly*, December 10, 1932.

A Collection of Reactionary Documents (反動文件彙編 Fan-tung wen-
chien hui-pien), compiled by the KMT Headquarters, Fourteenth Division of the Army (陸軍第十四師特別黨部), March 1, 1932; 4
vols. bound in 2 tomes, mimeographed; 008. 2129/7120/V. 1, Nos. 1-
2, 3-4, SSC.

A Collection of Red Bandit Documents (赤匪文件彙編 Ch'ih-fei
wen-chien hui-pien), compiled by the Fourth and later the Second
Department, Nanchang Headquarters, Chairman of the Military
Council (軍事委員會委員長南昌行營第二,第四廳), July, 1933-
October, 1934; 4 vols. (Vols. 1, 7, 8, and 11) on file; 008. 2129/
4070, SSC.

A Collection of Red Bandit Reactionary Documents (赤匪反動文件彙
編 Ch'ih-fei fan-tung wen-chien hui-pien), compiled under the
sponsorship of General Ch'en Ch'eng, June, 1935; reprinted May,
1960, 6 vols. , 008. 2129/4072, SSC.

A Collection of Red Bandit Secret Documents (赤匪機密文件彙編
Ch'ih-fei chi-mi wen-chien hui-pien), compiled by the First Bandit-
Suppression Propaganda Department, Headquarters of the Commander-in-chief of the Land, Sea, and Air Forces (陸海空軍總司令部
第一勦匪宣傳處), June-October, 1931; 6 vols. bound in 1 tome,
mimeographed; 008. 2129/4074, SSC.

Comintern Resolution on the Chinese Peasant Problem (國際對中國
農民問題決議案 Kuo-chi tui-yü chung-kuo nung-min wen-t'i
chüeh-i-an), n. d. ; reprinted by the North Route Subcommittee (北路
分委), February 18, 1931; reproduced in *A Collection of Red Bandit
Secret Documents*, Vol. 3, leaves 33-38, mimeographed.

Comintern Resolution on the Chinese Problem (共產國際關於中國
問題的議決案 Kung-ch'an kuo-chi kuan-yü chung-kuo wen-t'i ti
i-chüeh-an), adopted by the ECCI, February 25, 1928; reprinted in
The International Line, Vol. 3, pp. 45-52, and *Red Documents*, pp.
289-96.

The Conclusion of the ECCI Twelfth Plenum (共產國際執委第十二
次全會之總結 Kung-ch'an kuo-chi chih-wei ti shih-erh-tz'u ch'üan-
hui chih tsung-chieh), editorial of *Pravda*, October 2, 1932; Chinese
version reprinted in *Red Flag Weekly*, January 31, 1933.

A Confidential Letter of the Rebels (叛逆的秘密信 P'an-ni ti pi-
mi hsin), by the Kiangsi Provincial Action Committee (江西省行委),
Yungyang, December 20, 1930; produced as an appendix in *A Reply of
the General Front Committee;* reproduced in *A Collection of Reactionary Documents*, Vol. 3, leaves 16-18.

Constitution of the Chinese Communist Party (中國共產黨黨章
Chung-kuo kung-ch'an-tang tang-chang) (draft submitted to the Sixth
National Congress, 1928), reprinted by the Central Bureau, Soviet
Areas, December, 1931, lithographed, 008.221/5064, SSC; printed
by the China Press (中國出版社), August, 1938, 008.221/5062,
SSC.

Copy of a Letter from Mao Tse-tung to Ku Po (毛澤東給古柏的信
Mao-tse-tung chi ku-po ti hsin), December 10, 1930; produced as an
appendix to *A Reply of the General Front Committee;* reproduced in
A Collection of Reactionary Documents, Vol. 3, leaf 18.

Dallin, David J., *Soviet Russia and the Far East*, New Haven, Yale
University Press, 1948.

*Declaration Calling for the Convocation of the First National Congress
of the Chinese Workers', Peasants', and Soldiers' Council (Soviet)*
(號召中國工農兵會議(蘇維埃)第一次全國代表大會宣言
Hao-chao chung-kuo kung-nung-ping hui-i (su-wei-ai) ti-i-tz'u
ch'üan-kuo tai-piao ta-hui hsüan-yen), issued by the Presidium of the
National Conference of Delegates from Soviet Areas, July 7, 1930;
contained in *The Chinese Soviets*, Vol. 1.

*Declaration of the Central Government of the Chinese Soviet Republic
and the Revolutionary Military Council of the Chinese Workers' and
Peasants' Red Army on the March of the Chinese Workers' and
Peasants' Red Army to the North to Resist Japan* (中華蘇維埃共
和國中央政府中國工農紅軍革命軍事委員會為中國工農
紅軍北上抗日宣言 Chung-hua su-wei-ai kung-ho-kuo chung-yang
cheng-fu chung-kuo kung-nung hung-chün ko-ming chün-shih wei-
yüan-hui wei chung-kuo kung-nung hung-chün pei-shang k'ang-jih
hsüan-yen), issued July 15, 1934; printed in *Red China*, No. 221,
August 1, 1934, p. 1.

*Declaration of the Central Government of the Chinese Soviet Republic
on the Fukien Incident* (中華蘇維埃共和國中央政府為福建
事變宣言 Chung-hua su-wei-ai kung-ho-kuo chung-yang cheng-fu
wei fu-chien shih-pien hsüan-yen), issued February 11, 1934; printed
in *Red China*, No. 149, February 14, 1934, p. 3.

*Declaration of the Chinese Soviet Provisional Central Government and
the Revolutionary Military Council of the Workers' and Peasants'
Red Army* (中華蘇維埃臨時中央政府工農紅軍革命軍事委員
會宣言 Chung-hua su-wei-ai lin-shih chung-yang cheng-fu kung-
nung hung-chün ko-ming chün-shih wei-yüan-hui hsüan-yen), dated
January 17, 1933; printed in *Red China*, No. 48, January 28, 1933,
p. 1.

*Declaration of War against Japan by the Provisional Central Govern-
ment of the Chinese Soviet Republic* (中華蘇維埃共和國臨時中
央政府宣佈對日戰爭宣言 Chung-hua su-wei-ai kung-ho-kuo lin-
shih chung-yang cheng-fu hsüan-pu tui-jih chan-cheng hsüan-yen),
dated April 15, 1932; printed in *Red China*, No. 18, April 21, 1932,
p. 2.

Decision by the ECCI Thirteenth Plenum on the Convocation of the Comintern Seventh World Congress (共產國際執委十三次全會關於召集共產國際第七次世界大會的決定 Kung-ch'an kuo-chi chih-wei shih-san tz'u ch'üan-hui kuan-yü chao-chi kung-ch'an kuo-chi ti ch'i-tz'u shih-chiai ta-hui ti chüeh-ting); Chinese version printed in *Struggle* (Kiangsi), No. 55, April 14, 1934, pp. 15-16.

Decision by the ECCI Thirteenth Plenum on the ECCI Financial Statement (共產國際執委十三次全會關於共產國際執委財政報告的決定 Kung-ch'an kuo-chi chih-wei shih-san tz'u ch'üan-hui kuan-yü kung-ch'an kuo-chi chih-wei ts'ai-cheng pao-kao ti chüeh-ting); Chinese version printed in *Struggle* (Kiangsi), No. 55, April 14, 1934, p. 16.

Diagram of the Resolution of the Central Committee on Smashing the Imperialist-KMT Fifth "Campaign" (關於中央粉碎帝國主義國民黨五次"圍勦"決議案表解 Kuan-yü chung-yang fen-sui ti-kuo chu-i kuo-min-tang wu-tz'u "wei-chiao" chüeh-i-an piao-chiai), printed by the Political Department, School of the Workers' and Peasants' Red Army, September 8, 1933; 008. 222/5059, SSC.

A Directive Letter of the Central to the Soviet Areas (中央對蘇區指示信 Chung-yang tui su-ch'ü chih-shih hsin), September 1, 1931; 008. 222/5053, SSC.

Discussion of the Li-san Line by the Presidium of the ECCI (共產國際執委主席團對於立三路線的討論 Kung-ch'an kuo-chi chih-wei chu-hsi-t'uan tui-yü li-san lu-hsien ti t'ao-lun), December, 1930; Chinese version printed in *Bolshevik*, Vol. 4, No. 3, May 10, 1931, pp. 1-75, 300. 805/804, BIC.

Documents of or concerning the Enlarged Conference of the Provincial Committee of the Kiangsi Soviet Area (江西蘇區省委擴大會議文件 Chiang-hsi su-ch'ü sheng-wei k'uo-ta hui-i wen-chien), n. d., probably early 1932, n. p., probably Juichin; lithographed; 008. 236/5048-2/C. 2, SSC.

Documents of the CCP Sixth National Congress (中共第六次全國代表大會文件 Chung-kung ti-liu-tz'u ch'üan-kuo tai-piao ta-hui wen-chien), July 9(?), 1928; reprinted in *The International Line*, pp. 58-155, and Red Documents, pp. 136-234.

Documents of the Second Soviet Congress of the Chinese Soviet Republic (中華蘇維埃共和國第二次全國代表大會文獻 Chung-hua su-wei-ai kung-ho-kuo ti-erh-tz'u ch'üan-kuo tai-piao ta-hui wen-hsien), published by the Council of People's Commissars, March, 1934, Juichin; 008. 61029/5044, SSC.

Draft General Principles of the State Fundamental Law (Constitution) of the Chinese Soviet Republic (中華蘇維埃共和國國家根本法(憲法)大綱草案 Chung-hua su-wei-ai kung-ho-kuo kuo-chia ken-pen fa (hsien-fa) ta-kang ts'ao-an), prepared by the Central Preparatory Commission for adoption of the National Soviet Congress; printed in *The Chinese Soviets*, Vol. 1.

Draft Labor Law (勞働法草案 Lao-tung fa ts'ao-an), prepared by the CCP Central Committee in 1931; printed in *Draft Resolutions Introduced by the CCP Central Committee to the First National Soviet Congress*, pp. 15-25; also printed in *Red Flag of the North*, No. 15, October 25, 1932, pp. 63-73.

Draft Land Law (土地法草案 T'u-ti fa ts'ao-an), prepared by the CCP Central Committee in 1931; printed in *Draft Resolutions Introduced by the CCP Central Committee to the First National Soviet Congress*, pp. 9-14.

Draft of Comintern Eastern Department's Proposed Program—the Tasks of the CCP in the Labor Movement (共產國際東方部提綱草案——中共在職工運動中的任務 Kung-ch'an kuo-chi tung-fang-pu t'i-kang ts'ao-an—chung-kung tsai chih-kung yün-tung chung ti jen-wu), reference item No. 3 of the Third Plenum; reproduced in *A Collection of Red Bandit Secret Documents*, Vol. 3, leaves 45-50.

Draft Resolution of the First National Soviet Congress on the Question of the Red Army (全國蘇維埃第一次代表大會紅軍問題決議案草案 Ch'üan-kuo su-wei-ai ti-i-tz'u tai-piao ta-hui hung-chün wen-t'i chüeh-i-an ts'ao-an), prepared by the CCP Central Committee in 1931; printed in *Draft Resolutions Introduced by the CCP Central Committee to the First National Soviet Congress*, pp. 1-7.

Draft Resolution on the Land and Peasant Problems in Soviet Areas (蘇維埃區域土地農民問題議決案草案 Su-wei-ai ch'ü-yü t'u-ti nung-min wen-t'i i-chüeh-an ts'ao-an), by the Comintern Eastern Department n.d., reprinted by the CCP Central Secretariat, November (?) 20, 1930; a pamphlet 008.751/4424/C.1, SSC; reprinted by the CCP Want'ai Ho-tung Committee (萬泰河東委員會), April 22, 1931, mimeographed, 008.751/4424/C.2, SSC; reproduced in *A Collection of Red Bandit Secret Documents*, Vol. 3, pp. 38-45, and in *A Collection of Reactionary Documents*, Vol. 4, leaves 1-8, mimeographed.

Draft Resolutions Introduced by the Central Committee of the Chinese Communist Party to the First National Soviet Congress (中國共產黨中央委員會提出全國蘇維埃第一次代表大會草案 Chung-kuo kung-ch'an-tang chung-yang wei-yüan-hui t'i-ch'u ch'üan-kuo su-wei-ai ti-i-tz'u tai-piao ta-hui ts'ao-an), reprinted by the Political Department, Third Army Corps, First Route Army, Chinese Workers' and Peasants' Red Army, n.d., probably 1931; 008.631/8064.2, SSC.

Ehrenburg, G. B., *Sovetskii Kitai*, Moscow, 1933.

Fascism, Danger of War, and the Tasks of the Communist Parties in the Various Nations—Resolution of the ECCI Thirteenth Plenum on the Report of Comrade Kuusinen (法西主義，戰爭危險與各國共產黨的任務——共產國際執委十三次全會關於庫西寧同志底報告所通過的提綱 Fa-hsi chu-i, chan-cheng wei-hsien yü ko kuo kung-ch'an-tang ti jen-wu—kung-ch'an kuo-chi chih-wei shih-san-tz'u ch'üan-hui kuan-yü kuu-si-nen t'ung-chih ti pao-kao so t'ung-kuo ti t'i-kang), adopted in December, 1933; Chinese version appearing in *Struggle* (Kiangsi), No. 55, April 10, 1934, pp. 3-15.

A Fight for Leading the Masses in the Revolution and Establishing Their Soviet Regime (為領導民眾革命建立民眾的蘇維埃政權而鬥爭 Wei ling-tao min-chung ko-ming chien-li min-chung ti su-wei-ai cheng-ch'üan erh tou-cheng), a compendium of documents published by the Central Bureau, Soviet Areas, CCP, April, 1932; 008.1010/8137, SSC.

The First Telegram from the Chinese Soviet Provisional Central Government to the People's Revolutionary Government in Fukien and the Nineteenth Route Army (中華蘇維埃臨時中央政府致福建人民革命政府與十九路軍的第一電 Chung-hua su-wei-ai lin-shih chung-yang cheng-fu chih fu-chien jen-min ko-ming cheng-fu yü shih-chiu-lu-chün ti ti-i tien), dated December 20 (1933); printed in *Red China,* No. 149, February 14, 1934, p. 4.

[An Appeal] from the Central Government of the Chinese Soviet Republic and the Central Committee of the CCP to All the People of the Soviet Areas for Unfolding Mass Guerrilla Warfare (中華蘇維埃共和國中央政府中國共產黨中央委員會為發展群眾的游擊戰爭告全蘇區民眾 Chung-hua su-wei-ai kung-ho-kuo chung-yang cheng-fu chung-kuo kung-ch'an-tang chung-yang wei-yüan-hui wei fa-chan ch'ün-chung ti yu-chi chan-cheng kao ch'üan-su-ch'ü min-chung), dated October 3 (1934); printed in *Red China,* No. 240, October 3, 1934, p. 1.

Fundamental Anti-Japanese War Program of the Chinese People (中國人民對日作戰的基本綱領 Chung-kuo jen-min tui-jih tso-chan ti chi-pen kang-ling), issued on May 3, 1934; printed in *Red China,* No. 236, September 21, 1934, pp. 1-2.

General Principles of the Constitution of the Chinese Soviet Republic (中華蘇維埃共和國憲法大綱 Chung-hua su-wei-ai kung-ho-kuo hsien-fa ta-kang), adopted by the First National Soviet Congress on November 7, 1931; printed in *Red Flag Weekly,* No. 25, December 4 (?), 1931, pp. 2-7.

General Principles of the Constitution of the Chinese Soviet Republic (中華蘇維埃共和國憲法大綱 Chung-hua su-wei-ai kung-ho-kuo hsien-fa ta-kang), adopted by the Second National Soviet Congress in January, 1934; printed in *A Collection of Red Bandit Reactionary Documents,* Vol. 3, pp. 672-78.

Greet the Great Revolution of the Chinese Soviet Victory (迎接中國蘇維埃勝利的大革命 Ying-chieh chung-kuo su-wei-ai sheng-li ti ta ko-ming), editorial of *Red China,* Special Edition during the Second National Soviet Congress, No. 7, January 22, 1934, p. 1.

A Guide to the Anti-Imperialist Struggle and the Armed Protection of the Soviet Union (反帝國主義鬥爭與武裝保護蘇聯之南針 Fan ti-kuo chu-i tou-cheng yü wu-chuang pao-hu su-lien chih nan-chen), compiled and printed by the Propaganda Department, Central Bureau, Soviet Areas, CCP, September 18, 1932; 008.222/7106/C.1-2, SSC.

A Guide to the Land Investigation Drive (查田運動指南 Ch'a-tien yün-tung chih-nan), printed and issued by the Central Government, n.d., probably sometime between July and October, 1933; 008.743/4063-3/C.1, 2, SSC.

A History of the Chinese Communist Movement (支那共産黨運動史
Shina Kyōsantō Undōshi), compiled by the General Staff (Sambō Hom-
bu), Tokyo, 1931.

History of the Chinese Communist Party, 1932 (中國共産黨一九三二年
史), compiled under the auspices of the Intelligence Department,
Foreign Office, Tokyo.

History of the Chinese Communist Party, 1933 (中國共産黨一九三三年
史), compiled under the auspices of the Intelligence Department,
Foreign Office, Tokyo.

History of the Chinese Communist Party, 1934 (中國共産黨一九三四年
史), compiled under the auspices of the Intelligence Department,
Foreign Office, Tokyo.

*History of the Fifth Campaign by the Third Route Army of the Bandit-
Suppression Army* (北路勦匪軍第三路軍五次進勦戰史 Pei-lu
chiao-fei-chün ti-san-lu-chün wu-tz'u chin-chiao chan-shih), compiled by the Department of Staff, Third Route Army; 1st ed., 1937,
n. p., 2 vols.; 004.622/1033, SSC.

Ho Kan-chih 何幹之, *History of the Contemporary Chinese Revolution*
(中國現代革命史 Chung-kuo hsien-tai ko-ming-shih), Hongkong,
1958.

Hu Chiao-mu 胡喬木, *Thirty Years of the Chinese Communist Party*
(中國共産黨三十年 Chung-kuo kung-ch'an-tang san-shih nien), Peking, 1952.

Hu Hua 胡華, *History of the Chinese Revolution of New Democracy*
(中國新民主主義革命史 Chung-kuo hsin min-chu chu-i ko-ming-shih),
rev. ed., Peking, 1952.

Hu Shih 胡適, "China in Stalin's Grand Strategy, " *Foreign Affairs*,
October, 1950.

*Instruction No. 15 of the Central Executive Committee—concerning the
Question of Continuing the Reorganization of the Local Soviet Governments* (中央執行委員會第十五號訓令 —— 關於繼續改造地方蘇
維埃政府問題 Chung-yang chih-hsing wei-yüan-hui ti shih-wu hao
hsün-ling-kuan-yü chi-hsü kai-tsao ti-fang su-wei-ai cheng-fu wen-
t'i), issued September 22, 1932; printed in *Red China*, September
27, 1932, p. 1.

*Instructions of the Fifth Plenum to the Party Corps of the Second Na-
tional Soviet Congress* (五中全會給二次全蘇大會黨團的指令 Wu-
chung ch'üan-hui chi erh-tz'u ch'üan-su ta-hui tang-t'uan ti chih-
ling), printed in *Struggle* (Kiangsi), No. 47, February 16, 1934, pp.
16-20; also in *Documents of the Second National Soviet Congress of
the Chinese Soviet Republic*, pp. 9-22.

The International Line (國際路線 Kuo-chi lu-hsien), printed by the
Central Bureau, Soviet Areas, CCP, December, 1932, n. p., probably Juichin; 009.54/6076, SSC. Probably the first volume of a three-
volume collection of documents of the same title; the second volume
is unavailable.

The International Line, Vol. 3 (國際路線第三本 Kuo-chi lu-hsien ti-san pen), n. d., n. p.; 009. 54/6076/V. 3, SSC. Probably the last volume of a three-volume collection of documents.

The International Situation and the Tasks of the Various Comintern Branches–Resolution of the Comintern Twelfth Plenum on the Report of Comrade Kuusinen (國際情勢和共產國際各支部的任務 —— 國際第十二次全會關於庫西寧同志報告的決議 Kuo-chi ch'ing-chih han kung-ch'an kuo-chi ko chih-pu ti jen-wu–kuo-chi ti-shih-erh-tz'u ch'üan-hui kuan-yü kuu-si-nen t'ung-chih pao-kao ti chüeh-i), adopted in September, 1932; Chinese version appearing in *Struggle* (Shanghai), No. 31, December 5, 1932, pp. 2-8, and in *Red Flag Weekly*, No. 53, December 10, 1932, pp. 2-21.

Isaacs, Harold R., *The Tragedy of the Chinese Revolution*, 1st ed., London, Sacker and Warburg, 1938; 2d ed., Stanford, Stanford University Press, 1951.

Kung Ch'u 龔楚 , *The Red Army and I* (我與紅軍 Wo yü hung-chün), Hongkong, South Wind Publishing Co., 1954.

Labor Law (勞動法 Lao-tung fa), adopted by the First National Soviet Congress in November, 1931; reproduced in *A Collection of Red Bandit Reactionary Documents*, Vol. 5, pp. 1342-56.

Labor Law of the Chinese Soviet Republic (中華蘇維埃共和國勞動法 Chung-hua su-wei-ai kung-ho-kuo lao-tung fa), adopted and promulgated by the Central Executive Committee of the Chinese Soviet Republic, October 15, 1933; printed in *The Soviet Code*, Vol. 2, pp. 3-40.

Labor Protection Law (勞動保護法 Lao-tung pao-hu fa), adopted by the National Conference of Delegates from the Soviet Areas; printed in *The Chinese Soviets*, Vol. 1, compiled and printed by the Central Preparatory Commission for the National Soviet Congress, November 7, 1930.

Land Law (土地法 T'u-ti fa), promulgated by the Chinese Revolutionary Military Council, n. d.; reprinted by the General Political Department, First Army Corps, Red Army, 1930; reproduced in *A Collection of Red Bandit Secret Documents*, Vol. 5, leaves 1-4, and in *A Collection of Red Bandit Reactionary Documents*, Vol. 3, pp. 912-18.

Land Law of the Chinese Soviet Republic (中華蘇維埃共和國土地法 Chung-hua su-wei-ai kung-ho-kuo t'u-ti fa), adopted by the First National Soviet Congress in November, 1931; an original copy of the proclamation issued jointly by the Presidium of the Congress and the Central Executive Committee of the Chinese Soviet Government on December 1, 1931, 008. 742/4043, SSC; reproduced in (1) *The Soviet Code*, Vol. 2, pp. 41-47; (2) *A Collection of Red Bandit Documents*, Vol. 1, pp. 2-8; (3) *A Collection of Red Bandit Reactionary Documents*, Vol. 3, pp. 922-27.

Lei Hsiao-ch'en 雷嘯岑 , *Thirty Years of Turmoil in China* (卅年動亂中國 Sa nien tung-luan chung-kuo), 2 vols., Hongkong, The Asia Press, Ltd., 1955.

A Letter from the CCP Central Bureau of the Soviet Areas to the CCP Kiangsi Provincial Committee (中共蘇區中央局致中共江西省委信 Chung-kung su-ch'ü chung-yang-chü chih chung-kung chiang-hsi sheng-wei hsin), January 19, 1932; lithographed by the CCP Kiangsi Provincial Committee, February 7, 1932, contained in *Documents of or concerning the Enlarged Conference of the Provincial Committee of the Kiangsi Soviet Area,* leaves 16-21.

A Letter from the CCP Central Committee to Party Headquarters at All Levels—regarding Leadership of and Participation in a Campaign Week Dedicated to the Fight against Imperialists' Invasion of the Soviet Union and Their Partition of China As Well As to the Enlargement of the Revolutionary National War (中共中央致各級業部一封信 —— 關於領導和參加反對帝國主義進攻蘇聯瓜分中國與擴大革命民族戰爭的運動週 Chung-kung chung-yang chih ko chi tang-pu i-feng hsin—kuan-yü ling-tao han ts'an-chia fan-tui ti-kuo chu-i chin-kung su-lien kua-fen chung-kuo yü k'uo-ta ko-ming min-ch'u chan-cheng ti yün-tung-chou), March 30, 1932; printed in *True Words (Shih-hua),* No. 4, May 10, 1932, pp. 8-9.

Letter from the CCP Central Committee to the Party Headquarters in the Various Soviet Areas, Objecting to Imperialists' Invasion of Soviet Russia and Their Partition of China (中共中央為反對帝國主義進攻蘇聯瓜分中國給各蘇區業部信 Chung-kung chung-yang wei fan-tui ti-kuo chu-i chin-kung su-lien kua-fen chung-kuo chi ko su-ch'ü tang-pu hsin), dated April 14, 1932; printed in *A Guide to the Anti-Imperialist Struggle and the Armed Protection of the Soviet Union,* compiled and printed by the Propaganda Department, Central Bureau, Soviet Areas, September 18, 1932, pp. 13-22; also in *True Words (Shih-hua),* No. 4, May 10, 1932, pp. 5-8.

Letter from the ECCI to the CCP Central Committee, Received on November 16, 1930 (共產國際執行委員會給中國共產業中央委員會的信，一九三〇年十一月十六日收到 Kung-ch'an kuo-chi chih-hsing wei-yüan-hui chi chung-kuo kung-ch'an-tang chung-yang wei-yüan-hui ti hsin, i-chiu-san-ling nien shih-i yüeh shih-liu jih shou-tao), Chinese version, reprinted in *Red Documents,* February, 1938, n.p., pp. 362-75; reproduced in *A Collection of Red Bandit Reactionary Documents,* Vol. 2, pp. 434-47.

Letter from the ECCI to the Central Committee of the CCP (共產國際執委致中共中央委員會的信 Kung-ch'an kuo-chi chih-wei chih chung-kung chung-yang wei-yüan-hui ti hsin), Notice by the Comintern Political Secretariat, October 26, 1929; reprinted in *Red Documents,* pp. 334-45.

Letter from the ECCI to the Chinese Communist Party on the Peasant Problem (共產國際執行委員會與中國共產業書 —— 關於農民問題 Kung-ch'an kuo-chi chih-hsing wei-yüan-hui yü chung-kuo kung-ch'an-tang shu—kuan-yü nung-min wen-t'i), June 7, 1929; reprinted in *The International Line,* pp. 43-57, and *Red Documents,* pp. 319-33.

Letter from the ECCI to the Chinese Communist Party on the Political Situation and Present-Day Task (共產國際執行委員會與中國共產黨書—— 關於政治形勢與目前任務 Kung-ch'an kuo-chi chi-hsing wei-yüan-hui yü chung-kuo kung-ch'an-tang shu—kuan-yü cheng-chih hsing-shih yü mu-ch'ien jen-wu), n. d., probably early 1929; reprinted in *Red Documents*, pp. 297-318.

Letter of the ECCI Presidium, to the Chinese Communist Party (共產國際執委主席團給中國共產黨的信 Kung-ch'an kuo-chi chih-wei chu-hsi-t'uan chi chung-kuo kung-ch'an-tang ti hsin), adopted by the enlarged session of the ECCI Presidium, July, 1931; Chinese version reprinted in *Bolshevik* (Kiangsi), No. 1, July, 1934, pp. 1-41; also in *Red Documents*, pp. 376-404.

Li, *Der 1. Kongress der Vertreter der Sowjetgebiete Chinas*, published in *Die Kommunistische Internationale*, April 9, 1930, pp. 712-20.

Li Ang 李昂, *The Red Stage* (紅色舞台 Hung-se wu-t'ai); published by Sheng-li Ch'u-pan she, Chungking, 1942.

Lo Fu 洛甫, *Victories in Attacks of the Chinese Workers' and Peasants' Red Army* (中國工農紅軍在進攻中的勝利 Chung-kuo kung-nung hung-chün tsai chin-kung chung ti sheng-li), printed in *Red Flag Weekly*, No. 40, May 15, 1932, pp. 6-14.

Lu Ch'iang 盧強, *The "Hero" on the Chingkangshan* (井崗山上的「英雄」 Ching-kang-shan shang ti "ying-hsiung"), Hongkong, Liberty Press 自由出版社, 1951. Subtitled *Romances of Mao Tse-tung* (毛澤東外史 Mao Tse-tung wai-shih).

Mao Tse-tung 毛澤東, *Concluding Remarks on the Report of the Central Executive Committee* (關於中央執行委員會報告的結論 Kuan-yü chung-yang chih-hsing wei-yüan-hui pao-kao ti chieh-lun), printed in *Documents of the Second National Soviet Congress of the Chinese Soviet Republic*, pp. 125-39; also in *Red China*, Special Edition during the Second National Soviet Congress, No. 5, January 31, 1934, pp. 1-2.

――――. *A New Situation and a New Task* (新的形勢與新的任務 Hsin ti hsing-shih yü hsin ti jen-wu), printed in *Red China*, No. 97, July 29, 1933, p. 3.

――――. *On the Rectification of Incorrect Ideas in the Party* (關於糾正黨內的錯誤思想 Kuan-yü chiu-cheng tang nei ti ts'o-wu szu-hsiang), December, 1929; reprinted in *Selected Works of Mao Tse-tung*, Chinese ed., Vol. 1, pp. 87-99; English ed., Vol. 1, pp. 105-15.

――――. *On the Tactics of Fighting Japanese Imperialism* (論反對日本帝國主義的策略 Lun fan-tui jih-pen ti-kuo chu-i ti ts'e-lüeh), December 27, 1935; reprinted in *Selected Works of Mao Tse-tung*, Chinese ed., Vol. 1, pp. 137-62; English ed., Vol. 1, pp. 153-74.

――――. *Our Study and the Current Situation* (學習和時局 Hsüeh-hsi han shih-chü), April 12, 1944; reprinted in *Selected Works of Mao*

Tse-tung, Chinese ed., Vol. 3, pp. 941-54; English ed., Vol. 4, pp. 157-70.

————. *Rectify the Party's Style of Work* (整頓黨的作風 Cheng-tun tang ti tso-feng), February 1, 1943; reprinted in *Selected Works of Mao Tse-tung*, Chinese ed., Vol. 3, pp. 813-30; English ed., Vol. 4, pp. 28-45.

————. *Reform Our Study* (改造我們的學習 Kai-tsao wo-men ti hsüeh-hsi), May, 1941; reprinted in *Selected Works of Mao Tse-tung*, Chinese ed., Vol. 3, pp. 770-803; English ed., Vol. 4, pp. 12-20.

————. *Report of the Central Committee and the Council of People's Commissars of the Chinese Soviet Republic to the Second National Soviet Congress* (中華蘇維埃共和國中央執行委員會與人民委員會對二次全國蘇維埃代表大會的報告 Chung-hua su-wei-ai kung-ho-kuo chung-yang chih-hsing wei-yüan-hui yü jen-min wei-yüan-hui tui erh-tz'u ch'üan-kuo su-wei-ai tai-piao ta-hui ti pao-kao), printed in *Documents of the Second National Soviet Congress of the Chinese Soviet Republic*, pp. 122-24; also in *Red China*, Special Edition during the Second National Soviet Congress, No. 3, January 26, 1934, pp. 1-12 (pp. 5-8 missing).

————. *Selected Works of Mao Tse-tung* (毛澤東選集 Mao-tse-tung hsüan-chi), compiled by the Mao Tse-tung Selected Works Publishing Committee, CCP Central Committee (中共中央毛澤東選集出版委員會), published by the People's Publishing Company, [distributed by Hsin Hwa Book Company.] Chinese ed., 3 vols., Peking, Vol. 1, 1953, Vol. 2, 1956, Vol. 3, 1957. English ed., 4 vols., New York, International Publishers, 1954-56.

————. *A Single Spark Can Start a Prairie Fire* (星星之火，可以燎原 Hsing-hsing chih huo, k'o-i liao yüan), January 5, 1930; printed in a pamphlet published by *The Mass Daily* (群眾日報), Sian, n. d., 008.13/6063/C.2, SSC; also printed in *Selected Works of Mao Tse-tung*, Chinese ed., Vol. 1, pp. 101-11; English ed., Vol. 1, pp. 116-28.

————. *Strategic Problems of China's Revolutionary War* (中國革命戰爭的戰略問題 Chung-kuo ko-ming chan-cheng ti chan-lüeh wen-t'i), December, 1936; reprinted in *Selected Works of Mao Tse-tung*, Chinese ed., Vol. 1, pp. 163-236; English ed., Vol. 1, pp. 175-253.

————. *The Struggle in the Chingkangshan Mountains* (井岡山的鬥爭 Ching-kang-shan ti tou-cheng), November 25, 1928; reprinted in *Selected Works of Mao Tse-tung*, Chinese ed., Vol. 1, pp. 59-86; English ed., Vol. 1, pp. 71-104.

————. *Take Care of the Living Conditions of the Masses and Attend to the Methods of Work* (關心群眾生活，注意工作方法 Kuan-hsin ch'ün-chung sheng-huo, chu-i kung-tso fang-fa), January 27, 1934; printed in *Selected Works of Mao Tse-tung*, Chinese ed., Vol. 1, pp. 131-36; English ed., Vol. 1, pp. 147-52.

——. *Why Can China's Red Regime Exist?* (中國的紅色政權為什麼能夠存在? Chung-kuo ti hung-se cheng-ch'üan wei-shih-mo neng-kou ts'un-tsai?), October 5, 1928; reprinted in *Selected Works of Mao Tse-tung*, Chinese ed., Vol. 1, pp. 49-58; English ed., Vol. 1, pp. 63-70.

McLane, Charles B., *Soviet Policy and the Chinese Communists, 1931-1946*, New York, Columbia University Press, 1958.

Miao Ch'u-huang 繆楚黃, *A Short History of the Chinese Communist Party (First Draft)* (中國共產黨簡要歷史 [初稿] Chung-kuo kung-ch'an-tang chien-yao li-shih [ch'u-kao]), Peking, 1st printing, 1956, 4th printing, 1957.

Michael, Franz H., and George E. Taylor, *The Far East in the Modern World*, New York, Henry Holt and Company, 1956.

Mif, Pavel 米夫, *Heroic China: Fifteen Years of the Communist Party of China*, New York, 1937; Chinese version entitled 英勇奮鬥的十五年 (Ying-yung fen-tou ti shih-wu nien), 1936, 291/906, BIC.

——. *A New Phase of the Revolutionary Crisis in China* (中國革命危機的新階段 Chung-kuo ko-ming wei-chi ti hsin chieh-tuan), published in *Communist International*, April, 1933; Chinese version appeared in *Struggle* (Kiangsi), Nos. 22 and 23, August, 1933.

Minutes of the Politburo Enlarged Meeting (政治局擴大會紀錄 Cheng-chih-chü k'uo-ta-hui chi-lu), dated November 22, 1930; mimeographed; 255.21/809, BIC.

The New Revolutionary High Tide and Preliminary Successes in One or More Provinces—Resolution on the Present Political Tasks Adopted by the CCP Politburo on June 11, 1930 (新的革命高潮與一省或幾省首先勝利 一九三〇年六月十一日政治局會議通過日 前政治任務的決議 Hsin ti ko-ming kao-ch'ao yü i-sheng huo chi-sheng shou-hsien sheng-li-i-chiu-san-ling nien liu yüeh shih-i jih cheng-chih-chü hui-i t'ung-kuo mu-ch'ien cheng-chih jen-wu ti chüeh-i), reprinted by the Red Army Academy Party Committee 紅軍學校校委, Kian, Kiangsi, October 10, 1930, mimeographed, 008.235/5051, SSC; also in *A Collection of Red Bandit Secret Documents*, Vol. 3, leaves 12-24, and *A Collection of Red Bandit Documents*, Vol. 7, pp. 4-37.

North, Robert C., *Moscow and Chinese Communists*, Stanford, Stanford University Press, 1953.

Oppose the White Terror (Declaration of the ECCI Thirteenth Plenum) (反對白色恐怖 Fan-tui pai-se k'ung-pu) (共產國際執委第十三次全會宣言 Kung-ch'an kuo-chi chih-wei ti shih-san-tz'u ch'üan-hui hsüan-yen), adopted in December, 1933; Chinese version appeared in *Struggle* (Kiangsi), No. 54, April 7, 1934, pp. 1-3.

Order No. 12 of the Central Executive Committee—concerning Emergency War Mobilization (中央執行委員會第十二號命令——關於戰爭緊急動員 Chung-yang chih-hsing wei-yüan-hui ti shih-erh hao ming-ling—kuan-yü chan-cheng chin-chi tung-yüan), issued October 13, 1932; printed in *Red China*, No. 36, October 16, 1932, pp. 1-2.

Organic Law of the Central Soviet of the Chinese Soviet Republic (中華 蘇維埃共和國中央蘇維埃組織法 Chung-hua su-wei-ai kung-ho-kuo chung-yang su-wei-ai tsu-chih fa), promulgated on February 17, 1934; printed in *Documents of the Second National Soviet Congress of the Chinese Soviet Republic*, pp. 152-66.

Po Ku 博古 (Ch'in Pang-hsien), *Conclusion of the CCP Central Committee Fifth Plenum* (中國共產黨中央委員會第五次全會總結 Chung-kuo kung-ch'an-tang chung-yang wei-yüan-hui ti-wu-tz'u ch'üan-hui tsung-chieh), printed in *Struggle* (Kiangsi), No. 48, February 23, 1934, pp. 1-6.

————. "My Position is Over There, on the Front, Standing in the Forefront of the Battle Line!" ("我的位置在那邊, 在前線上, 站在戰 線的最前面 ! " "Wo-ti wei-chih tsai na-pien, tsai ch'ien-hsien shang, chan-tsai chan-hsien ti tsui-ch'ien mien!"), May 12 (1934); printed in *Red China*, No. 189, May 16, 1934, p. 1.

————. *Struggle for Smashing the Enemy's Fifth "Campaign" and for Winning an Independent, Free Soviet China* (為粉碎敵人的五次"圍 勦"與爭取獨立自由的蘇維埃中國而鬥爭 Wei fen-sui ti-jen ti wu-tz'u "wei-chiao" yü cheng-ch'ü tu-li tzu-yu ti su-wei-ai chung-kuo erh tou-cheng), a speech delivered before a meeting of the party's active elements of the central level on July 24, 1933; printed in *Red China*, No. 99, August 4, 1933, pp. 1-6.

————. *Support the Bolshevik Forward and Offensive Line of the Party* (擁護黨的布爾塞維克的進攻路線 Yung-hu tang ti pu-erh-se-wei-k'e ti chin-kung lu-hsien), February 16, 1933; printed in *Struggle* (Kiangsi), No. 3, February 23, 1933, pp. 4-10; reproduced in *A Collection of Red Bandit Documents*, Vol. 7, pp. 225-46.

Political Resolution Adopted by the Enlarged Conference of the CCP Provincial Committee of the Kiangsi Soviet Area (中共江西蘇區省委 擴大會議政治決議案 Chung-kung chiang-hsi su-ch'ü sheng-wei k'uo-ta hui-i cheng-chih chüeh-i-an), December, 1931; lithographed, 008. 236/5048-2/C. 1, SSC; also printed in *Documents of or concerning the Enlarged Conference of the Provincial Committee of the Kiangsi Soviet Area.*

Political Resolution Adopted by the First Party Congress of the (Central) Soviet Area (蘇區黨第一次代表大會通過政治決議案 Su-ch'ü tang ti-i-tz'u tai-piao ta-hui t'ung-kuo cheng-chih chüeh-i-an), printed by the Central Bureau, Soviet Areas, November, 1931; 008. 235/1833/C. 1-2, SSC.

Political Resolution of the Sixth National Congress (六次大會政治決 議案 Liu-tz'u ta-hui cheng-chih chüeh-i-an), July 9(?), 1928; reprinted in *The International Line*, pp. 58-94, and *Red Documents*, pp. 136-72.

Provincial Committee Correspondence (省委通訊 Sheng-wei t'ung-hsin), issued by the Kiangsi Provincial Committee of the CCP, 1933-34, n. p. ; 008. 2105/9025, SSC. Scattered issues bound in 1 volume, mimeographed. Published every three or four days. The earliest number on file (No. 11) bears the date of July 6, 1933, and the last issue available (a special edition) is dated May 15, 1934.

Provisional Land Law (土 地 暫 行 法 T'u-ti tsan-hsing fa), adopted by the National Conference of Delegates from the Soviet Areas; reproduced in *A Collection of Red Bandit Documents,* Vol. 1, pp. 11-17, and *A Collection of Red Bandit Reactionary Documents,* Vol. 3, pp. 918-21.

The Recent Organizational Tasks of the CCP-Resolution of the Comintern Eastern Department (中 國 共 產 黨 的 最 近 組 織 任 務 —— 共 產 國 際 東 方 部 議 決 案 Chung-kuo kung-ch'an-tang ti tsui-chin tsu-chih jen-wu-kung-ch'an kuo-chi tung-fang-pu i-chüeh-an), August, 1930; a pamphlet, 009.54/6032, SSC; also reproduced in *A Collection of Red Bandit Secret Documents,* Vol. 3, leaves 24-33.

Reconstruction of the Party (黨 的 建 設 Tang ti chien-she) (Shanghai); a party organ founded after the Fourth Plenum. Twelve numbers are on file in BIC, 052.1/804. The first three numbers appeared every ten days, the first issue bearing the date of January 25, 1931. Nos. 4 and 5 appeared monthly. Thereafter the magazine was published at irregular intervals. The last issue available was printed on March 8, 1933.

Reconstruction of the Party (黨 的 建 設 Tang ti chien-she) (Kiangsi), a party periodical published by the Department of Organization, Central Bureau, Soviet Areas, CCP. Appeared irregularly; 6 numbers available (Nos. 1-6), bound in 1 tome, 008.2126/9021, SSC. No. 1 is dated June 10, 1932, and No. 6, November 11, 1932.

Red China (紅 色 中 華 Hung-se chung-hua), organ of the Provisional Central Government of the Chinese Soviet Republic. Founded in Juichin, December 11, 1931, and carried on right up to the evacuation of the Chinese Communists from Kiangsi, the last issue available bearing the date of October 20, 1934. Appeared first once a week, then every ten days, then every three days. For the most part, one issue consists of four pages, sometimes six, very often up to eight. Bound in 8 volumes with some scattered issues missing. Bearing the call number 008.1052/2125, SSC, the newspaper is the richest and most complete store of information about the Kiangsi Soviet ever known to the world.

Red Documents (紅 色 文 獻 Hung-se wen-hsien), printed by Chiaifang-she (解 放 社), February, 1938; 008.2129/2703, SSC.

Red Flag Daily (紅 旗 日 報 Hung-ch'i jih-pao), Organ of the Central Committee, CCP, published in Shanghai. First issue (August 15, 1930) to No. 42 (September 25, 1930) published daily; No. 43 appeared September 27, and No. 44 September 30, 1930. On file in BIC, bearing no call number.

Red Flag of the North (北 方 紅 旗 Pei-fang hung-ch'i), published by Pei-fan hung-ch'i she (北 方 紅 旗 社). Scattered issues published in 1932 on file in BIC, 052.1/806.

Red Flag Weekly (紅旗週報 Hung-ch'i chou-pao), published in
Shanghai by the Central Department of Propaganda, CCP. Nos. 10-
58 and 63 on file in BIC bearing the call number 052.1/809; Nos. 1-
9 and 59-62 not available. No. 10 appeared July 20, 1931, and No.
63 January 1, 1934.

Red Star Journal (紅星報 Hung-hsing pao), published by the General Political Department, Chinese Workers' and Peasants' Red
Army (中國工農紅軍總政治部), July, 1933, to September
(?), 1934, n. p., probably Juichin. Fifty-three issues bound in 1 volume, 008.1052/2160, SSC. It was first published as a weekly of four
pages, but from No. 40 on appeared every five days, containing six
to sometimes eight pages. The earliest issue on file (No. 4) bears
the date of August 27, 1933, and the last (No. 66) that of September
25, 1934.

Reference Items of the Third Plenum (三中全會材料 San-chung
ch'üan-hui ts'ai-liao), an official collection of 22 released documents
of and concerning the Third Enlarged Plenum of the CC, CCP; printed
by the Central Bureau of Soviet Areas (?), October 6, 1930 (?); reproduced in part in *A Collection of Red Bandit Documents*, Vol. 3,
leaves 2-55, mimeographed. A number of the listed documents are
not available.

*Report of the Comintern Eastern Department on the Errors of the
Chinese Party Third Plenum and of Comrade Li Li-san* (國際東方
部關於中國黨三中全會與李立三同志的錯誤的報告 Kuo-
chi tung-fang-pu kuan-yü chung-kuo tang san-chung ch'üan-hui yü
li-li-san t'ung-chih ti ts'o-wu ti pao-kao), dated December, 1930,
Moscow; Chinese version as appendix to "The Discussion of the Li-
san Line by the Presidium of the ECCI, " printed in *Bolshevik* (Shanghai), Vol. 4, No. 3, May 10, 1931, pp. 66-75.

*Report on the Plenum of the Central Preparatory Commission for the
National Soviet Congress* (全國蘇維埃大會中央準備委員會全
體會議經過 Ch'üan-kuo su-wei-ai ta-hui chung-yang chun-pei
wei-yüan-hui ch'üan-t'i hui-i ching-kuo), printed in *Red Flag Daily*,
No. 36, September 19, 1930; also in the appendixes to *The Chinese
Soviets*, Vol. 1.

*Resolution and Statements Adopted by the First Enlarged Meeting of
the CCP Central Bureau of the Soviet Areas* (中共蘇區中央局第一
次擴大會議決案與報告 Chung-kung su-ch'ü chung-yang-chü ti-
i-tz'u k'uo-ta-hui i-chüeh-an yü pao-kao), adopted probably in late
March, 1931; reprinted by the CCP Wan-t'ai-tung Committee (萬泰
東委), May 8, 1931, mimeographed, 008.235/5048-2, SSC.

*Resolution concerning the Expulsion of Ch'en Tu-hsiu and Approving
the Expulsion by the Kiangsu Provincial Committee of P'eng Shu-
chih, Wang Tse-chieh, Ma Yü-fu, and Ts'ai Chen-te* (開除陳獨秀
黨籍並批准江蘇省委開除彭述之汪澤楷馬玉夫蔡振德四
人決議案 K'ai-ch'u ch'en-tu-hsiu tang-chi ping pi-chun chiang-su
sheng-wei k'ai-ch'u p'eng-shu-chih wang-tse-chieh ma-yü-fu ts'ai

chen-te szu-jen chüeh-i-an), adopted by the Central Politburo, November 15, 1929; 262.3/804, BIC.

Resolution concerning the Reports of the Meeting of the Party Corps of the National Labor Federation and the Kiangsu Provincial Committee, Both Taking Place on January 17 (關於一月十七日全總黨團會議與江蘇省委報告的決議 Kuan-yü i yüeh shih-ch'i jih ch'üan-tsung tang-t'uan hui-i yü chiang-su sheng-wei pao-kao ti chüeh-i), adopted by the Central Politburo, January 20, 1931; printed in *Reconstruction of the Party*, No. 2, February 5, 1931, pp. 29-31.

Resolution of the CCP Central concerning the Imperialist-KMT Fifth "Campaign" and the Task of Our Party (中共中央關於帝國主義國民黨五次圍勦與我們黨的任務的決議 Chung-kung chung-yang kuan-yü ti-kuo chu-i kuo-min-tang wu-tz'u "wei-chiao" yü wo-men tang ti jen-wu ti chüeh-i), adopted July 24, 1933; printed in *Struggle* (Kiangsi), No. 21, August 12, 1933, pp. 1-7.

Resolution of the Central Bureau, Reviewing the Emergency Mobilization Work of Local Party Headquarters to Crush the Massive Attack of the Enemy (中央局關於粉碎敵人大舉進攻地方黨部緊急動員工作檢閱的決議 Chung-yang-chü kuan-yü fen-sui ti-jen ta-chü chin-kung ti-fang tang-pu chin-chi tung-yüan kung-tso chien-yüeh ti chüeh-i), adopted November 21, 1932; printed in *True Words (Shih-hua)*, No. 10, November 30, 1932, pp. 4-7.

Resolution of the Central Bureau, Soviet Areas, CCP, concerning Leadership of and Participation in the Campaign Week Dedicated to the Fight against Imperialists' Invasion of the Soviet Union and Their Partition of China As Well As to the Enlargement of the Revolutionary War (中共蘇區中央局關於領導和參加反對帝國主義進攻蘇聯瓜分中國與擴大革命戰爭運動週的決議 Chung-kung su-ch'ü chung-yang-chü kuan-yü ling-tao han ts'an-chia fan-tui ti-kuo chu-i chin-kung su-lien kua-fen chung-kuo yü k'uo-ta ko-ming chan-cheng yün-tung-chou ti chüeh-i), dated May 11, 1932; printed in *True Words (Shih-hua)*, No. 4, May 10, 1932, pp. 9-12; also contained in *A Guide to the Anti-Imperialist Struggle and the Armed Protection of the Soviet Union*, pp. 22-32.

Resolution of the Eleventh Plenum of the ECCI (共產國際執委第十一次全會決議案 Kung-ch'an kuo-chi chih-wei ti-shih-i-tz'u ch'üan-hui chüeh-i-an), adopted in April, 1931; Chinese version appearing in *The International Line*, December, 1932, pp. 1-26.

Resolution of the Enlarged Fourth Plenum of the CCP Central Committee (中國共產黨中央委員會擴大會第四次全體會議議決案 Chung-kuo kung-ch'an-tang chung-yang wei-yüan-hui k'uo-ta-hui ti-szu-tz'u ch'üan-t'i hui-i i-chüeh-an), January, 1931, 008.235/5948/C.1, SSC; reprinted by Wan-t'ai Ho-tung Committee, CCP, April 21 (1931), 008.235/5948/C.2, SSC; *Red Documents*, pp. 235-44; also reproduced in *A Collection of Red Bandit Reactionary Documents*, Vol. 2, pp. 424-34.

Resolution of the Fifth Plenum concerning the Economic Struggle and the Work of Labor Unions in White Areas (五中全會關於白色區域中經濟鬥爭與工會工作的決議 Wu-chung ch'üan-hui kuan-yü pai-se ch'ü-yü chung ching-chi tou-cheng yü kung-hui kung-tso ti ch'üeh-i), printed in *Struggle* (Kiangsi), No. 50, March 11, 1934, pp. 1-12.

Resolution of the Sixth National Congress on the Land Problem (六次大會土地問題決議案 Liu-tz'u ta-hui t'u-ti wen-t'i chüeh-i-an), July 9 (?), 1928; reprinted in *The International Line*, pp. 118-44, and *Red Documents*, pp. 196-222.

Resolution of the Sixth National Congress on the Peasant Problem (六次大會農民問題決議案 Liu-tz'u ta-hui nung-min wen-t'i chüeh-i-an), July 9 (?), 1928; reprinted in *The International Line*, pp. 145-55, and *Red Documents*, pp. 228-34.

Resolution on the Chinese Problem (中國問題決議案 Chung-kuo wen-t'i chüeh-i-an), adopted by the Seventh Enlarged Session of the ECCI, November, 1926; reprinted in *The International Line*, Vol. 3, pp. 1-21, and *Red Documents*, pp. 245-66.

Resolution on the Chinese Problem (中國問題決議案 Chung-kuo wen-t'i chüeh-i-an), adopted by the Eighth Plenum of the ECCI, May, 1927; reprinted in *The International Line*, Vol. 3, pp. 22-43, and *Red Documents*, pp. 267-88.

Resolution on the Chinese Problem, Adopted by the ECCI Political Secretariat on July 23, 1930 (中國問題決議案——共產國際執委政治秘書處一九三〇年七月二十三日通過 Chung-kuo wen-t'i chüeh-i-an–kung-ch'an kuo-chi chih-wei cheng-chih pi-shu-ch'u i-chiu-san-ling nien ch'i yüeh erh-shih-san jih t'ung-kuo), Chinese version, reprinted in *Red Documents*, pp. 346-61; reproduced in *A Collection of Red Bandit Secret Documents*, Vol. 3, leaves 3-12, mimeographed.

Resolution on the Current Situation and the Tasks of the Party (目前的形勢與黨的任務決議 Mu-ch'ien ti hsing-shih yü tang ti jen-wu chüeh-i), adopted by the Fifth Plenum of the Central Committee, January 18, 1934; printed in *Struggle* (Kiangsi), No. 47, February 16, 1934, pp. 1-16.

Resolution on the Political Situation and the Party's General Tasks–Resolution for Accepting the ECCI Political Secretariat Resolution on the Chinese Question, July, 1930 (政治狀況和黨的總任務議決案——接受共產國際執行委員會政治秘書處一九三〇年七月的中國問題議決案的決議 Cheng-chih chuang-k'uang han tang ti tsung jen-wu i-chüeh-an–chieh-shou kung-ch'an kuo-chi chih-hsing wei-yüan-hui cheng-chih pi-shu-ch'u i-chiu-san-ling nien ch'i yüeh ti chung-kuo wen-t'i i-chüeh-an ti chüeh-i), adopted by the CCP Central Committee Third Plenum, September, 1930; mimeographed, 330.3/808, BIC.

Resolution on the Problem of the Red Army (紅軍問題決議案 Hung-chün wen-t'i chüeh-i-an), adopted by the First National Soviet Congress; 008.5526/2137-2, SSC.

Resolution on the Question of Comrade Ho Ch'ang and Others (關於賀昌等同志問題的決議案 Kuan-yü ho-ch'ang teng t'ung-chih wen-t'i ti chüeh-i-an), adopted by the Central Politburo on January 27, 1931; printed in *Reconstruction of the Party*, No. 3, February 15, 1931, pp. 39-40.

Resolution on the Question of Party Reconstruction Adopted by the First Party Congress of the (Central) Soviet Area (蘇區黨第一次代表大會通過黨的建設問題決議案 Su-ch'ü tang ti-i-tz'u tai-piao ta-hui t'ung-kuo tang ti chien-she wen-t'i chüeh-i-an), printed by the Central Bureau, Soviet Areas, November, 1931; 008.235/9021, SSC.

[CCP] Resolution on the Resolution of the Eleventh Plenum of the ECCI (關於國際執委第十一次全會總結的決議 Kuan-yü kuo-chi chih-wei ti shih-i-tz'u ch'üan-hui tsung-chieh ti chüeh-i), adopted in August, 1931; printed in *The International Line*, pp. 27-42.

Resolution on Some Historical Problems (關於若干歷史問題的決議 Kuan-yü jo-kan li-shih wen-t'i ti chüeh-i), adopted by the Seventh Enlarged Plenary Session of the CCP Sixth Central Committee, April 20, 1945; reprinted in *Selected Works of Mao Tse-tung*, Chinese ed., Vol. 3, pp. 955-1002; English ed., Vol. 4, pp. 171-218; also a one-volume reprint in circulation, published by the People's Publishing Co., Peking, 1953.

Revolution and War (革命與戰爭 Ko-ming yü chan-cheng), a magazine published by the General Political Department, Chinese Workers' and Peasants' Red Army, Juichin; 008.105/4487-2, SSC. Two numbers available in the SSC: No. 1, August 1, 1932; No. 2, August 15, 1932.

The Revolutionary Crisis in China and the Responsibility of the Members of the CCP (中國革命危機與中國共產黨黨員的任務 Chung-kuo ko-ming wei-chi yü chung-kuo kung-ch'an-tang tang-yüan ti jen-wu), an editorial of the Comintern organ *Communist International*, November 11, 1931; Chinese version reprinted in *True Words*, No. 3, April 20, 1932.

Schwartz, Benjamin I., *Chinese Communism and the Rise of Mao*, Cambridge, Harvard University Press, 1951.

The Second Statement of the CCP Central Committee on the Fukien Incident (中國共產黨中央委員會為福建事變第二次宣言 Chung-kuo kung-ch'an-tang chung-yang wei-yüan-hui wei fu-chien shih-pien ti-erh-tz'u hsüan-yen), dated January 26, 1934; printed in (1) *Red China*, Special Edition during the Second National Soviet Congress, No. 4, January, 1934, p. 2; (2) *Struggle* (Kiangsi), No. 45, February 2, 1934, pp. 1-3; (3) in a leaflet, 008.222/3115, SSC.

Shao Shan 少山 (Chou En-lai), The Shao Shan Report—*Reference Item No. 9 of the Third Plenum* (少山報告——三中全會材料第九號 Shao-shan pao-kao—san chung ch'üan-hui ts'ai-liao ti-chiu hao), September, 1930; mimeographed; 255.21/934, BIC.

Snow, Edgar, *Red Star over China*, New York, Modern Library, 1944.

Snow, Helen Foster (Nym Wales), *Red Dust,* Stanford, Stanford University Press, 1952.

The Soviet Code, Vol. 2 (蘇維埃法典第二集 Su-wei-ai fa-tien ti-erh chi), compiled by the People's Judicial Commissariat, July, 1934; 008.542/4424/V.2, SSC.

Stalin, J., *Problems of Leninism,* English ed., Moscow, Foreign Language Publishing House, 1954.

Statement by Chu Teh, P'eng Teh-huai, and Huang Kung-lüeh on the Fut'ien Incident (朱德彭德懷黃公略為富田事變宣言 Chu-teh p'eng-teh-huai huang-kung-lüeh wei fu-t'ien shih-pien hsüan-yen), December 17 (1930), at Huangp'i, Kiangsi; reprinted by the Hsinkuo County Soviet Government, January 23 (1931); mimeographed; 008.222/3065, SSC.

Statement of Comrade Ch'iu-pai (秋白同志聲明書 Ch'iu-pai t'ung-chih sheng-ming-shu), dated January 28, 1931; printed in *Reconstruction of the Party,* No. 3, February 15, 1931, pp. 48-50.

Statement of Comrade Li-san to the Politburo and the Fourth Plenum (立三同志給政治局與四中全會的聲明書 Li-san t'ung-chih chi cheng-chih-chü yü szu-chung ch'üan-hui ti sheng-ming-shu), printed in *Reconstruction of the Party,* No. 3, February 15, 1931, pp. 44-45.

A Statement of the CCP Central Committee to the People of the Whole Country on the Japanese Imperialists' Invasion of North China and Their Threat of Conquest of the Entire Nation (中國共產黨中央委員會為日本帝國主義強佔華北併吞中國告全國民眾書 Chung-kuo kung-ch'an-tang chung-yang wei-yüan-hui wei jih-pen ti-kuo chu-i ch'iang-chan hua-pei ping-t'un chung-kuo kao ch'üan-kuo min-chung shu), dated April 10, 1934; printed in *Struggle* (Kiangsi), No. 59, May 15, 1934, pp. 1-6.

Statement of the CCP Central Committee to the People of the Whole Nation with Respect to the Fukien Incident (中國共產黨中央委員會為福建事變告全國民眾 Chung-kuo kung-ch'an-tang chung-yang wei-yüan-hui wei fu-chien shih-pien kao ch'üan-kuo min-chung), dated December 5, 1933; printed in *Struggle* (Kiangsi), No. 38, December 12, 1933, pp. 1-3; reprinted by the Minkan Provincial Committee, CCP, 008.234/3115, SSC.

Statement of the CCP on the Current Situation (中國共產黨對於時局的主張 Chung-kuo kung-ch'an-tang tui-yü shih-chü ti chu-chang), January 1, 1932; printed in *A Fight for Leading the Masses in the Revolution and Establishing Their Soviet Regime,* pp. 1-7.

A Statement of the Central Government of the Chinese Soviet Republic and the Central Committee of the Chinese Communist Party to the People of the Whole Soviet Area on Developing Mass Guerrilla Warfare (中華蘇維埃共和國中央政府中國共產黨中央委員會為發展群眾的游擊戰爭告全蘇區民眾 Chung-hua su-wei-ai kung-ho-kuo chung-yang cheng-fu chung-kuo kung-ch'an-tang chung-yang wei-yüan-hui wei fa-chan ch'ün-chung ti yu-chi chan-cheng kao ch'üan-su-ch'ü min-chung), issued October 3, 1934; printed in *Red China*, No. 240, October 3, 1934, p. 1.

A Statement of the Views of Ho Meng-hsiung (何孟雄意見書 Ho-meng-hsiung i-chien-shu), dated September 8, 1930; released by the Central Secretariat, January 6, 1931; mimeographed; 262.9/159, BIC.

Struggle (鬥爭 Tou-cheng) (Shanghai), organ of the CCP, published every ten days, but sometimes at irregular intervals. Seventy numbers on file in BIC, 052.1/809, from the first issue to No. 72; Nos. 4 and 65 missing; mimeographed. The first issue bears the date of January 21, 1932, and the last issue available appeared May 8, 1934.

Struggle (鬥爭 Tou-cheng) (Kiangsi); Organ of the Central Bureau of the Soviet Areas of the CCP, published by the Party Press Committee (黨報委員會), Central Bureau, Soviet Areas, CCP, February 4, 1933-September 30, 1934, n.p., probably Juichin; 73 numbers bound in 6 volumes (18 scattered numbers missing); 008.2105/7720, SSC.

T'e Sheng 特生 (Hsiang Chung-fa), *Report on the Work of the Central Politburo* (中央政治局工作報告 Chung-yang cheng-chih-chü kung-tso pao-kao), September, 1930, mimeographed; 257/940, BIC. Generally known as *The T'e Sheng Report* (特生報告 T'e-sheng pao-kao).

Telegram from the Chinese Soviet Congress to the CCP Central (中華蘇維埃代表大會給中共中央電 Chung-hua su-wei-ai tai-piao ta-hui chi chung-kung chung-yang tien), dated November 18, 1931, signed by the Presidium of the Congress; printed in *Red Flag Weekly*, No. 25, December 4 (?), 1931, pp. 1-2.

The Ten Great Demands of the Chinese Revolution (中國革命之十大要求 Chung-kuo ko-ming chih shih-ta yao-ch'iu), contained in the Political Resolution of the CCP Sixth National Congress (中共六次大會政治決議案); *The International Line*, pp. 63-64; *Red Documents*, pp. 141-42.

Trotsky, Leon, *The Third International after Lenin*, trans. by John G. Wright, New York, Pioneer Publishers, 1st ed., 1936, 2d ed., 1957.

True Words (實話 Shih-hua), Organ of the CCP Central Bureau of the Soviet Areas, published by the Central Bureau, Soviet Areas, CCP (中國共產黨蘇區中央局), February 14-November 30, 1932, n.p., probably Juichin; 7 numbers bound in 1 volume; 008.2105/3002, SSC.

True Words of Youth (青年實話 Ch'ing-nien shih-hua), Organ of the Central Bureau of the Soviet Areas of the Chinese Communist Youth Corps (中國共產青年團蘇區中央局), published by the Chinese Communist Youth Corps, July, 1931-September, 1934, at Yungfung, Juichin, or Tingchow at different times; scattered issues bound in 7 volumes; 008.2105/5083, SSC.

The Urgent Task of the Party in a Decisive Fight against the Enemy's Fourth "Campaign" (關於在粉碎敵人四次"圍剿"的決戰前面

業的緊急任務 Kuan-yü tsai fen-sui ti-jen szu-tz'u "wei-ch'ao" ti chüeh-chan ch'ien-mien tang ti chin-chi jen-wu), by the Central Bureau, CCP, February 8, 1933; printed in *Struggle* (Kiangsi), No. 2, February 4, 1933, pp. 1-3.

Wang Ming 王明 (Ch'en Shao-yü), *The CCP Is the Only Leader in the Anti-Imperialist and Agrarian Revolution in China* (中國共產黨是中國反帝與土地革命中的唯一的領袖 Chung-kuo kung-ch'antang shih chung-kuo fan-ti yü t'u-ti ko-ming chung ti wei-i ti linghsiu), printed in *Struggle* (Kiangsi), No. 66, June 30, 1934, pp. 1-12.

The Weekly Service Program in Memory of Comrade Hsiang-Chung-fa (向忠發同志紀念週工作大綱 Hsiang chung-fa t'ung chih chinien-chou kung-tso ta-kang), issued by the Yungchit'ai Special Committee (永昌泰特委), August 23, 1931; 008.234/2751, SSC.

Wei Jen 為人, *The Fight against Li-sanism Should Be Linked with the Reform of the Party Leadership* (反立三主義要與改造黨的領導機關聯系起來 Fan li-san chu-i yao yü kai-tsao tang ti ling-tao chi-kuan lien-hsi ch'i-lai), December 23 (1930); printed in *Reconstruction of the Party*, No. 1, January 25, 1931, pp. 17-21.

Wittfogel, Karl, *A Short History of Chinese Communism*, an unpublished manuscript on file in the Far Eastern and Russian Institute, University of Washington, 1956.

Yakhontoff, Victor A., *The Chinese Soviets*, New York, Coward-McCann, Inc., 1934.

Yoshikawa, Shigezō, *Handbook on Current China* (中國手覽 Chukyo Soran), Tokyo, 1950.

Alphabetical List of Documents

Index

A-B League: in Fut'ien incident, 98, 99, 101, 102, 103, 104, 105, 107, 108, 109, 110, 112-13; and Tuan Hsi-p'eng, 100, 101; in Kiangsi and western Fukien, 100, 104, 159, 160; meaning of, 100; in Red Army, 101, 105, 107, 108; and Second Plenum of Southwest Kiangsi Special Committee, 103, 105, 106; in Oyuwan, 194, 195

Action Committee: established by Li Li-san, 32, 51, 64, 94, 103, 124, 142; responsibility of, 32, 94, 103; and Ho Meng-hsiung, 56; ceased to function, 64; abolished, 151
– of Kiangsu province: punished Ho Meng-hsiung, 95
– of Kiangsi province: and A-B League, 102; and Fut'ien incident, 102, 103, 104, 108, 110; leaders of, arrested by Mao, 107

Agrarian revolution: advocated by Mao, 4, 5, 7-8, 17-18, 99, 101, 106, 110, 111, 161, 165, 170, 180, 205, 240; Comintern impact on, 5, 30, 89, 196; overlooked by Li Li-san, 79, 84, 87, 89; under Russian Returned Student leadership, 161, 178-79, 180, 204-5, 265, 288. *See also* Land laws; Peasant movement

Anti-Japanese vanguard: organization of, announced, 291, 292, 293, 295, 296, 297; as first step of Long March, 293-94; made break-through, 293, 298, 299

Armed uprising: as Comintern policy, 10, 26, 40; opposed by Ch'en Tu-hsiu, 10; advocated by Li Li-san, 15, 17, 19, 33, 34, 51, 75, 76, 81, 83, 87, 124, 137; relations with political strikes, 34, 36-37; Ho Meng-hsiung's comments on, 51, 54

"Ascend mountainism," 78

August 7 (1927) Conference, 5n, 97, 115, 141, 142

Bela Kun, 87

Blind Actionism, 10, 76, 79

Borodin, Michael, 83, 84

Bourgeois-democratic revolution: as understood by Li Li-san, 22, 26; as prescribed by Comintern, 26, 31; as understood by Chou En-lai, 62; as understood by Mao, 205, 272; as viewed by Russian Returned Student leadership, 272

Brandt, Conrad, Benjamin Schwartz, and John K. Fairbank. *(A Documentary History of Chinese Communism)*, 24, 27, 30n, 31n, 65, 78n, 118, 147n, 174, 178, 260, 271

Bukharin, Nikolai Ivanovich, 72

"C" cadres, 104

Canton Commune, 43, 44, 82

Cease-fire terms (January 17, 1933), 225, 226, 258, 292, 293, 296

policy of Russian Returned Student
leadership, 186, 189, 190, 191,
199, 200, 201, 212; urged by Chou
En-lai, 202; stressed by Central
Bureau, 191, 209-10, 211
Wittfogel, Karl, 24
Workers' and Peasants' Inspection
Commissar, 173, 184
Wu Hao, 75, 144. *See also* Chou En-
lai
Wu Liang-p'ing, 276
Wuhan: as Li Li-san's target of at-
tack, 15, 22, 25, 30, 32, 33, 36,
37, 41, 75, 77; CCP's break with
KMT Left at, 10; suggested as seat
of government, 41; as Oyuwan's
target of attack, 195

Yakhontoff, Victor A., 18, 172, 178,
182, 188, 260, 270-71
Yang Wen-chung, 234-35, 237
Yangtse Bureau, 151
Yoshikawa, Shigezo, 147n
Yü Fei: and others, led separatist
move, 119, 126-27, 130, 144,
197; recalled to China, 144; as
member of Central Bureau, 150
Yü Tse-hung, 243
Yü Tu-san, 144
Yüehkan province, 244, 245
Yün Tai-ying: executed, 147
Yungyang, 102

Zinoviev, 69